BEYOND MODERN SCULPTURE

BEYOND MODERN SCULPTURE

THE EFFECTS OF SCIENCE AND TECHNOLOGY

ON THE SCULPTURE OF THIS CENTURY

JACK BURNHAM

GEORGE BRAZILLER · NEW YORK

THIS VOLUME IS DEDICATED TO MY MOTHER
WHOSE APPROVAL AND SUPPORT WERE CRUCIAL.

For information address the publisher:

George Braziller, Inc.
One Park Avenue
New York, New York 10016

Library of Congress Catalog Card Number: 68–16106

Printed in the Netherlands.

First printing, October 1968
Second printing, July 1969
Third printing, April 1973

Acknowledgments

No book comes into being without the advice and support of many people. The majority of these in the case of this volume are the artists who have generously given their time and insights to the author. They need not be named because evidence of their presence is the book itself. They are, however, warmly thanked.

My appreciation extends to everyone who has in some way contributed to the style and factual content of the manuscript. This includes Professors G. Haydn Huntley, George Bauer, Gustave Rath, Miss Davida Fineman, Miss Van Ftergiotis, and Ingeborg Burnham. For her expert labors I extend gratitude to my typist, Miss Grace Olsen.

I feel fortunate in my association with a publisher whose enthusiasm for the arts is tempered by considerable taste and perception. As for the details of publication, sympathetic editing and adroit handling of all matters pertaining to illustrations and quotes are always a godsend to any author. For these I heartily thank Miss Janice Pargh and her assistant, Miss Cindy Hills.

A Key to the Reference Bibliography

Each quotation in the text is immediately preceded or followed by date of publication, page number and, where appropriate, author of the work quoted. The full listing of works can be found in the Reference Bibliography which begins on page 379. Titles are grouped alphabetically by author under the relevant chapter heading, and with earliest publication date. Where more than one work by an author has appeared in a given year, an *a*, *b*, or *c* follows the date to identify the title both in the text and in the bibliographical references.

Preface

In the years since modern sculpture has come of age the literature on the subject has grown, though only in restricted directions. There have been several short histories and some good anthologies, plus a number of brilliant monographs on individual sculptors, but as yet no synoptic overview has been attempted defining the influences responsible for modern sculpture. This book is such an attempt, and while to some such a task may seem premature, there are sufficient signs giving us at least a beginning for such an undertaking. In trying to uncover the foundations of modern sculptural form, several questions have dominated my concerns, namely: What are the intellectual and psychical origins of modern abstraction? What forces precipitate the rapid stylistic changes of modern sculpture? Where have these forces shifted and why? What are the formal foundations of modern sculpture? Does sculpture conform to a pattern which can give us intimations of its future?

These questions, among others, have become important in the last few years as sculpture has risen in prominence and painting continues to show signs of failing vitality. Sculpture is, however, far from being a monolithic set of interests. Thus, much of the most contemporary and provocative three-dimensional art is only generically related to the figurative sculpture of the past. Recent modes, particularly Kinetic, Luminous, and Environmental Art, are all stuffed uneasily under the category of sculpture, but as yet they are too problematic to be classified.

The subtitle of this book may appear to limit its scope; however, I feel that it covers the prime controlling forces of modern sculpture. As I sought the origins of these influences, it seemed more obvious that these origins were founded in the philosophies of rationalism and materialism.

Consequently the development of modern sculpture very closely parallels the intellectual framework produced by our scientific culture. This study is, admittedly, not unbiased in its choice of sculptors. It must be understood by the reader that while the amount of text allotted varies greatly from artist to artist, this in no way has been meant to be an indication of any individual's artistic worth. Rather, considerations of space have been primarily determined by each artist's influence on the theme of the book. While I have tried to maintain some objectivity concerning individual works, my preferences are certainly evident. But here too they largely hinge on the nature of my subtopic, thus if American artists seem to dominate sections of this book, it is mainly because their commitment to technology has been more easily gratified, if not fulfilled. Certainly in the past ten years many artists from other continents have chosen the New York City environment for just that reason: its technological facilities and stimulation.

It would be misleading to regard the fundamental assumptions behind this book as completely original. They are what might be loosely categorized as "instrumentalist": stemming from the theory that art is the fruit of various social contingencies. Some of my assumptions have their spiritual antecedents in the writings of the nineteenth century German architect Gottfried Semper. I had nearly finished writing this book when my attention was called to Semper's *Der Stil in den technischen und tektonischen Künsten oder praktische Ästhetik* (1863). Semper in this work and subsequent essays laid the foundations for viewing all the arts as the combined result of "purpose, material, and technique." Yet this famous trinity is hardly the ethical essence of Semper's philosophy, which rests on viewing art as a clear reflection of the economic, technical, and social relationships which form any society. As one of the first to detect this, Semper was certain that traditional art had scant future in a society where the means of production and technical advancement had been diverted from the general welfare.

Not until thirty years afterward were the extremely influential views of Semper challenged by the Viennese art historian Alois Riegl, in his *Stilfragen* (1893). It was not Semper's political concern that Riegl attacked but his *Kunstmaterialismus* (Riegl, p. vi), an alleged desire to interpret art entirely in the light of material conditions. In its place Riegl substituted a theory of *Kunstwollen* (Riegl, p. vii) or artistic volition. This could also be interpreted as some intangible drive accounting for stylistic changes from epoch to epoch. The essence of this theory was that art stems from ideal not material sources. Later, some critics compared the intellectual basis of Riegl's *Kunstwollen* with the concepts of "phlogiston," a mystical substance invented by eighteenth-century chemists, and Henri Bergson's elusive "*élan vital*," both spurious doctrines that employed impressive terms to cover phenomena that had no satisfactory physical explanation. But, as Sigfried Giedion has made clear (1962, pp. 15, 40–43), Riegl's *Kunstwollen* was to become the impetus for a mode of German aesthetics which has preserved its influence up to the present. This philosophy, concerned as it is with the spiritual-artistic motivations of man, has its basis in psychological discoveries of the late nineteenth and early twentieth centuries. Its founders were the psychologist Theodor Lipps and the art historian Wilhelm Worringer. In asserting the perpetual duality between the drive toward abstract and that toward naturalistic creation, Worringer paved the way for the eventual academic justification of modern abstraction—and this on purely psychical terms. To a large degree this accounts for the subsequent lack of attention focused on the material developments which accompanied the growth of abstract sculpture.

Since the 1920's two generations of art historians have been studiously taught to shun the crass manifestations of the technical milieu while probing the intentions of the modern artist. And, to no small extent, many artists have discouraged such comparisons as being shallow and not to the point. The tools of scholarly criticism—stylistics, iconographical analysis, historical context, and formal analysis in the last fifty years—remain as trusted now as ever. Yet they explain with diminishing clarity what has happened after 1800, and almost nothing of what has happened in sculpture in the last sixty years.

I am sure that my lack of success with the tools of art scholarship is in part responsible for the present book. Had the tools served their purpose, I might not have sought out others less respected. But these I have found in the materialist parallelisms so despised by Riegl. I heartily confess to their use. Moreover, the situation has changed drastically since Riegl's time. At the turn of the century a firm, though not air-tight, case could still have been drawn up for the supremacy of spiritual forces in the shaping of art. How untrue this is today—unless one is ready to admit that our spiritual aspirations are entirely bound to the scientific-technical impulse! Those who desire this, or even admit to it, are far in the minority. As expected, the bulk of artists strenuously resist identification with materialism—even those committed to it through the creation of industrially fabricated sculpture. How they reconcile their sentiments with their physical productions is a central theme of this book. Idealism, in any shape or form, does not die easily.

In behalf of materialism, I will say just this. It survives in our culture because it is incredibly vital. Science and technology, the handmaidens of materialism, not only tell us most of what we know about the world, they constantly alter our relationship to ourselves and to our surroundings. These alterations are not just quantitative. When they exceed a certain threshold, they *must* become qualitative. Increasingly, materialism embraces those activities which were once thought to be purely spiritual in substance and origin. It is not spirituality which has diminished—in art or any other activity—but materialism which has grown to vast proportions. If this materialism is not to become a lethal incubus, we must understand it for what it really is. Retreat into outmoded forms of idealism is no solution. Rather, new spiritual insights into the normality of materialism are needed, insights which give it proper balance in the human psyche. A small beginning is to record its effects upon one art form. This book is directed toward that task.

Evanston, Illinois
July, 1967   J. B.

Contents

BEYOND MODERN SCULPTURE

Introduction

One must then ask a devastating question: to what extent does the art remain in any traditional (or semantic) sense *sculpture?* From its inception in prehistoric times down through the ages and until comparatively recently sculpture was conceived as an art of solid form, of *mass*, and its virtues were related to spatial occupancy.

—HERBERT READ (1964, p. 250)

Form and Indecision

For nearly twenty-five centuries the beauty and potency of sculpture was connected with an obsession for the free-standing human form and its life-emitting properties. Today sculpture has just barely preserved the prime attribute of palpable form: it remains a class of visible objects mirroring the process of psychic disbelief in its own being. With unmatched pathos it suggests still visible roots in the magic totemic objects of earlier ages while seeking sustenance in the austere soil of the scientific model and technical invention.

In his history of modern sculpture, Herbert Read characterizes (1964, p. 253) the tortuous dematerialization of post-World War II sculpture as a reduction to a "scribble in the air." For Read, extension rather than containment, dynamicism instead of mass, have become the values carrying modern sculpture further away from its original stability—a quality which he views as its only salvation. Recalling Read's early articulate defenses of Arp, Brancusi, and Moore, this mien of disappointment, amounting almost to a gap between the generations, signals the end of an era.

Read's questioning of the turns taken recently by sculpture goes beyond a general indictment of the art. As with other critics of his generation, he senses that three-dimensional art has embarked upon a course which could make it totally unrelated—both materially and psychically—to the functions of all past sculpture. Sculpture, in fact, may cease to have meaning even within those broad boundaries which remain the temporary conveniences of art history.

This book explains that premonition. It reveals *why* sculpture has undergone such drastic alteration in the past three-quarters of a century. Unfortunately, past art criticism has never been explicit about the foundations of modern sculpture, while the categorizing of sculpture has become enmeshed in its own system of tautologies. Thus names of movements and styles, usually the invention of journalists, have become the means by which critics define the very phenomena they set out to explain. Simple attachments of nomenclature are meaningless because sculpture has been diverted by pressures far stronger than those implied by literary concoctions or biographical studies.

By examining the phenomenon of sculpture in depth, this book probes beneath the veneer of stylistic emphasis to reveal sculpture as the result of a set of coherent metamorphic forces: the impetus generated by the psychic and intellectual authority increasingly invested in science and technology. This invested authority has fluctuated in philosophical emphasis, from decade to decade, a rising influence but not a monolithic one.

It may be argued that science and technology (or *technics*—to link them into a single word) are only one means in a large spectrum of influences which have turned sculpture away from its original course. But most aspects of Western culture are to some degree ramifications of technics. While retaining vestiges of a humanistic or nontechnical ethos, they have become systematically undermined and subsumed. Religion, literary imagery, craft technique, drama, architecture, painting—all the forces which have touched sculpture in the past—have not escaped the technological demiurge. Both physically and spiritually technics are responsible for sculpture's impending rupture with the past. A central aim of this book, therefore, will be to show the coercive nature of technics. In this respect, the essayist Friedrich Jünger conceded over forty years ago that technology is the metaphysics of our century; time has not diminished the accuracy of Jünger's apprehension.

The continued influence of technics on sculpture is not obvious. Rather, it is a subtle maneuver of our culture that all innovations are canonized under the heading of the "new." Rarely is the "new" regarded as part of a long-term trend—the "new" being that which is disembodied from tradition. The desire for the "new" partly stems from the unconscious desire of most artists to retain the illusion of private innovation, intuitive capability, and autonomy; partly this is abetted by critics who consider their own efforts creative acts sustained by the appearance of the "new." In such an atmosphere the ability to see sculpture in the cold light of connected formal invention is hardly encouraged.

This book attempts to detail the destructive-creative duality of technics as it affects the *archaic* endeavor of making sculpture. Quite broadly sculpture and technics are related in that they are both extensions of an urge to control and shape a limited part of man's environment. In this respect C. G. Jung has called archaic man "pre-logical" and has suggested that he differs from technological man only in his suppositions about the forces which control the world. This may have been a passing observation for Jung, but its implications for sculpture have been critical. Sculpture, in this study then, is seen as an archaic mode of form realization unwillingly thrust into a hostile and ultimately explosive frame of reference. What is happening now in sculpture can be anticipated from earlier studies of the transition from magic to science during the Middle Ages: this became a secular and churchly dispute resulting in the exchange of an older value and technical system for another more effective.

Modern sculpture has shown evidence for some time of its fate: not death through formal exhaustion as has appeared imminent, but time extinction through the attainment of goals as old as sculpture itself. For sculpture reached its apogee when human anatomy triumphed through realism and became spiritually renewed through naturalistic vitalism. (We have learned to look upon such an attitude as a reflection of the classical prejudice.)

Less than seventy years ago abstraction and geometric formalism were considered a necessary antithesis to naturalism. For the art historian Wilhelm Worringer, artistic abstraction became the means by which man periodically sought relief from "cosmic anguish," confronted as he was with a world admitting to no outward order; while abstraction's counterpart, classical naturalism, was symptomatic of human confidence to face the problems of an indifferent world. Abstraction, moreover, was an artistic phenomenon particularly appearing when a culture was confronted with existential doubt. The fortuitous appearance of Worringer's thesis a few years before the general acceptance of abstraction among avant-garde artists (ca. 1910) remains one of the inspired juxtapositions of modern scholarship. It made logical the demise of figure sculpture, which, nevertheless, had had brief moments of greatness during the previous century.

This study departs considerably from Worringer's view of the function of abstraction and formalism—or at least as they have appeared in recent times. In a pre-scientific society abstraction may well have served as a form

3

of psychic protection from the dangers of an indifferent environment. But in an industrial society the role of artistic abstraction *is* nothing less than psychic preparation for the entire re-creation of society, including remaking the biological composition of its inhabitants. In such cultures, once an unspecified threshold of scientific understanding has been crossed, *abstraction no longer functions as an adjunct to ritual which has become hollow; to remain culturally potent abstraction or formalism must gravitate toward a merger with the types of symbolic reasoning employed by science.* Formalist art in a culture devoted to technological evolution seeks and finds its *raison d'être* in more pervasive types of formalism, while in an archaic culture formalism remains latent and decorative in character.

The term "threshold of scientific understanding" as it is used above requires clarification if the real meaning of artistic formalism in a scientific age is to be understood. It is important to realize that for the first time in the known history of the world this "threshold" has been reached. This is our uniqueness within the continuum of events; there are many historical awakenings from which this threshold can be determined. One might be the sequential mastery through mathematics of the invisible energies which pervade the universe. Any such list must include Newton's proofs for universal gravitation in his *Principia*, the equations of Clerk Maxwell for light and electromagnetism, and Einstein's famous ratio for the interconversion of mass and energy. Each in its way is a delicate web of symbols; but only upon such ephemeral creations could the present technology have been built.

Both artistic and technical abstraction, having common distant origins in the rituals of everyday living, finally reconverge, this preordained by the integrative pressures of technology—an assumption which eliminates the pretense that contemporary art is tied to the art history karma of stylistic cycles: Archaic, Classical, Mannerist, Romantic, Abstract, and so on. Stylistic cycles are a self-evident impossibility as art becomes a psychical manifestation of the scientific demiurge, which moves ceaselessly in a single irreversible direction. Art thus becomes a dwindling part of an unstoppable scheme of events. We must see present art for what it is: the unique child of a unique age.

Nevertheless, this raises an important point. Science historians have speculated that science cannot indefinitely maintain its exponential rate of growth without turning the whole world into a race of scientists. A leveling-off process must begin. Hopefully this will happen *as* a world-wide stabilizing ecology is reached. In such a world the need for totemic artifacts would have disappeared as a psychic task. Another alternative is the reduction of the world to a pre-scientific state through a series of man-precipitated disasters. Here is a world ripe again for the reappearance of sculptural images.

Such a prognostication views modern sculpture as a preparatory stage representing steps toward the simulation of biological life, a point in human evolution when the sculptor begins to imitate the machine maker and the creator of scientific models, unaware that the artifacts of technology are meant to do the same things as his own forms, and that they do them more successfully. The drive that finally prompted the sculptor to forsake naturalism and the human figure was not that of the desire to destroy the biological replica, but the realization that if he was serious in his quest to bring inert matter to life anthropomorphism would not accomplish it. The machine, he intuitively realized, as unsubtle and inefficient as it was, remained the only means by which man would eventually reconstruct intelligent life, or what might be called life-bearing artifacts. As a result, much modern sculpture has been concerned with the creation of pseudo-machines which haphazardly approximate the life impulse.

What connects art to science is an abiding similarity between the artistic and scientific mind: it is as if both were motivated by the same pangs of discovery and a desire for the consummation of ideas into beautiful totalities. Words such as *progress* and *evolution* appear to have meaning connected to the history of science but none, or a suspected and slight amount, when attached to art. Perhaps the concept of progress, of progression from a less sophisticated to a more encompassing state, both materially and psychically, is a quality that can only be identified with art in a technologically dynamic culture, and then only because art ceases to be art in the traditional sense. It is difficult to ignore the common purposes of art and science, though less so when we consider that in prehistoric times the artist and the magician were both latent scientists. If we remember the joint origins of art, magic, religion, and science, it seems possible that each was part of a common goal which could only be ascertained as one of the four disciplines to achieve some degree of irremeable control over the environment.

Twentieth-century sculpture, future retrospection will show, was a highly transitional process, a brief labyrinth of changes. Already as a means of description, the term "sculpture" has lost its identity; it has become a misnomer for an art once concerned with carving and modeling for the purpose of simulating biological appearances, but which now generically designates all three-dimensional art construction.

Much of the confusion which surrounds sculpture today revolves around the classical intention of sculpture as a segregated endeavor, instead of as a vestigial biological activity closely related to the technological drive. It becomes important, therefore, that we look upon sculpture as an indication of man's changing conception of biology, as an indication of his biological role, and especially as a form of biological activity in itself.

Reification

Perhaps the most dynamic concept used by Karl Marx for viewing the capitalist system was the dialectical convenience of reification or "thingification" *(Verdinglichung)*. For Marx "thingification" was a term which described how certain societies transformed all ideas into objects. By this means, man himself became an exchangeable object, a commodity. This process typified for Marx the way in which man accomplished his own alienation from self: in part this consisted in the separation of human involvement from the work process, sundering ritual from intellectual knowledge, and the isolation of the human spirit from all sensual and psychical contact with the environment. This Introduction will not consider if Marx's economic solutions could reverse the effects of reification to restore man's sense of wholeness. Reification will be described from another point of view.

Historically science has transformed itself by stages. These are characterized by the general acceptance of the same paradigms which produce uniformity between world views and experimental techniques among scientists, at a given time. "Copernican astronomy" and "Newtonian mechanics" typify such encompassing frames of reference. Each paradigm of major importance has produced not only a scientific but a subsequent cultural revolution, one profoundly coloring the popular view of reality. The world *seems* and *is* altered accordingly as the views of men are transformed. Similarly, reification is the means by which the world is made anew, through sculpture or other artifacts, in a scientific culture. *Thus the process of "thingification" which has given birth to modern sculpture is the constant resynchronization of artistic sensibility with a disclosed form-world of scientific theory.*

As the primacy of the scientific world picture has become almost undisputed, sculpture has become engaged in a trade-off between its strivings toward science-oriented "objective" reality and the necessity for retaining some vestiges of idealism for survival's sake. "Thingification" brings sculpture away from its traditional modes of existence; as it does several trends are detectable.

a. The transition of sculpture from craft methodology to a reflection of the modern production of goods.

b. The sporadic passage of sculpture from idealism (as expressed through the traditional hieratic values of the sculpted object) to materialism.

c. The evolution of sculpture from a psychically-impregnated totemic object toward a more literal adaptation of scientific reality via the model or technologically inspired artifact.

d. And the replacement of inanimate sculpture with life-simulating systems through the use of technology.

Steadily we move toward a "scientific artistry," one that rejects whatever is inconsistent with contemporary science. Nevertheless, sculptors, though to a diminishing degree, outwardly reject scientific and technological influences despite the larger roles these same forces continue to play in their creative ambitions. It is the nature of cultural revolutions that we outwardly eschew their values while accepting them inwardly.

There is an ironic twist to reification in modern sculpture. The very paradigms by which science expands in conceptual mastery over the forces of nature are increasingly difficult to approximate through the traditional means of sculpture. Sculptors continue to "thingify" only at the risk of not being able to verify the sources of their creations—except as they are the output of a higher authority, namely, technics. The problem of what is real and what becomes real remains. Thus C. G. Jung in an essay, "The Basic Postulates of Analytical Psychology" (1933, p. 200), stated that "Under the influence of scientific materialism, everything that could not be seen with the eyes or touched with the hands was held in doubt: such things were even laughed at because of their supposed affinity with metaphysics." Disbelief in the immaterial was held by Jung as the prime reason why many scientists refused to study the human psyche as a legitimate problem of psychology.

Jung's conception of mechanistic science fits a nineteenth-century biologist or chemist, but was largely untrue after 1900. Far from being committed to a Humian materialism, science, epistemology observed, has long gravitated toward types of experimentation and hypothesis which are quite removed from direct sensory confirmation. This has forced significant areas of science, reluctantly, toward metaphysical speculation. However, within Western society scientific reality has steadily become the measure of all reality; thus Jünger's comment that technology is the metaphysics of this century is even more true of science in its role as a speculative agent. When metaphysical considerations and the accepted notion of reality fuse into a single view of the world, the result is an operational system as psychologically and intellectually pervasive as any monolithic religion. Hence the contemporary icon *par excellence* becomes the scientific model which interprets principles believed to be operative in the real world. In part, this explains why "thingification" has redirected sculpture away from its traditional anthropomorphic course.

Science, nevertheless, has not worked upon sculpture as a consistent materialist influence. Much of the most original formalist and geometric sculpture of the past half century owes its existence to what could be called "scientific idealism." Such an idealism attempts to view essential reality through the theories and models put forth provisionally by scientists; their use as sculpture or icon transforms them into ideational verities. As sculptors have sought embodiments of the essence of reality in scientific prototypes, some remain unaware that science is in no position to establish or define reality. By necessity, attempts to create sculpture within any context of scientific idealism are eventually undermined by the problematic and fluid condition of science, though sculpture created under these circumstances may have historical validity, as does any famous though now discredited scientific paradigm. Modes of scientific idealism have consistently stimulated the development of nonrepresentational sculpture: thus the so-called biomorphic idiom relied on vitalism; Constructivism found its impetus in the evanescences of modern structural engineering, mathematics, and physics; Surrealist sculpture vested its validity in Freudian interpretation of the subconscious mind; while the object sculpture of today seeks transcendence through the seeming rationality of materialism colored with phenomenological considerations.

Reification moves sculpture from its passive state as contemplative art toward more precise approximations of the systems which underlie operational reality. It is no coincidence that Spengler foresaw this happening as static figurative sculpture moved away from the classicism of Euclidean proportions and toward the Faustian dynamicism of the mathematical function (realized incompletely in Kinetic and some Object Art). Such a transition does not happen all at once, but has been in the making for hundreds of years; nor has sculpture been all transitional. As Thomas Kuhn points out in his study *The Structure of Scientific Revolutions* (1962), scientific paradigms do not follow one another in close procession, but are spaced apart so that they color and determine the types of experimentation undertaken during the time of their influence. Kuhn calls these periods of experimentation sustained by a major paradigm "normal science," or science which is nonrevolutionary in that its experimentation *elaborates* an already existent paradigm. This profile is essentially the one followed by sculpture.

There are "major reifications" by which sculpture comes to entirely new modes of form consciousness, and what could be called "minor reifications" where a given form consciousness is elaborated. Both, but particularly the former, are dependent on the evolving scientific world picture.

In Chapter One, "Sculpture's Vanishing Base," the dynamics of reification will be observed symptomatically through its effect on the sculpture base. Sculpture has for much of its duration been predicated on the conviction that artistic vitality could be substituted for biological vitality. Therefore the sculpture base was a convention for recognizing sculpture's innate lack of biological autonomy and mobility. In the last eighty years this condition has altered because of the following factors: the demise of idealism, the gradual realization of sculpture's material status simply as object, and the rise of the conviction that physicochemical conditions rather than spiritual energies are responsible for the origination of biological life.

Early in the present century the process of reification began to draw the sculptor away from an exhausted naturalism and toward an analytical awareness of biological life supported by vitalism. Thus, in a chapter entitled "The Biotic Sources of Modern Sculpture," vitalism is introduced both as a scientific doctrine and a sculpture aesthetic. It is shown that vitalism, as a source of artistic reification, lasted as long as it remained tenable as a scientific philosophy.

The essence of formalism in sculpture resided in its power for imbuing sculpture with varieties of proto-mechanical stylization. It is a thesis of this book that formalist and vitalist sculpture represent two preparatory tendencies which symbolically anticipate the re-creation of life through nonbiological means, that is, through technology. In this instance classical machine parts such as gears, pins, cams, and bearing plates (reduced to their basic geometric equivalents) are equated in the subconscious of industrial society with the life force itself. As a result, these and other geometrical configurations have become the formal vocabulary of much nonrepresentational sculpture. In part, formal sculpture became the reconstruction of life through the simulation of machine forms, and Chapter Three, "Formalism: The Weary Vocabulary," explains why the classical machine has become an inadequate archetype for this purpose.

In a final chapter in the first part of the book, formalism and vitalism are regarded as anachronistic dead ends. "Form Exhaustion and the Rise of Phenomenalism" records the decline of modern sculpture as it has been understood via the abstract idiom. Several options seemed to be left to the avant-garde: a return to stylized realism, direct involvement with the machine through Kinetic Art, or the creation of an aesthetic which could make formalism plausible again.

The last alternative has produced Object or Minimal sculpture, along with a desire to preserve the static, material consistency of past sculpture. In theory at least, Object sculpture is art which has been cut free of all previous iconic influences; it is sculpture de-idealized. Object sculpture, nevertheless, is not free of the idiosyncrasies of human perception. An object's origins are related to its ability to exist in the human mind, free and unattached, while its shape is ambiguously interpreted through viewer ambience. Object sculpture, however, is quite likely not the last step in the process toward absolute "thingification." Reification works in other directions, particularly as it allows sculpture the chance to approximate biological activities.

Sculpture has become an art form addicted to ideas which threaten its material substantiality. Yet, by definition, it remains slavishly attached to the idea of physical mass. Driven on by the dynamic influences of science and technology, sculpture has ceased to be an art with a sense of traditional continuity, surviving only through constant threats to its own origins.

Object and System

The two parts of this book divide modern sculpture respectively into *object* and *system*. The object denotes sculpture in its traditional physical form, whereas the system (an interacting assembly of varying complexity) is the means by which sculpture gradually departs from its object state and assumes some measure of lifelike activity. Attempts to preserve sculpture as object have already been touched on. What then are those psychological and socioeconomic properties which give objects their importance?

From prehistoric times the object—palpable, finite in dimensions, varying in preciousness, a direct result of the human formative urge—has been the means by which environment has been subdivided into transportable units. By contrast, the term *real estate*, denoting fixed property (houses and land), came to mean that which cannot be destroyed, that which by its very nature gives man wealth and, more importantly, the means for sustenance. Yet, compared with the provisional quality of systems, the object has more in common with real estate in the traditional sense. The object, although it can be destroyed, *is* real and lasting, and the sculpted object in particular has provided a large and unreplaceable record of all cultural history. Durability, compactness, and changing concern for the meaning of human anatomy have given sculpture a position as an intimate, psychical chronicle unmatched by other arts or artifacts. However, today, perishable sculpture and moving, energy-controlled sculpture possess uncertain durations as objects which disconnect them from traditional values of the sculpted object.

This impermanence is directly related to the industrial trend toward a *systematized* environment. Furniture, books, cooking utensils, tools, toys, and reliquaries were only some of the objects which made existence *objectively* real, which could be handed down from generation to generation, and which were made to last as self-contained entities. In contrast, the object now is a replaceable component in an interlocking system of production and need fulfillment. When we buy an automobile we no longer buy an object in the old sense of the word, but instead we purchase a three- to five-year lease for participation in the state-recognized private transportation system, a highway system, a traffic safety system, an industrial parts-replacement system, a costly insurance system, an outdoor advertising system, a state park recreation system, a drive-in eating and entertainment system—and, not least of all, the general economic system. Granted, objects were always the means by which man participated in systematic social activities; still there has been a gradual shift of emphasis from the object to systems which make the object useful primarily as an economic instrument.

To a marked extent the object has lost its independent status in technological society; the object becomes one of many means by which a systems-oriented culture functions at increasing levels of complexity tempered by efficiency. Ironically, we are capable of manufacturing more objects than ever before; yet, like the realistic portrait after the invention of photography, the object has been debased by its profusion.

It is difficult to describe this debasement. Certainly we are capable of creating articles more elaborate, valuable, useful, and finished; articles far more powerful and efficacious than any before in history. Do today's objects lack human warmth, the feel of care and personal attention? If we say they are less beautiful, what does that mean? It is easy to romanticize the importance of human craftsmanship. Perhaps what has changed most drastically is Western man's lack of need for objects of intrinsic worth, his casual attitude toward the buying and using of items for daily existence.

During the 1930's Stuart Chase and other critics of the social fabric introduced the term "technological tenuousness" to describe the vulnerability of a society dependent on interwoven electrical power and communication systems. It remains evident that the object has certain properties of endurance which the system does not yet, and perhaps never will, possess. The city itself epitomizes human systemization and, as one designer has pointed out, before modern civilization its average probable life span was about three hundred years. We know those cities by the vestiges of their street layouts and the objects buried under their ruins. Yet how do we define where the object leaves off and the system begins?

Above all the object occupies a specific space: it has *place*, remaining inert and stationary. A system is an aggregate of components; first, its parts are mutually dependent; and second, it may manifest some of the fundamental characteristics natural to life: self-organization, growth, internal or external mobility, irritability or sensitivity, input and output, kinetically sustained equilibrium and eventual death (humans are the most dramatic instances of systems which die). The advantages of a system over an object are flexibility of use, adaptability, and the capacity for measured reaction. Objects, on the other hand, may be more reliable and, because of their greater inherent physical stability, last longer than systems. For economy, though, the modern engineer designs his systems in terms of a given life span. A longer than necessary life span would probably be a waste of materials and precision.

A systems-oriented world is a milieu completely given over to what Jacques Ellul calls *technique*. Science and technology for Ellul are simply the most efficient forms of technique. For most of man's early existence art, magic, religion, hunting, shelter building, and medicine were merged into a single ritualistic program of survival. Civilization brought about an inevitable division of labor, a partitioning of instincts, and a segregation of psychic preoccupations from physical duties. In time each task had its implicit societal value, its methodology for maximum return, and its separate traditions. Technique in Ellul's estimation has become *the* means by which the patterns of unified social living have progressively degenerated. The pervasive invisibility of systems, systems which seem to operate more for their own sake than for the people they serve, has gradually replaced earlier, direct, more sensual modes of expressing the phenomenon of being alive.

The modern network of artificial systems remains the most sophisticated form of materialism devised to date. These systems presuppose that man is master of his environment solely through the domination of known forms of energy and matter. The object, therefore, becomes a transient state of man's attempt to *further* objectify (or reify) the properties of nature. Thus the system becomes a logical extension of the object through intellectual domination of the environment.

Although Ellul disavows any signs of overt pessimism, he regards technique as a force which will in time destroy all traces of biological life; so technique remains a pernicious disease which Ellul, as a doctor diagnosing a terminal case, sees no hope of curing. It is enough to say about technique, as Ellul interprets it, that its flower is modern Western science; it has no psychic or ethical strictures; it is self-aggrandizing and, most alarming, irreversible. As for its effects on art, Ellul has this to say about the future of art in a technique-bound society (1954, p. 423):

It was held that, with the development of a purely materialistic society, a struggle was inevitable between the machine and the economy, on one side, and the ideal realm of religion, art and culture, on the other. But we can no longer hold such a boundless simplistic view. Ecstasy is subject to the world of technique and is its servant.

Not only does technique facilitate centralized control over human action and destroy the capacity for individual reflection, but according to Ellul it also channels and diffuses those instincts in man which account for much of his artistic motivation. Ellul thinks that satisfying the ecstatic impulse of the human psyche by chemical or mechanical means would in time eliminate the underpinnings of human culture, but he does not specify if a society based on high-level technology could allow art to be made even by those not entirely integrated into its scheme of values. Perhaps he would say that it does not matter since the artist has no access to the mass communications media.

This book makes a case for at least the temporary survival of sculpture through transition from the object to the system. The system, as expressed through Kinetic Art, Light sculpture, some Environmental Art, and Cybernetic Art, has become a viable, if evanescent, aesthetic preoccupation. All of these art movements stand defiant, counter to the subtler implications of the object; they are technique in the driver's seat. Moreover, Ellul's pessimistic view of technique is based on a value system which views the fallibility of the human situation as the greatest good worth saving. Even with all its pathos, indecision, and sorrow it demonstrates a nobility of existence not replaced by the effectiveness of technique for its own sake. Technique for Ellul remains implacable, without doubts or second thoughts; it remains inhuman in the most essential meaning of the word.

Less emotionally charged, there exists another way to look at the inroads created by artificial systems. Since the mid-nineteenth century, physicists have used the term *entropy* to express the work potential in a measurable system. Entropy is a curiously negative term, a kind of dissipation factor which expresses the level of disorganization to be found in a system. The more disorganized or chaotic the system, the less work it can do, the higher its level of entropy will be. Entropy also measures the probability that a system exists; the more structured the system, the less probable its existence. Viewed in terms of entropy, the Earth has been running downhill, out of energy (dissipation of internal thermal heat and raw materials), thus

13

becoming a more probable system for over a billion years. Technology has speeded up the dissipation of energy from the Earth, but at the same time has reorganized energy stores into compact usable sources so that materials could be ordered into more improbable and structured forms. Such a trend has led one cyberneticist to define technology as the development of pockets of decreasing entropy on a planet where the general level of entropy is rising.

The economist Kenneth Boulding expresses this same procedure in a more fanciful way (1964, p. 140):

The universe then is seen to be like a man, who is spending his capital so that his total capital in the form of potential continually diminishes, but who continually builds up the diminishing capital into ever more elaborate works of art. Thus when a sculptor makes a statue out of a piece of stone, there is more organization in the statue than in the stone, in the sense that the shape of the statue is much less probable than that of the stone. But if we look at the whole system, the stone, the statue, the chips, and the sculptor himself, we shall find that the organization of the statue has been bought at the cost of disorganization in the chips and perhaps in a diminuation of the potential of the sculptor.

Boulding's sculpture analogy is relevant on a certain level, but it is the first sentence of his statement which provides a clue for the place of systems in art. Complex systems in all phases of modern life *are* the "ever more elaborate works of art" which begin to approximate those of nature. Thus a pail of sand, a spring-wound machine, a plant, and a human being represent systems of decreasing entropy. In each succeeding case a level of structure and complexity is bought only through the dissipation of greater amounts of energy.

For this reason some social scientists see a common effect linking social, technical, and biological evolution. Each in its own way moves toward a higher life form; each seeks to lower its entropy rate at the expense of the general environment. In effect, what this creates according to Boulding is "more order at some points at the cost of creating less order elsewhere." *Technique, then, may be the means by which society eventually becomes one giant, interconnected, living system, structured to reduce individual differences between components and to facilitate integration and communication within the whole.* Sculpture, then, in a technological society must be regarded as a tiny microcosm of the entire socio-technical-biological evolution.

Often the most modern developments have ancient antecedents, and such is the case with moving sculpture. "Sculpture and Automata," the first chapter of the second part of this study, shows systems as the primitive devices and mechanisms by which moving sculptures have been powered and controlled throughout history. Automata have rarely functioned as high art, but always as the by-play of religious, magical, theatrical, or proto-scientific obsessions. The robot has been the collective obsession of a technological population dreaming of its own replacement. Though graceful, there was something aesthetically clumsy in the automatic manikins of the eighteenth century. They were an ambition better forgotten. Yet the contemporary merging of sculpture with automata is recognition that sculpture had to become deformed, mutilated, encased, and rendered sensually repellent before it could rightfully be called a machine.

Sociologically the succeeding chapter holds no dire juxtapositions; rather the machine's strict formalism (in action) is seen clumsily dominating, sometimes with genius, the evolution of contemporary Kinetic Art. Cogently explained are the limitations of the classical machine wedded to sculpture.

After "Kineticism: The Unrequited Art" the difficulties and special attractions of Light sculpture are brought forth. As with Kinetic sculpture, emphasis is put on the fact that illuminated art is preeminently the result of an electromechanical system. Effects well outside the range of traditional sculpture may be achieved, but only at the expense of stability and life duration.

In many ways the last chapter culminates and justifies many of the ideas put forward in this book. Nothing more spectacular heralds the beginnings of the sculpture of the future than the slow emergence of what is called "Cyborg Art" (the art of cybernetic organisms). Cybernetic theory is discussed and some of industry's labor- and thought-performing robots are contrasted with the mock robots of contemporary sculpture. Much of this section is devoted to attempts by sculptors to make "sculptures" or three-dimensional systems which actually operate on cybernetic principles. It may be difficult to accept some of the conclusions presented, which read as a kind of "art fiction" (related to the better-known genre of science fiction). Yet, after reading this section, there should be no doubt that experiments in artificial intelligence are already fruitful. It is only a step from here to suppose that in time an aesthetics of artificial intelligence will evolve. Unless the world is substantially altered for the worst, the logical outcome of technology's influence on art before the end of this century should be a series of art forms that manifest true intelligence, but perhaps more meaningfully, with a capacity for reciprocal relationships with human beings (in this case the word *viewer* seems quite antiquated). The need for intelligent response and self-recognition which we have instinctively sought, and sometimes found, in art will reappear in fantastically powerful forms. But in return for fulfillment of our needs, we must loosen our psychological grasp on traditional art.

Bizarre?—Yet attempts throughout history to produce automata show that the human will devoted to synthetic re-creation is almost as urgent as that of natural procreation. A portion of human existence is readily identifiable with successive attempts to concede a soul or indwelling vitality to inanimate objects. Nevertheless we know we cannot invest vitality in shaped stone, nor can vitality rise out of any need for "truth to materials"—even in its day a profane dogma ineffectually supplanting the sacred object. Nearing the end of an age which sought vitality in latent visual metaphor, the "*élan vital*" will be looked upon as the old prime mover, while the Greek "*kybernētēs*" (derived from *steersman* and the basis of the word cybernetics) becomes the expression of a new and even more effective prime mover.

PART ONE

SCULPTURE AS OBJECT

CHAPTER ONE

Sculpture's Vanishing Base

Functions of the Sculpture Base

The base is the sculptor's convention for rooting his art to surrounding reality while permitting it to stand apart. As such, the base creates a twilight zone both physically and psychically. It says, in effect, that this sculpted object has a life, a "presence" of its own. Its use to support various top-heavy standing figures, and to provide a perch to minimize damage, are the obvious physical reasons for its existence; beyond that, the base helps to create an aura of distance and dignity around the favored object. Moreover, Western tradition has been consistent in its use of the base as an appendage to sculpture. Within the representational idiom in general, the base has served to isolate and emphasize the particular psychology and anecdotal content of the activity it supports.

Modern abstract and nonobjective art has produced a considerable shift from this general use of the base. Steadily the base has declined in its purpose of psychological segregation to become the means of physically isolating one class of objects from all others—namely, *sculpture*. That sculpture could be created by setting any object upon a base became a chief dialectical dilemma of modern sculpture. *All* objects, thereby, could be considered sculpture; a popularization which has turned modern sculpture away from the base as a means of identification. If the base was rendered meaningless—both physically and psychically—sculpture could only regain meaning free of its confines.

While practical and aesthetic questions of mounting sculpture have confronted artists for thousands of years, it is revealing how little attention the problem receives in historical texts and technical treatises. Except for certain arbitrary proportional canons, the base has remained a minor detail of the craft. Until the advent of gallery-size sculpture in the eighteenth century, the substructure was usually an architectural detail, designed to harmonize with an architectural setting, or planned according to elements of an architectural order as in the case of statuary groups by Renaissance wood-carvers and metalsmiths. Until the present century, architecture was considered the mother of sculpture.

Nomenclature for the substructure of sculpture is ill-defined. *Plinth*, *base*, and *pedestal* are the most commonly used terms, and sculpture may employ any or all of these elements. These terms may be defined as such: the base, the greatest mass upon which a sculpture rests, it refers to the support as a whole; the pedestal, a shaftlike form which elevates the sculpture; the plinth, a flat, planar support which separates the sculpture from the ground or from a pedestal. Until recently students were taught that a base should be unobtrusive while providing maximum enhancement for any sculpture set on top of it. Bases consequently tended to be strong geometric shapes with an architectonic simplicity separating them from the organic activity above.

Not surprisingly the greatest innovators in modern sculpture have had the most to do with the reorganization of bases. This stems from a realization that sculpture continues beyond its material periphery with a spatial sphere of influence, which varies and emanates in all directions. The modern sensibility has progressively attempted to break down the psychic barrier, the traditional object-viewer relationship, that accounts for the transcendent qualities of sculpture. It has tried to substitute an environment where observer and object are given a like status; raising an object to humanness or superhumanness is no longer an issue. What is important is a naturalness where things, both objects and organisms, are accepted for what they are, not for what they represent. As a result, the destruction or withering away of the base is very much a part of the "secularization" of sculpture. Withdrawn from sculpture are all the old reverberations and implications of the "art object." In its place sculpture without a base functions with all the casualness of an umbrella stand or the early-morning fog over a field. In a sense, the sculptor has asked the observer to forget about the heroics of past art and to concentrate on the nature of the everyday here and now. As a consequence, two trends have dominated the modern base: the first incorporates the base into the sculpture itself, to the point where sculpture rests directly on the floor or ground; the second attempts to free sculpture from all earthly contact or means of visible support, making sculpture not so much airborne as gravity defying.

These solutions for mounting modern sculpture have another more far-reaching implication. Traditionally the base with its limited area has implied a fixed situation where the "frozen" condition of the sculpture necessitated no room for mobility. Traditional sculpture is virtually life that cannot move. Consequently it is given nowhere to go. From the second half of the nineteenth century there seemed to be a collective consciousness at work among avant-garde sculptors working both to disturb this traditional biological immobility, this fixity which the base ordains, and the sense of gravitational dependence so inherent in the anatomy of man. Besides being a field of action, the base becomes an orientational device; it is a tacit acknowledgment that all mammals have a top and bottom or head and feet, plus a ventral and dorsal side. The base is a biological reaffirmation that man is constructed to walk the ground, to gain his mobility through successive contacts with the earth. It was preordained that for sculpture not rooted to the ground or made inanimate, the base had lost its reason for being.

This chapter will show through successive examples that the sculptural will toward spatial mobility and a non-idealistic art are intimately tied to innovations in the function of the base. This is an involved transition; it continues today; and the evolutionary pattern is not always clear. As a sign, though, of great transformations which are taking place in sculpture, the base is symptomatic and deserves to be given the closest attention.

Works by Four Early Modern Sculptors

It is fitting to begin this study with an analysis of figurative works. These are by sculptors whose unorthodox conceptions of the human form and its actions are in part defined by their very personal approaches to presentation. Certainly one of the earliest for our purposes was an artist who had already revolutionized the psychology of portrait painting before taking up sculpture.

During the past ninety years much has been made of Edgar Degas's bronzed creature clothed in a real cloth bodice, dancing shoes, net tutu, and hair ribbon. *The Little Dancer of Fourteen* (FIG. 1), as she was called by Degas, is neither sculpture nor doll, but an attempt to bring art into the area of living activity. This was the only sculpture exhibited by Degas during his lifetime and, since he used great care in its preparation, there is—if one is aware of Degas's personal problems—a hint of the Pygmalion impulse in its creation. It was certainly more than an anatomical exercise. The *Dancer* may be an alter ego, reflecting aspects of Degas's personality: among them physical plainness, a sang-froid attitude and a remarkably aggressive frailty. Also there is a resilience of character which is not without its pathos. It may be that the infusion of perverse vitality into this child figure has something to do with Degas's propensity for inventing and solving formal problems in figure sculpture at the expense of feminine grace and dignity.

The *Dancer*'s feet are in fourth position with knees, hips, and elbows

2. Edgar Degas, *The Tub*, circa 1886.

1. Edgar Degas, *The Little Dancer of Fourteen*, 1876.

locked in a posture of disciplined repose. Actually this position would not be painful because the girl's body is not in constant muscular tension. Rather, her skeletal framework, locked in position, supports the main weight of the body. This is not "frozen" activity but a position which could be held for some time. More relevant is the slab of polished hardwood under the *Dancer*'s feet that serves as both a plinth and a replica of a ballet practice floor. The base, like the real costume, is a part of the environment, an abbreviated tableau helping to establish the ambivalent reality-ideality of the piece.

More indicative of Degas's revolutionary attitude toward the sculpture base is his small bronze of a woman bathing, *The Tub* (FIG. 2). This eighteen-and-a-half-inch high work shows a woman one-third submerged in a round tub partially filled with water. Her left knee is drawn up and grasped by the right hand in a typical Degas pose. Photographs of this piece ordinarily show

22

a crudely-textured plinth under the bathing tub. Knowing Degas's inclination toward directness and immediacy, one suspects that this plinth was not a part of the original ensemble. The difference in the modeling between the two would bear this out. John Rewald (1944, pp. 78–79) has included an overhead view of the original wax cast which shows the plinth as an afterthought of the caster. It did not exist in the original.

Obviously Degas conceived of the tub, half filled with water, as the base for his composition of the woman bathing. There are previous examples in sculpture (for instance, the monumental cadavers and biers of Roman antiquity) where the base has become a part of a figurative composition. Yet here, with Degas's bronze casting also depicting the water in the tub, the figure seems to emerge from the base. All considered, the Dada and tableau aspects of this piece are so radically new that plaster castings fitted into their dry-cleaning shop environments of the 1960's seem passé by comparison. If a bathtub can function as a base, what prevents us from considering the bathtub as pure sculpture in itself? Degas was breaking ground for such a line of reasoning.

The impressionism of Medardo Rosso made for the first fusion between base and subject, the figures and the structure upon which they are mounted. Very early in the sculptor's career, before his mature style of group impressionism, he completed a work in which the relationship to the base displayed the same modern sensitivity as Degas's. The genius of Rosso was such that he displayed an almost pathological inability to execute the expected solution to any problem in sculpture.

During his first year in art school in Milan, Rosso had been commissioned to design a funerary monument for a Milanese client. Circumstances surrounding the transaction are most obscure. The work, in some respects, is a typical Italian funerary theme of the times and is called *The Kiss on the Tomb* (FIG. 3). It depicts, in life size, a woman fully prostrated on the tomb of her just deceased husband, bestowing a last kiss before the tomb is sealed. In terms of emotional directness, the subject was not unduly histrionic for the urban cemeteries of Genoa and Milan at the end of the century. Rosso treats the modeling of his stricken woman, especially her clothes, almost as a sketch and with an amazing lack of slickness. The slab or face of the tomb is handled with the same vigor. For some unexplained reason the municipality of Milan had the work removed from the city cemetery and melted it down on the advice of the local art commission.

It could be surmised that Rosso's aggressive, slaglike treatment of the modeling—so out of character with the usual grand finish of Italian carving—

23

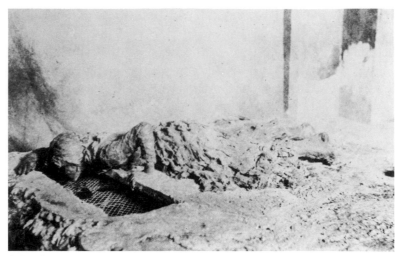

3. Medardo Rosso, *The Kiss on the Tomb*, 1886.

4. Auguste Rodin, *The Burghers of Calais*, 1884–1886.

offended the sensibilities of the commission. This plastic fusion of base and figure may have produced a public or official reaction. One suspects, considering Rosso's hectic and aborted art schooling, that the crudeness of the work evoked certain political and revolutionary overtones unacceptable at that time. *The Kiss on the Tomb* exhibits little pomp, that emotional protection which anesthetizes the pain of death. Instead, the prevailing feeling is one of naked pathos.

In a series of conversations with his secretary, Paul Gsell, Auguste Rodin comments on Gsell's character analysis of *The Burghers of Calais* (FIG. 4), a monument which caused Rodin much rethinking (1912, pp. 88–89):

> . . . you have justly placed my burghers in the scale according to their degree of heroism. To emphasize this effect still more I wished, as you perhaps know, to fix my statues one behind the other on the stones of the Place, before the Town Hall of Calais, like a living chaplet of suffering and of sacrifice.
>
> My figures would so have appeared to direct their steps from the municipal building toward the camp of Edward III; and the people of Calais of today, almost elbowing them, would have felt more deeply the tradition of solidarity which unites them to these heroes. It would have been, I believe, intensely impressive. But my proposal was rejected, and they insisted upon a pedestal which is as unsightly as it is unnecessary. They were wrong. I am sure of it....

If sculpture of the past twenty years is any indication, Rodin was considerably ahead of his time. On more than one occasion Giacometti has used precisely Rodin's suggestion with impressive results. Yet, ironically enough, the choice which Rodin was forced to make resulted in a base with multiple bodings for the future. If there is any straight line of evolving conceptions concerning the development of bases, they remain obscure. Rather, many paths have evolved leading toward the situation existing today.

The town council of Calais ordered the sculptor to assemble the *Burghers* as a single group composition so that it could be mounted on a tall base in the city square. It is easy to imagine how all of Rodin's thoughts about the intimacy of the individual statues were destroyed. However, other possibilities began to appear. Originally each figure was created to stand on its own plinth. These plinths are not simply flat tablets; they are sloped, uneven perches giving each figure some degree of imbalance or tilt from an imaginary axis perpendicular to the ground (FIG. 5). Throughout the ensemble this creates a concurrent forward and backward thrust, a type of twisting momentum which revolves around no one figure. With these six oddly-integrated figures Rodin cast the whole into a single eight-inch-thick plinth.

25

5. *The Burghers of Calais*, Detail of Plinth, 1884–1886.

Albert Elsen (1963, p. 83) has described the sequence of shadows and concavities that a viewer encounters while walking around *The Burghers of Calais*. The ever varying spaces, hollows, and angles tend to make the group extremely difficult to read as a coherent sequence. Any impact of drama and unity is sensed through the group as a mass. Arms invading pockets of interior space, and the tilted, almost falling, position of some of the bodies stem from the erratic contours of the plinth underfoot. Viewed alone, this craggy slab of bronze has all the ambiguity of a Cubist relief whose projected planes slip past one another opening deep crevices. Each statue's center of gravity is partly defined by the slope of its footing. Figures tend to lean forward and toward the center of the composition. Yet added complications—projected arms and contorted bodies—produce a sense of indeterminacy.

It is possible to disagree with Rodin's final placement of the *Burghers;* the focused intensity of his original plan (a column of figures) is lost so that some of the gestures within the group are wasted effect. But an immediacy and improvisational quality are gained, in which semi-random placement is played off against a strictly determined psychology of human emotions. With both the figures and the unified base, the effects gained by shattering, then reforming the totality have slowly gained an importance through later sculpture experiments.

Christopher Gray (1953, pp. 92–93) says this about the relationship of space to solid matter in Cubist painting: ". . . both solid form and space itself are treated as if they had a positive material existence. Space itself is given form and modulated with color in the same manner as material form." In contrast, the Cubist or Futurist sculptor worked without the advantage of illusionism and was tied down to an analytical approach to compact volumes. Ambiguities of space and matter could only be implied through devices such as negative silhouette and perforation.

The Futurist Umberto Boccioni saw the possibility for a more literal fusion between the material subject of a sculpture and the illusionary environment surrounding it. This was made evident in the *Technical Manifesto of Futurist Sculpture*, in which he stated (quoted in Herbert, 1964, pp. 78–79): "Let us…proclaim the complete abolition of the finished line and the closed statue. Let us open up the figure like a window and enclose within it the environment in which it lives. Let us proclaim that the environment must form part of the plastic block as a special world regulated by its own laws."

Boccioni's determination to realize these aims of the manifesto proved far more ambitious than the intentions of the Paris Cubist sculptors. His *Fusion of a Head and Window* (1912), with its awkward assembly of parts, is one of the earliest efforts in this direction. The assemblage consists of a real window sash without glass panes, penetrated by a sheath of wooden sun rays more substantial than the carved head they illuminate. The result is a futile attempt to introduce ephemeral environment; plastically the work is too chaotic and simplistic to justify the high aims of the manifesto.

In *Development of a Bottle in Space* (FIG. 6), Boccioni comes closer to

6. Umberto Boccioni, *Development of a Bottle in Space*, 1912.

transforming Futurist ideology into palpable bronze. The composition moves through a succession of discontinuous spiral edges toward an apex at the mouth of the bottle. The dish, the cloth, and other obscure objects surrounding the bottle become part of the base while, compositionally, the base is part of the sculpture; therefore Boccioni has come closer to his original intention. Formally, the base appears as a row of shifting, inclined planes which level by level appear to penetrate the space of the bottle itself. Plastically, this solution is vastly superior to the earlier one of heavy-handed sun rays passing through a nonexistent glass. As in *The Burghers of Calais*, the base functions as a stage set, a baroque platform impelling flux and activity. Within the humble limits of a few still-life objects, Boccioni contrived a small structure whose coherence and related forces approach true monumentality.

Shortly before his death in the First World War, Boccioni turned from the depiction of flux, physical and psychical, between juxtaposed objects to the expression of mechanistic-organic dynamism. This he achieved with a sculptural synthesis of flayed muscles and streamlined forms. His masterpiece in this style is *Unique Forms of Continuity in Space* (FIG. 7). A vaguely striding figure stands supported on rectangular impost blocks as part of a single casting. These two pedestals, executed with precise geometry, contrast sharply with the imprecision and slightly aerodynamical expression of the forms they support. The base no longer circumscribes activity but serves as a launching pad for all movement. The staticity of the two separate blocks is tied together by the arch of the figure's striding legs. What Boccioni accomplishes with the underlying plinth and two blocks is an effect of optical closure where action between two defined points is filled in by the viewer.

The Base as Anti-Base

Even before 1913 and the appearance of nonobjective sculpture, the function of the base was changing. More radical figure sculptors tried to make their statues fit into daily life, curtailing the hieratic function of the base in favor of environmental naturalness. In some cases the base satisfied no more than a convention, provided a means for allowing a work to stand with the least evidence of support. One exception to this resulted from the desire of some Cubist and abstract sculptors to leave no doubt in the mind of the public that their work *was* sculpture. In this instance elaborate and imposing bases were used. Today no such caution is necessary and the sophisticated public has few preconceptions about what is or is not sculpture.

Tangent to these attitudes were the evolving presentation techniques in nonobjective sculpture or sculpture of "pure form." More breath-taking methods were sought to release essential form from the confines of the base.

7. Umberto Boccioni, *Unique Forms of Continuity in Space*, 1913.

Since idealized form approached hyper-physical being, the base no longer served the primeval biotic function of providing solid "earth" for repose. Several works by Brancusi, and later the Constructivists, contain a number of overlapping attempts to rid sculpture of mass, the effects of gravitation and, even at times, spatial orientation.

The situation, however, was not so straightforward as simply accommodating the base to a new set of plastic values. Marcel Duchamp conceived of a more imposing threat to the idealism of the sculpted object. Duchamp produced a series of ordinary objects, frequently utilitarian, which, through a "laying on of hands" by the artist, were raised to the status of fine art. Part of the irony of the "Readymades" is their very idealism—a consequence of being all idea with no deliberate construction technique on the part of the artist. Rather than dying out as an ontological caper, the Readymade has become one of the pervasive influences in modern sculpture, a sort of Goedel's Theorem of aesthetics, which has proved the provisional quality of art.

The installation of a Duchamp exhibition, until recently, always stirred interest because the mode of display varied with a given director's assessment of the Readymades as works of art. They could be displayed as "art," as historically important curios, or merely as the interesting results of a wayward talent. The usual cautious, neutral, and probably fitting decision was to set the Readymades in plexiglas cases—neither mocking nor accepting the Readymades as art—a wise precaution considering today's deluge of post-Duchampian art and the ascendancy of the "cool." Now fewer things begin on a pedestal, but all receive wary respect.

Yet if one cult sought to denigrate sculpture to the status of mundane object, another more powerful faction strove to "iconize" sculpture via bodiless formal conceptualizations.

Constantin Brancusi

Brancusi's ability to create psychical associations with his materials has resulted in the most amazing array of presentation techniques. No one can grasp the development of modern sculpture without understanding how Brancusi rethought the relationship of sculpture to its environment. As frequently observed, his bases are more than appendages to his sculpture; they are sculpture. In a way the bases have their origins in the senses and memories of the perceiver; like the reveries of children, they are the phenomenal outgrowth of all the hyper-physical properties of substances. The relationship between the subject and base resembles that of a flowering plant; to separate the stem and flower from the roots makes for an abbreviated beauty, committing an offense to both biology and art.

Many of Brancusi's ideas for the mounting of sculpture are original inventions. And, like all organically conceived innovations, they developed slowly from work to work. Effects were modified and heightened until they reached a climax. Later Brancusi would reemploy them in a new context. To all but a few contemporaries his ideas for displaying sculpture seemed very strange, even more so in some cases than the sculpture itself. Their acceptance into the idiom of modern sculpture is staggering; in the past forty years thousands of sculptors have borrowed from Brancusi's ideas. Rather than examine an abundance of individual works, a few examples support this enumeration of Brancusi's display techniques:

1. Frequently his bases confront the observer with rough and handhewn textures in direct contrast to the finished precision of the subject above. For instance the bronze *Bird in Space* (FIG. 8) culminates the forms of wood and stone below it. Moreover, these textures establish a psychical hierarchy. Usually, the lower portions of a base are the roughest, like the rusticated façades of Renaissance palaces. This spectrum of crude to fine finishes has its symbolic implications, some revealed by Brancusi in conversation: com-

8. Constantin Brancusi, *Bird in Space*, 1919.

monness opposed to preciousness, the creative seed in the mother, emergent life, the storyteller and the myth, natural and sublime origins, geometry and organism, etc.

2. A sculptor like a good builder opposes the mere application of materials. Still only intuition, not engineering finesse, exists in the way Brancusi sandwiched assorted shapes into what appears to be a precarious pile. These piles do not seem to be structural solutions; rather they substitute the visual equations of a poet for a builder's logic. Often a metal dowel, a bit of glue or cement keeps such an equation intact. To support a portrait head, there is no reason why an eighteen-inch cruciform of light buff-gray limestone should have a six-inch-diameter pink marble cylinder placed on top of it.

3. The bases often give the impression of a child's precarious pile of building blocks. A single added block could topple an entire structure. That Brancusi has securely fastened the parts together is not for the viewer to know. What lingers is the faintest expectation of collapse, thereby releasing

a bird or fish from all firm contact. The sculptor developed the visual power of sources of potential energy, with great overhanging weights. In the veined gray marble version of *The Fish* (FIG. 9) a millstone, supported by a much smaller cylinder, hovers just off the ground. As counterpoint a sleek fish hovers a few inches above the ponderous millstone.

4. It was Brancusi's practice to align the vertical axis of the sections of his bases in rigorous symmetry. Sometimes, as a gesture of provocation, a sculpture would be placed off-center or rotated to a nonfrontal position. For objects, symmetry offers one of the highest forms of organization; any artistic volition which calls for its destruction must establish an even higher call to order. There is a biological truth here: within the total regularity of a crystal or organism only an imprecision spurs on further growth or formation; in sculpture as well, a calculated irregularity separates the living from the dead.

5. The "breathing" bases are pedestal forms with saw-tooth sides or cylinders carved with ringlike involutions similar to the lining of an esophagus. Usually, Brancusi would place such a form between two rectangular blocks. The result is purely optical; a faint retinal pulsation gives the effect of a minute rhythmic contraction and expansion.

6. A mirror surface placed directly beneath some versions of his fish sculpture (FIG. 10) is most effective when the area of contact between the reflective surface and the fish form are minimal. The resulting impression of depthlessness is as close as he comes to "floating" his sculptures or disengaging them from earthly contact.

7. The type of contact that a sculpture had with its base was of the utmost importance to Brancusi. This *touching* of two surfaces, the ground below and the touching object above, signifies the essential dynamic relationship of the delicate film of life covering the earth. A sculpture with a great deal of under surface in contact with the base is analogous to a plant reaching into the earth, or an iceberg with its mass underwater. In contrast, Brancusi's egg-shaped sculptures rest on a single tangential point. Their point of contact with the flat surface of the base is completely visible. However, the center of gravity of these sculptures is such that normal tilt suggests tranquility. Brancusi does not always position his sculptures according to their inherent equilibrium (FIG. 11). Occasionally he defies a sculpture's center of gravity by pinning it with a dowel in a position of unrest. The result is a sense of precariousness and momentary gesture.

As with the sculptures themselves, Brancusi infused his bases with an ancient and logical sense of animism. They are logical because they fulfill a primitive need to provide for the psychic security of a living spirit. Their

9. Constantin Brancusi, *The Fish*, 1930.

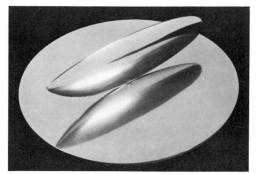

10. Constantin Brancusi, *The Fish*, 1924.

11. Constantin Brancusi, *Leda*, 1924.

height above the ground promises protection from dangers real and imagined. Their material represent natural habitat for the spirit of the sculpture. In many cultures the living set out food, utensils, and even doll servants for the dead; just so the bases of Brancusi provide a liberating and sympathetic environment for any latent life which they embrace.

The Constructivists

While some of Brancusi's bases are metaphorical attempts to release earthbound masses from the pull of gravity, this one desire becomes the *raison d'être* for the Constructivists. During the "heroic" period of the Russian Revolution, when the Constructivists had visions of revising art according to the technological and scientific landscape, all factions recognized the importance of using modern engineering techniques. If their earliest analogies for sculpture ran to bridges, structural steel towers, and rigid-frame air ships, their solutions for bases bore a relation to abutments and foundations, but perhaps more to dirigible moorings. Three considerations seemed to be of uppermost importance: that the base express a dynamism consistent with the construction on top of it; that it be an extension of a construction (structually as well as visually); and, perhaps most important, that an illusion of separation be produced between the base and its superstructure. As the Constructivist movement became more involved in absolute conceptions of self-contained objects, this last became a primary concern.

A remaining evidence of these three functions can be found in some of the photographs of the Vkhutemas student exhibition in Moscow (May, 1920) held under the direction of Tatlin, Rodchenko and Gabo. While these constructions no longer exist, the surviving photographs reveal that the bases for these works were fragile pedestals supported by the thinnest wooden struts and tension wires. These constructions, intended to teach students the properties of materials for engineering purposes, were not for pure sculptural experimentation. Nevertheless, the idea behind the structural integration of base and construction has had a lasting effect on sculpture. It epitomized the means by which modern engineering erected structures through the least visible and lightest members.

What motivated the Constructivist sculptors to support masses by nearly invisible means? Recent successes with heavier-than-air flight might have been influential, but more important were the conceptual models of science. After 1921 Soviet aesthetic policies aborted progress within the Constructivist movement; work continued outside Russia by the brothers Naum Gabo and Antoine Pevsner. Gabo led this later development. By 1921 the anthropomorphic character of his earliest works had completely disappeared. The bases for his constructions lost all their traditional implications, and, as in the works of Brancusi, their new function was discovered only through experimentation. The next phase of Gabo's work approached the architectonic mockups of futuristic skyscrapers. Between 1922 and 1925 Gabo's bases consisted mostly of raised polished disks, sometimes mirror smooth and close in character to Brancusi's solution. Both sculptors realized by 1928 that their constructions, receding from the human and architectonic images, had evolved to become creations of pure imagination (though ruled by a host of subconscious images culled from the realm of engineering and science). Unlike anthropomorphic statuary, these new constructions lacked biotic orientation. They had no up or down, no front, back or sides. As a class of objects existing in real space, the symmetry and congruity of these constructions became visually obscured, if not destroyed, when they were placed on a flat, opaque surface.

Gabo's construction *Torsion* (1929) is the forerunner of several attempts to produce a kinetic relationship (kinetic in the sense of embodying latent energy, not movement) between a construction and its base. This had already been attempted by the Vkhutemas group with working models of string and bowed wood. Gabo's work with heat-formed plastics could only imply some system of tension and compression. Raised by small metal pins above the plastic underbase, a circular sheet of clear plastic acts as a plane of contact

12. Naum Gabo, *Construction in Space with Balance on Two Points*, 1925.

with the construction. This superstructure is fastened to the periphery of the plastic disk while two attached projections curve inward and meet over the center of the work. The twisting counter-stress of these projections, of course, accounts for the name *Torsion*. Here Gabo uses the transparency of plastic to make pellucid the consistency of his structure, to express continuity of space, and especially to produce the illusion of separation between structure and base. Visually this is a better solution than his 1925 *Construction in Space with Balance on Two Points* (FIG. 12) where he tries to use two circular edges of glass segments as the only points of contact with the base. Structural difficulties impelled him to reinforce the glass with metal supports.

Though Gabo's solutions for mounting his constructions increased in daring, his brother (after the 1920's) reverted to more conventional ideas. In part, this was in keeping with Pevsner's sturdier technique of brazing bronze rods into warped planes. *The Dancer* (1925) was one of Pevsner's last attempts at anthropomorphic sculpture. It balances a large rhombic form on an apex of minimum dimensions. This area of contact with a thin plinth of sheet bronze is defined by a small, intricate set of plastic and metal parts, very precisely assembled with small set screws.

The 1935 *Construction for an Airport* (FIG. 13) represents Pevsner's desire to provoke the feeling of lift and flight. This model for a monument consists of a row of triangular planes making contact with the ground on one edge and one point, though the edge is raised a quarter of an inch to preserve the autonomy of the model. This hovering quality disappeared from later works as Pevsner pursued a more baroque conception. Interior space subsequently did not imply airiness and suspension; rather it invited the eye to move perpendicularly over curved and ambiguous planes of bronze.

Though intent on freeing his works from the ground plane, the Constructivist sculptor usually refrained from simply suspending his constructions from an overhead wire. He found that, even poised in the air, a work needed one or more visual points of reference. This was necessitated by the viewer's desire for spatial orientation. Yet few suspended sculptures, until this decade, have been designed for specific spaces or positioned for a given architectural context. However, for gallery sculpture, the early Constructivists discovered that a work held barely off the ground (by one or two inches) seemed much more airbound and aloft than one suspended quite isolated thirty feet in the air.

An instance where such a ground reference plane was employed is Gabo's *Construction in Space* (1953). A typical Constructivist solution, the base consists of a circular plinth in black plastic. The sculpture hangs suspended from above, attached to its base by a thin guy wire. When Gabo devised

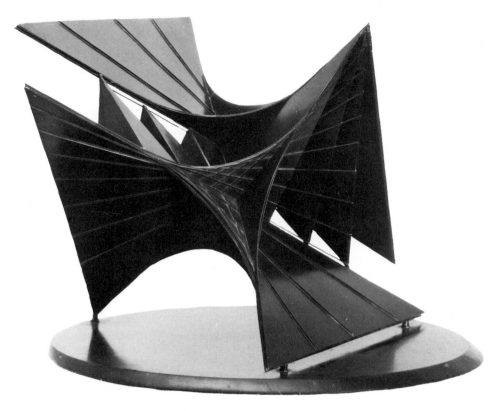

13. Antoine Pevsner, *Construction for an Airport*, 1934.

a construction to hang very high in the air, as with a work, *Construction Suspended in Space*, for the Baltimore Museum in 1953, he carefully used the surrounding circular staircase as a visual point of reference. Some fixed point nearby helps to give any air-bound sculpture a sense of proximity and relatedness, which defines the difference between something hovering in space and limply hanging.

In an essay on the war monuments of Rotterdam (1963, pp. 31–40) Lewis Mumford presents a moving description of the festive but difficult installation of Gabo's *Bijenkorf Monument* (FIG. 14). A great token of hope for the people of that destroyed city, Gabo envisioned his twisting vertical structure as a tree which would be the symbol of growth and regeneration. The construction, eighty-one feet high, needed a very deep substructure of steel girders embedded in concrete to withstand lateral and bending stresses above ground, Gabo speaks of this steel-concrete substructure as the "roots" of his construction. These "roots" above ground are clad with slabs of black marble. In effect this base is simply a very practical form of protection against the abrasion of daily street wear. It is perhaps providential that one of the first artists to fully employ technological means should seize upon an organic metaphor as a symbol of regeneration of hope for the urban domain.

Postwar Withering of the Base

Methodically examining the role of sculpture display techniques after the Second World War is no easy task. Many trends have appeared, the most important being the disappearance of the base from floor-standing sculpture. Concurrent with this is the repeated placing of sculpture on a few points in contact with the base.

The development of the base provides an evolutionary parallel which has its counterpart in nature. Imagine the growth of a young bird in the nest; finally it climbs out of the nest and begins to use its feet and wings; as time passes flight becomes its primary means of locomotion. On a different biological time scale, another species of birds may have decided to come out of the trees and walk along the ground. This analogy may be an oversimplification; however, it is not unlike what has happened to sculpture in the past few decades. The base, or the perch, no longer seems to have much meaning for the sculpture produced today.

Environmental *Merzbau* (nonsense constructions) by Kurt Schwitters and Calder's larger constructions are the most obvious attempts to transcend or ignore the sculpture base. Calder's work particularly in plate steel precipitated the move toward positional informality. His first large-scale stabile was a giant, room-filling structure shown at the Curt Valentin Gallery, New York, in 1940. A second version of this (FIG. 15) was commissioned and made because of the structural instability of the original. Here Calder used heavier plate steel, ribs, and gusset plates that considerably added to its sculptural richness.

Later Reuben Nakian and Herbert Ferber used immense size to provide environmental experiences. However, Calder's stabiles, because of their subtle articulation and abruptly changing contours, still make the most sense as ambiant adventures.

In *The Poetics of Space*, Gaston Bachelard takes up the question of size in a spatial context. In a chapter entiled "Intimate Immensity" he states (1958, p. 184):

Immensity is within ourselves. It is attached to a sort of expansion of being which life curbs and caution arrests, but which starts again when we are alone. As soon as we become motionless, we are elsewhere; we are dreaming in a world that is immense. Indeed, immensity is the movement of a motionless man.

As Bachelard later points out, size is those instances when the mind can expand in ideal space far beyond itself. In this respect, and considering Bachelard's remark about immensity within a motionless man, a tiny group of six-inch-high Giacometti figures positioned on a massive plinth has infinitely more monumentality than most room-size environmental sculptures.

During the early 1950's Harry Bertoia created not only sculptured wall screens, but a type of open suspended construction consisting of thousands of brass rods randomly joined, giving the impression of a meshlike metallic cloud. Even at the time, when the statistical format of Jackson Pollock and Mark Tobey had found fairly wide circulation among artists, Bertoia's con-

14. Naum Gabo, *Construction for the Bijenkorf*, 1954–1957.

15. Alexander Calder, *Black Beast*, 1957 version of 1940 original.

structions represented a new sculpture sensibility, one that dealt with large masses in space without allowing them to appear painfully heavy and trapped.

At this time, Richard Lippold found a more formal and precise answer to the obstacles surrounding suspended wire constructions. This relied on the fact that most suspended objects seem to hang; they have a rather undynamic affinity with their environment. Many of Lippold's works are held in suspension by guy wires radiating in all directions. Each wire construction is the nucleus of a series of variable tensions, so that supporting wires become part of the construction itself. Lippold has played down these supporting wires by diminishing their brightness and thickness, making them less visible also by the control of lighting sources.

A *tour de force*, Lippold's *The Sun* (FIG. 16) is kept poised in the air by dozens of wires fastened and recessed into the walls, ceiling, and floor. Similar to the block-and-tackle rig of a large tent, excess tensions and slacknesses are taken up by small turnbuckles attached to each guy wire. Most of the wires in the construction describe radial *pencils* of lines in segmented planes. Guy wires, on the other hand, are nearly invisible because they run singly and in different directions. In this type of installation, the entire room serves as a base for the construction. A statistical phenomenon gives this work its hovering effect: a radial massing of wires produces a readable form while single strands of thin tension wire stay invisible and hold the work in place.

An example of a sculpture almost balanced on a single point is David von Schlegell's *Twisted Column* (FIG. 17). The connection with the inverted-L-shaped steel member lying on the floor is particularly subtle because the column seems to be cantilevered so that its center of gravity would put it out of balance. This is not the case. The column, consisting of sheets of heat-formed wood veneer, bends so that the counter-weighted top accommodates the odd angle of the channel member connecting the inverted base to the underside of the column.

Floor-Bound Sculpture

Despite a flat sheet-iron plinth welded to its legs, Picasso's *Design for a Construction in Iron Rods* (1928) served as an important forerunner for the tradition of floor-standing metal sculpture. Undoubtedly the very crude utilitarian consistency of welded iron and steel made the preciousness of the base seem an affectation. Both the geometric and biomorphic idioms gained a robustness from direct welding techniques; also unfinished surface treatment contradicted the exclusive status which the base gives to objects. Large welded and brazed constructions (ca. 1955) by David Smith and Ibram Lassaw were raised from the floor by only the thinnest plinths. Much of the

40

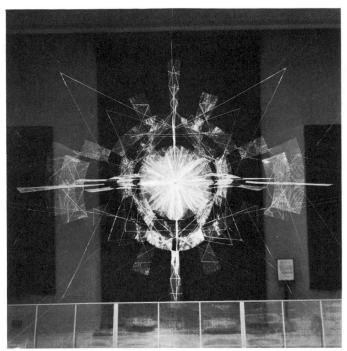

16. Richard Lippold, *Variation within a Sphere, No. 10: the Sun*, 1954–1956.

17. David von Schlegell, *Twisted Column*, 1963.

floor-size "New York School" sculpture, following the lead of Picasso and the postwar British metal sculptors such as Lynn Chadwick, Kenneth Armitage, and Reg Butler, began to grow leglike appendages instead of bases.

Within the last six or seven years floorbound sculpture has become more the rule than the exception—though many small works, to facilitate inspection, are still set upon pedestals not designed as part of an ensemble. For a growing number of sculptors, to the point of affectation, sculpture is not just *set* upon the floor but has an obligation to *lie* upon the floor—or better, to be casually propped up by a wall. In a number of cases these sculptures do not reach the standing eye-level of the viewer but are designed to be seen from above.

The German sculptor Jochen Hiltmann and the Englishman Anthony Caro are two early producers of floorbound sculpture. Hiltmann's sculptures

18. Harry Bertoia, *Untitled*, 1960.

made between 1960 and 1964 have the fascination of small meteoric steel spheres posing as found objects. Set upon the floor, they assume the casualness of beach stones. In contrast, many of Caro's sculptures (see Chapter Three, FIG. 39) are obviously floor-oriented, with a dominant horizontal axis. Thus, the ground or floor beneath acts as a stabilizing plane for oddly pitched structural steel members which make irregular contact with it. That a sculpture or construction can be made to look unquestionably floorbound was made evident in a series of vibrating works (ca. 1960–1961) by Harry Bertoia. An example (FIG. 18) consists of a tubular stainless-steel frame (rectangular and close in spirit to some early Marcel Breuer furniture) housing gridlike clusters of thin steel rods. Seen in the context of other sculpture then in vogue, Bertoia's brushed stainless steel was staggeringly severe and cool to the touch. The fact that his constructions have functional legs now seems both less surprising and more reasonable.

The wave of "new sculpture," with its main entrances in London,

New York, and Los Angeles has made the schism with the formal base complete. New York Hard-Center, Minimal, or Object sculptors (Don Judd, Robert Morris, Ann Truitt, and Mike Nevelson were some of the earliest) created a school which makes blanket rejection of all the older dynamic-geometric and vitalist theories. Their solution offers a three-dimensional form as inert as it is massive. In some instances these severely geometrical shapes resemble bases more than sculpture. A typical reaction was that of the critic Barbara Rose. For her these objects asked such questions as (1965, p. 36): "What are the bases of sculpture? What is structure, what is construction, and what is their relationship?" Object sculpture retorts to the first question set forth by Miss Rose. It might be saying that sculpture, as we have known it, is only one kind of three-dimensional object, and that it conforms to its own particular standards of aesthetic presence. As much as Object sculpture seems to be a denial of past sculpture values, it reminds us uncategorically that sculpture is eminently three-dimensional. To desire sculpture which is solid, palpable, and *real* may appear tautological, but in truth these characteristics reaffirm those qualities which have been methodically removed from modern sculpture. What comes next in the quest for ephemerality after the fine-wire constructions of Lippold or the plastic transparencies of Gabo? Pure energy itself? As we shall see later in the investigation of sculpture as system, both these questions now receive answers—and the resulting solutions threaten the existence of sculpture as it has traditionally been conceived. When sculpture is less and less tangible, the base becomes the only aspect which continues to show presence and substantiality. Perhaps an inverse premise is at work. If Brancusi can incorporate the base into his sculptures, what is to prevent the base, in later hands, from becoming sculpture?

There is also another possibility, which might be called "ceiling-bound" sculpture. Robert Grosvenor creates the most dramatic of these constructions. *Transoxiana* (FIG. 19), suspended by channels from the ceiling, teasingly misses the floor by inches. Such a switch in gravitational orientation destroys not only the base, but the spectator's sense of "up" and "down."

The base belongs to an older conception of art, typified by a reverence for irreplaceable objects. In some cases the art object emanated transcendental qualities. Thus, the sculpture base bestowed an *apartness;* it physically defined the aesthetic distance which necessarily remained between the viewer and art object. To a marked degree this relationship has changed. Gross familiarity with objects, artistic or not, results from the mass proliferation of man-made things. This has undermined the protocol of the viewer-object relationship.

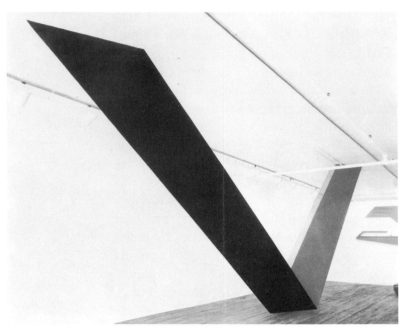

19. Robert Grosvenor, *Transoxiana*, 1965.

A desire to bring art directly into the flux of life has produced some doubtful consequences. Some recent construction has been presented on the basis of store window display or the *tableau vivant*. These consist of assemblages of dressed figures given the benefit of real materials and objects for a setting. Here the problems of the base do not exist. In psychological effect, this type of manikin expressionism and environmental tableau relates to similar efforts in the European courts and Catholic Church during and after the Middle Ages. Their fragility probably excluded those objects from being considered high art in the sense of painting and sculpture.

Air-Borne Sculpture

Within the past ten years attempts varying in resourcefulness have been made which go beyond the Constructivist ambition of the total liberation of sculpture from the base. Short of shooting sculpture into orbit (which has been suggested as a real possibility by Takis), some sculptors have tried to free their forms from all physical contact with the Earth.

One attempt, though missing the goal, has been the use of discontinuous compression and continuous tension systems, the *tensegrity* principle first developed by Kenneth Snelson (see Chapter Three, FIG. 65) under the guidance of R. Buckminster Fuller. The Japanese sculptor Morio Shinoda has worked with balloon-type, sheet-metal forms suspended by the tensegrity

20. Morio Shinoda, *Tension and Compression 32*, 1965.

principle. Where Snelson has been involved in lifting small, thin compression members off the ground, Shinoda's forms, because of their apparent bulk, are much more dramatic. These steel globes (FIG. 20) hover a foot or so off the floor with the help of only a few fine stainless-steel wires. (Since these comments about Shinoda, Kenneth Snelson has held his first show of tensegrity constructions in New York during the spring of 1966. Significantly, in his larger works Snelson has enlarged his compression members. These thick, hollow tubular aluminum units have the same feeling of bulk as Shinoda's constructions.)

Since 1959, the sculptor Takis has produced numbers of what he calls Telemagnetic constructions (see Chapter Six, FIG. 100). The base in this instance is a wall or metal plate which serves as an anchor for the system. Takis attaches found or self-made forms to flexible wires, which are tied to fixed posts. These metallic forms are set within range of the magnetic field of electromagnets. The forms stand straight out in the air, attracted toward but not touching the magnet. Repeated interruption of the electric current makes these objects fall limply or quiver at attention in the direction of the electromagnet.

The yearning to free sculpture from the confines of gravity has been met by subjecting forms to even more powerful kinds of energy. Such forces can produce a condition of equilibrium. Thus Alberto Collie has designed a

21. Alberto Collie, *Floatile No. II*, 1967.

number of titanium disks (a nonmagnetic metal which is repelled rather than attracted by a strong electromagnetic field) that seem to vibrate at a distance from their bases (FIG. 21). Early models stabilized and held the disk within range of the base by a tiny, almost invisible thread tied to the bottom of the sculpture. The systems technology of a Cambridge, Massachusetts, laboratory has enabled Collie to eliminate even this tiny thread. Here the disk is subjected to another stronger magnetic field produced by an electromagnetic coil which keeps the piece within the field of the first, or levitating, coil. Any attempt to dislodge the disk relays a feedback signal which strengthens the magnetic field opposite the force pushing the disk out of equilibrium. Hence, the base has vanished altogether!

In a newspaper article, Collie insists that Brancusi would have sent some of his forms aloft if it then had been possible (anonymous, October 26, 1964): "He was working to the ultimate of what was scientifically available to him at the time. I am able to free my form from gravity because technology has moved so far ahead."

The technological significance of Collie's art is impressive, but not because of its association with Brancusi's sculpture. The purpose behind technological acceleration is not the creation of better Brancusis. His work already represents a particular era and attitude toward sculpture. Collie's plastic and aesthetic problems are in another realm, though his reasoning for the use of electromagnetism touches upon a long unsolved dilemma (anony-

22. Robert Grosvenor, *Floating Sculpture*, 1966–1967.

mous, October 26, 1964): "It is like describing an egg. No matter how much
of an egg a person can see, there is still a tiny place at the base where it cannot
be seen. Now I have been able to take the art form and place it so that it can
be viewed in its entirety."

This statement echoes the Constructivist dilemma with self-contained
constructions whose symmetry is destroyed by laying them on a flat surface.
Collie's difficulty had earlier been surmounted with the aid of guy wires, point
contacts, and suspended objects. Now, with sculpture completely liberated
from its base it becomes a different animal! Its *raison d'être* is no longer that
it embodies formal qualities, but that it exists as a physical system including
invisible forces. The duality between matter and energy enters a new phase.

Finally, there are the gestures of unrealized liberation. These include the
Group Zero night exhibitions, *vernissages* held by Otto Piene and Heinz Mack
in the streets of Düsseldorf. Under the night sky in 1960 dozens of white
balloons were set adrift and followed up into the heavens by searchlights. In
part propaganda for the group, more importantly these balloons signaled the
migration of material forms toward another area of activity.

However, we should not avoid mention of Andy Warhol's silver-colored
pillows filled with lighter-than-air gas, produced by the "Factory" for his
May, 1966, show in New York. These floated at all heights, slowly discharging
their contents. The water-borne sculptures of Robert Grosvenor (FIG. 22)
attain another form of floating. These are meant for sea travel as a buoylike

47

23. Hans Haacke, *Sphere in Oblique Air-Jet*, 1967.

structure carries a T form above the waves. This superstructure, triangular in cross-section, projects out of the water at an angle. For four years Hans Haacke has worked with large weather balloons stably balanced on columns of forced air (FIG. 23). Lately, these have been perfected to the point where the balloon moves at some distance and in a trajectory from its source of air support. In fact, the currents of air used are almost unnoticeable.

Actual "flying sculptures" (beginning in 1966) are now being constructed by the New Yorker Charles Frazier. Besides various sculptural helicopters, rockets, and inflated shapes, Frazier's most ambitious undertakings are a series of fantastic, doughnut-shaped hovercraft which operate by moving over the ground on a sixteen-inch cushion of air.

The trend toward mobility, particularly through the air, will probably continue. Perhaps visions of space capsules, appearing stark still but hurtling through space at thousands of miles per hour, represent a new collective dream. Surely artists will make a role for themselves in these exobiotic ventures.

CHAPTER TWO

The Biotic Sources of Modern Sculpture

Organicism as an Evolving Creed

Over thirty years ago Lewis Mumford in *Technics and Civilization*, a pioneering study of the interaction between machines and societies, charted an increasing gravitation toward what he termed "an organic ideology." Mumford held that scientists in the first stages of the modern machine culture, with meager means at hand, were frightfully deficient in their explanations of the complexities of nature. And life, being the greatest complexity, was altogether too mercurial and perplexing to serve as anything but a metaphysical hobbyhorse for theologians and philosophers. Only the bravest or most foolish scientists made any projections about life's actual basis. Yet, in the early part of this century, with the development of atomic physics, the relationships between states of matter came much more clearly into view. A most important discovery was that matter, both organic and inorganic, constituted a continuum and could be analyzed as a series of connected energy states. From that time on, the meaning of the machine gradually changed. Mumford, in countering the social philosopher Werner Sombard's earlier idea that the drive of technology would eventually displace the organic or living beings of society, insisted that *the real destiny of the machine was to merge itself with natural organisms.*

Mumford cited 1870 as a turning point when the designer, industrial and architectural, began to realize that all further development necessitated a return of technology to organic models. Many advanced social thinkers realized that progress could no longer be equated with more mechanical invention. As a consequence, models based on equilibrium and the subtle interrelation between living organisms and technology became an ideal of every planner and designer. Organicism was the harmonious fusion of the natural and the man-made. Today, more than thirty-five years after Mumford's prognosis, society has yet to realize, except in isolated instances, this ideal.

But, if anything, the need for implementing such a goal has increased to almost tragic proportions.

In the area of sculpture the term *organic* has suffered a number of ambiguous and ill-defined applications. It has not enjoyed the moral imperative connected with the desire to unite technics with the best interests of natural life. While we try to integrate sculpture into our lives, the aim of sculpture has always been to stand somewhat aloof from life's activity. Moreover, at its greatest popularity the most that the term *organic sculpture* implied was a certain suprastylistic emphasis on biological characteristics. Even criteria for what is natural and what is biological have been altered through scientific discovery—changing the life-giving properties of sculpture as these criteria become less identified with each other.

Most civilizations, even the most primitive, have manifested in their social life, food-gathering, and arts, a high degree of what has been termed *organic unity*. Speed, quickly shifting social patterns, psychological insecurity signal that our culture feels a lack of organic cohesiveness. The visionary designers and artists of our technological society have searched for it continuously, found it fragmentarily, only to have it slip out of sight again. The sculptor has sought it on his own terms in chiseled rock and chunks of wood. He has not made our life any more organic but he has given us signposts for the conduct of a more normal existence.

Much of this chapter is concerned with the philosophy of *vitalism* as it has been reflected in sculpture. In several important ways vitalism has served for some sixty or more years as the sculptor's counterpart to an aesthetic based on organicism. Vitalism is a preeminently poetic view of life, a celebration of the natural condition, while organicism is a beautiful view of the utilitarian evolution of systems, both biological and nonbiological. As modes of awareness, organicism and vitalism have influenced each other; in some essential ways they remain in polar opposition. But to understand the growth and popularity of vitalism, we must first review the effects of organic thinking upon modern life.

Expressed as a conscious concern of the designer, *organicism* could be defined as the awareness of the interrelation between systems and their components within larger systems so that behavior of the whole ensemble can be understood and manipulated. Organicism could also be defined as any arrangement possessing the attributes of life. Certainly these meanings are not equivalent—though they overlap. The first relates closely to machines, factories, and social systems; the second is obviously tied to biological life. The nature of the second definition is often the working objective of the first. Psychically and theoretically, the "bringing to life" of machines, industrial and social systems has become the unconscious obsession of the twentieth-century technician. The "bringing to life" of wood and stone has always been the obsession of the sculptor; however, we live in a period where for the first time the sculptor sees the virtual achievement of his goal through the technician. Now the sculptor seems well on the way to doing so.

For the vitalist sculptor in the recent past, the "life" of his works was a criterion of artistic success and developed from his ability to create a plastic unity; for the biologist, "life" remains a question of systematically understanding the nature of living matter. By way of redefining "life" in future biology, machine theory, and sculpture—and unquestionably one of the central ideas of this book—*the meaning of organicism for all three disciplines has already begun to converge toward a single end result—the understanding of living matter through its creation.*

According to the writer Lancelot Law Whyte, the term *organicism*, implying a "harmonious arrangement of parts," came into modern usage only between 1720 and 1750 (1954, p. 233). Occasionally the term found its way into treatises on architecture and related subjects before 1840, but it was Horatio Greenough in America who first extolled organicism as a virtue of right living and thinking. Sensing the need for the same parsimony that an artisan has in shaping his tools, or a plant in growing branches, Greenough advocated a "simplicity-complexity" design quotient for all man-made objects. And while the idea was never implemented to any significant degree in Greenough's own sculpture, his employment of the phrase "organic beauty" is totally modern in its transcendent yearnings—being at one with nature in the shaping of the environment through an eye for practical detail and appropriate use of materials. Organicism has come to mean a certain sympathetic alliance with the natural forces maintaining the ecological balance of the Earth. Moreover, the word rings with the purity of unqualified virtue. For an object to receive the designation *organic* is for it to rest above criticism. Not only has *organic* as an adjective been thoroughly abused, but the term and its application have seldom received sufficient scrutiny. It has been, though less now, the plaything of the tastemakers.

More important, the recent sense of what is *organic* lies in a spiritual free zone for the artist and natural scientist. It has offered one of the few uncontested meeting places where both could share intuitions and common concerns without feeling threatened. If organicism led a moral cause, its only demand of the architect, for example, has been the possession of genius and, as Louis Sullivan stated, the chance to create one's vision of what was "natural" and "right." There have been no rules for organic creation, and somehow only the elect had it within themselves to do what was, or what seemed in hindsight, natural and right.

Actually the modern sense of *organic*, as applied to the arts, grows out of several nineteenth-century developments. The sudden popularity of L'Art Nouveau style during the 1890's was due, in part, to an awareness of a new style of biological drawing. The lower forms of life, some microscopic, inspired increasing appreciation for their symmetry and structure. They were depicted with keen artistic sensitivity and precision. In 1899 Ernst Haeckel, zoologist and fiery defender in the German-speaking countries of Darwin's theories, came out with his now rightfully famous book *Kunstformen der Natur*. Already Haeckel had written a number of books both poetically polemical and massively erudite in their defense of evolution as the authentic and beautiful explanation of man's gradual ascent from one-celled existence. *Kunstformen der Natur* is a selection of watercolor drawings of various fragile specimens of undersea life. More than a naturalist's album, the book, as the title implies, tried to arouse an intelligent lay public to the exquisite symmetries and transparencies of tiny animals not ordinarily observed. For later abstract sculpture this type of book drove home the possibility that organic forms could also be basically geometric in their structure. Also for L'Art Nouveau–influenced architects like Sullivan, Victor Horta, Hector Guimard, and possibly Charles Rennie Mackintosh, Haeckel's book and others served to provide the designer with a new vocabulary of organic forms—one free from the sterile repetition of classic plant motifs.

For a building to look organic was just one side of the coin. The shapes and functions of its structural members became the more fundamental concerns within organic investigations, one in which visual traces of nature became manifestly less evident and less important. Very early in the trend toward organic architecture, Joseph Paxton used the leaf structure of the South American water lily, Victoria regia, for the glassed-in structure of a greenhouse at Chatsworth, and later modified it for the glazed ridged vaults in the Crystal Palace (1851). First transported to England during the 1830's, the Victoria regia fascinated early Victorians both by the beautiful complexity of the venation on its underside and its ability to support heavy weights while floating on water. Various photographs of the leaf's understructure and Paxton's vaulted glass roofs make one of the most graphic comparisons of organically derived distribution of stresses. Paxton never tired of emphasizing their visual and structural similarities. What has been pointed out in relation to Paxton's buildings, though far less organically implicit, is the standardization of parts: the modular detailing, the mechanical connectors, and the steel tension members—all of organic origin, but virtually unused building devices in the 1850's. The organic character of modern building is, in fact, machine technique itself.

This point Frank Lloyd Wright made clear in an early essay, "The Art and Craft of the Machine" (1901). The machine, still not adequately defined, was beginning to be looked upon as an invisible extension of the application of organic principles; where the visual illustration of the plant or animal organism is no longer apt or visually translatable, the machine takes over and translates organic function in principle. All too well, Wright understood the artist's fear of accepting what he could not see, or deal with, on traditional terms (1960, p. 71):

Upon this faith in art as the organic heart quality of the scientific frame of things, I base a belief that we must look to the artist brain, of all brains, to grasp the significance to society of this thing we call the Machine, if that brain be not blinded, gagged, and bound by false tradition, the letter of precedent. For this thing we call Art is it not as prophetic as a primrose or an oak? Therefore, of the essence of this thing we call the Machine, which is no more or less than the principle of organic growth working irresistibly the Will of Life through the medium of man.

Infinitely more than applied organic decoration, the extension of machine technology shaped the rationale of late-nineteenth-century architecture. The rolled steel beam, the space-frame concept of steel-girder construction, factory-assembled detailing, reinforced concrete—all were essential for producing the modern office building. The use of reinforced concrete, particularly in Europe and later in Latin American countries, in the hands of a few exceptional designers, resulted in a design ideology recognized in years to come as the essence of organic thinking. With a freedom that designing in ferro-concrete allowed, the engineer became the prime, though unwitting, "form giver" of large structures instead of the architect, "form giver" in the sense that the engineer could exert his special talents in the direction of minimal and therefore organic-appearing forms.

This was exemplified by the bridges of Robert Maillart. These structures were calculated, mathematically and empirically, with an exactitude that made the resultant forms and their curves almost readable stress diagrams. Using ferro-concrete to its fullest capacity, with less emphasis on mathematical analysis than on testing and model making, Maillart demonstrated that parsimony and a feeling for uncalculatable consequences were as applicable to civil engineering as to natural order. Maillart also demonstrated the more important inspiration, one that had already been absorbed by naturalists: that nature was beautiful, not because it tried to be decorative, but because millions of mutative efforts within each species allowed the organism to strive for a reasonably economical form-function solution.

Thirty years ago when Sigfried Giedion, in his essay "Construction and Aesthetics" (Martin *et al.*, 1937, pp. 220–237), spoke out for more studies on the interrelationships between sculpture, painting, and architecture, the world held a popular hope for a truly "organic" architecture. Modern building techniques had matured by then, but the hope for organicism lay in new planning methodologies, new studies in sociology and psychology, and a greater understanding of mankind's shelter needs. Since this idealism of the 1930's, organic architecture, with sporadic exceptions, has become a rallying cry of the past.

Concurrently the aura of organicism spread from architecture to sculpture. *In their own words, sculptors have wrongly referred to their work as being "organic."* Only a few sculptors such as Henry Moore saw the inappropriateness of the word and supplied "vitalistic" in its stead. Where organicism in architecture correctly implied the workings of systems and subsystems in harmony, no such functional approach applied to sculpture. Sculpture's ability to *look* plantlike, rocklike or animal-like, without being representational, was its sole claim to the organic title.

Yet curiously, since the Second World War a number of scientific and technological disciplines have recognized the need for restructuring along organic organizational lines. This trend has not as yet spilled over into building or artistic endeavors. The largest and most comprehensive attempt to use the analogues of biological organization has been systems analysis and development. During the Second World War man-machine units (in bombers, gun stations, radar installations, etc.) were for the first time deemed too complex to be controlled by human reflexes. As a result, studies in the systematic organization and control of such groups were undertaken. Since the 1950's countless corporations have redesigned their procedures from a systems point of view. Systems development now stands as *the* means of integrating humans into increasingly automated industries and services.

Some experts regard the organization of men and machines into optimally functioning systems as tantamount to creating synthetic organisms. The designing of high-speed aircraft, computer systems, or atomic submarines undergoes a processing cycle very similar to that of an evolving organism. As of now, the analogy between the two remains more metaphorical than literal. Men and machines working together manifest many of the growth, stability, and continuity symptoms of organisms, but much remains to make the term "organic" more than a design ideal.

In some respects the craving for an organic sculpture was another reaction to the technological way of life, an isolated cry for a return to an older sense of spiritual and physical equilibrium. As such, it had more to do with the intimate needs for sensuous, visual tactility than with the more public needs of architectural, commercial, and service organization. Sculpture, ever since the end of the last century, has tried to solve the craving for organic presence by its own restricted means: those of mass, form, and surface. In spite of the upheavals in various engineering technologies, sculpture—with very few exceptions—has remained an art of metaphor and not an actual demonstration of structural principles. Yet, doubtless, the influence of biological discoveries has also made an indirect impact on the changing characteristics of sculpture. Since the subject matter of sculpture almost always concerned the biological, it was to be expected that sculptors would be influenced by ideas related to the phenomenon of life. This, at the end of the nineteenth century, seemed to be the kernel of sculpture, the sole reason for its existence. Perhaps this found its best expression in the romantic, vitalistic pantheism of Rodin. Rodin's sentiments, in fact, are not unlike those found in the notebooks of Michelangelo, his great hero. As quoted by his secretary, Rodin said with full conviction (1912, p. 166):

This is because the artist, full of feeling, can imagine nothing that is not endowed like himself. He suspects in Nature a great consciousness like his own. There is not a living organism, not an inert object, not a cloud in the sky, not a green shoot in the meadow, which does not hold for him the secret of the great power hidden in all things.

Yet the organicism of which Rodin speaks, if anything, is more emotive and less literal, more metaphysical in its transference of sensibilities (that of *organicness* to inert matter), than any outright adherence to a creed or variation of the functionalist equation. Rodin reiterated (1912, p. 178): "When a good sculptor models a torso, he not only represents the muscles, but the life...which animates them—more than the life, the force that fashioned them...." Rodin hints that the sculptor's job is not to imitate life, but to *convey* it, perhaps as a runner in a relay hands his baton on to the next runner, or as genetic traits are passed on and modified by each generation; the sculptor, as Rodin saw him, not only created life, but had the task of constantly renewing it.

With no deliberate use of the term, Rodin was one of the first modern sculptors to express openly the vitalistic ideal. He did this at a time when vitalism had reached its literary and scientific peak. Not only was the vitalist doctrine subtly suited to artistic uses, it also possessed intellectual respectability. Rodin was onto a powerful idea—something that would provide the reigning aesthetic for many years in modern sculpture.

Generally accepted scientific theories, particularly those appealing to the emotional bias of the public, have a way of filtering down in "common sense" form with sizable cultural authority. Vitalism is one instance in the history of scientific ideas where a theory can be seen to wane, not only in its scientific form but as an aesthetic. As vitalism fell from favor in biology, so it did in sculpture—in fact, owing to a time lag, it remained slightly longer in its artistic form.

Thus, to chart the gradual entry of vitalist thought into modern sculpture, it seems advisable to outline the long history of vitalism as a philosophical and scientific idea. To give so much attention to a theory in biology may seem a roundabout way of explaining sculpture, but it will prepare us to answer this question: Why, if vitalism played such a reactionary role in the biological sciences, did it provide some of the most advanced justification for avant-garde abstract sculpture?

The Mechanist Versus Vitalist Dispute

Mechanistic theory of organic matter can be summarily defined as a belief in a physical basis, usually electrochemical, for all phenomena of life including human consciousness. *Pure mechanism* is the view that life can be interpreted on all levels solely in terms of analyzable physical functions and combinations of matter. More often than not, the mechanistic approach has derived its greatest support from the more analytically minded physical scientists—especially physiologists and biochemists.

The vitalist, whether theologian, metaphysician, or medical doctor, often retained emotional and professional interest in not seeking rational mechanistic explanations for the processes of life. Either that, or with true humility the vitalist sensed the impossibility of ever completely understanding living structure. To the vitalist, life at its core is metaphysically instigated. It consists of an "entelechy," to use Aristotle's word, a nonmaterial center of being making it different in quality and in kind from inorganic matter. From its modern beginnings starting in the seventeenth century, the strategy of vitalism has drawn attention to those aspects of life which could not be explained by physical means. As Ludwig von Bertalanffy states in his *Problems of Life* (1949, p. 8): "The history of biology is the refutation of vitalism...." Because vitalism centered its reasoning on noncausal and nonphysical beliefs, it has functioned as a conservative, if not reactionary, agent. The nature of a "vital essence" has evolved only as the basis for claiming its existence in the human body and has been consistently undermined by biology. Biology's attacks on vitalism were not pat polemical speeches or writings, but the weight of new discoveries.

The immense complexity of the life processes has been vitalism's biggest asset. As the biologist Edmund Sinnott makes clear, *organism* is a wonderfully fit name for living entities. The word *organism*, no matter to what size system it applies, expresses the hierarchical arrangement of systems which function at incredibly high levels of organization. Because doctors have been in the unique position of observing life in all its manifestations, thus wondering at its constant surprises, vitalism found ardent support in the medical profession. In earlier times physicians had good reason to be repelled by the inadequacy of mechanistic explanations in dealing with subtle biological relationships. Crude mechanical analogies (i.e., early theories of the circulatory system, breathing, or muscle contraction) did not suffice. Mechanistic materialism has traditionally drawn its inspiration from whatever theories were currently popular in physics and inorganic chemistry. Often in the seventeenth, eighteenth, and nineteenth centuries these theories were far from adequate assumptions on which to base medical knowledge; if anything, early explanations of body functions only helped to make vitalism more credible.

The absolute uniqueness and transcendent nature of life has traditionally been one of the most jealously guarded tenets of Christian theology. Well into the nineteenth century, an accusation of heresy or personal corruption was the most likely churchly response to the assertions of the mechanists. The one drawback to this line of attack was that the Church opened itself to ridicule when mechanist theories of biological functioning proved to be correct— which increasingly they did. Time and time again the Church retracted its stand, not by admission but by conveniently forgetting what it had proclaimed earlier as one of the mysteries of God's creative powers. The mechanists, on the other hand, had the freedom to propose any number of hypotheses for a given problem; they needed but one correct solution to destroy a religious-vitalist point of dogma. This exposes the self-critical and dynamic element of science. For a biologist or chemist to invoke a vital spirit or mystical fluid in the explanation of life—as the vitalist did—would have been to admit defeat and to negate the spirit of inquiry. Nevertheless, some scientists assumed this limiting attitude. Yet, essentially, both vitalists and mechanists have based belief in their respective causes on *faith*. For the vitalist faith was clearly of a religious or mystical persuasion. At best, the mechanistic researcher had to adopt some open, yet highly provisional, attitude toward unexplained biological functions. The great physiologist

Charles Sherrington thought the true scientist should remember that adequate explanations had always been lacking in the past, but because so much had been discovered subsequently it was worth assuming that what is still unknown would also eventually turn up.

This book cannot give a detailed account of mechanistic thinking and the reaction to it, yet it will be helpful to touch upon some of the key thinkers and experimentalists responsible for the steady decline of vitalist pretensions. If anything, they forced the vitalists out of doctrinaire positions and toward more subtle and lyrical arguments, which would, in fact, be effective in poetry and the plastic arts.

For over two hundred years there has been a steady recession in the number of biological problems left unsolved, beginning with the understanding of muscular contraction and approaching the present with an incipient mastery of the structure of proteins. Though as yet many more questions remain than have been answered, as science has laid bare what are euphemistically called "nature's secrets," it has been up to the vitalist to redefine the "life force" in terms of an ever-receding sphere of influence over the properties of living organisms. For instance, in the last century the fact that mammals must maintain a fairly steady body temperature was interpreted by the vitalists as a unique attribute, a God-given sign of higher life. The discovery of self-regulating systems in organisms, and the realization that these were explainable in mechanical terms, did much to undermine that quasi-religious contention. The mechanists are still not out of the woods. As the situation stands, there remain a number of mysteries connected with the life processes that defy basic explanation; many phases of self-organization, growth control, enzyme distribution, aging, and thought process are areas still in semidarkness.

If we had thought, as Descartes did, of the body as an "animal machine" —according to seventeenth-century mechanical principles—our knowledge of physiology would have barely progressed during the last three hundred years. Animals are not reducible to clockworks. Descartes's real contribution was a *method* of investigating living matter. This was the beginning of modern physiology. In a later chapter devoted to automata more mention will be made of Descartes's innovational attempt to understand physiological functions. Physiology was a state of mind, as Sherrington later defined it, in which successful mechanistic analysis depended upon extensive research. Consequently, by the eighteenth-century experimentation on muscle fiber, the lungs, blood circulation, the digestive tract, and the sensory organs had led to rudimentary, and, in certain instances, reliable information. Yet, the brain, the nervous system, and the reproductive organs remained the centers of metaphysical speculation for vitalistic belief. Theologists continued to concede that much could be explained about life from a materialistic standpoint, while they happily saw little hope of reducing the human soul, human thought, and reproduction to the level of mechanisms, no matter how complex the mechanistic theory.

As an exercise in human objectivity, one of the most remarkable documents of the enlightenment is Julien de la Mettrie's treatise "Man A Machine" (*L'Homme Machine*, 1748). De la Mettrie not only challenged the notion, long a part of Christian doctrine, of a soul in the human body, but he was the first philosopher with medical training to state categorically that the brain and its processes could ultimately be described by physical principles. In our eyes many of de la Mettrie's mechanistic proofs sound purely specious, more casuistic chatter than physical experimentation. However, de la Mettrie did introduce relevant physiological demonstrations (such as muscle contraction showing the irritability concept) to stress the autonomous motive power common to all living matter.

Organization is the prime concept of de la Mettrie's man machine; he defined the principle of biological organization so that it no longer resembled the dependent, animal automaton of Descartes. Though Descartes refused to defy the Church by extending the machine concept to the areas of thought, emotions, and complex reactions, de la Mettrie had no such inhibitions. In fact, he constructed a model of reasoning in which the psychologist would base much of his experimentation on what he knew to be true physiologically. Concerning the higher faculties, the Cartesian mechanistic model could only rely on vitalism; which is to say, it had no functional theory.

If de la Mettrie's key concept is organization itself, it is also to his credit that he regarded consciousness as one of its highest forms. For all orthodox philosophers and scientific men it was unthinkable that the mental capacities could be contained in matter. For this reason de la Mettrie's theories of physically based consciousness posed an extremely grave challenge to organized religion. Soon the question was asked: how far could scientific investigation and conjecture proceed before destroying the spiritual inviolability of the human intellect and the soul? Much polemical nineteenth-century theology can be interpreted as an attempt to preserve some sphere of the human psyche from the insatiable investigatory powers of science—and particularly to thwart any unifying comparisons made between man and all other animals.

De la Mettrie spelled out man's favored though not sublime position less explicitly than most nineteenth-century evolutionists. He grasped the essence of nature as a series of hierarchically organized bodies of matter but did not attempt to relate man to the animals through common biological origins (quoted in Vartanian, 1960, pp. 189–190):

It can be seen that there is only one [type of organization] in the Universe and of its examples Man is the most perfect. He is to the Monkey or to the most intelligent of Animals, what the planetary clock of Huygens is to the Watch of Julien Leroy. If more works, more cogs and more springs were required to indicate the movements of the Planets than to indicate the Hours, or to strike them; if more art was required of Vaucanson in order to create his *Flutist* rather than his *Duck*, even more would have been necessary in order to make his "Talking Man": a Machine which cannot be considered impossible, especially in the hands of a new Prometheus. In the same way it was necessary for Nature to use more art and more apparatus in order to make and to maintain a Machine capable of marking all the beats of the heart and impulses of the mind for an entire century; because if one does not see the hours in the pulsation of the heart, it is at least a Barometer of warmth and vivacity by which the nature of the Soul can be judged. I am *not* wrong! The human body is a clock, but an immense one constructed with such great skill and craft that if the wheel used to mark the seconds happens to stop, that of the minutes turns and continues its rate; in a like manner the wheel which marks the quarter-hour continues to move: and all the others too, when the operation of the first is interrupted by rust or put out of order by any cause whatever. (Translated from the French by George Bauer.)

Of interest to us in a later chapter will be the reference by de la Mettrie to Vaucanson's automata, assembled a decade before "Man A Machine" was written. To no small degree Vaucanson's facsimiles of animals and men excited the imagination of his century in a manner not too unlike our present attachment to the computer. Not only did de la Mettrie grasp the principle of mechanical complexity but he was also aware of the body's special metabolic capacity for self-repair. It fell to the following century to prove that this state of self-repair was a never-ceasing process of cell replacement. However, owing to de la Mettrie's incisive talent for comparison, the machine analogy was once and for all firmly fixed in the mind of the public.

For many of us, bred on the results of scientific rationalism, there is great beauty in the partial evidence that matter alone is the autonomous generator of life and development. Yet for the bulk of humanity in centuries past, and for many today outside the orbit of modern science, the assertion that life evolves without need of a divine impetus remains a horrible suggestion, a frontal attack on the higher origins of man. Such an idea, on the other hand, rather appealed to the cruel rationalism of the French Encyclopedists and later, for different reasons, to the German Romantics. Mechanistic thinking is not without a certain element of perversity, and far into the nineteenth century some materialists, mainly chemists, insisted on the supremacy of electrical and chemical processes—even when their models and concepts were plainly unworkable. An early scientific, and therefore excusable, example of this kind of paradigm can be found in the *Codice Atlantico* of Leonardo da Vinci where he pursues an analogy between the waters rising in the earth, and the same process in plants, and the blood circulation as it exists in animals; all are witnessed as separate types of organisms operating on a similar principle. German medical materialists of the middle of the nineteenth century produced far more outrageous conjunctions of matter and the organic processes. Some are that man is the sum of his foods; thought is a secretive process like urine from the kidneys; and genius is established according to the bodily intake of phosphorus. In common with the theories of the mechanistic physiologists, this type of theory desired to explain functioning in terms of matter; still, it had no semblance of scientific method, lacking the patience to verify its conclusions. At best it made the role of the vitalists that much easier. It took a visionary mind to realize that if nature held on to its secrets it succeeded because the mechanist had yet to gather the proper tools and the knowledge of molecular structure necessary to penetrate into the workings of organic tissue.

The synthesis of urea by Wöhler in 1828 is often regarded as the turning point in the mechanist-vitalist controversy. For the first time an organic substance was derived from the usual techniques of inorganic chemistry. Actually, at the time of the discovery, this made no such impact. And later at the beginning of the next century the neo-vitalist Henri Bergson depreciated synthetic urea by referring to it as merely a bodily waste material, something dead, as if this had nothing in common with living matter.

Gradually through the nineteenth century, the idea that organic materials possessed indefinable properties gave way to the sentiment, true but vastly understated, that they were only more complex in degree than inorganic substances. On another level, by proving the interconnection of the body's organs, the physiologist Claude Bernard set up the experimental criteria for viewing an organism as a network of interrelated systems. His disclosure of the various regulatory mechanisms (systems utilizing negative feedback circuits) proved essential to any comprehension of the sympathetic functioning of the nervous system, the blood system, and the digestive processes. No longer considered a static system, the human body was viewed as a vast web of balanced processes—some tearing the body down and others replacing what was destroyed. Bernard's nineteenth-century biological explanations became the control concepts for machines in the twentieth century.

The mysteries of fermentation, cell structure, and reproduction by the end of the nineteenth century began to give way to new biochemical techniques and more powerful microscopes. Admittedly, even then, indications in favor of a completely mechanistic approach were not all that clear. For this reason some of the great pioneers of cellular and microbial analysis refused to become dogmatic about a materialistic basis of life. The pathologist Rudolf Virchow had such reservations. Virchow sharply defined the dividing line in matter theory between the living and nonliving. And, while he helped to establish the metabolic nature of organisms as "societies of living cells," he viewed as unproven assertions that life was merely the very complex organization of matter.

In spite of Virchow's contribution, Ernst Haeckel, the German chief exponent of Darwinism (and author of *Kunstformen der Natur*), felt obliged in the name of victorious materialism to attack his fellow researcher. Haeckel did little to endear himself even to those sympathetic to his cause, and his literary verbosity and aggressive atheism are often illustrated by his statement that "the cell consists of matter called protoplasm, composed chiefly of carbon, with an admixture of hydrogen, nitrogen and sulphur. These component parts, properly united, produce the soul and body of the animated world, and suitably nursed become man. With this single argument the mystery of the universe is explained, the Deity annulled and a new era of infinite knowledge ushered in" (quoted in Eiseley, 1958, p. 346).

Even more cavalier than de la Mettrie's assertions a century and a half before, Haeckel's analysis of life was similar to saying that violin music is *only* the noise that results from a certain assembly of wood and catgut. As much as for the cause of science, Haeckel's expositions of phyla and evolutionary divisions of animal life directly aimed at undermining the intellectual authority of the Church—but for the first time without pseudonymity. Haeckel, nevertheless, must be given his due; his desire to attack the Church was not without a desire to draw blood for hundreds of years of physical and intellectual bullying perpetrated by the Church on the scientists of Europe. If his ontological, political, and social projections were unfounded and directly shaped by his view of evolutionary theory, at least he brought into the open some of the central philosophical issues of the day. After leaving the theologians in perhaps permanent disarray, Haeckel next succeeded in drawing the big names of metaphysical philosophy into battle under the generic banner of "neo-vitalism."

One further observation must be made. Since Haeckel's era at the end of nineteenth century and the beginning of the twentieth, advancement toward a thorough comprehension of life has steadily persisted. Although even elementary "life in a test tube," the popular conception of scientific supremacy over the elements of nature, stands a long step from complete knowledge of organic organization. Much, much research remains to be done, and recent developments in providing a clearer picture of protein structure, isolating genetic material in the cell and analyzing its base as the DNA molecule, the synthesis of DNA, and the first successful attempts to crack the genetic code are only the first few constructive stages toward reconstructing organisms.

For the present, the forces of vitalism in science have been slowed down considerably, if not entirely abated. But it should not be forgotten that as late as 1947 the highly considered and devoutly religious biologist Pierre Lecomte du Noüy proclaimed in his book, *Human Destiny*, the statistical impossibility of spontaneous generation and self-organization among the first forms of life. By the time of du Noüy's book the prime movers behind neo-vitalism had to drop the strategy of a vital essence as the motive force in organisms, and instead they adopted a new plan of attack. Briefly du Noüy's argument was that, given the condition of the Earth a billion years ago when life was first made possible, and given the complexity of even the simplest example of cellular life, the numerical probability of life evolving as a result of the right chemical and climatic circumstances was mathematically almost null. Armed with an impressive set of calculations, the author made his point; and, by doing it, sought to reinforce the division between organic and inorganic matter, a relationship which was then, as now, rapidly being eroded into a single continuum by the biochemists.

Du Noüy proceeded on the basis of scientific rationalism harnessed to a personal sense of revelation. His main enemy, besides materialism, was the probabilistic techniques of modern science, illustrated, for instance, when he maintained that (1947, p. 37): "To believe that we shall ever be able to explain biological phenomena in general, and the evolution of living beings, through the use of the same calculations employed to estimate the number of houses which will burn or the pressure of gas in a vessel, is an act of faith and not a scientific statement."

Granted, classical evolutionary theory has come under justified scrutiny in the past few years, but du Noüy's simplistic analogy of statistical technique neither proves nor disproves its application to biology. Six years after *Human Destiny* S. L. Miller produced a number of organic compounds by allowing an electrical discharge to pass through an oxygen-free space containing hydrogen, ammonia, methane, and water vapor. The lack of oxygen in the experiment seemed to discredit the results as a reconstruction of how the first life on Earth could have evolved. But the very complex substances produced in this experiment surprised even scientists and destroyed du Noüy's notions about biological probability.

Since Marshall Nirenberg's synthesis and testing of simplified RNA strands in the early 1960's, molecular biologists have constructed many synthetic nucleotide chains for which the exact genetic sequence is known. These in time will be linked to specific proteins. It is hypothesized, and partially verified, that all life derives from a complex series of catalytic and autocatalytic chemical reactions between nucleic acids (RNA and DNA molecules) and proteins. The growing complexity of life is assured because each of the two building blocks tends to consume the less well-adapted, and usually simpler, types of its counterparts. Pre-cellular life is established when proteins form boundary layers around a parent nucleic acid molecule; thus the molecule is protected and allowed to ingest food and reproduce under the right circumstances. Through evolution the boundary layer becomes less passive as it surrounds food and stores energy; in time it becomes the basis for the cell.

A more problematic question is the origin of life as it might have evolved from the Earth's composition while the seas cooled billions of years ago. Until 1966 A. I. Oparin's primordial atmosphere (a mixture of methane, hydrogen, water, and ammonia), energized by the sun's rays and capable of producing organic substances, had seemed the most probable way in which life evolved. Since then, P. H. Abelson has theorized that hydrogen cyanide (composed of hydrogen, carbon, and nitrogen) was a most likely substance of the Earth's atmosphere; when this was mixed with water and subjected to the sun's rays, complex organic molecules resulted. In experimentation Abelson has been able to produce many organic chemicals with this combination.

Until recently there has been little laboratory evidence that basic organic matter could evolve without the help of radiation, electrical charges or other external help. Yet now, basic chemicals subjected to 570° Fahrenheit heat have been transformed into organic matter. Sol Spiegelman carried this several steps forward by very nearly synthesizing organisms from basic chemicals at the University of Illinois in 1965.

Today the hierarchy of the Roman Catholic Church has been forced to accept the creation of life by man as a proven fact but has retreated to the position that true creation means the creation of matter and energy out of nothing—this last, according to one monsignor in New York, remains the option of God.

Twenty years ago du Noüy's book enjoyed a sizable popularity (and it is still in print); then as now it appealed not only to an educated public with a need for spiritual assurance, but also to those who desired the authority of a scientifically trained mind. Yet scientists, no matter how dedicated and brilliant, are notoriously human once they depart from their specialty. Today the intellectual sights of vitalism are aimed at another target: the realm of computer technology, which encompasses artificial intelligence and computer creativity. It remains to be seen if this new "offense to the human spirit" will be crushed—or will become another triumph for the mechanists. Slowly the criterion of vitalistic life has changed from physiological to neural perspectives.

A profound struggle has been in progress for several hundred years, a controversy in which the supreme intellectual authority of the world has changed hands: a transition from Church to science. If traditional sculpture imitated life through lifeless materials, it could not but be influenced by the outcome of this larger spiritual and intellectual conflict.

Bergson: The Poetics of Vitalism

Fifty years before the two-cultures debate, one man had the literary power, the grasp of science, and the verbal articulation to fabricate both a beautiful and a logical picture of man's place in a universe of matter and void.

Enid Starkie observes that the writings of Henri Bergson must be studied as literature before considering them as philosophy. Indeed, all contemporary evidence of the reaction to Bergson's words mark him as a poet, an unparalleled charmer of audiences. If his ideas, in spite of their frequent use of scientific terms, often failed to impress scientists or analytically minded philosophers, they invariably found great sympathy among writers and artists (it should be kept in mind that the "vitalist versus mechanist" argument was essentially one, not of the right facts, but of the right sensibilities toward all that makes life bearable as a state of consciousness). For the poet, beauty and an elegant style transcend the tiresome collection of fact. Objective truth and conviction through poetry are not identical, although it has been the gift of many artists to produce the impression of such a fusion. As for belief through poetics, Bergson's unique rhetorical effect on a lecture platform has been recorded by Miss Starkie (quoted in Hanna, 1962, pp. 94–95).

Bergson's eloquent and precise language held his audience enthralled, so that no distraction was possible. The attention of his listeners did not wander for a moment, nothing could break the thread of the discourse. It was like perfect and beautiful music, captivating the mind, just as music's richness does, allowing it no escape. The absence of heavy technical vocabulary made it a joy to hear, and he was the least Germanic of philosophers. His words slipped out as if on silk, and the rhythm lulled the senses of his hearers so that they felt that they saw with his eyes, with the eyes of a poet.

Each lecture, each essay by Bergson was presented as a polished *objet d'art*. All that Bergson touched had a fragile air of lyricism, and he methodically fought the trend which implied that life could be wholly interpreted through materialism alone—even when this trend was elevated to the complexity of modern biochemistry. In the presence of art—for what else offers more identification with life?—physical matter has something unclean and defiled about it. Furthermore, vitalism did have its scientifically respectable side. The vitalist image of the life force conquering inert matter had already found root in the theories of the biologists Oken, Blumenback, Treviranus, and the physiologist Johannes Müller, so that even into the twentieth century scientists, focusing on certain biological problems where material evidence was scant, tended to draw vitalist conclusions.

The experiment of Hans Driesch in which he cut the blastula of sea urchins into tiny pieces and then observed the pieces reorganizing themselves into full but smaller embryos, led Driesch to posit a theory of a vital carrier running throughout the organism. This and other experiments presenting parallel conclusions were regarded by Bergson with utmost sympathy. In 1904 at the International Congress of Philosophy, attended and partially presided over by Bergson, the great biologist Reinke, grand-priest of German neo-vitalism, attacked what he considered the stupidity of trying to reconstruct the human senses according to the functions of chemical elements. He pointed out that a living organism was no more a chemical problem than a great sonata was a mechanical one—as far as music was concerned, Reinke would have found no opposition in his day (though today some musicians might give him an argument). At the turn of the century Bergson had no lack of reputable scientific support; he had only to choose what best fitted his evolving philosophy.

To characterize the prime defect of Bergson's mechanistic opponents in the eyes of the philosopher would be to call their theories of evolutionary life unartistic and *not* beautiful. On the other hand, the phenomena of genetic inheritance and eventual death of the individual organism, as pictured by Bergson, are more than functions of the life cycle; they are what he termed the *vital process*. In this context the word *process*, as used by the philosopher, takes on an aura of reflective beauty that has its parallel in the symbolist technique of writing a poem which describes the creative act of writing a poem. Structurally embedded in his prose lie the poetic clues of the vitalist process of life which he seeks to explain. As a poet, he conveys without the hindrance of empirical proofs; he explains by explaining the futility of explanation. Thereby stands the strategy of his philosophy: the use of intellect to undermine intellect—through the aid of artistry.

Thus, *Creative Evolution* (1907) by Bergson is a strange, lovely admixture of poetic exposition and seemingly scientific rationalism. All his scientific evidence leads to his assumption that inert matter is entered by a life force in order to instill animation, like a block of uncut stone on the sculptor's bench; this analogy received literal acceptance by some of the next generation of sculptors, whose task it became to psychically force the shape of life into the fragments of material which came their way.

Best remembered of Bergson's ideas is the phrase *élan vital*, the vital impetus, or, in George Bernard Shaw's words, the "life force." This was vitalism regenerated and made the rallying cry for one of the twentieth century's most powerful aesthetics, a term raised in authority by some of the most impressive names in science. The general popularity of the *élan vital* had much to do with the natural inclination of most people with a touch of idealism in their souls to *want* to believe in its validity. In contrast to the mechanistic theories of physiology and evolution, in no way did the *élan vital* denigrate the existence of man, nor nullify the divinity of his origins; it was, simply put, one of those ideas in the history of philosophy that seemed too good and pure not to be true. Furthermore, the concept of an essence which made life possible in inert matter—which was life itself—possessed a persuasive dignity and charm which made it difficult even for a die-hard materialist to resist.

But there were those of a scientific bent who could resist Bergson's magic and call it claptrap. However, even when these men managed to devastate the philosopher's scientific explanations, the literary quality of their attacks fell considerably below Bergson's prose standard. In their rejection of psychic alternatives for an explanation of life, and in their manipulation of an inflexible leaden materialism, the mechanists demonstrated a clear insensitivity, if not a dearth of aesthetic authority, which tended to repel educated people—not only Bergsonians. Scientists as a rule have rarely attempted to refute interpretations of the kind mounted by Bergson; rather they have allowed them an unnoticed, gradual demise—suffocation by the weight of subsequent discovery.

Can we forget, though, what it is like for the mass of humanity to suffer under the knowledge that every living entity on the earth is harnessed to the same set of physical laws without exception, laws immensely complex in their ramifications and whose only claim to mystery lies in our incomprehension of them? Bergson understood this, and the singular beauty of the *élan vital* lay in its ability to penetrate reality on both the psychical and physical levels. It explained without explaining away. Rather than existing as a fixed law, the vital force had the power of cutting into the temporal continuum on its own volition. Physical laws, while a necessary aspect of reality, seemed to Bergson only to explain the outer shell of life, with little or no regard for the flow of events that comprised the stream of pure experience—manifested for instance through the uniqueness of thought as opposed to interpretation of it solely as a problem of electrochemical circuitry. Life was more than a state of material forces. Life flowed in and about every living being and it was up to the sensitive individual to feel the penetration of the *life force* through the strength of the psychical magnetism which it generated. Bergson's appeal to sensitivity made it as difficult to deny directly the presence of the *élan vital* as to prove its existence. In the form of an idea, therein lies a good part of its durability. Yet, in the last fifteen years the development of molecular biology has given us the beginning of a poetic view of living systems which may well in time far outshine the delicate imprecisions of Bergson.

Read, Focillon, and the Aesthetics of Neo-Vitalism

It is difficult to know which came first, circa 1910, abstract vitalist sculpture or the neo-vitalist aesthetic which supported it. Very probably both ideas were a *fait accompli* which sought each other out. Given an open society – even one with predominantly hostile critics and galleries—the desire among a small minority of sculptors to produce abstract forms in this age generated one of those secret and powerful urges that, once let loose, could not be contained or nullified. In an expanding technological culture dealing with new levels of abstraction, it could hardly have been different.

The neo-vitalist aesthetic, as embodied in Bergson's *élan vital*, was ready-made for a sculpture that seemed not to be *carved* but to grow from an inner direction. Already the *élan vital* had left its soothing imprecision in contemporary French poetry, philosophy, and biology. For Parisian artists of the first two decades of this century, it was one of many new and useful ideas "in the air." Without overt commitment to mechanism, mathematics, or primitive magic, sculptors created a geometric-organic idiom which seemed to leap over centuries of Western classical idealism and align itself with age-old values of sculpture. The fragile banalities of the nineteenth century were rejected for much cruder but fundamental sensibilities. It was imperative that the modern abstract vitalist create "life" as Rodin had done— but in a radical form that would appear to be anything but a copy of life. With the right circumstances and a degree of genius a sculptor could—in fact, *had* to—liberate the vital essence from the dormant heart of his material before he could call the result sculpture. Such a sentiment may sound ludicrous today—though as an idea it has propelled a good portion of the modern idiom for the past fifty years. It endured as one of those great sophisticated folk myths capable of turning museum directors into beasts of prey at the sight of a prime work of Henry Moore up for sale.

By nature art historians are pattern-creating creatures, and patterns abound in art history; but, like so many broad conceptions, they begin to show serious flaws when applied to specific cases. Such a theory is one that tries to account—through opposing world views—for the development of art styles in history and prehistory. These polar sources are the *organic* (also referred to as the *representational* and *amorphic)* and the *geometric* (also termed the *linear* and *abstract)* tendencies. Submitting that this division is to some extent active in all art periods from paleolithic to modern times, Wilhelm Worringer and Arnold Hauser are but two of a number of art historians who attempt to explain stylistics and its underlying meaning for a culture in terms of how cultures gravitate toward one tendency or another.

A case can usually be made that either the *geometric* or the *organic* tendency prevailed in the art or decoration of a past culture. Most extinct societies displayed a mixture of both tendencies—a plurality not always easy to reconcile in terms of the nature and activities of a society. Contradiction becomes readily apparent when the *geometric* is exclusively identified with abstraction, and *organic* tendencies are thought to coincide with naturalism and representationalism. Such a categorization induces semantic acrobatics when art historians are confronted with modern abstract art, which is obviously organic in origin. One of the first champions of modern art, Herbert Read, observed that throughout the history of cultures there have been repeated attempts to merge the organic and geometric tendencies. Read found a solution for modern sculpture by calling the merger of organic appearing forms with abstraction *vitalistic art.*

This question of the *organic-geometric fusion* figures prominently in conceptualizations of the historians Herbert Read and Henri Focillon. Yet as separate categories the organic and geometric nearly vanish with the emergence of abstract vitalistic sculpture. In fact, never before in the history of art had there been such a conscious merger—both intellectual and plastic—between these two opposing forces.

For the first time in history our culture has the option of literally fusing organic activities with the linear-geometric precision of machines. This has come about recently by the growth of both theoretical and applied sciences: cybernetics, electronic circuit theory, information theory, systems analysis, etc. The result of course is neither *amorphic* or *representational*—as we describe natural organicism—nor *linear* or *abstract*—as we interpret classical machines—but a fusion of the two which transcends the existing stylistic polarity. In a sense, much of what we have taken for style in the past will be absorbed eventually into an anti-style or no-style aesthetic. Here the means of designing objects and fitting them together will result in optimal, quasi-organic solutions. Much of what has gone on in the past in the way of arbitrary stylistics, fluctuations from century to century or year to year, may eventually *not be possible*. In a sense, we are transcending style—in that style will be absorbed in optimum technological manipulation. Certainly this is not a new dream. Every technological innovation has produced the impression of an optimum style form. Style itself has been a combination of technical necessity, tradition, and inventive whim. Yet the stylistically *invisible* technology and environmental planning which we are gradually weaving around ourselves might very well make stylistic option a dead issue.

As the problems of environmental planning and resource development become increasingly critical factors for human survival, the present latitude in stylistic flexibility will become less and less permissible. In the future stylistics will be relegated to increasingly trivial forms of expression—as has always been the case in tradition-oriented cultures. Certainly every culture has a *style*. But when arbitrary stylistics are synthetically devised simply to sell unneeded products, waste resources, and rearrange the landscape in a less than humane way, then style no longer ranks as a form of intracultural expression, but as a disease threatening the very basis of human existence.

Vitalism in sculpture can be viewed as a prototype of the trend toward stylistic transcendence. It attempted, at the beginning of the century, to conjoin idealism to a new awareness of biological capability. In one sense, vitalism stood not even halfway between the two sensibilities; it took a step—a large one—out of the old world of representational idealism.

A source of intense belief was needed, something that would replace fast-dying faith in realism. Because of his timely and successful attacks on materialism, Henri Bergson became the high priest of a new cult—that of instilling life, by way of the vital essence transferred by the sculptor's fervor, into inert matter. It imparted spiritual energy and hope to writers and poets contemporary to Bergson. Essays abound by writers attesting their debt to him. A devotee to the *élan vital* was George Bernard Shaw. In an article written in 1932, Shaw described the metamorphic process by which Rodin fashioned a portrait bust of him. He marveled at Rodin's ability to transform clay through a series of sharply different stylistic types (quoted in Elsen, 1963, p. 126).

Once again, a century rolled by in a single night, and the bust became a bust by Rodin and it was the living reproduction of the head that reposes on my shoulders. It was a process that seemed to belong to the study of an embryologist and not to an artist. The hand of Rodin worked, not as the hand of the sculptor works, but as the work of *Élan Vital*.... The hand of God is his own hand....

After the literary smoke clears, it appears that Shaw was only indicating what Rodin wanted the world to believe. Rodin tried every conceivable means, including some rather doubtful illusionistic tricks, to simulate life in clay. The technical resources used by the sculptor originate in many instances as his own invention and they vary from *fin de siècle* banality to pure genius. Following Rodin, other sculptors, both representational and abstract in their work, adopted the vitalistic attitude. Curiously, it was one of the few ideas in modern sculpture that sculptors often mentioned when explaining their work process and attitudes toward materials. Yet the idea took a long time to penetrate the minds of critics who had to write about modern sculpture. Perhaps the personal, almost religious, fervor of the *vital impetus* made it incomprehensible to the non-artist. In this instance the critic had to confront both a literary or overtly stylistic influence, and a *biological* relationship between the artist and his materials. Not until the 1950's did any critic really begin to look at vitalism as a separate and specific philosophy for the creation of sculpture.

Although Sir Herbert Read is gifted with consummate literary skill, at times a tendency to polemicize comes through in his writings. Nonetheless, no bibliography of modern sculpture is complete without two or three books by this critic and aesthetician. His writings must be examined, if for no other reason than that he has probed, as no other writer, under the surface appearances of modern sculpture. Where colleagues have been content to write about the procession of sculpture styles, Read has concerned himself with far more knotty problems such as the rediscovery and evolution of formal properties.

It is worthwhile devoting some space to Read's gradual awareness of the central position of vitalism as a ruling principle of modern sculpture. Read is fortunate in having established close friendships with two major sculptors: the Constructivist Naum Gabo and the Vitalist Henry Moore. These relationships have acted as an interpretive bridge between two extreme positions in the modern abstract idiom. One should mention Read's partiality in the 1930's for the informalist leanings of the Surrealists. At the time this produced a more obvious, if synthetic, polarity between modern realism and abstraction in his writings.

The first evidence of a more basic duality appears in Read's *The Anatomy*

71

of Art, published in 1931. He notes that organic and geometrical art appear and reappear throughout history, and he voices a distinct preference for organic art (1932, p. 51): "It is the art of joy in living, of confidence in the world." This proclivity grows stronger in later books, but not without an attempt to seem impartial.

Art Now (1933) appears with nothing new concerning the geometric-organic opposition, but includes a small section devoted to what Read terms "the genetic concept of art." This he sees embedded in the philosophy of Giambattista Vico, whose conception of society as a developing organism greatly appeals to Read—who, furthermore, wishes to find a place for art in such a model of society. Here, at least, the influence of Bergson can be anticipated.

By 1937 in *Art and Society* Read rationalizes the appearance of geometric art in the Neolithic Age by explaining it as the symbolic atrophying of the artistic impulse in man, and then compares this with the modern industrial situation. Also in the same year Read contributed to the anthology *Circle: International Survey of Constructive Art.* The idea of a vital impetus behind their works is expressed by several artists; constructive organicism is a central theme; neither idea is mentioned by Read. It must be remembered that in 1934 in the group anthology *Unit One*, edited by Read, Henry Moore made a clear statement of a belief in artistic vitalism. Read therefore had direct access to the philosophy.

The first overt example of Read's formulation of the vitalistic principle appears in a small book entitled *Art and the Evolution of Man* (1951, p. 34). "I have to confess," writes the author, "at this point, that I am an unregenerate Bergsonian. From the scientist's point of view Bergson has been dismissed as a 'good poet but a bad scientist,' and no doubt he was unscientific in method. But he had what the scientist so often lacks—a synoptic vision." Read goes on to frame the breadth of Bergson's evolutionary vision of human development, with special considerations for intellect, and intuition as if these formed a set of disembodied components flitting in and out of physical matter. Read, like many literary persons, felt drawn to the totality of Bergson's theory; as a description of evolution it is preeminently suited to explaining the evolving role of art as a critical aspect of human consciousness; almost biologically it intertwines thought with the artistic objects resulting from thought. Bergson's explication is beautiful—like a slow-motion movie of a flower blooming. Moreover, it appealed to Read's need, due in part to the encouragement of Lancelot Law Whyte, for a "unitary principle" capable of operating on both animate and inanimate levels. "The point I am trying to make..." says Read, "is that the work of art is not an analogy—it is the essential act of transformation; not merely *pattern* of mental evolution, but the vital process itself" (1951, p. 39).

The notion of vitalism is finally produced outright in an essay on Henry Moore which appears in *The Philosophy of Modern Art* (1952). In this essay the author views representationalism as the disease which cyclically destroys sculpture, and Rodin as the modern master who nursed it back to health. Moore, of course, plays the part of therapist (1952, p. 203):

Henry Moore, in common with artists of his type throughout the ages, believes that behind the appearance of things there is some kind of spiritual essence, a force or immanent being which is only partially revealed in actual living forms.

In another passage Read states (1952, p. 202):

The division which used to be made between the organic and the inorganic in science has been abandoned by science itself, but nevertheless a distinction which is popularly associated with the phenomenon of "life" does exist, and Henry Moore himself has suggested that *vital* rather than *organic* might therefore be a better word to describe the art which is the antithesis of constructivism.

Read goes on to discuss the inherent ambiguities of the word *vital*, also pointing out all the associations gathered by the word in modern usage in relation to the machine, so that it is clear, even to Read, that *vital* expresses qualities that extend beyond the flesh-and-blood category, the realm of natural life where he wishes to fix it. In one passage, the author tries desperately, but unsuccessfully, to unravel the frustrations of the two principles: the organic and the *constructive*—that is, the *geometric*—which seem to present a dichotomy, but in reality continue to merge and interrelate toward some unseen end. It is worth quoting Read at length because the dilemma that he poses was a very real one for two generations of sculptors, and is only beginning to be understood in terms of its internal contradictions (1952, p. 201).

The story of modern sculpture between Rodin and Henry Moore is the story of a wholly unintelligent strife between these two principles—a strife which sometimes take place within the conscience of the artist. Brancusi, Archipenko, Lipchitz, Laurens, Duchamp-Villon, Giacometti, Arp, Schlemmer, Tatlin, Pevsner, Gabo and Barbara Hepworth are the names of some of the participants in this confused movement, from which, however, the antithesis of organic and constructive does finally emerge in all its clarity and inevitability.

I have explained the scientific justification for both terms of the antithesis, but in the appreciation of art we tend to dispense with theory, and rely on the obvious and apparent differences. No one is likely to confuse the "constructive" with the "organic" if faced with typical examples of both types of art; and however much we may insist that the constructive work is no less justified in nature than the organic work, there will always be a tendency to associate the organic with the vital and therefore with the human. We have seen that constructive elements underlie all natural phenomena; that organic growth follows laws, and involves structures, which are as geometrical, or mathematical, as anything created by a constructive artist.

At this point we might ask ourselves, why did it take Read until 1951 to recognize the nature of vitalism, and the apparent schism between organic and constructive (i.e., geometric) sculpture? Probably because it was not clear to artists themselves. The vitalist aesthetic was confined to a rather small number of artists. The fact that they comprised many of the best sculptors of the period from 1910 to 1940 only began to become self-evident after the Second World War. And, more importantly, the vitalist aesthetic only took hold and began to take on the dimensions of an academy *after* the war.

By 1964 when Read published *A Concise History of Modern Sculpture*, an entire section was given over to vitalistic sculptors, whose works range from extreme amorphism to recognizable organic creatures and precise crystalline structures; but for Read what seems to identify them all as vitalist is a certain sympathetic affinity with the natural environment. In other words, vitalistic art is not an art of alienation; the vitalist sculptor is bent on extorting humanistic life symbols from his surroundings, rather than fabricating icons of despair and rejection. Throughout a final chapter of the book, "A Diffusion of Styles," Read's disturbance at the emasculation of sculpture in the form of *junk* and *linear* assemblages is manifestly evident. He views this eating away at the rotund healthy body of sculpture as a kind of cancer of the age and he quotes Ruskin on change and excitement—instead of contemplation—and the deleterious effects of these first two stimulants on the art forms of a culture.

To define what Read wishes sculpture to be almost demands that one set down Read's definition of sculpture. This is not easy since Read, as a major writer on sculpture, never commits himself in so many words to a precise description. At the times when he describes the attributes of sculpture he comes closest to a definition. In *The Art of Sculpture* (1956) Read views sculpture as arising from a special sensibility that deals, unlike painterly perception, with three-dimensional masses in space (1956, p. 71): "The specifically plastic sensibility is, I believe, more complex than the specifically visual sensibility. It involves three factors: A sensation of the tactile quality of surfaces; a sensation of volume as denoted by plane surfaces; and a synthetic realization of the mass ponderability of the object."

Read later repeats these attributes with a slightly different emphasis (1964, p. 18): "A gulf separates the work of Rodin from that of Arp or Henry

Moore; but all three sculptors share the same concern for the virtues proper to the art of sculpture—sensibility to volume and mass, the interplay of hollows and protuberances, the rhythmical articulation of planes and contours, unity of conception. The ends differ but the means are the same...."

Significantly, Read's definition of the concerns of sculpture is not far removed from the definitions of Ruskin and Wilenski. But from his choice of sculptors it seems obvious that his preferences lie toward the vitalistic idiom. It is clear from many of Read's statements—though not true of either Wilenski or Ruskin—that linear, mechanical, or geometric characteristics do not satisfy his ultimate concern for what sculpture should be. In *A Concise History of Modern Sculpture* (1964) Read presents the Constructivists' (Tatlin, Rodchenko, Pevsner, and Gabo) viewpoint and acknowledges their continued influence—yet with no great enthusiasm. In fact, some years ago Read's friendship with Gabo was strained by Gabo's insistence on "space" and linear elements as a legitimate path to sculptural exploration. There was a reconciliation; still, several questions remain. Is Gabo's and the Post-Constructivist school's involvement with "open" linear sculpture really the beginning of the death of sculpture as Read implies in his history? Is "healthy" sculpture necessarily vitalistic, and how can "healthy" sculpture be defined? Surely recent American and British "Object" sculpture complies with Read's list of sculpture concerns—but some of it at least, it is fair to conclude, Read would not consider healthy.

Of interest and typically Bergsonian is Read's final analysis (1964, p. 253), in which vitalism becomes a moral imperative, a force which can save sculpture from ultimate withering away. He states: "Virtually everything, one must say, has been lost that has characterized the art of sculpture in the past. This new sculpture (linear, welded metal sculpture), essentially open in form, dynamic in intention, seeks to disguise its mass and ponderability."

The *contemplative* aspects of Moore's ponderous reclining figures finally provide the only sanctuary for a mind aroused by the "horror and hatred" of the newest modes. Earlier (1964, pp. 76–77) he describes this latent inner force:

I have by no means exhausted the sculptural inventions of Picasso, but from 1930 onwards he was to be more and more exclusively preoccupied with *magic:* he is concerned to represent in his figures certain vital forces of social significance—the *anima* that we project into all subjects, animate or inanimate, the quality the Chinese call *ch'i,* the universal force that flows through all things, and which the artist must transmit to his creations if they are to affect other people. This *vitalism,* as I prefer to call it, has been the desire and pursuit of one main type of modern sculptor. (Italics added.)

It should be apparent by now that Herbert Read's aesthetic doctrine of sculptural vitalism is heir to Bergson's vitalism; as such, it is emotionally and intellectually attached to the attack on mechanism in the biological sciences. What Bergson, and later Read, sought was a viable metaphysical explanation of organic life and the expression of life in art, an explanation which would merge the two. Significantly, neither man could be described as antiscientific and both have possessed better than average understanding of the underlying structure of science. But neither has been satisfied with science as an ultimate arbiter of values. Bergson and Read felt that the core of vitalism resides in the intuition of the individual to feel the "life pulse" in objects or other beings about him. Nor was either thinker anti-intellectual, rather they supported the position that analysis must be accompanied by faith, intuition, and sensitivity. As an attempt to inject a humanistic rationale into modern life, vitalism presented a relevant position. But, as a synoptic view of the real meaning of science and technology and their carry-over into the arts, it is now both outmoded and inadequate.

The organic ideology and its vitalistic manifestations must be looked upon as part of a continuum of evolving attitudes within the social conception of what defines *organic*. In other words, the nature of what are considered *organic* changes has altered in the past hundred years. At one technological period *organic* might have been interpreted, as Lewis Mumford makes clear (1934, p. 345), in the Queen Anne legs and painted flower and scroll work that adorned the nineteenth-century machine. This is an extreme example of the literal application of representational organicism. By and large, organicism has gradually moved from completely natural and primitive forms to a new set of meanings circumscribed by technological capability. The modern meaning of the organic lies in *the gradual moving away from biotic appearances toward biotic functioning via the machine;* vitalism is a transitional step in this process from inanimate object to system. In sculpture the vitalistic synthesis owes a good deal to other influences concurrent with Rodin and Bergson. In the sense that Ruskin conceives of architecture as the abstract massing of forms for functional and aesthetic reasons, he could be considered a precursor of modern vitalism. But, in general, the vitalistic yearning to reproduce nature's forms was stimulated by a heightened graphic awareness of visible organic structure.

Haeckel's *Kunstformen der Natur* (1899) has already been mentioned as a new vision of the naturalist's album, presenting various forms of organic life on a more abstract level, with symmetry, transparency, and linear pattern as dominant features. Books stressing the abstract affinities between art and nature have been especially popular in Germany. Blossfeldt's *Urformen der Kunst* (1929) used magnified photographs to heighten and emphasize the geometrical and sculptural aspects of nature. Another, *Kunstgebilde des Meeres, Muscheln und Schneckengehäuse* (1936) by Paul André Robert was one of the Iris series of books on nature and art. A still more recent example of the genre is Schmidt's *Kunst und Naturform* (1960).

As early as 1872 in England Frederick Edward Hulme published *Art-Studies from Nature as Applied to Design*, and although this early work is less scientifically bent than its German counterparts, it is a methodical attempt—in the modern sense—to "abstract" from Nature.

The book that stands as the definitive work of classical biology in its effort to show how form and function are linked organistically through geometry is D'Arcy Wentworth Thompson's *On Growth and Form* (1917). Not simply a set of volumes containing many striking drawings and photographs, it is an attempt, prior to biophysics, to discern the laws of growth according to classical physics. The method used is a mathematical analysis of the formative tendencies of organisms according to their processes and growth patterns, discernible on the visual physicochemical level. Before commencing, Thompson insisted that his study was not meant to prove the ultimate causation of organic forms according to physical laws operating on a molecular level; instead, he interpreted the organic world according to the familiar horizon of what can be seen with the unaided eye.

In a very real sense *On Growth and Form* stands on the threshold between that world of natural forms which is still accessible to the sculptor, and the world of molecular bonds and protein chains completely out of his reach. Herbert Read and other essayists have repeatedly referred to Thompson's analysis of cellular formations, evolutionary form developments, tissue structure as a function of magnitude, the shaping of bones, differentials in growth rates, the mathematics of spiral growth, and the development of hollow three-dimensional bone trusses, so as to parallel the vitalist sculptor's forms with the products of nature.

Finally, a major influence on vitalistic thought in art was a slim volume, *La Vie des formes* (1934), by Henri Focillon. During Bergson's revival of a rational, antimechanistic philosophy, Focillon attended his famous Thursday-afternoon lectures at the Collège de France as an attentive listener. Very probably, Bergson's example of the evolutionary potential of art forms was eventually taken up by Focillon as the foundation for his theory of the transmutation of forms.

Not surprisingly, in an essay on Henry Moore (1952, pp. 195–215), Read acknowledges his debt to Focillon and reiterates Focillon's theory of formal metamorphosis and its counterpart in the evolutionary morphogenic development of forms in nature. Two ideas appear in *The Life of Forms in Art (La Vie des formes)* which are instrumental in Read's gradual shift toward the vitalistic theory of sculpture. In the chapter "The World of Forms," Focillon states (1934, p. 4):

Can form, then, be nothing more than a void? Is it only a cipher wandering through space, forever in pursuit of a number that forever flees from it? By no means. Form has meaning—but it is a meaning entirely its own, a personal and specific value that must not be confused with the attributes we impose upon it. Form has significance, and form is open to interpretation.... Their physiognomic quality [speaking of forms in general] may closely resemble that of nature, but it must not be confused with nature. Any likening of form to sign is a tacit admission of the conventional distinction between form and subject-matter—a distinction that may become misleading if we forget that the fundamental content of form is a formal one. Form is never the catch-as-catch-can garment of subject-matter.

Inadvertently perhaps, in trying to establish the ontological basis of form, Focillon set down reasoning which holds true for most nonobjective sculpture until the present; namely, the meaning of form lies within itself and the enjoyment of form is for its own sake. In allowing that form springs mysteriously from form, Focillon's attitude was vitalistic; but in its disassociation from the organic metaphor it was certainly not. Rather than connecting form with living matter, Focillon attempted to establish the separate integrity and identity of form in art. Read, obviously, disregarded this aspect of Focillon's reasoning. Whatever else it is, sculpture must deal with palpable matter. Form generation for Focillon was an abstract ideal; for Read sculptural form, if it is to be vital, must spring from the geometry of organic matter.

What may have been important to Read, though, is Focillon's encouragement of the inductive analysis of form, that is, the viewing of form in all of its manifestations and stages very much as a classical biologist might have observed the stages of an organism's development. There is also something else to be considered. Focillon did not conceive of form as altogether palpable and geometric. Form for him had a larger meaning, one verging on the term *Gestalt*, the shape of form change. Form in this case becomes metamorphosis in space-time more than anything geometrically substantial— though Focillon leaves an enticing, perhaps intentional, ambiguity between the two.

In a later chapter entitled "Forms in the Realm of Space" Focillon quite deftly ruled out vast areas of modern sculpture, even those considered vitalistic, as a part of the realm of sculpture proper (1934, p. 26):

Sculpture may indeed suggest the content of life and its inner articulation, but it is perfectly obvious that its design does not and cannot suggest to us anything re-sembling a void. Nor are we likely to confuse sculpture with those anatomical figures made up of parts indiscriminately thrown together into a single body that is no bet-ter than a kind of physiological carry-all. Sculpture is not an envelope. It bears down with all the weight of its density. The interplay of the internal component parts has no importance save as it comes up to and affects the surfaces, without, of course, compromising them as the outward expression of the volume....The abuse of the word "volume" in the artistic vocabulary of our time is indicative of the fundamental need to recapture the immediate data of sculpture—or of sculp-tural quality.

Not only did Focillon take issue with Constructivism, but it would seem that his definition of sculpture ruled out Cubism, extreme Expressionism, and every sort of "open" abstract sculpture. In this respect Focillon's old-fashioned ideas about the true nature of sculpture must have been something of an embarrassment to some of his admirers. Unintentionally, he contributed to the ideal of an abstract vitalistic sculpture, but there is one point which he and Read do agree upon—that is, the limits of sculpture. In a sense, a contained void, if pushed too far, is regarded by both as the destroyer of sculptural volume.

Read suggests (1956, p. 72) that, "Ideally each [individual]...should be provided...with a piece of sculpture to hug, cuddle, fondle—primitive verbs that indicate a desire to treat an object with plastic sensibility." Here is a graphic example of what Read finds to be the prime quality of sculpture. Vitalism somehow goes hand in hand with "the sensation of volume," "ponderability," and "tactile quality."

This discussion has tried to show how the fabrication of the vitalistic myth flourished on many levels—scientific, theological, philosophical, literary—and finally in the mainstream of sculpture exposition itself. If anything, Read and Focillon provided a *post facto* intellectual justification for vitalism's existence. The real originators of the vitalistic aesthetic were sculptors themselves. Not dogmatically, but through casual conversation and statements of personal goals, these sculptors informed the public that the stimulus of the vitalistic idea was responsible for the energy and freshness of their work.

Motives and Analyses of Five Vitalist Sculptors

If Bergson proposed neo-vitalism as a philosophical doctrine at the beginning of this century, then why did it take nearly half a century for a major art critic to identify vitalism as a central doctrine of modern sculpture?

Actually the reason is fairly apparent. The vitalist sculptor thought of his vitalistic beliefs as a personal stimulus, an emotional incentive, rather than as a public philosophy that could be formulated into doctrine for a manifesto. There were literally a score of *isms* in vogue during the period from 1910 to 1940, and nearly every vitalistic sculptor was connected to a different set of them. The very fact that vitalism spanned so many schools of modern sculpture gives it a validity and position of importance above most. Also, the vitalists—perhaps more than other modern sculptors—tended toward vagueness and imprecision concerning their most profound allegiances. It took some time for the public and critics alike to realize that no human or natural beauty in the old sense, but the raw, sometimes unlovely, motive force of nature lay behind a vitalist sculptor's creative desires.

Superficially all the pioneer vitalists seemed to be involved in other concerns. This was most apparent with Gaudier-Brzeska's diversified output. Brancusi on the other hand rarely compromised himself, yet personified the indefinable spirit with many contrasting facets: Cubist for some, or Surrealist, primitive, baroque, oriental, byzantine, classical—according to one's propensities—but nevertheless, always Brancusi. Until the late 1940's Arp was regarded as a prankster Dada poet whose reliefs and plaster forms were largely the result of Surrealist whimsy. To consider Arp a great classicist of the modern idiom—at that time—would have been absurd. Barbara Hepworth for a considerable portion of her career was identified with the Neo-Plastic intentions of the Abstraction-Création group in Paris. Henry Moore, on the other hand, oscillated between the Surrealist wave of the 1930's and, to a lesser degree, the Constructivists as represented by the spirit of *Circle* in 1937.

All the above sculptors have made strongly vitalistic statements concerning their methods and intentions. However vitalism as a movement or a cohesive expression of belief never crystallized. This was also true of the American "organic" sculptors, such as Theodore Roszak, Ibram Lassaw and Seymour Lipton who worked in brazed metal after the Second World War. What is common for the sculptors mentioned was their sense of discovery linked to the natural process, an abiding awareness of the living characteristics of natural forms. Also they were sensitive to the fact that the work habits of the sculptor could be a physical extension of the morphogenic processes of nature. In theory, at least, or as much as his temperament allows, the sculptor may commit himself to what the Chinese call the *Tao*, or the *Way*—that expression of nature which has to do with the unified, inexorable forces of the universe. As concrete expression of the natural environment, vitalistic sculpture contains certain common features.

It copies nature through example and metaphor, not primarily through mimeticism. Whatever symbolism vitalism employs is related to the growth properties of materials, those at least which can be made visible. Vitalism generates an *intuition* that life is not literally, but plastically, present in a sculpted object. However, a viewer is never left to doubt that a vitalist sculpture is a man-made product rather than the result of natural forces. *Intuition*—a prime Bergsonian concept—is the origin, not analysis or reason, for all good vitalist sculpture.

As an idea, vitalism had no boundaries; it remained a personal declaration rather than a formal aesthetic. If at its inception it came to life in Rodin's utterances and was carried to abstraction by Gaudier-Brzeska and Brancusi, then it is important to remember that vitalism affected the work of hundreds of sculptors for the next forty years. As a contagious influence, the vitalistic mystique spread among sculptors almost religiously. As with all dogmas, its propagation depended upon the fact that it went unanalyzed and, to a great extent, undetected.

For our purposes it is a serious loss that Henri Gaudier-Brzeska's proposed essay "The Need of Organic Forms in Sculpture" was never written. Ezra Pound recounted how this piece was to have appeared in the second issue of *Blast* (house organ for the London-based art movement Vorticism); but before it could be written, the war and then death at the front in 1915 removed Gaudier-Brzeska (along with Duchamp-Villon and Boccioni, also lost in the great war, this represented the slaughter of fully half the generation's best sculptors). Of all the Cubist and proto-Cubist sculptors working before the war Gaudier alone possessed an attitude that gave some inkling to the vitalistic synthesis, then evolving between the world of geometric and organic forms.

In Gaudier-Brzeska's last abstract works—*Stags* (1914) and *Birds Erect* (FIG. 24) are the best examples—there exist evidences of both the mechanomorphic impersonality of Duchamp-Villon and the doctrinaire geometric Cubism which became so favored in Paris, especially in the work of Lipchitz. The organic effect in Gaudier's sculpture touches on crystal structure, yet all the blocklike planes employed are kept gently convex and their edges are slightly rounded.

Horace Brodsky in his book on the sculptor attributes the indeterminant plant-rock quality of *Birds Erect* to some cacti that the sculptor kept in his studio. "These he liked," says Brodsky, "because of their strangeness and because they suggested new ideas. All the time, he was going to nature for his forms. He was not carving jig-saw puzzles. Fishes, birds and plants

24. Henri Gaudier-Brzeska, *Birds Erect*, 1914.

were his guides, and he was continually drawing from the nude" (1938, p. 92).
Brodsky also seems to think that Gaudier-Brzeska attempted these last
works as shock experiments and publicity stunts, adding that Gaudier
wanted to emulate several well-known Cubist painters. Some or all of this
may be true, for it is difficult to see Gaudier-Brzeska as a consistent force in
modern sculpture. His works—a good cross-section—alternately show the
sculptor as a romantic realist, a rather flabby imitation of Jacob Epstein,
and a pasticheur of all that was wrong with English sculpture at the time.
With his friend and loyal supporter, the poet Ezra Pound, Gaudier-Brzeska
should be remembered for his meaningful innovations and a few master-

pieces; also, his youth and poverty are factors which must mitigate any evaluation of his stature.

For both these late works, *Stags* and *Birds Erect*, "soft bluntness" was Wyndham Lewis's very apt term. To exploit the surface properties of stone, its veins and imperfections, as an analogue to organic matter, to carve nature-originated forms without betraying their source, to derive power from the lines and surfaces of materials without giving way to a machinelike inflexibility—this was Gaudier's method and the beginning of vitalist dogma.

Just as Bergson had ruled that instinct prevailed over intellect in the conduct of the human mind, so instinct became paramount in the new sculpture. Gaudier-Brzeska's reply to a critic printed in the *Egoist* supports this (quoted in Pound, 1960, p. 37). "The modern sculptor is a man who works with instinct as his inspiring force. His work is emotional. The shape of a leg, or the curve of an eyebrow, etc., etc., have to him no significance whatsoever; light voluptuous modeling is to him insipid—what he feels he does so intensely and his work is nothing more or less than the abstraction of this intense feeling...."

Gaudier had been very much taken by Brancusi's sculpture in a London exhibition and had actually, during this event, talked to Brancusi—before beginning *Stags* and *Birds Erect*. It is difficult to say, and more impossible to speculate upon the eventual effect of the meeting, except to note that the tendency toward simplification of organic form had already begun in Brancusi's work as early as 1908.

Some men create their own mythological aura; for others, myths rise up about them like the rainbowed haze around a waterfall. Brancusi caused a bit of both. If early in his career he rejected the patronage afforded by an apprenticeship under Rodin, he learned by example from the Master that what is unnoticed and mundane always contains the magical beginnings of art; moreover, the search and the effort to fabricate art are inseparable; to allow either aspect to dominate or slip out of harmony is to destroy the vitality of the result. In one way Brancusi personifies the heartfelt desire of our civilization to be modern and old-fashioned at the same time—and to share the benefits of both worlds. Friends and biographers of the sculptor collected his *bons mots*, aphorisms, and little observations. These sum up his philosophy in a hundred different ways. In essence it is: *man must live in harmony with nature; my sculptures reflect such a union.*

Myth encompasses the ability to act out a role so that drama becomes more desired than reality. In this sense Brancusi's reception of visitors during his declining years was a performance that enhanced his sculptures.

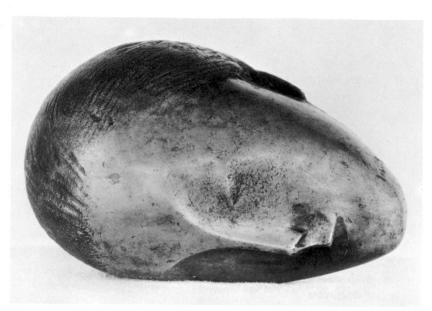

25. Constantin Brancusi, *Sleeping Muse*, 1910.

As food for the myth (and the word *myth* is used in its most innocent and least provocative sense, instead of *image* which has its own modern connotations of manufactured fame), Brancusi's appearance was flawless: he was diminished by age, quite short and delicate, slow but agile in the way of older people who still enjoy life, troll-like with a white beard and pointed lamb's wool cap, gracious yet reserved with strangers. On a first visit the conversation soon narrowed to showing pieces in the studio. This "animation" of the sculpture was a ritual performance that can best be described by envisioning the little dance of Spalanzani in the *Tales of Hoffman* where the inventor goes from one figure to the next setting his automata in motion. Brancusi, much like a conjurer at a side show for children, would flick the dust cloths from a succession of gleaming sculptures—all with the timing of an actor who knows when to proceed to the next effect. The tall-ceilinged, white studio rooms were pierced by a sun which transformed the sculptures into vessels of light. This atmosphere was touched with Brancusi's sense of pagan serenity, a remedy for a world which had witnessed too much false religion. In a very literal way Brancusi's studio was a temple to uncorrupted sensuality.

For an insight into the Brancusi myth it is futile to dwell on his folk heritage, the archetypes that seem to well up out of the legends of his childhood, the calculated fine then the calculated rough handling of materials, or the naturalist's desire for simplicity—these are all aspects of vitalist

26. Constantin Brancusi, *The Beginning of the World* (Sculpture for the Blind), 1924.

technique. Gesture, not representation, transmits this secret of life. The great dialectical mood of Brancusi's sculpture resides in a fusion of machine-like, inward-dwelling precision and an antithesis, a blind rootedness to the earth.

That life was invested in geometry became a realization of nineteenth-century biology. The first attempts at extreme shape reduction are probably as old as sculpture itself; evidences of it are to be found in Cycladic, Minoan, and Aztec sculpture. Brancusi's *Sleeping Muse* (FIG. 25) in bronze was a distinct simplification toward a perfect ovoid shape. Antecedents for Brancusi's reduction, besides the examples of Elie Nadelman's carvings and certain primitive sculptures, can be traced back to the impressionism of Medardo Rosso and to a few hyper-romantic Italian sculptors whose obscuration of facial features produced a sense of dreamlike reverie. Yet, Brancusi pushed the reductive impulse toward a destination never before explored. Facial features became more obscure with the *Prometheus* of 1911; the ovoid was completely geometrized in *The New Born* of 1915; and finally, the ovoid, in *The Beginning of the World* (FIG. 26) was reduced to formal perfection.

The reductivism of *The Beginning of the World* provoked one of Brancusi's biographers, Ionel Jianou, to comment on the place of the egg in the folk customs of the Slavic tradition. The egg, colored and decorated, is not only an Easter symbol, but all that implies eternal life through regeneration.

85

As early as 1912 the critic Jacques Doucet realized that the subtlety of these near egg forms by Brancusi was accentuated by slight impressions and textures that interrupted otherwise symmetrical surfaces. If the ovoid form, polished and gleaming, is the perfect collector of light, then any imperfection on its surface would act as a premonition, a visual hint of the forces of internal organization harbored within.

According to D'Arcy Thompson, the formula for the envelope of the ovoid form is essentially the same for all fluid, membrane-covered eggs. The miracle of the egg is that constant radial pressure within an animal's oviduct makes it, within amazing tolerance, a series of near-perfect circles around a straight axis. Thompson suggests that, if mounted on a lathe, the egg would "turn true."

Perhaps this explains Brancusi's affinity in the finish of his sculptures for machine forms. More often than not, he sought organic forms possessing a high degree of symmetry, and this was accentuated by slight irregularities and off-center displacements of related parts. Apparently Brancusi appreciated that most eggs have two unequal minor radii of curvature—one at each end—and this, because of the change of curvature and slight displacement in the center of gravity, produces a slight tilting in the ovoid when rested on a flat surface. In his *Prometheus* this tilt is quite integral to the feeling of tortured resignation characterized by the collapse of the head. It must be noted that Brancusi added to the interest of his egg form by also varying the two major radii.

The mirrorlike, impenetrable surfaces which border the sculptor's forms are really visual metaphors for these enlarged magical seeds which generate activity from within. In this respect, the yolk inside a perfectly shaped shell membrane is in reality a single giant cell which begins its own development by the process of cleavage (subdivision into cells); yet, at the same time, the yolk embodies an "organizing principle" that arranges new cells into different organs for various functions. The processes of embryonic differentiation are among the most complex and beautiful in all biology, and possibly by giving us the outer shell of these functions Brancusi has made materially evident a central tenet of his philosophy; that is, in nature simplicity and complexity are one and the same; they are unity.

It must be reiterated, Focillon observed, that form begets progeny and a single form embedded in the mind of an artist can propagate an entire family of new variations. More methodically than either Brancusi or Henry Moore, Jean (or Hans) Arp managed to produce sculpture in this germinal fashion. And the statement by Arp, much repeated by others, that "Art is the fruit that grows in man, like a fruit on a plant, or a child in its mother's womb" (1948, p. 50) lies close enough to the reality of an artist's creative processes to be regarded as more than an apt poetic metaphor.

Arp was an Alsatian, educated in France and Germany, whose artistic and intellectual turning point coincided with a stay in Zürich during the First World War. Here the Dadaist movement came into being at the Café Voltaire. Numerous essays plus Arp's own writing explain the effects of Dada on his work.

Dada, as practiced by its founders, was a methodical (though not outwardly appearing) exploitation of artistic forms. These were used in rebellion against the seemingly rational, but essentially hypocritical and corrupt, governments of a monarchical structure then crumbling in Europe. The members of the Zürich Dada group, most of them more political than Arp, looked upon war as mass slaughter benefiting certain social classes—those with the means of production and those ruling. They viewed the solemn attempts of politicians, bankers, academics, and theologians to solve crises through codes of international morality as so much legalized insanity. There had to be an answer to a technological society that turned its citizens into progressively more efficient war machines in the name of Christian morality. The reaction of the Zürich Dadaists was to numb the senses through acts of creative destruction; artistic insanity was made the final reclusion for minds that refused to be bent toward acceptance of official but death-breeding values.

Arp's solution, if it can be viewed specifically as that, sought to forsake artistic representationalism for an *Urwelt* (primeval world) of seeming irrational and random form—a reality where all objects and elements of everyday life existed and merged in the same psychical level of appearances. Arp's poems and prose at the time, (e.g., "walking on the arm of a somnambulist box of sardines" or "Einstein's poems have nothing to do with modern alarm clocks") are typical of the discordances introduced into his first painted reliefs.

Not readily understood is that his use of "alarm clocks," "thoughts," "mustaches," "forks," "eggs," and "navels"– all in apparently random combinations—harbors the seeds of its own secret and serene reason. As Arp tried to explain, it has to do, in part, with the democratic temperament of animals. This is the inability of animals, unless spoiled, to live by the same set of false values and prestige inflation that makes so much human life a misery. Clearly, the shape of Arp's cosmogony was that of a mystic: for him life assumed a leveling off, a unification and a delight in being alive. The simple existence led by Arp and his wife supported their attempts to find art in what is natural and uncomplicated.

An indispensable concept of the vitalist (something which Duchamp had touched upon as early as 1913) was a discovery by Arp that a "controlled" random arrangement of forms would produce imagery of a certain unobvious playfulness. This, in part, was precipitated by the fact that physicists had become aware of important problems in dynamics unsolvable by the application of classical physics. By 1900, statistical mechanics, using a theory of random numbers, was developed to unravel these problems. In biology statistical techniques had just come into wide use. And presently, with high-speed computers, randomness itself has become an expedient for solving problems in high-energy physics. Thus the Dada propensity for nonsensical formlessness can be regarded as a cultural-technical parallel to some of the most sophisticated mathematical techniques available in our century. Moreover, the Dada obliteration of causality as a logical basis for artistic perception echoes in Einstein's earliest theories of relativity. The overwhelming freedom which characterizes random operations in organisms and perception had been seized upon, not only as an emotional release for an increasingly deterministic society, but on a technical level for the deeper investigation of all phenomena.

By 1930 Arp's interests had jumped from wooden reliefs and paper cutouts to free-standing three-dimensional sculpture. For lack of money most of these early forms remained models in plaster. Moving beyond the flat cutout quality of his reliefs of the 1920's, the plaster carvings attempted not merely to reproduce nature, but to "grow," to "come to life" as natural organisms do. Here the credo of vitalism is most obvious. Ultimately, the idea of artistic creativity is no longer sufficient; in effect, the vitalist sculptor thought of himself as a kind of fabulous organism capable of bearing young in a multitude of shapes. Arp called these shapes concretions and remarked about them (1958, pp. 14–15):

Concretion signifies the natural process of condensation, hardening, coagulation, thickening, growing together. Concretion designates the solidification of a mass. Concretion designates curdling, the curdling of the earth and the heavenly bodies. Concretion designates solidification, the mass of the stone, the plant, the animal, the man. Concretion is something that has grown. I wanted my work to finds its humble, anonymous place in the woods, the mountains, in nature.

The closest Arp came to producing "like a plant that produces fruit" is in the sensitive employment of surface disturbances and growth manifestations which appear in organisms, but without the use of an entire contour of any single plant or animal. Many of Arp's rounded forms are inherently inert, and it is through a series of subtle clues, signs of growth, mitosis, or metamorphic activity, that a beholder is induced to sense life encased in some rock-hard material. As for these outer contours, considerable light is shed on Arp's awareness and poetical application of growth processes as they appear in simple cellular forms. The biologist Edmund Sinnott describes some of these (1963, pp. 6–7):

An organic body that is made up, at least in its early stages, of watery cells tends to show rounded contours.... Really flat surfaces and acute angles are rare save in occasional special structures. In this respect living forms thus differ from crystals, with which they are often compared.

Second, an organic form is not static but is continually undergoing change. Materials are constantly entering it and leaving it, so that its form is more comparable to that of a waterfall than a crystal. Form is the result of progress. It is in equilibrium, but this equilibrium is dynamic, not static. Furthermore, these external and internal changes are not such as simply to maintain a constant state but rather to produce a a specific and orderly development. An organism has been called a slice of space-time, since it changes in respect to both. It has a definite pattern of growth and differentiation which can often be expressed in mathematical terms. The slow rate of change sometimes obscures this relation in time, however, as does the fact that organic forms are commonly studied in dead specimens where growth and change have ceased.

Third and most important, an organic form is the visible expression of an organized living system. Its spatial configuration is the result of growth correlations among different parts and its various dimensions. The amount of growth in one direction or dimension is precisely related to that in others, and local differences in cellular character are so controlled that tissues and organs differentiate in a definite spatial order.

There is little doubt that Arp was acutely aware of the organic formative processes; his early nature studies and enthusiastic walks through the Swiss and German countrysides are testimonies to that. What is far less discernible is his consistent application of biological principles—both those seen and those understood.

In a work such as *Human Concretion* (FIG. 27), a viewer never possesses any certainty that what he is looking at is either animal or vegetable. But generally this work, as with Arp's other forms of the period, tends toward a state that resembles a one-celled organism, one that could be found floating freely in a liquid. As Sinnott states, the organism is in a constant condition of dynamic equilibrium, not only chemically but in terms of pressures external and internal to the outer cell wall. The wall itself is a container membrane with flexible geometry, or nearly so; hence the frighteningly free, amorphic

27. Jean Arp, *Human Concretion*, 1949, cast stone after 1935 original plaster.

quality which has become the trademark of Arp's concretions. With this, as with other early concretions, we are coaxed into believing that the outer boundary of the plaster represents, approximately, a minimal surface for thin films suspended in a liquid. Hydrodynamic pressure on the internal and external sides of these outer walls is equal so that the form appears stable, subject to water currents and internal movement. Arp, therefore, presents an extremely fluid, tenuous system frozen in plaster or bronze. Plainly Arp is aiming at metaphor. While his globular shapes stand in space, they allude to laws of dynamics which apply to systems suspended in another atmospheric density, namely water. Sculpture had traditionally implied some form of structural rigidity in its subject matter, but implicit in Arp's forms is an impression of immense flexibility, where the slightest external current or movement produces noticeable deformations.

In *Human Concretion* there are at least two variations of growth. First, it is well to remember that growth, as we perceive it, takes place in terms of enlargements impossible to see because of their slowness. A more dynamic level of growth takes place among cells or in a foetus where shape is actually being created and rearranged. Arp's growth patterns apparently spring from the microscopic level and are mixtures of both plant and animal processes. The tendency of cell cleavage is manifest in *Human Concretion*, whereby the parent cell splits into two cells, then into four, and a geometrical explosion ensues—at least this is hinted in the fold of one small protuberance in this sculpture. More striking in the series of organic metaphors is the process of *morphogenetic movement*, or the transfer of protoplasm so that an organism assumes a new form. The biologist John Tyler Bonner compares this with Aristotle's description of the sculptor who takes a lump of clay and, without adding or subtracting from the original mass, manipulates his clay into the desired form; except, as Bonner points out, in the case of an organism the cells themselves are the sculptor. Part of the vitalistic aesthetic employed by Brancusi and Arp is that their sculpture gives no outward hints, no gouged surfaces or finger marks *à la Rodin*, which indicate an external forming agent; all is made to seem rearranged from the inside, the growth center of the piece.

D'Arcy Thompson explains the protuberances, buds, and growing points which begin their emergence from a single point on the wall of a cell. A purposeful weakening of the membrane occurs at that spot—like a bulge caused by the thin area on an inflated balloon. Why one point rather than another should protrude, or what causes this protrusion, is difficult to explain. Many theories have been discounted, and Bonner, writing in 1963, offers a hypothesis based on the internal pressures generated by the cytoplasm—but admits that there is no proven theory for the "budding" of a cell. In terms of appearances, Thompson many years earlier posed the formation of this budding most beautifully: the bud forms a node or growing point from which the cell continues to subdivide along an axis of growth; the point is sharp, tender, and sensitive and seems to propel itself forward by means of some internal force. *Human Concretion* produces the same sharpened projecting edges, giving the illusion of forward thrust, that seem to stem from internal conditions in a real cell formation. In *Crown of Buds* (FIG. 28) the idea of growth points is made much more emphatically, and these "buds" contain the added implication of a young girl's breasts. Finally, a prime effort by Arp in this direction is a sculpture entitled *Growth* (FIG. 29). The bottom of the form is truncated, not rounded naturally, so as to stand vertically on its base; yet it rises into the air like a vine seeking the sunlight.

Toward the late 1930's Arp's experiments were directed toward increasingly complex and irrational shapes. One-celled forms were gradually replaced by partly open, tendril-like shapes. The geometry of organic end-development took precedent over growth. Both Brancusi and Surrealism

28. Jean Arp, *Crown of Buds*, 1936.

have been cited as influences for one particular device which entered Arp's concretions at the time. This is the abrupt lopping off or truncation of his remarkably soft and vulnerable forms—something like a cloud run through a meat slicer. Arp's pseudo-organisms seemed to simulate food gathering, growth, and mobility by the very nubility of their protuberances and cleaved surfaces. With the added decisiveness of the truncations, all this had the somnambulant reality of a dream execution. In reflection there is only a sense of mild, disquieting shock to these lopped-off sections. Arp's sculpture, in spite of these incisions, continues to live, but the "organicism" of these pieces is somehow provisional. On the other hand, Brancusi's incisions in his *Bird in Space*, such as the truncation at the top, do not sever the form; they function as a normal termination of the bird's contour.

In his last ten years, because of age, Arp did much less direct carving; instead his main body of work returned to the early reliefs. Some of these were free-standing, stainless-steel fabrications—very inorganic, precision-executed like corporation trademarks. The dialectic of these pieces seems not to be the precision of organisms, alive, but the irrationality of machine-conceived surfaces—a complete turnabout. His philosophy implied at this point that the machine is best able to create like nature; if not that, then this is raising the principle of vitalism to a position of impotency and nonvalidity. If a word must be coined, it is the *iconization* of the vitalistic image.

Arp's influence was decisive, perhaps more important than either Picasso's or Brancusi's, for the future work of two young English sculptors.

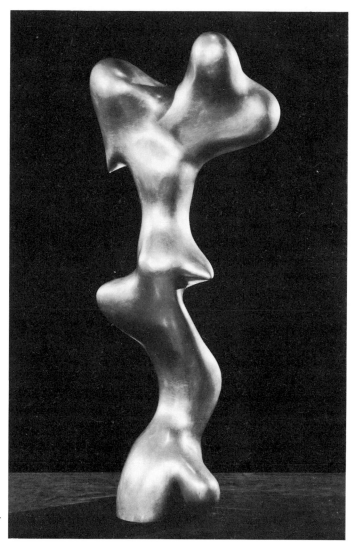

29. Jean Arp, *Growth*, 1938.

It is most probable that the mature work of Henry Moore and Barbara Hepworth would not have been what it was without the example or philosophy of Jean Arp. Barbara Hepworth's trip to Paris in 1932 and her visits to the studios of Arp, Brancusi, and Picasso acted, in her word, as a "ratification," or aesthetic endorsement for works developing parallel to Moore's efforts.

The idea—the imaginative concept—actually *is* the giving of life and vitality to material.... When we say that a great sculpture has vision, power, vitality, scale, poise, form or beauty, we are not speaking of physical attributes. Vitality is not a physical, organic attribute of sculpture—it is a spiritual inner life. Power is not man power or physical capacity—it is inner force and energy (quoted in Martin, 1937, p. 113).

Written by Barbara Hepworth for publication in *Circle* (1937), the above statement once again demonstrates the metaphysical, almost religious, capability of vitalism. As a contributor to the literature of vitalism, Barbara Hepworth makes perhaps a slight addition, yet it would be wrong not to mention her influence on Moore's work in the early 1930's, a time when both artists came closest to a merger of intentions and means. Beyond the influence of Leon Underwood, it was Hepworth's knowledge of Continental art, especially that of Paris, which brought home to Moore the basic weaknesses of English sculpture.

Through the 1930's Barbara Hepworth's sculpture developed a serenity and lack of emotional tension which has been regarded as almost classical in its cast. Some of the vigor of her mature work is drawn off by the premeditated geometry, painted surfaces, and stringed components which she frequently uses. The work, nevertheless, is handsome and at times near great, though perhaps a bit too controlled and craftlike to provoke the sensation of an autonomous inner life in the sense of successful vitalistic sculpture.

No sculptor has brought out with such bluntness, or described with greater precision, the vitalist position than Henry Moore. Where previous sculptors felt content to imbue themselves with a tacit aesthetic based on the organic influence, Moore has always been quite candid about the origins and techniques of his synthesis of natural elements. He has never regarded himself as a magician but simply as a sensitive and observant artist obeying the characteristics of his materials. If, strictly speaking, vitalist doctrine is concerned with the infusion of "life" into the materials of sculpture, then it should be emphasized that Moore has been quite specific in recommending that the word *vital* be used to describe this infusion, rather than *organic*. On the surface the difference may seem small, but *organic* implies a functionalism, an application of materials to various duties, which runs well beyond the range of vitalism.

Vitalism, based as it is on nonphysical substances and states of life, is a metaphysical doctrine concerned with the irreducible effects and manifestations of living things. It was the great discovery of twentieth-century sculpture that these did not have to be appreciated through strict representationalism. Visual biological metaphors exist on many levels besides the obvious total configuration of an animal or human. The aesthetic of true organicism, on the other hand, is not grounded in the appearances of natural forms and their carryover into sculptural materials, but is concerned with the organization of processes and interacting systems.

94

Moore's vitalism, in no way scientifically analytical, is the vitalism of the naturalist and sensitive craftsman. Besides the sculpture itself, the most obvious example of this lies in Moore's writings. A statement in the anthology *Unit I* (1934) describes the program which Moore set for himself, and which, with a few interruptions, he has followed for the past thirty-five years. Some essential parts read as follows (quoted in Read, 1934, pp. 29–30):

Truth to material. Every material has its own individual qualities. It is only when the sculptor works direct, when there is an active relationship with his material, that the material can take its part in the shaping of an idea. Stone, for example, is hard and concentrated and should not be falsified to look like soft flesh—it should not be forced beyond its constructive build to a point of weakness. It should keep its hard tense stoniness.

Observation of Natural Objects. The observation of nature is part of an artist's life, it enlarges his form-knowledge, keeps him fresh and from working only by formula, and feeds inspiration.

The human figure is what interests me most deeply, but I have found principles of form and rhythm from the study of natural objects such as pebbles, rocks, bones, trees, plants, etc.

Pebbles and rocks show Nature's way of working stone. Smooth, sea-worn pebbles show the wearing away, rubbed treatment of stone and principles of asymmetry.

Rocks show the hacked, hewn treatment of stone, and have a jagged nervous block rhythm.

Bones have marvelous structural strength and hard tenseness of form, subtle transition of one shape into the next and great variety in section.

Trees (tree trunks) show principles of growth and strength of joints, with easy twisting movement.

Shells show Nature's hard but hollow form (metal sculpture) and have a wonderful completeness of single shape.

There is in Nature a limitless variety of shapes and rhythms (and the telescope and microscope have enlarged the field) from which the sculptor can enlarge his form-knowledge experience.

Vitality and Power of Expression. For me a work must first have a vitality of its own. I do not mean a reflection of the vitality of life, of movement, physical action, frisking, dancing figures and so on, but that work can have in it a pent-up energy, an intense life of its own, independent of the object it may represent.

In several essays Herbert Read has already elaborated on this and other statements by Moore. But, in truth, what Moore has to say is quite clear to anyone who has taken the trouble to observe his work. Still, at least two things could be said about Moore's doctrine which are only realizable since the early 1960's.

"Truth to material," first of all, is an ambiguous premise. However, during the 1930's, the 1940's and a good deal of the 1950's, it approached the stature of a universal dictum for a number of sculptors other than Moore. "Truth to material" followed to its ultimate conclusions is a *reductio ad absurdum*. Any forming or shaping must take advantage of the plasticity of each material, and, more importantly, no material will do what it is not meant to do. Moore, as a reaction to the falsity of much Neoclassical and Romantic carving, was only setting up an antidote, not an iron law, for the use of materials. The attraction for a great many sculptors to "truth to material" is its ring of moral equilibrium and natural propriety. But, like Humpty-Dumpty's assertion to Alice over the meaning of words, the post-vitalist in reaction to "truth to material" has declared, I can make materials mean anything I want them to mean; after all, who is to be the master?

Another observation has to do with "vitality and power of expression," Moore's limiting criterion of what is *vital* in sculpture. Vitalism, by its very purpose of seeking to imbue physical mass with psychic energy, is an idealistic mechanism for controlling attitudes about inert, nonmoving matter. It is a surrogate for actual physical vitality. The trend toward Kineticism in the 1960's, inelegant as it may be aesthetically, cannot help but undermine and change our attitudes and sensory apprehension of nonmoving art. Increasingly we will regard the traits of vitalistic sculpture with the same amused tolerance that we now reserve for obvious antiquing in nineteenth-century Neoclassical sculpture.

"Natural" is a diabolical term because it can be used with almost unlimited intentions. The biologist C. H. Waddington, in a remarkably penetrating essay (Whyte, 1951, pp. 43–56), presents a statistically oriented view of what is "natural" and its applications to Moore's vitalistic sculpture. He makes the point that abstract forms which seem to be the most accurate expression of life are lifelike because they display a multifunction visual complexity; inorganic forms, on the other hand, are single purposed and show a lack of multiple purpose. Moore, working with natural forms, both inorganic and organic, shifts back and forth to all magnitude of sizes for his ideas—then merges the results. Waddington explains this in terms of one of Moore's favorite subjects, beach pebbles. Tidal and rhythmic forces of the ocean, the various consistencies of stone, their texture and grain, etc., all subject stone fragments along a beach to many formative abrasive pressures. In Waddington's words (Whyte, 1951, p. 50):

It represents not the equilibrium or balancing of many conflicting tendencies, but the chance outcome of a series of random and unrelated events, in fact, Whitehead's mere confusion of detail.... But if the number of detailed events (forms of abrasion)

30. Henry Moore, *Four Piece Composition (Reclining Figure)*, 1934.

are large enough, and if they are approximately the same magnitude, a certain statistical regularity will emerge, and there will be a tendency for the production of some reasonably definite shape, which may simulate an organic shape produced by internal equilibrium.

In connection with this idea of organic and inorganic shapes, Waddington makes an observation about the basic man-made and unnatural appearance of a Picasso pen-and-ink sketch for a monumental sculpture of the late 1920's. This drawing, or one quite like it, must have been seen by Moore and impressed him. In a book on Moore, edited by David Sylvester (1957, p. 190), there appears a chalk, pen, wash, and water-color drawing executed in 1933 which closely resembles Waddington's Picasso drawing. The forms, their assembly, and even the pen-and-ink technique are straight out of *Cahiers d'Art.*

The drawing by Moore represents a turning point for him for two reasons. First, it appeared at a time when Moore was still carrying on a search for a way to "open" his figure sculpture by means other than simple penetrations; clearly the Picasso bone technique was considered by Moore and rejected—although in the multi-piece compositions of 1934 by Moore (FIG. 30) the Picasso forms do make their appearance in a less linear presentation. Secondly, Waddington is correct; Moore was searching for a system of organic analogues that imply equilibrium, and the seeming erosion of rock forms by the natural elements begins to appear in a wooden reclining figure of 1935. Bone shapes, stone abrasion, and geological formations are fused into the same figure, not separately arranged as in earlier attempts.

Not surprisingly, Moore's sculpture has only become devitalized and weakened when he has strayed too far from the tenets of his 1934 statement. This is true of some of his work just prior to the Second World War and particularly during the 1950's. Various half-hearted attempts at formalism, totemism, and realism are in no way consistent with the strengths of Moore's sensibilities.

During the present decade Moore has produced some of the most powerful work of his career—much of it in very large bronze castings. No longer are the plaster models finished in smooth perfection, but instead the plaster rasp and the pick hammer simulate the kind of graininess and sedimentary stratification which Moore relates to the rock formations in the Yorkshire countryside. At the same time, the tendency of bones to appear smooth-hard or porous, depending upon the function of a bone at a given area, is of more importance to Moore. Some of the figurative conceptions relate to earlier two-piece and three-piece compositions, and, with the aid of polychrome patinas, completely detached sets of shoulders and knees jut up from a plinth's flat surface like the upright rock promontories off the coast of Brittany (FIG. 31).

Question by David Sylvester: In a series of multiple-piece reclining figures, in which particular ones did you use found objects?

Answer by Henry Moore: Well, for example, in the first of the three-piece sculptures which is going to be shown soon, one of the pieces, the middle piece, was suggested by a vertebra—of I don't know what animal it was—that I found in the garden. And the connection of the one piece through to the other is the kind of connection that a backbone will have with one section through to the next section. But they've been separated. It's as though you've left the slipped disc out of them, but it's there. That's the only one I can immediately think of (Moore, June 7, 1963).

Moore's sculpture at the present time involves some of the most literal adaptations to be found in his work. In these new locking pieces (FIG. 32) the sculptor looks more closely at the various hinge mechanisms and contact points between bones in a skeletal position. Included between the larger segments are thinner members, shock cushions so to speak, resembling the cartilage wrapped around the contacting surfaces of bones. Earlier in the interview with David Sylvester, Moore mentions the truncated surfaces produced by sawed cross-sections of the discovered bones. These truncated surfaces are a new aspect of an idea already adapted by Arp, Brancusi, and others. In sum, the locking forms are Moore's lexicon of touching surfaces, some close together in fine, barely perceivable seams, while others open, tapering toward rounded raised edges. It is interesting that the vitalism in these later pieces has come full circle through abstraction to a kind of tran-

31. Henry Moore, *Reclining Figure, II*, 1960.

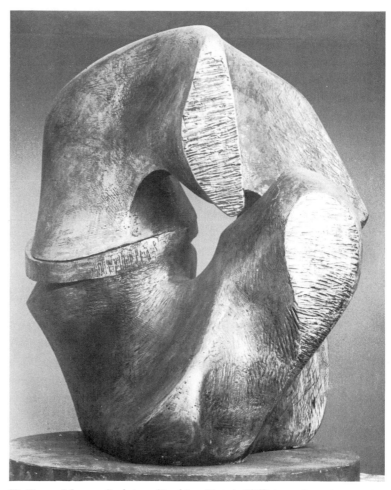

32. Henry Moore, *Sculpture (Locking Piece)*, 1962.

scendent realism: a realism not too far removed from the realm of the naturalist and classical biologist.

D'Arcy Thompson has alluded (1917, p. 10) to a morality implicit in natural forms. Very much like Louis Sullivan's dictum that *all* trees grow naturally, it recognizes that man seeks and finds a positive moral position in the earth-born phenomena about him, as a kind of stabilizing factor for his powers of cognition and creativity. This seems to be a fundamental reaction to the industrial age. Thompson refers also to the fact that the analysis of natural effects for the physicist constitutes just so many problems of a mechanical or mathematical nature, but, as to relationships of nature, "…it is on another plane of thought from the physicist's that we contemplate their intrinsic harmony and perfection and 'see that they are good.'"

While this last phrase may seem no more than an echo from the biblical injunction, for a sculptor such as Moore, living in an industrial society, it contains the essence of an authentic moral stricture. Yet perhaps we can look at this peculiarly modern homage to nature more realistically. Slightly tinged with romantic loneliness, the vitalist sculptor, according to the image nurtured for the last forty years, works in single-minded harmony with the forces and shapes of nature, somehow quelling on a macrocosmic level the eroding torrents of science—and all that follows in technology. But nevertheless, when one thinks of the machinery which a sculptor with Moore's output must use, the subcontracts to foundries, the advertising media and the marketing techniques that keep his work before a world public, then the idea of constant rapport with nature, the craftsman's intimacy with his materials, seems like an innocent conceit—not too dissimilar to the courtiers of Louis XV's entourage playing shepherd and shepherdess in the woods surrounding Versailles.

Vitalism in Postwar American Sculpture

Contrary to what Focillon has written, no artistic analogue to biotic generation of form types can assure art of an infinite supply of new forms. Sculptural form and its varieties constitute a decidedly finite grouping. While form can be endlessly multiplied in minor variation through permutation, there are real limits to what can be considered "significant form." Even within the great range of biotic models, formal variation in sculpture is readily exhausted after the archetypes of a class have been repeatedly used. It is one of the prime strategies of nature that it uses the same shapes over and over again in a multiplicity of roles.

Modern abstract sculpture is given over, almost entirely, to the task of formal invention; and nothing is so important in this respect as the invention of form itself. Dealing with psychological and compositional variations of human situations, representational sculpture never encountered this problem. The vitality of representationalism in no way depended on morphological development. Characteristic of present technology is its voracious appetite for forms and ideas. The modern arts are especially addicted in this respect. Abstract vitalistic sculpture—throughout its life span—has been dependent on form possibilities. When these were exhausted, the idiom was finished.

After the Second World War the category of biotic forms least explored was that of open shapes: roots, branches, plant and mineral fiber, pods, shells, flowers, etc. While this portion of the form continuum was being explored to some degree by postwar British metal sculptors, it thrived to its fullest extent in the New York environs. This biotic metaphor did not yield up the soft, undulating, maternal shapes of Arp and Moore; instead, its direction was persistently aggressive and high-strung—not tactile, but threatening. This sculpture bore all the marks of urban mentalities seeking some reconnection with the underlying structure of nature.

The names usually connected with the American contribution to vitalistic sculpture, or what was wrongly called "organic" sculpture, are Theodore Roszak, Ibram Lassaw, Seymour Lipton and, less biotically directed, Herbert Ferber and Harry Bertoia. In outlook, style, and technique all five display sharp parallels—though the first three named are of more interest at this point. Many of the goals and sensibilities shaping American painting just after the war were also current in sculpture: the desire for a transcendent apparition, the feeling for casual textures, the desire to break away from European prototypes, and a willingness to explore nontraditional mediums and materials.

Prior to the war, Roszak, Lassaw, and Lipton formed part of the small group of serious abstract and Neo-Plastic artists working around New York City. Each had the problem of assimilating, yet getting out from under, the domination of European sculpture idioms. Also each sensed the trend, through Constructivism, toward the construction of open, spatial forms instead of sculpting in massive materials. Technically, all three felt the need to move beyond casting and carving, and into some area of additive construction without the formal limitations of Constructivism.

What developed was a technique for working and joining metals. Steel, monel metal, or brass (in wire, rod, or sheet form) were first shaped and then joined by welding or brazing. This much certainly was not new, and their work had nothing of the careful, workmanlike industrial finish of Julio Gonzalez or David Smith. The new technique was exacting in its own way, but as a kind of controlled imprecision; joining metals were covered and fused with parent metals in a shaping process in which intense heat was one of the major formative elements. Instead of welded or brazed seams being hidden by filing or grinding, an entire sculpture was covered with a coating of low-temperature brazing metal so that no distinction remained between joints and the surface area of a work (this process of braze-coating metallic forms gave the surface an agreeable vitality of rippled, pocked, and flowing textures). Looking toward Europe at the time (the late 1940's), the sensitive brutalization of surfaces enacted by Alberto Giacometti, and the application of scabrous, slaglike textures in both paintings and sculpture by Jean Dubuffet at least confirmed that a new aesthetic had jointly arisen. However, the American sensibility was less caught up in *Angst* and unnaturalness; it rejected the antibeauty implication of the Europeans.

One cannot underestimate the influence of the vitalistic idiom for American sculptors at the time. Cubism was defunct; Constructivism remained too restrictive in its formal vocabulary; and the desire to create "as nature creates" (but not like Brancusi, Arp, or Moore) seemed a hopeful and less-explored direction. Charmion von Wiegand (1957, pp. 55–68) has stressed that Zen and various Oriental aesthetics, no matter how poorly grasped, played a part in the postwar American consciousness. They were a segment of the cultural transformation, just as Kandinsky's and Mondrian's interest in theosophy had helped to stimulate the first nonobjective painting. *Shibui*, the Japanese cultivation of seemingly unappealing and ill-formed surfaces, has its kinship with an appreciation of the unformed, globular metal surfaces. It appeared that precision was not the only means of merging man-made shape with nature—a certain casualness, a tendency to let brazed forms flow and be shaped by the natural results of intense heat, became identified with the random and asymmetrical aspects of organic matter. Life did not just contain living, perfected forms; natural forms were prone to withering and decay. Hence, nature could be sharp, dry, repellent, and untactile.

It is difficult now to remember the slogans, clichés, and stylistic anachronisms which beset American sculpture before 1945. To a great extent, postwar vitalism was a flight from the *isms;* it was nature with a small *n* involved in a soul-searching attempt at originality. As early as 1945 Theodore Roszak concocted out of steel and welding rod the beginnings of a neo-baroque, organic expressionism (FIG. 33). By his method metals were directly assembled into complex open compositions without the difficulties of casting. The idea of brutal, ever-changing aspects of nature, nature as a series of conquering systems, predatory and threatening, became the center of Ros-

33. Theodore Roszak, *Thorn Blossom*, 1948.

zak's vision. According to H. H. Arnason (1957, p. 33), the "pitted surfaces and thorny projections" of these first works "… all communicate the artist's awareness of something unhealthy and dangerous." Bones became inter-locking spiny vertebrae instead of Moore's gentle, transitional monoliths with rounded knobs. Plants were not tender shoots but thorns magnified into gleaming and threatening spikes.

Thorn Blossom is characteristic of Roszak's early mature work. Dried seed pods, roots drawn from the earth, a kind of linear flowerlike cluster, a great thorn or horn perhaps part of the jawbone of some prehistoric animal: all these disparate forms are welded into a plausible but unpleasant unity. Roszak scaled his surfaces with fire or used a patina before polishing the smoother, more accessible surfaces to create a web of highlights. Quite possibly a throwback to his Constructivist work, *Thorn Blossom* is more bilaterally symmetrical than anything composed by the European vitalists. It hints at machine origins.

Similar to the "space cage" experiments of Giacometti and Calder in

34. Ibram Lassaw, *Kwannon*, 1952.

the 1930's, in some of Ibram Lassaw's first iron structures are searching
attempts that wander in a nether land between Miró and Neo-Plasticism. As
with other American vitalists, he immersed himself in the literature of
Oriental and Western mysticism and in the romance of modern science.
Lassaw in his learning phases moved through the sculpture of Gonzalez, the
Constructivists, and Paris Surrealists, gathering what he would later use
from each. The transition to a mature style came about 1950. He had learned
welding during the Second World War, and the crucial step, after five years
of experimentation in other mediums, was the purchase of oxyacetylene
equipment for welding and brazing.

Open wire forms, fused and covered with brazing metal, immediately
became his *matière*. Lassaw's rectilinear structures of encrusted lines are
hauntingly organic, yet unlike any forms to be found in nature. A clue to his
approach is found in a sentence from Meister Eckhart: "To find nature
herself, all of her likenesses must be shattered." Lassaw copied this into one
of his notebooks. In this case nature becomes a skeletonized vision of fussed-
over, liquified metal, oscillating between Zen indeterminacy and a science-

fiction environment of crystallized plant life. With the production of his very first all-metal construction Lassaw spoke of a certain elation—a breaking into an area of recognition—perhaps akin to the Zen state of *satori*. The six-foot *Kwannon* (FIG. 34) in bronze and silver continues to hold on to the rectilinearity of the earlier *de Stijl* constructions. Gradually from this point his constructions increased in complexity; *The Awakened One* (1956–1957) sprouts a kind of nerve ganglia in the interstices between its right-angled elements. By 1958 Lassaw was creating giant lunar plant forms complete with roots and tubers rising upward from strange metallic husks; the seven-and-a-half-foot *Quaternity* (1956–1958) is one of the best examples. During the 1960's the biotic element has become increasingly apparent in Lassaw's work, yet interestingly, his work is, if anything, less forceful and vital than the earlier, more graceful constructions. There is a transcendent, chimerical quality to the *Kwannon*, hovering white-gold networks which vanish with the literalism of the later fantastic plants.

For sheer formal inventiveness during the 1950's, a single American sculptor has outdistanced his contemporaries on both sides of the Atlantic. Seymour Lipton is not the first dentist to become involved in sculpture—either through dental casting techniques or because of the natural sculptural quality of teeth. Lipton's work, beginning in the early 1940's, shows evidences of the Surrealist-organic idiom then prevailing in the New York City area. His sculpture, open, bony, and aggressive like Roszak's, had limitations defined by the drawbacks of lead casting and a certain unresolved bulkiness.

The year 1950 or 1951 marked the introduction by Lipton of sheet-metal shapes: formed, tacked into place and completely covered with brazing metal.

At first the shell—formed by hammered sheet metal—and then the semi-open pod became the basic formal units of his style. Until approximately 1957 most of Lipton's ideas contained an unashamed blending of organic forms, not aggregates of dissimilar types such as Roszak has used, but more often exotic plant forms. To this the sculptor brought a formidable under-standing of the Constructivist vocabulary of formal relationships: rotational symmetry, knot configurations, inside and outside opposition of elements, concentric form, and a sense of spatial flow and release. As pure idea, Lipton's work represents the fullest use of formalism employed with the vitalist idiom.

To a large extent this was made possible by Lipton's handling of welded metals. Here are a flexibility and freedom, a complexity of sheet forms interpenetrating, and a teasing playfulness in the partial opening and closing of welded seams never attained in any sculpture before. More so than the Constructivists, Lipton has become a master in luring the eye of the viewer into the interior of his works.

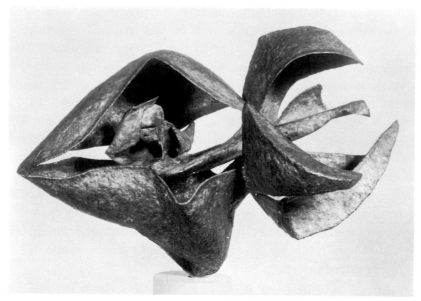

35. Seymour A. Lipton, *Jungle Bloom*, 1954. Yale University
Art Gallery. Gift of Mrs. Frederick W. Hilles.

One of Lipton's most successful biomorphic treatments is his construction *Jungle Bloom* (FIG. 35). The near horizontal axis of the piece gives the impression of bilateral symmetry whereas in reality every side and every view has a different aspect. A small broken seam appears at a point where the base meets the pedestal and reveals an otherwise inaccessible spatial pocket. The front of the flower consists of three curious cuplike petals, and, like the best of the metal-working abstractionists, Lipton has avoided all obvious planar arrangements and joining edges. One petal defies botanical order by supporting the linear center of the bloom. This center is a kind of rolled anther and filament which hangs suspended instead of extending from the throat of the blossom.

The beauty of Lipton's technique is that it allows the fabrication of solid or near-solid forms, sheet forms of any curvature, or linear forms. Lipton, moreover, never has to worry about the usual problems of joining or matching different materials. All of his metals are completely covered with melted brazing rod so that there are no joints or different-colored metals to hide. When Lipton fabricates a sheet form in which both sides are to be made visible, the form must be constructed of two sheets of metal fitted together and brazed on one side each. This is so because the liquid metal from the brazing rod will only adhere to one side of a piece of sheet metal. Much of Lipton's constructions are therefore a matter of inside-outside duplication

36. Seymour Lipton, *Sentinel*, 1959.
Yale University Art Gallery.

of surfaces. However, this has the advantage of letting the sculptor control the apparent thickness of his sheet forms.

Sentinel (FIG. 36) is a good example of Lipton's tendency in the last ten years to drop the use of strictly biomorphic forms in favor of box-type metaphors: these include rooms, books, bells, and liturgical objects. This the art historian Albert Elsen terms Lipton's propensity for *analogizing*. It began with the use of vaguely anthropomorphic figures—concurrent with the early 1960's "new image of man" vogue—and has continued, not only with the adoption of man-made objects, but with a fusion of highly personal forms. Much like Arp, Lipton has felt the urge to merge both objects and non-physical conceptions into a personal amalgam of formal relationships.

Following some of the best scholarship available on Rodin's sculpture,

Albert Elsen has drawn a relationship between Lipton and Rodin—a tie which Lipton accepts. This is interesting if only for the reason that it juxtaposes one of the first and possibly one of the last of the vitalists in the modern tradition—a span of approximately ninety years.

Presently we have reached the end of the vitalist phase, and the possibilities of formal invention open to Rodin have been successively reduced with each passing decade. Lipton since the early 1950's has never failed to please the public and please with good cause, while Rodin, in a far more enviable position historically, provoked both great pleasure and outrage. With no slight to Lipton, the mechanics of historical entrance and innovational priority are not on his side, but on Rodin's. The inventive possibilities and, consequently, the power of influence open to the two men has been completely different: Lipton remains a conservative in the best sense of the word. It is simply the nature of events and genius that Rodin's best work, hanging between illumination and passion, has a demonic terribleness—in the archaic sense—which is light years away from the studied aggressiveness of Lipton's art.

One suspects that in the 1960's the flower of vitalism in sculpture has budded, bloomed, and withered into a dried reminder of more fertile times. But what the revival of postwar vitalism has meant is that *all* the sequences of a flower's existence are equally valid for study and appreciation. Withered stalks and young shoots have had their influences alike, and it must be remembered that the flower—though it appears to be the culmination of a plant form—is only one stage in the organic cycle. It was fitting, too, that vitalism in American sculpture could not have come into being without the perfection of a new piece of technology—namely oxyacetylene brazing.

Vitalism and Artistic Values

At the beginning of this century when abstraction entered art from many directions, vitalism reinvested sculpture with some of the conviction and emotional substance lost with the decline of realism. It sought to make a beautiful metaphor of sculpting itself. By attaching itself to the platonic ideal of essences, an idea that had probably outlived its scientific and perhaps philosophic value, vitalism prepared the way for an organic view of existence based on machine values. Though vitalism denied the full extent of the scientific position, it was actually very conducive to the introduction of mechanistic-organic properties into sculpture. Arp, Moore, and Brancusi— to name the most significant contributors—produced instances of biological awareness in their sculpture and statements which would have been impossible with representationalism. In fact, these contained a more thorough analysis of the underlying consistency of biological form than all types of past sculpture combined.

Vitalism, therefore, has been traditionally allied to a concern for protecting religion, metaphysics, and subsequently art, against the erosive effects of scientific rationalism. Moreover, it was not alone among sculpture influences in its attempt to play down the centrality of technological values. Even an aesthetic ideology as sympathetic to the scientific vision as Constructivism sought to set limits on the influences of scientific-technological methodology in the arts. Yet the invasion of the artistic sensibility by these twin influences goes on unhindered. We have yet to define the scope or pattern of the situation.

CHAPTER THREE

Formalism: The Weary Vocabulary

Formalism in Sculpture

Precisely what is *formal* in sculpture today? One answer would be that it is those material-optical-tactile features of sculpture which can be identified and logically examined as separate physical entities. The formal qualities are those that still give form in the original classical sense: shape, proportion, scale, structure, texture, color, context—those aspects of the visual reality to which we turn for our nonliterary meanings in objects.

Formal qualities in sculpture (just as in painting) have both changed and decreased since the beginning of the century. Inspect any critique on sculpture composed before 1920. When sculpture was universally figurative, composition *was* the positioning of the human figure; proportion *was* derived from various anatomical canons: Classical, Renaissance, Mannerist, Romantic, Expressionist, modern medical, etc.; structure *was* anatomy and the problems inherent in carving and casting limbs; texture *was* the simulation of natural surfaces; and color was all but unheard of. Observed differently, all these features are nothing more than a nineteenth-century biologist's morphological conception, a categorizing of form templates according to the visual properties of different species. If biology and biophysics have steadily relied less on the importance of organic external appearances, this has also happened in sculpture. The problem of modern sculpture is no longer, how long will formalism last? Rather critics ask, what remains in formalism that has not been discovered and rediscovered, and what lies beyond formalism capable of carrying on the evolutionary trends of the past eighty years?

Aside from the periodic reappearance of "new realism" and "new figuration" tendencies, often potent holding actions, very few signs have appeared to indicate options other than formalism. This is one of the realities of sculpture today. The ingenuous belief by many members of the early pioneering avant-garde that formalism would in time develop into a "new language of vision" has been realized, but what was not anticipated was that the formalist vocabulary, in order to maintain its vigor, must constantly change and grow. This has happened only marginally. The result has been a certain contempt by the pioneers of modern sculpture for work being done today and a not-well-disguised sense of envy and frustration from the younger generation. Saddled more or less with the formalist vocabulary, each succeeding generation of sculptors has had to answer the charge of imitation—without too much success. Generally, they take their legacy in silence and plan palace revolts around marginal innovations. It is a world of fifty-year-old manifestoes for them, one that promised artistic nirvana and ended up in dry wells and "museums of modern art" for those who once planned to tear down the established repositories.

In spite of a subtraction of traditional formal properties, sculpture has thrived because it has learned other means of formal invention. With the degeneration of form in the classical-Euclidean sense, and the decline of figurative sculpture, a dependence upon formalism has grown in its place. But, as the mechanism of formalism exhausts itself, sculptors are left with the fact that they cannot rid themselves of the presence of objects. That is their métier. Ironically, as sculpture dematerializes, denies presence, reduces its mass, the sculptor is bound to a theory of matter (inasmuch as it expresses what he is doing) not much more contemporary than that of the Greek atomists—twenty-five centuries old. The three variables of matter according to Democritus: *shape*, *order*, and *placing*, are just as necessary to sculpture conceptualization now as in the time of Polyclitus.

Where the contemporary sculptor is beset by a phenomenal world of technology—much of it powered by nonvisible energy—and where he is cognizant of the subvisual levels of matter, it is not too surprising that strong elements of pathos and frustration creep into his efforts to deal meaningfully with materials.

Formalism has been a strategic necessity; it does not fit comfortably into the traditional lexicon of art. In daily language it is interesting how the words *formal* and *formalism* generate antipathetic connotations. *Formal* hints at stiffness, boredom, and a lack of vitality. *Formality* is closely connected with the idea of trivial routine, while in the terminology of socialist realism *formalism* denotes soullessness and a subservience to decadent irrelevancies. The philosopher Hegel sensed that the truth-bearing efficacy of art belonged to the past, and that the scientific-philosophical spirit held a more exacting standard of truth—one that would not allow the truth of art to survive.

From this it might appear that formalism is a kind of transitional phase, a "phasing out" of art toward scientific rationalism. As a manifestation of materialism, formalism has both revitalized and demoralized sculpture. Modern formalist analysis is possibly *a stricter application of prescientific methodology to the arts.* Importantly enough, as formalism grows more daring in its techniques, it becomes more pervasively influential within the plastic arts.

Formalist tendencies during the development of figurative sculpture had the exactness and surety of geometrical regularity. Only with the coming of modern sculpture has formalist analysis increasingly depended on *intuition* rather than *regulation.* In this way most sculptors have tried to counter the scientific incursions of formalistic thinking. Moreover, no sets of rules exist today in sculpture as they did in the past. All modern canons of formalism are the more or less acknowledged property of their inventors. However, aesthetic rules that are shared are usually not arbitrary but have some common basis in visual perception. The problem of formalism remains that of sustaining irrationality within a framework of increasingly rational technique.

Attitudes: The Scientific Demiurge

The desire to *explain* the quantitative and qualitative consistency of physical phenomena stands behind the spirit of scientific inquiry. This drive also provides the psychic basis for modern formalism in sculpture. The passion of each is to reveal and analyze underlying truths. Where such methodology consistently leads to an understanding of more fundamental realms of order (usually invisible) in science, this same drive has resulted in growing stasis when applied to sculpture. A present dilemma of sculpture is its inability to move beyond phenomenological means and into those very areas of nonvisual analysis established by science. Much of the great sculpture of this century already stems from conscious or unconscious acknowledgements of the directions taken by scientific analysis. In an essay Naum Gabo (1957, p. 176) reveals this fact with clarity:

...we have gotten familiar with a world in which forces are permitted to become mass and matter is permitted to become light; a world which is pictured to us as a conglomeration of oscillating electrons, protons, neutrons, particles which behave like waves, which in their turn behave like particles. If the scientist is permitted to picture to us an image of an electron which under certain conditions has less than zero energy (in common language, it means that it weighs less than nothing) and if he is permitted to see behind this simple common table, an image of the curvature of space—why, may I ask, is not the contemporary artist to be permitted to search for and bring forward an image of the world more in accordance with the achievements of our developed mind, even if it is different from the image presented in the paintings and sculptures of our predecessors?

The time between 1890 and 1910 was a period of acute transition from classical physics to modern atomic theory. Before 1890 physics had separated matter from radiation, with results that seemed to balance with all the known natural laws. Gradually, unexplained phenomena disrupted the stability of the classical picture. Planck's first paper on quantum theory in 1899 and Einstein's on relativity six years later secured (or would shortly for all concerned) the fact that mass and energy were fundamentally united and, under certain conditions, were mutually convertible. That matter had lost its supremacy in human conception became a subliminal element in the shifting horizon of the sculptor's attitude. The world of sculpture, fixed and immobile —essentially classical in Spengler's eyes—had suddenly begun to lose its foundations.

Artistic homage to the "natural world" slipped into meaningless gesture. Nature no longer revealed itself directly to the eye, but was conveyed more accurately through scientific hypothesis and its resultant models. Much of the seeming irrationality of modern art was no more than (witness relativity theory) the mirror of science confronted with the fallibility of "common sense" perception. Physics asked, the still unresolved, what is *real* on the sub-atomic level? If matter were actually a series of extremely brief, highly connected "events," then why was the sculptor creating a private and hermetic "reality" in bronze and marble?

Technology provided a similar dilemma. The tool in many ways has always been the practical counterpart of the sculpted work, and in prehistoric times they were often the same object. Before modern industrialization the tool possessed a readable external form which left its function apparent. Like the human organism, the functional explanation of the modern machine is internalized; it remains a black box to all but the most initiated. As a result, while the machine's simplified metal coverings were safety and protective features, they also served as symbols of psychic inaccessibility. It is no accident, therefore, that much modern sculpture appears to have the externalized efficacy of a hooded machine—promising minor miracles if only its outer canopy could be lifted to reveal an inner sense of life force. Such a rationalization is vitalism applied to the machine.

Another important consequence of technology has been the growing tendency to relate materials, energy sources, transportable objects, events, and signals into a unified network above and beyond natural order. In such a situation the object was bound to lose out as a cumbersome element in the information-energy network. Sculpture in the past had been dependent on the inviolable separateness of objects. The demands of technology are such that separate, unique entities are a cardinal sin against the technological strategy of duplication and interchangeability. To a degree difficult to calculate sculpture has already suffered, not only from the proliferation of common goods, but from the surrogate effect of mass-produced proto-sculpture. These are anything from cement garden dwarfs to Rodin's *Thinker* in the form of bronzed bookends. On a seemingly more ethical level, the trend toward low-priced, mass-produced sculpture has proceeded in the form of "multiples" or the serial production of simple works by "name" artists controlled by galleries and museums. In terms of uniqueness, sculpture has been handed a death blow because, as Arthur Clarke, the science popularizer, has observed, the idea of ownership gradually erodes as all articles are made commonly accessible. Uniqueness and scarcity value derived from a single human hand no longer hold meaning in a technological society. At this stage of technical evolution the uniqueness of an artist can only be proven by the generative power of his ideas, not by material output.

Art consequently has been forced to adopt the advertising techniques used to sell other mass-produced goods—and even then only to secure a minute portion of the public's wealth. To an extent, something like this has happened in the areas of applied scientific research, but the ethical and psychological incursions have not been so damaging as to the arts.

To a greater extent than now suspected, the relative freedom from want and undue pressure afforded the scientist is envied, covertly, by the artist as an ideal situation where legitimate development is possible. Made-to-order working conditions, ample support, and a defined sense of purpose are other objects of cupidity. The same holds true for the manipulators of the public media today. Teamwork, empirical results, communication potency, and immense funds are only some of the advantages, real or imagined, which the artist connects with the technological way of doing things.

As early as 1910 the values of teamwork and an anonymous style were evident to Picasso and Braque. In her autobiography Françoise Gilot recalls a conversation with Picasso in which he allegedly says (1964, p. 75): "That was the reason we abandoned color, emotion, sensation, and everything that had been introduced into painting by the Impressionists, to search again for an architectonic basis in the composition, trying to make an order of it. People didn't understand very well at the time why very often we didn't sign our canvases. Most of those that are signed we signed years later. It was because we felt the temptation, the hope, of an anonymous art, not in its expression but in its point of departure." Picasso goes on to explain that the experiment was a failure because individualism lies too deeply embedded in the structure of the artistic temperament.

This oscillation between anonymity and personal fame has been present in most twentieth-century art movements. In one recollection Jean Arp speaks of the collective and anonymous tendencies of some of the early Zürich Dadaists. In more rigorous form, elements of scientific objectivity and impersonality were constant themes in the writings of the Suprematicist Kasimir Malevich, and also of members of *de Stijl*. In *The New Vision* (1938, p. 79) the Bauhaus master László Moholy-Nagy wrote:

My desire was to go beyond vanity into the realm of objective validity, serving the public as an anonymous agent. An airbrush and spray gun, for example, can produce a smooth and impersonal surface treatment which is beyond the skill of the hand....I even gave up signing my paintings. I put numbers and letters with necessary data on the back of the canvas, as if they were cars, airplanes, or other industrial products.

The avant-garde's blatancy in proclaiming total addiction to the new ruling order of technology reached a peak as witnessed by Theo van Doesburg (quoted in Banham, 1960, p. 187): "This International [Foundation Manifesto of the Constructivist International, 1922] is not the result of some humanitarian, idealistic or political sentiment, but of that amoral and elementary principle on which science and technology are based."

In some important ways the 1920's represented a high-water mark in the consternation over technology, and not until the late 1950's did a similar phenomenon reappear. Then between 1958 and 1962 at least eight groups arose in Europe committed to programs that not only embraced the visible results of technics, but were structured to varying degrees around scientific-technical protocol for achieving those results.

Later this book will speculate on the future of scientific methodology applied to sculpture, and where this is likely to lead. As early as 1930 Georges Vantongerloo, a member of *de Stijl*, made a prediction that must have seemed very far fetched at the time (1948, p. 41):

But already we see art disengaging itself from a quasi-philosophical artiness to become more and more a science and form *one* with a new society. (Do not confuse this with utilitarian art.) But the field of action for the artist is not open yet. The artist is still condemned to exhibit art as an object; art is still part of the old organization. But since this organization cannot persist forever, it must one day cede its place to an organization better adapted to the present.

If expressions of artistic alliance with science and technics did reach a zenith during the 1920's, it was nevertheless the beginning of the end of the "First Machine Age"—to borrow a term from the design historian Reyner Banham. Banham is correct in his observation that since the end of the First Machine Age we have been content to coast along on an aesthetic designed in the spirit of a far less complex technology. With this earlier conception of technology prevailed the notion that art and science would and could coexist, and for those artists oriented toward the new methodology science was actually a symbol of hope and optimism—though in some instances there were signs of caution from artists who saw Western culture dangerously careening to one extreme.

The published writings of Piet Mondrian explicitly circumscribe the progressive relationship between art and science. No artist felt as intuitively the relevance of his art to the theoretical and utilitarian changes taking place. Yet, the inventor of Neo-Plasticism was thoroughly certain that art would remain *art* even though subsumed into the operational fabric of society. He felt that the patterns of technological invention and economic and political control would ultimately conform to his rational and balanced view of art (1945, p. 31):

But man, evolving toward the equilibrium of his duality, *will create in an even greater degree, in life as in art, equivalent relationships and therefore, equilibrium....* Nor will our moral life always be oppressed by the domination of material existence. Increasingly, science succeeds in maintaining our physical well-being. Through superior technics, primitive materials are brought closer to the needs of man. Human life, although dependent on the physical and material, *will not always remain dominated by Nature.*

The position of another pioneer nonobjective painter, Kasimir Malevich, is in no way as well thought out as that of Mondrian. Ambiguous and confusing, Malevich's writing on science and art—while the subject matter of his paintings pays due homage to the "technological landscape"—reveals little about technics' effects on the ultimate values of art (1927, p. 36):

We therefore differentiate two categories of creative work: the artistic-aesthetic (the province of the artist) and the productive-technical (the field of the engineer—of the scientist).
Out of artistic-aesthetic creation proceed absolute enduring values; out of scientific (productive-technical) creation proceed relative, transitory values.

The above statement typifies an ambivalence characteristic of a growing number of modern artists: a love-hate relationship with science, an emotion which is half aware of the potency of science but fears its ascendancy over art. What Malevich failed to understand, and what Mondrian so consummately recognized, was the strong parallelism inherent in the evolution of both systems. To consider art as a system of "enduring values" remains as near-sighted as attempting to minimize the changing "perceptual set" of people exposed to an evolving technology.

With foresight the most technologically-oriented sculptors of the era never doubted art's ability to be influenced without being overwhelmed by newer technics. The analytical-technical spirit was fully operative in Alexander Archipenko; nevertheless, for all of his innovations in penetrated forms, new materials, reductionism, light and color, Archipenko remained a sculptor more dependent on formal traditions in art than on the utilization of new scientific insights (1960, p. 39):

The Gothic and modern styles seem to be analogous in their striving to be detached from matter, in search of spirit. The form of art of our era emanates from abstract causes, from the same realm in which contemporary science finds its causes for modern invention. Contemporary art and science both tend towards abstract forces. Art becomes preoccupied with the expression of transcendency; science with the materialization of abstract energy, such as radio, electrical and atomic.

Slightly further on in this essay on style, Archipenko notes the telescoping process (with its analogy to technology) by which the turnover of art stylistics increases at a steep geometric rate (1960, p. 40):

Unlike past eras, our contemporary mechanization and speed for the economy of time are the causes for rapid changes of forms in modern art. The production of the Egyptian style existed over 5,000 years; the Gothic, 500; modern Cubism, 10 years. Now in our tempo, art seems to be deteriorating into a seasonal performance, particularly in the United States. The history of art has known no such turbulent period or varied stylistic experimentation as in the present day.

Yet Archipenko believed that such a culture could and would continue to produce art.

One of the most unequivocal users of the electrical technology, László Moholy-Nagy, saw art as only part of the functional equation for giving man a new and better array of sensory refinements. Moholy-Nagy emphasizes this objective and collective approach to the problem of visual re-education, and further (1928, p. 13):

This does not mean that "art" must be cast aside, nor that the great individual values within the domain of art are to be questioned. Quite the contrary—it is precisely those values which are firmly anchored in the elemental. But this fact is obscured for the great majority by the unique character of the individual interpretation, and of our tendency to place art on a pedestal.

Added to Moholy-Nagy's denial that technics meant the end of art are the writing of one of the few modern sculptors to directly employ mathematical formulae, Georges Vantongerloo:

> Let us grant that mathematics is not a product of experience alone and that Euclid's postulate is indemonstrable by Euclid's geometry. Art thus can well be a product of great sensitivity, and even though it has science as a base, it will never be a scientific art, which is a contradiction in terms. Does the knowledge, the science, that has served to establish a work of art, constitute the artistic value of the work? The knowledge may be useful, but in itself it is devoid of artistic value. The wish to reduce art to mathematics is nonsense.

Taken literally, the above paragraph (1948, p. 9) directly contradicts the quote by the same artist given here a few pages earlier. The first quote, in which Vantongerloo saw art becoming a science, appeared five years after the statement above. Obviously he began to have second thoughts about the future independence of art.

Two sculptors inextricably bound to the scientific-technical spirit, the Pevsner brothers, have been entirely consistent in their rejection of the fusion of art with science. Naum (Pevsner) Gabo, the younger of the two, has perhaps been the most eloquent on this separation and the reasons for it. In an essay of 1937 (1957, p. 164) he states as follows:

> The Constructive idea does not see that the function of Art is to represent the World. It does not impose on Art the function of Science. Art and science are two different streams which rise from the same creative source and flow into the same ocean of the common culture, but the currents of these two streams flow in different beds. Science teaches, Art asserts; Science persuades, Art acts; Science explores and apprehends, informs and proves.

A line of reasoning could be constructed, and Herbert Read has done so, to show that the verbs used by Gabo to distinguish art from science are, with a little effort, interchangeable. In a later essay of 1956, Gabo with more precision points out that art is essentially irrational and that it is conveyed through human feeling and intuition. Science, on the other hand, means logical manipulation within an assigned set of values. Some philosophers of science might even argue that point, too. Yet Gabo seems to be on more solid ground when he states at the end of his essay (1957, p. 180):

> The new scientific vision of the world may affect and enhance the vision of the artist as a human being but from there on the artist goes his own way and his art

remains independent of sciences; from there on he carries his own vision bringing forth visual images which react on the common human psychology and transfer his feelings to the feelings of men in general, including the scientists.

With few exceptions the artists quoted, while sympathetic to the new order of technics, draw a firm boundary between art and the purpose of science. For artists of the *de Stijl* movement some ambiguity and doubt existed. For the most part, this division was in effect for three decades following the 1920's.

By the late 1950's and early 1960's a new sensibility had evolved. This inclination, which was by no means totally nonobjective in its aesthetics, had in its most general outlines the appearance of a fulfillment of the Hegelian prophecy concerning the extinction of art. This force has appeared under many names: Pop Art, Optical Art, the New Nihilism (whatever happened to the old nihilism?), New Tendency, the New Objectivism, Kinetic Art, Robot Art, Structuralism—all intimately connected with technics.

All of these movements reflect reactions to an environment where organizational methodology has become a way of life: in communication, advertising, industrial production, scientific research, and, not least of all, the vocational fragmentation of human beings. Concomitantly, several trends seem to be growing: a psychological diminishment of the relation between art and everyday environmental experience; a heightened sense of competition between art and the most potent media; a feeling that any means for the production of art can, should, and will be used.

In the strictest sense the emotional stance of the present avant-garde artist is an-emotional, an-idealistic, an-ethical, and in many instances an-aesthetic. To paraphrase Jacques Ellul: technique uses what is at hand, regardless of the implications. He refers to this as the principal law of the age and goes on to quote the French politician Jacques Soustelle's observation concerning his country's construction of an atomic bomb, "Since it was possible, it was necessary."—"Really a master phrase," says Ellul, for the operation of today's society. (1954, p. 99).

In the remainder of this book Soustelle's imperative should become apparent. The fine old, almost genteel, distinctions between art and science-technology—even those contrived by the nonobjective pioneers of the 1920's—have lost their reasoning edge. Scientists and engineers not only inadvertently make some of the most effective Kinetic and Optical Art today; often they are the most effective critics of these genres. Fewer artists think about the separations between art and technics, and more dwell on the practical problems of acquiring the use of efficient mass-production techniques, the latest in miniature programmers and more expert technical assistance. Forty years ago artists adamantly asserted the sovereignty of their art, today a significant faction want nothing more than a quiet, profitable *mariage de convenance* with technics.

Invention in Sculpture

At present invention in art is courted, respected, and analyzed in a way not dissimilar from the "significant breakthroughs" arranged in think factories and research corporations. As William Gordon, one of the inventors of corporation "brainstorming" points out, while it was taken for granted in the past that the criterion for accepting an artistic solution was some degree of "like" or "dislike"—an emotional response—this type of response was distrusted in the areas of science and technical invention; cold, analytical responses were needed for judging an engineering solution. Gordon found that, on the contrary, the selection of possible solutions in *all areas of creativity* are accompanied by various degrees of irrational "pleasure." Even the most technical obstacles are surmounted on an aesthetic basis.

For civilization it is understood that invention is the source of all technical advancement. The remarkable acceleration of inventions produced in Western culture has actually made invention, its methodology and acceptance, a normal procedure, a way of life. While divergent aims separate the purposes of art and science, both areas are beset with the common obsession: invention. Neither evolves without the *will to invent*.

Even as a manufacturer produces a product that is only marginally different from his competitor's, the same proliferation of hybrids from prime inventions takes place in sculpture. Many sculptors are loath to admit this. An ego-centered blocking mechanism prevents most artists from admitting how much they owe to other artists. In art there are few patent rights and the idea of artistic invention remains a sensitive area. However, it is something that should and can be openly aired. The purpose of this discussion is to trace a segment of one sculptural invention. This is the *hollow*, fully enclosed box form, of importance in Hard-Center and Object sculpture during the past five years.

Nominally, David Smith is credited with this invention as a result of his *Cubi* series beginning in 1963 (FIGS. 37, 38). The essence of this type of construction was the fabrication out of plate stainless-steel of a group of hollow rectangular boxes. These were joined edge-to-edge, edge-to-face, partial face-to-face, etc.; the idea being that the quite large and imposing forms themselves could be readily attached in any number of rational or irrational joining sequences. These hollow welded boxes lent themselves to a flexi-

37. David Smith, *Cubi XVIII*, 1964.

38. David Smith, *Cubi XXIII*, 1964.

bility that had few precedents in the arrangement of massive sculptural shapes.

As antecedents to David Smith's *Cubi* series several possibilities exist. One is the increased use of various box forms (mostly single and open) by assemblage artists, culminating with the early 1964 "Boxes" show at the Dwan Gallery in Los Angeles. With the general demise of "open sculpture" the containment possibilities of the box form, its space-defining properties, seemed an obvious next step.

Another antecedent for the enclosed box form were the gigantic steel constructions of the underrated painter-sculptor-architect Mathias Goeritz. First invited to teach in Mexico in 1949, Goeritz four years later produced his famous experimental museum, "The Echo." Standing in the courtyard of the museum is a construction by Goeritz, a truly prophetic, space-filling object with all the earmarks of work produced over a decade later in England and the United States. This construction is hollow, welded plate steel, baseless, with an abrupt and angular relationship to the ground plane that has, in the past four years, become part of the new sculpture lexicon. Only Goeritz's long lack of exposure and publicity in the art capitals accounts for his restricted reputation.

A third antecedent for David Smith's forms, and one probably closer to Smith's source, is American neon box-sign construction. Since the early 1920's the neon belt and stickout signs have become, for better or worse, fixtures of the American landscape. By the 1940's a new genre had been invented: the roadside pylon sign. Massively tall, supported by steel H-beams or lally columns, these polychromed structures have used neon and incandescent light to great effect. Later these were supplemented with fluorescent-lighted, plastic-face inserts with enameled and stainless-steel skirts. Without a doubt, the illuminated pylon sign of the 1950's was *the* arch-underground American art form; its influence on contemporary American sculpture has been overpowering.

Tom Wolfe, among others, discovered the Mecca of American pylon art (1965, p. 8):

One can look at Las Vegas from a mile away on Route 91 and see no buildings, no trees, only signs. But such signs! They tower. They revolve, oscillate, they soar in shapes before which the existing vocabulary is helpless. I can only attempt to supply names—Boomerang Modern, Palette Curvilinear, Flash Gordon Ming-Alert Spiral, McDonald's Hamburger Parabola, Mint Casino Elliptical, Miami Beach Kidney. Las Vegas' sign makers work so far out beyond the frontiers of conventional studio art that they have no names themselves for the forms they create.

Concerning sign makers two things should be added. The sign designer, as underground artist, had in the past an even sharper eye for new effects and techniques than the average sculptor. Formally it has been the task of the sign maker to appropriate dated, corny, modern art shapes, revitalizing them through the techniques of the sign man's vocabulary.

Moreover, the economics of Smith's box forms compared to neon box construction present some interesting contrasts. The neon box sign is of thin-gauge galvanized sheet steel, reinforced internally by sheet metal braces and angle irons; the box itself contains only neon housing units, a few transformers and flashers. Structurally, large-scale pylon signs are aggregates of these boxes bolted together and supported upright by structural steel members. The development of the pylon sign during the past thirty years has derived from the transformation of sign lettering styles, but, even more, the daring use of box form combinations. A similar evolution, though compressed, is evident in David Smith's *Cubi* sculptures. Smith, capable of affording the staggering expense of large amounts of plate stainless steel, welded the faces and edges of his volumes directly together. No internal skeleton was necessary and, unlike pylon signs, the anti-structural consistency of his sculptures was assured.

Considering the daring formalism of Smith's last pieces in the *Cubi* series, an interesting case of mutual influence has been noted by the art journals. The English sculptor Anthony Caro adopted Smith's idiom of direct structural-steel welding shortly after a visit to America in 1961; in turn, Caro became a noticeable influence on Smith's work after 1964. Some of the last *Cubi* pieces (FIG. 38) are without a base—one of Smith's enduring problems—and, in fact, show a sensitivity to the ground plane and a propensity for irrational assembly found only in Caro's work (FIG. 39). Thus the vertical "display" value of the pylon sign moved toward eclipse.

Concurrent with Smith's stainless-steel constructions, the closed box form was used in sculptures by Donald Judd, Robert Morris, and Ann Truitt. They and other creators of Minimal and Object sculpture made their box forms from plywood at much less cost. But massiveness and precision demand craft solutions which plywood could not yield. Thus, with the increased salability of object sculpture, the tendency has been to rely more on the commercial fabrications of plastics and metals.

While object sculpture represents a drive to move beyond traditional modes of idealistic formalism, it also fills the plenum of possibilities developed by industrial plastics. Since the Second World War a number of texts have advertised the potential of plastics in sculpture. With a few exceptions the sculptures illustrated have been classic cases of misalliance. Plastics have an aggressive neutrality which runs counter to the emotionalism of most

39. Anthony Caro, *Homage to David Smith*, 1966.

figurative and semi-abstract work. In general plastics are equated with total alienation of the senses. Hence, the implacability and resilient nature of Object sculpture is aesthetically consistent with polyester resins, epoxy and in fiberglass, formica laminates, and styrene.

Clearly invention has become an ascendant criterion in both technology and sculpture; if doubt exists, then perhaps the following caption and explanation from the *New York Times* (April 17, 1966) can dispel any lingering skepticism. Here the idea of conjoined invention or mutants is sanctified into an unsubtle parody of what could be called "consensus art" (FIG. 40).

...At Your Friendly Hybrid Dealer

Hybrid, a mass art object reflecting the 1965 tastes of savvy "art consumers," has finally been hatched. A bland construction of painted, neon trimmed Plexiglas on an aluminum base, it was conceived last year by British artists Gerald Laing and Peter Phillips. With midgit consumer research kits, they did a mass market study of 137 art professionals; ran the results through a computer. Out came Hybrid's profile. The process says Laing, "is the re-enactment of the motor industry techniques."

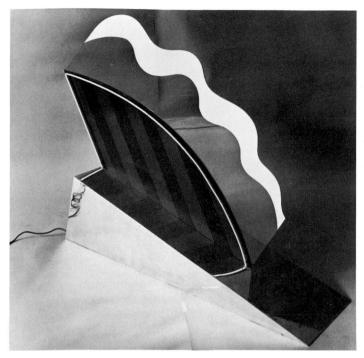

40. Gerald Laing and Peter Phillips, *Hybrid*, 1965.

The Scientific Model

Doubtless, machinery and the principles of mechanics have left their mark on modern sculpture. However, science model making gave the artist a more unworldly and idealistic vocabulary of sculptural forms. The sculptor learned to invent by discovering the world about him, and, aside from visible nature, the theoretical constructs of science constituted one of the most exotic reservoirs of forms. In many instances these constructs resembled nothing existent; thus their attraction was obvious. By the end of the nineteenth century display cases in every German mathematics department were filled with exotic plaster casts and models of stringed figures; while in physics, molecular, then atomic, models gave rise to a new and deceptive sensibility concerning the real nature of space and matter. Indirectly, the sculptor's ability to use these other worldly forms is tied to the scientific philosophy of model making.

For hundreds of years scientists have attested to the value of models for the development of new theories. The model serves as an analogy of a proposed system or set of relationships, though not necessarily as a physical object. In its function, the model is not too far removed from some of the purposes of sculpture. Models can be divided into two categories, the *formal* and the *substantive*. The *formal* model consists of mathematical relationships, those instances when a set of equations for a theory may have terms in common with the verified equations of another physical system. The category of model which has caught the imagination of the sculptor is the *substantive*, but only one type of that model.

Many substantive models are physical systems used as analogies to explain other physical systems; for example, known facts about the flow of liquids were used by Fourier to express his theory of heat conduction; the kinetic theory of gases was compared to the activity generated by great quantities of elastic particles in a defined space; and magnetism was explained in the nineteenth century, imperfectly, by the stresses encountered in an elastic solid. A passion for physical analogies clarifying new theories became so strong in the last century that scientists such as Lord Kelvin rejected theories unless they could be explained with a physical model. A need for visible conceptualization has still not diminished entirely among scientists. It has its uses.

The other type of substantive model, and one that affected sculptors above all, is the construction by the mathematician or physicist of a model describing a theory in space. As an overview, these models are a means for grasping certain facts about a system. The validity of these models revolves around such concerns as: the state of the science employing the model, how successful such models have been in the past, the fidelity achieved in transferring a nonvisual concept to a visual level, the degree and mode of abstraction which a model represents, the means of correcting or making known distortions within a model, and the limitations of single-state models in depicting processes.

The model gives the scientist the opportunity to inspect and build on the theory embedded in it. And just as long as he is fully aware of the limitations of his model, it should prove a stable basis for his projections. On the other hand, inessential features, particularly in substantive models, may be misleading. The model itself is occasionally mistaken for the theory.

In science, the model is a device for reviewing theoretical possibilities, while its use, when adapted to sculpture, becomes an end in itself. For the scientist, the model represents a subtle array of epistemological problems; he is concerned with these because model making always implies some degree of simplification or distortion.

The sculptor, on the other hand, was fascinated by the model because it seemed to represent the creation of form purely through mental activity with no reference to visible reality. The role of the model, particularly in atomic

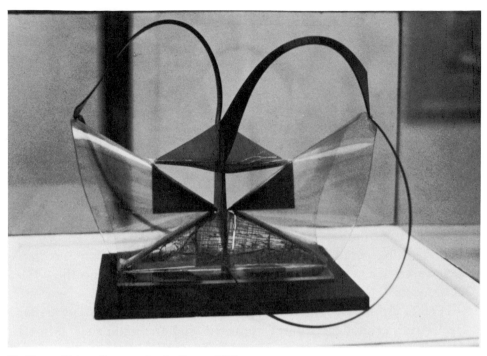

41. Naum Gabo, *Construction in Space*, 1928.

theory, has declined since the early 1920's. However, at that time atomic and mathematical models were first viewed by sculptors as exciting configurations. The Constructivist sculptor especially found himself confronted with the problem: How can the spirit of science be represented without debasing it or duplicating its methods? The solution was to use the techniques of model making, the unifying order of models, and especially their spatial openness, without slavishly copying the concepts behind them.

While mathematical influences will be considered in the next few pages, it is revealing to look at an early construction by Gabo (FIG. 41) illustrating the model and its artistic use. The work might be a figure out of a text for analytical geometry: being a convex conical surface generated by a line revolving around a single point. The ends of the cone are obliquely truncated and two opposing right angles at the apex define the cone's angle of revolution. A set of curved lines symmetrically rotated connect the edges of each cone with the apex. Yet this remains a study in pure spatial relationships, not a theorem on the areas of conic sections.

In physics, such spatial relationships were first contrived in the 1870's to represent the carbon molecule. Spatially, the atom was represented for the first time by the Rutherford-Bohr model (1912). This nucleus surrounded by shells of revolving electrons has remained the most popular, if inaccurate, representation of the atom. Eventually, this image of matter as "open" and essentially disconnected became the ideal prototype for much open sculpture.

In a series of lectures given in 1926 Bertrand Russell expressed a doubt shared by a growing number of physicists; he questioned the ultimate reality of the solar model. Russell made the accurate prediction that perhaps future provisional images of the atom would not be pictoral but relatable only through mathematical formulae. The usefulness of quantum theory and Heisenberg's uncertainty principle have since confirmed Russell's skepticism. It was finally accepted that atomic particles, unlike matter of classical physics, defied the laws of causality by appearing in different places without traversing the points between. The physicist Schrödinger wrote of the "lack of individuality of the particle." In *The Analysis of Matter* (1927) Russell goes into considerable detail over the shift from primitive perception of material substances to a new scientific-philosophical position implying the end of "sight-physics."

That electrons are cloud formations or that wave and probability characteristics cannot be adduced from ball and stick models is now well understood. Yet for the purposes of basic education, such models, particularly molecular configurations, remain useful teaching devices. Moreover, there existed almost a half-century time lag between the development of ball and stick models and their modification in so-called "open-sculpture." With time, it became increasingly clear to sculptors that their works attempted visible representation of the invisible relationships of physical reality. This accounts in part for the steady dematerialization of sculpture from 1910 to the 1950's. The model has been simply one way for the sculptor to cling to a tenuous reality.

The effect that modern theories of space and matter have had upon sculpture are in opposition to traditional ideas of form. Sculptors such as Vantongerloo, Bill, Lippold, Bertoia, and the Pevsner brothers in particular have been cognizant of the new space-time sensibilities, and one of their problems has been to express these adequately in material form. Sculptors wishing to express modern conscious reality, not primitive visual truth, but the "truer" physicist's reality, have the same dilemma as the maker of scientific models. With all the use of fragmented surfaces, string and wire construction, reflective illusory surfaces and openness, Constructivist and other types of formal expression remained essentially pre-1925. The images of the sculptor may be illusive, breathtaking, exquisite—nevertheless, they relate to a period when a ball-and-stick atomic model formed a creditable picture of matter. It is ironic that some sculptors of the 1920's felt influ-

42. Kenneth Snelson, *Atom*, 1964.

enced by scientific models precisely at the time when models were beginning
to lose their importance for the mathematician and physicist. Moreover,
various types of *object* models used in the sciences have steadily given way
to *field* models (extremely difficult to represent spatially) and pure mathematics. Yet many scientists concede that the decline of the physical model
has been a loss for purposes of conceptualization—making it now more
difficult to grasp problems through common-sense perception.

A recent attempt to depict the atom has been made by the structural
designer Kenneth Snelson. His *Atom* (FIG. 42) is a sculpture formed of concentric polyhedrons of touching metal rings, a configuration growing out
of the artist's long investigation of tension and compression elements and
their relation to molecular and atomic structure. This "atom" is significant
in that it attempts to present a *visually logical* model of tellurium. Here the

129

geometric qualities of the element coincide with the periodic table of electron shells. Although it has yet to find favor among scientists, Snelson's atom tries to define electrons spatially. About this he explains (July, 1966, pp. 174–175):

The picture of the atom we have now is a very garbled one; there is no consistent picture existing through the different sciences. There is a magnetic atom, an optical atom, a chemical atom, a spectroscopic atom, but they are all different atoms. I feel these are quite arbitrary and essentially questions of convenience or even aesthetic judgement in some cases, about why something should be thought to be a certain way when there is no evidence whatsoever that it *is* that way. So I think I have a fairly consistent picture of an atom, although it cannot at this point do what the scientists require of a model—that is give them more satisfactory statistical data than they have now.

While abstract sculpture occasionally has a strong affinity with the scientific model, sculpture as an imitation of the model is a theory hotly refuted by the Constructivists, particularly Gabo. In an essay of 1937 his position is that (1957, p. 169): "The shapes we are creating are not abstract, they are absolute. They are released from an already existent thing in nature and their content lies in themselves."

The constructing of objects free of visual allusions is a major tenet of Constructivist and much post-Constructivist sculpture. Yet one cannot but feel, on reviewing more of Gabo's work, that his constructions do in part stem from scientific models. In the past Gabo has denied this. Nevertheless, establishing the absolute apartness of the Constructivist approach is difficult. Objects do not automatically arise out of the minds of men—without reference to the phenomenal world—and in recent years Gabo has stated as much. In his essay *On Constructive Realism* (1948) Gabo explains the attitudes people take in regarding the cognitive efforts of scientists and artists (1957, p. 176). The gist of this is that the scientist *verifies* the images that he constructs, while the public feels insecure with the unverified images of the artist.

Gabo's example accounts for the defensive attitude which many artists have had until quite recently. His word *image* could easily be replaced by the word *model*. What Gabo implies is that the artist constructs his models of reality—but without the hope of receiving some orthodox approval for them. In the case of art, though, time and respected opinion seem to be the arbiters of whose *model* (i.e., sculpture image) best expresses the realities and sensations of a culture.

In scientific model making another area has become prominent since the obsolescence of models in particle physics and in most fields of mathematics. In the past fifteen years subcellular and molecular models have become vivid instruments for comprehending the latest developments in biochemistry and biophysics. Model-making technique has progressed to the point where tens and even hundreds of thousands of dollars are spent on complex, and often animated, models of biomolecular assemblies. The scientific convention and technology museum have come into their own as showplaces for these costly mockups. The uses by the makers of these models of vacuum-molded transparent acrylics, brightly colored thermosetting plastics, polarized and stroboscopic lighting, motor units and fluorescent-lighted large-scale photographic transparencies are, doubtless, every bit as innovational as any sculpture produced today. An overlapping in both form and technique exists between recent scientific models and the polychrome Object, and Kinetic sculpture of the past few years. Sculptors, while their affinities for the scientific model are less overt than a generation ago, are considerably indebted to the recent breed of experimental model maker. It is not unknown for artists to plunder each issue of *Scientific American* for its technical diagrams and illustrations.

In the physical sciences there is almost a discernible pattern in the changing importance of model making. Visual models are constructed only when a science has reached a stage where they are possible and visual conceptualization is helpful; then, as the science develops, visual models are forsaken in favor of mathematical analysis. This evolution has taken place in many areas of atomic physics and mathematics. It is happening now in biophysics. Important discoveries in biophysics in the past three decades have popularized the visual evidences of organic molecular chains. Without an emphasis on vitalism, as stressed before, much of the new sculpture has been influenced by these recent models of subcellular mechanics. In time, as submolecular activities become more important and more understood, this type of biological model will possibly pass into obsolescence.

The most recent and useful models are computer-generated "simulation" models of systems. It no longer helps to display a system as a static entity. Rather, digital computer programs are devised to simulate the history of finite states that comprise a given system as a set of chronological instants. If a changing system—for example, a flexible solid or set of atomic particles—is fundamentally altered in real time, one of the properties of a model must be to study these changes and their interactions. Thus the computer may approximate a dynamic system because it has the ability to handle a number of variables simultaneously. In biology, industrial control, logistics, and the social sciences these models are in practical use. In time we may expect artists to devise their own computer simulations with visual effects through computer display panels.

Where it does not manifest direct influence, the scientific model has evidently taken hold of the form-producing functions of sculptors in terms of spatial awareness and machine-precision finishes. The scientific model in the first decades of this century opened a totally unexplored field of forms to the sculptor, one not invested with functionalist overtones. And, though ever larger sectors of science have become too abstract for the employment of visual models, the sculptor's dependence on this type of influence has grown—not decreased. It is hardly imprudent to predict that, as the model maker is forced to invent new techniques to cope with the visual qualities of kinetic and submicroscopic systems, the sculptor will not hesitate to use them.

Mathematical Influences

For a majority of critics mathematics and modern sculpture juxtaposed have always seemed like Bunyan's "Slough of Despond," where the true believer in art was destined to become mired in the pitilessness of formal reasoning. Mathematical ideas have been influential in so-called nonobjective sculpture, but it is difficult to separate where artistic intuition left off and mathematical intuition began. Moreover, much apparently geometrical sculpture is the result of a desire for essence and simplification and less a craving for geometry in any formal sense of the word. One can readily see that Brancusi's shapes derive their simplicity from biotic origins; Picasso's influential rod constructions of the late 1920's were essentially Surrealist; many of the reductivist forms of the Bauhaus drew upon Neo-Platonic ideas; while the majority of sculptors working in a geometric idiom were more impressed with technology than with the theoretical sciences.

There were exceptions, important ones. For a few sculptors mathematics represented an invisible force, a powerful, wholly intelligent and man-made cogency let loose upon the world. For these men both the physical forms and the intellectual potency of mathematics represented a source of lofty inspiration. There are several reasons for this. Chief among them is the fact that modern formalism in sculpture is based not so much on the idea of *improvisation*, as in classical or figurative sculpture, but derives its vitality from *invention* and discovery. As implied earlier in the discussion of models, it seemed destined that the intriguing constructions of mathematical formulae would with time be "discovered" by the artist.

For mathematical influences to have taken hold at all in the arts necessitated enormous prestige. Not only has the "queen of sciences" proven itself as the greatest practical and theoretical tool, but some philosophers believed that certain areas of mathematics provided the only reasonable form of metaphysical speculation for the twentieth century. With such a tool, questions of proof, limit, and identity could be weighed in the hope of receiving rational answers not tied to sensory limitations or past metaphysical systematizing.

What appears plastically significant about the work of those few sculptors who adopted mathematics as a stimulus for their formal inventions is the type of mathematics chosen. In a progressive tendency these sculptors expropriated three-dimensional forms from areas of geometry which grew less sensual and metric. A parallel to this trend is clearly perceived when Oswald Spengler characterizes the relationship between Greek sculpture and classical mathematics. In "The Meaning of Numbers" (1918, pp. 46–47), Spengler makes no mention of modern sculpture in his comparison of classical and modern Western mathematics. He defines the psychical and physical conditions which tempered new approaches to numbers and spatial ordering; here he attempts to relate the classical notion of number to the spatio-tactile qualities of Greek sculpture.

The most valuable thing in the Classical mathematics is its proposition that number is the essence of all things *perceptible to the senses*. Defining number as measure, it contains the whole world-feeling of a soul passionately devoted to the "here" and the "now." Measurement in this sense means the measurement of something near and corporeal. Consider the content of the Classical art-work, say the free-standing statue of a naked man; here every essential and important element of Being, its whole rhythm, is exhaustively rendered by surfaces, dimensions and the sensuous relations of parts.... The worked stone is only something insofar as it has considered limits and measured form; what it *is* is what it *has become* under the sculptor's chisel.

Spengler then elaborated the notion that classical mathematical thinking is by necessity tied to the finite tangibility of solid geometry. Everyday perception, on the other hand, is not the impetus for Western modern mathematics, rather, it is the idea of *function:* two terms logically related so that the variable values of one correspond to those of the other. Imaginary points in a given manifold—not classical two- or three-dimensional space—control this new notion of mathematics. As in physics, reliance on the senses steadily declined in mathematics; and the power of the new form, according to Spengler, arose from its ability to create *pure thought images*—an idea which also occurs to the modern sculptor.

In another comparison Spengler proposed a second parallel between the two mathematical philosophies. He insisted that the essence of classical mathematics lay in *construction*, while every *operation*, the new mode of manipulation, "denies appearances." Dematerialization of sculpted form has its basis, not only in physics and technology, but in the thought processes of the mathematician. What is more, the overview of the mathematician increasingly becomes less concerned with the local proportional properties of objects and their magnitudes and more concerned with, as Spengler puts it, the *"general morphology of mathematical operation."*

This same morphological concern pervades sculpture. The immense enthusiasm of many nonobjective sculptors during the first half of the twentieth century grew out of their faith in the inexhaustibility of formal relationships and appearances. The feeling prevailed that form had intrinsic morphological channels open to exploration and exploitation in the same way that whole families of forms, real or imaginary, were open to Gaussian and topological analysis.

Concurrent with these realizations emerged an obvious source of "pure form"—the mathematical model. Here a certain element of Neo-Platonic idealism took hold of the sculptor's desire to go beyond the meaning of the physical object. Mathematical models derived their existence, not from nature or the man-made environment, but from the purely mental constructs of man. They were, to parallel Arp's explanation of art, "the fruit of the brain."

The priority by which nonobjective sculptors investigated post-Euclidean geometries closely approximated the chronological order of discovery of these geometries by mathematicians. Not surprisingly the first severely abstract work—that of the geometrical Cubist sculptors—approached forms derived from the solid geometry which is an extension of Euclid's plane geometry. With other Cubists, Archipenko occasionally, and more with early Lipchitz and Henri Laurens, the notion of embedded rectilinear form is never actually tied to geometry in any theoretical sense.

Yet the impending presence of a mathematical consciousness could be detected in Georges Vantongerloo's *Spherical Construction* of 1917. This artist's approach to nonobjective sculpture was unique for several reasons—not least of all for his understanding of the implications of modern formal analysis applied to art. He was probably the first avant-garde sculptor to acknowledge openly the use of a system of geometrical proportions (FIGS. 43, 44). Taking his lead from the proportional systems devised or rediscovered by the builders of Gothic cathedrals, Vantongerloo proposed an overlay of geometrical construction lines for the orthographic views of his constructions, claiming a higher validity for his proportions than for those

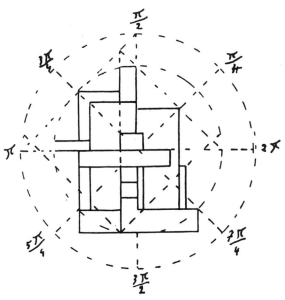

43. Georges Vantongerloo, *Drawing for a Construction
in an Inscribed and Circumscribed Square
of a Circle*, 1924.

44. Georges Vantongerloo, *Construction in an Inscribed
and Circumscribed Square of a Circle*, 1924.

reached by intuitive judgment. For most avant-garde sculptors of that time
all canons of mathematical proportions were identified with the various
academies—hence attempts to employ methods of classical divisioning were
considered an attempt to return to the *beaux-arts* tradition. This kind of
traditional methodology the modern sculptor rejected, favoring intuitive
manipulation of composition as a means to personal freedom. Hence, in
many quarters, among sculptors who otherwise would have been sympathetic to Vantongerloo's efforts, a great deal of antipathy and misunderstanding existed toward his unashamed use of mathematics.

By 1919 Vantongerloo converted to Neo-Plasticism with its obsession
for right-angle geometry. In line with Mondrian and Doesburg, he regarded
symmetrical composition as classical sterility and the death of form generation; however, his use of a Gothic proportioning system, through a rather
carefree choice of intersecting lines which only define the corners of his
rectilinear constructions is arbitrary if not needless. This is not unlike com-
puting the structural members for a building from standard handbook

135

values by substituting for unknowns a throw of the dice. It is clear that Vantongerloo relied on intuitive approximation for deriving his forms as much as any sculptor; it was the mathematical protocol used to arrive at these intuitions that upset most of his critics. This extraordinary mixture of precision and randomness might be called the integration of ritual and mathematical efficacy.

By 1929 a notable change had occurred with Vantongerloo's choice of mathematical tools. Instead of plane figures, diagonals, and bisecting lines according to Euclidean principles, Vantongerloo's *Construction Based on an Equilateral Hyperbola: XY=K* (FIGS. 45, 46) derives directly from the methods of Cartesian analytical geometry; and, as Spengler had earlier pointed out, the algebraic geometry of Descartes formed the first significant move away from the classical sensibilities of point, line, plane, and negative space. Here the sculptor used a Cartesian coordinate system with parabolic trajectories described by the equation of his title. This new mathematics does not alter the arbitrariness of Vantongerloo's proportions, but it does give them a horizontal elongated elegance missing from his earlier compact works. With these Cartesian-derived constructions the masses become thinner, more open, and cantilevered to an extreme. These manifestations might have had more to do with the development of Vantongerloo's sense of spatial consciousness than with the change in geometry itself. However, the horizontal slenderness of some of these constructions coincides with the limits of infinity derived from the upper values of his paraboloidal forms.

In time Vantongerloo chose the best course by ignoring critics who attacked him for giving some of his sculptures equations for titles. One answer posed the rhetorical question: why shouldn't a sculptor name his works after equations, doesn't this make as much sense as naming them after people, emotions, poetic imagery, or ideals? In an essay of 1927 Vantongerloo gave an eloquent defense of the scientific rationale applied to sculpture (1948, p. 22):

To say that I wish to create a purely mathematical art is as absurd as to say that anyone creates by pure intuition. Mathematics is only the means, the instrument, used as one uses hammer and chisel to cut marble.... Mathematics helps us understand the relations existing between geometrical forms. The new art, being abstract in the positive sense of the word, is created by abstract forms and means.

During the 1920's and 1930's investigation of mathematical form through the medium of sculpture centered around Paris, primarily through Vantongerloo and Pevsner, though later with Bill and Gabo. It would hardly

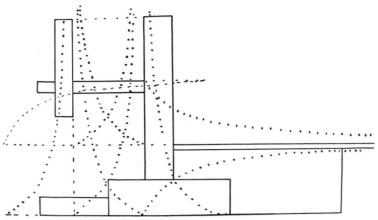

45. Georges Vantongerloo, *Drawing for a Construction
Based on an Equilateral Hyperbola, XY = K*, 1929.

46. Georges Vantongerloo, *Construction Based on an
Equilateral Hyperbola, XY = K*, 1929.

be accurate to suggest that the mathematical influence held sway outside
the sphere of these few committed artists. Mathematics did not bring about
the coherence of a group effort. More important was its reductivist and
form-giving influence on later generations.

Antoine Pevsner's constructions in the 1920's consisted mainly of sheet
copper and plastic, often fitted together with machine screws. As a student
Pevsner had an aptitude for geometry. Partly as a consequence of this, his
precise and elegant constructions of the 1920's—often a mixture of symmetries—displayed one of this century's subtlest minds focused on the construction of planar relationships.

47. Antoine Pevsner, *Developable Surface*, 1936.

48. Antoine Pevsner, *Developable Column*, 1942.

In an interview that appeared in *L'Oeil* in 1956 Pevsner spoke of beginning a search (about 1930) for a new kind of surface. A sketch of 1933 showing developments of skew and radial lines became the obvious genesis for a subsequent discovery. The new technique made its appearance in a construction of 1935; one plane of this is a section of a hyperbolic paraboloid. Interestingly enough, an engineer at Dreux (1933) built the first two-sided cantilevered paraboloidal structure. By 1935 in Paris the future of such constructions was discussed at a construction engineers' convention.

Pevsner's first work in his mature style appeared in 1936, *Developable Surface* (FIG. 47). Since then steady confusion has resulted from the sculptor's occasional habit of naming his constructions after this mathematically descriptive surface. Somehow the impression circulated that Pevsner used calculations and that this was work preceded by the use of mathematical logic, hence, not sensual sculpture. This is hardly true since the developable surface—a singly-curved surface (a plane curved in only one direction) found in descriptive and differential geometry—became Pevsner's means for liberating the surfaces of his constructions from the limitations of Euclidean planes and edges. It mainly gave the artist both an extremely rich surface texture and a flexibility in joining straight-line edges to curved surfaces. Moreover, Pevsner's technique for constructing surfaces with rows of bronze wire demanded several brazing temperatures and an extraordinary degree of skill and patience. A series of exotic interlocking surfaces resulted; nevertheless, it should be pointed out that the underlying hypothesis of Constructivist sculpture technique always focused on lines and edges generated by planes, rarely on surfaces for their own sake.

In the sculptor's *Projection into Space* (1938–1939) and *Developable Column* (FIG. 48) lie certain immediate similarities—at least to the layman—between these constructions and mathematical models. Pevsner throughout his life adamantly denied this. And Mme. Pevsner in the 1956 *L'Oeil* interview recounts in this respect the outcome of the 1952 "Art of the Twentieth Century" exhibition in Paris. At that time students and professors from the Sorbonne spent much time and effort taking measurements of Pevsner's constructions in order to determine whether they contained traces of mathematical systems or formulae. In every case the results were negative.

Generally speaking, a construction such as Pevsner's *Developable Column* may have some connection formally with the string model for a left-hand helical convolute, yet it is impossible from the sculpture itself to construct the helicoidal line which could generate the required tangents. Formally, the beauty of the *Developable Column* lies, not in any mathematical associations, but in Pevsner's genius for making a relatively simple surface visually inobvious. One convoluted edge of the construction is tucked into the darkened interior of the piece, so that there is in no sense an abrupt ending; the other edge swings up in an arc intersecting the turning plane at the center of the work. Pevsner often repeated the idea of inducing the eye to follow the perpendicular path of his serrated surfaces, thus instigating some intriguing perceptual ambiguities.

Naum Gabo, the slightly younger brother of Pevsner, has been the more theoretically inclined of the two men. Gabo's training in engineering, mathematics, physics, and medicine has helped to produce one of the most thoughtful artistic minds ever to write on the relationships between art and science. As was evident from previous quotes by Gabo, both he and his brother admit to being susceptible to the spirit and beauty of the scientific method—yet consistently he has eschewed all direct scientific influences. One aspect of controversy centers about the influence of certain types of mathematical models on Constructivist works.

In a letter written some ten years ago to the author, Gabo suggested that there is (or was) an evolution of visual influences which determined the form conception of Constructivist sculpture: this begins with the stereometric constructions of the human figure, proceeding from there to ideas analogous with building technology, from there to scientific apparatus, and ends with the liberation of the artist, leaving him free to devise from his own mental constructs. As if he was thinking of a pilgrimage of the spirit, Gabo envisioned the artist (and there is good reason to think that he was writing of his own experience) as a soul taken by the technological spirit yet free of its functionalism. As a result Gabo's images from the 1920's and 1930's slowly evolved from utilitarian appearances toward the purely conceptual.

Mathematical influences in Gabo's constructions appear more sensual than theoretical, having more to do with the optical consistency of mathematical models—in terms of their airiness, fragility, and intricacy—than with formal meaning. Some time ago the author asked Gabo what mathematical training he thought would be useful for a nonfigurative sculptor. None was needed, insisted Gabo, but a practical knowledge of descriptive geometry would be helpful in plotting and fitting together various planar patterns. Beyond this, he stated, a grasp of modern mathematics would be helpful.

Vestiges of projective and analytical geometry appear in Gabo's constructions during the later 1920's and 1930's. It is not doing an injustice to Gabo's work to point out that he recognized the incredible ethereality of the stringed and transparent model and sought to heighten this singular effect.

Moreover, Gabo was one of the first pioneers of modern art to perceive the engineering potential in the theoretical constructions of scientists. His linear constructions of the 1940's (FIG. 49) have a clear antecedent in the string models of a number of ruled surfaces. Nylon and plexiglas are the means by which Gabo stressed their visual penetrability. Yet perhaps the most significant investigation of the artist, touching nearer the core of modern geometrical concerns, began with his *Spheric Theme* series in 1937 (FIG. 50). The prototype for this series was made in opaque plastic, while later versions were transparent. In a subsequent statement Gabo reiterated that no graphic picture of space as it was known to science satisfied him, thus his desire to create upon the *Spheric Theme*, a symbol of space folding back upon itself as an infinite loop. The edges of this construction resemble the pattern in three dimensions created by the seams of a baseball. The surface from which these edges are created remains impossible to fabricate from a single flat sheet of plastic. If the *Spheric Theme* were flattened, it would resemble a circular disk with a circular hole in its center, except that it would contain twice the circumference of a regular circle. Topologically this represents a circular disk, but, according to a topologist, one that has been *stretched* or *deformed* so as to actually contain two flat disks cut open and attached edge to edge.

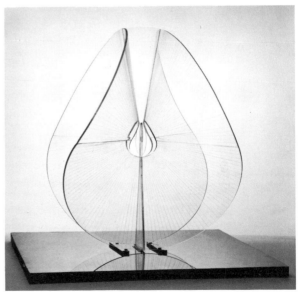

50. Naum Gabo, *Translucent Variation on Spheric Theme*, 1951 version of 1937 original.

49. Naum Gabo, *Linear Construction*, 1942.

Topology is the study of the innate properties of objects in space. These properties remain unaffected by changes in magnitude, position, or proportion and are only altered by the tearing or joining of an object's parts. Recalling Spengler's characterization of modern mathematics, it seems that many nonobjective sculptors, including Gabo, became less concerned with proportional metric relationships and more interested in the universal properties of planes, edges, penetrations, and spaces. This, then, became the basis of new sculptural formalism. Insideness and outsideness, connectivity, complex symmetry, and ambiguity—while they were intriguing properties for the topologist to ponder from the point of view of mathematical logic—became the most important plastic considerations for Gabo and other formalist sculptors.

Half a generation younger than the other sculptors just discussed, Max Bill is the incarnation of an artist whose inspiration stems from mathematical lucidity. Born in Switzerland, Bill's multiple roles as an architect, writer, designer, teacher, and painter have not prevented him from making some of the most powerful formalist works to be found in modern sculpture. Bill's first constructions were coincident with his membership in the Abstraction-Création group in Paris during the 1930's. Unlike Gabo and Pevsner, Bill has always been quite open about his debt to mathematics, and in particular the visual enigmas of that science. In an essay on his working philosophy Bill has stated (quoted in Maldonado, 1955, p. 37):

The mainspring of all visual art is Geo-metry, the correlation of elements on a surface or in space. Thus, even as mathematics is one of the essential forms of primary thought and consequently one of the principal means by which we take cognizance of the world that surrounds us, it is also intrinsically a science of the relationship of object to object, group to group and movement to movement.... Such mathematical representations have long been known to us. They emanate undeniable aesthetic appeal such as goes out from mathematical space-models, as, for instance, those that stand in the Musée Poincaré in Paris.

Continuing in the same essay:

The mystery of mathematical problems, the inexplicableness of space, the nearness of distance of the infinite, the surprise afforded by a space beginning on one side and ending in a different form on another side, congruent with the first; limitations without fixed boundary lines; the manifold which is nonetheless unity; uniformity which is changed by the presence of a single stress; a Field of Force; parallels that meet and the infinite that turns back upon itself as presence; and then again the square, in all its stability, the straight line untouched by relativity, and the curve, each point of which forms a straight line,—all these things that do not seem to have bearing on our daily needs are nevertheless of the greatest significance. These forces with which we are in contact are the elemental forces underlying all human order and are present in all forms of order which we recognize.

Clearly Bill uncovered something forgotten since the Renaissance; he revealed the sensuality of a form logic long under the veil of austerity and hyperintellectualism. His words are those of an artistic mentality convinced of the special *visual* logic of the mathematical model. A bystander could claim that his images are more "mathematics" and less artistic than, say, the constructions of Gabo. Inasmuch as the core of formal logic is made manifestly clear in a sculpture by Bill, this contains a grain of truth. However Gabo's forte continues to reside in the transcendent power of his images, and Bill's in the transformation of formal relationships.

Bill's special fascination with topology is perhaps due to the fact that topological properties are the most innate and unchanging to be found in three-dimensional objects. While this is a meaningless game for the layman, objects can be twisted and distorted beyond recognition without losing their topological characteristics in terms of edges, faces, and vertices. The *metric* properties (straightness, the measurement of angles and edges, cross-sectional areas, etc.) of the other geometries do not afford this type of plasticity. In this respect Bill's approach to making sculpture represents an important aspect of modern stylistics: the intention of the artist to use the same mathematical-structural properties repeatedly, though distorting them so that they remain unrecognizable as the original configuration. By doing this Max Bill demonstrates both a topological truth and an artistic principle: there are no "perfect forms," only the ability of the artist to reveal meaningful aspects of the same reality.

Toward the middle of the nineteenth century the German mathematician and astronomer A. G. Möbius discovered that a single strip of paper could have only one edge and one side. This was accomplished by twisting one end of the strip 180° before joining the two ends together. Since discovery, the Möbius strip has become one of the key visual examples of the topologist's special logic. As a construction with the unique property of one side, the Möbius band inspired Max Bill to create from it a series of variations.

One of the first, if not the first, is the *Endless Ribbon* (FIG. 51), a rather closed, undulant, ribbon shape. The same Möbius band appears in a polished brass form called *Monoangulated Surface in Space* (FIG. 52). Here the ribbon shape has been altered to a near cylinder where the twisted edge is prominently exposed so that it runs symmetrically traversing the bottom of the piece. Again the Möbius band took the form of a split ribbon of brass, as

Continuous Surface in the Form of a Column (FIG. 53). Bill chose to twist the top of this column at right angles with the bottom, so that one band of polished brass slowly twists 90° while the other moves through 270°. The Möbius band takes form again in a deceptive construction entitled *Transition* (1958): locked in a flat sheet of steel is a small ribbon turned 180° and smoothly joined at top and bottom to the interior edges of the sheet surface. Fashioned in different materials, placed in different positions, and designed to exploit different plastic properties of the same configuration, topologically these four sculptures *are* the same piece.

Ambiguity through spatial deception thus remains the *modus operandi* of much of Max Bill's sculpture. However, and this is important for any quality found in a scientific model and appropriated for artistic purposes, visual ambiguity is not the purpose of the mathematical model; visual ambiguity is simply the characteristic of a formal property which the sculptor later notices. Moreover, most three-dimensional topological models possess a level of complexity which makes them awkward and confusing as sculpture.

Much of the visual ambiguity attained by Gabo, Pevsner, and Bill in their work has a basis in seeming irrationality of continuous plane surfaces in three dimensions. In all cases these ambiguities are aesthetically valid only if a viewer first feels that he understands the form and its construction —but then realizes that its *Gestalt* is more complicated than he first supposed. Initial simplicity is necessary to evoke this "poetic indecision." If this is prevented by the overcomplicatedness of a configuration, a sculpture readily loses its power as a strong aesthetic statement—no matter how logical or unique it may be as a mathematical statement.

What is too much ambiguity? Most three-space topological figures are not only more complicated than the Möbius band, they are ugly. Their multiple twists, handles, punctures, holes, embedments, and cross-caps are much too ungainly and inelegant to be used purely as sculpture—or as sculpture as we know it now. Furthermore, most topology concerns itself with configurations and hypothetical spaces virtually unreproducible in three-dimensional form. Thus purist topologists often refuse to look at two- and three-dimensional figures for inferences. They prefer the lucidity of written mathematics because of the deceptions encountered in models constructed in real space.

For the reasons above it is not surprising that the use of topological exploration has not been carried further by sculptors. As in the case of physical models, used for sculptural purposes, there came a point in the 1950's when mathematical models were "used up" and those remaining suffered an analogous fate of conceptual invisibility. Theory in mathematics has out-

51. Max Bill, *Endless Ribbon*, 1935–1953.

52. Max Bill, *Monoangulated Surface in Space*, 1959.

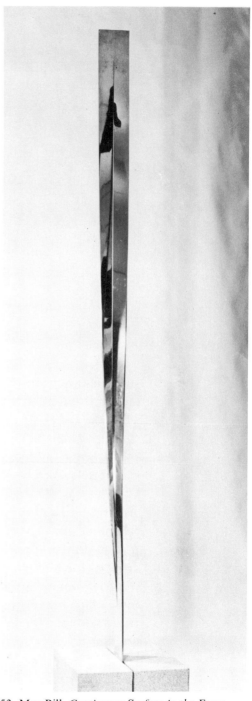

53. Max Bill, *Continuous Surface in the Form of a Column*, 1953–1958.

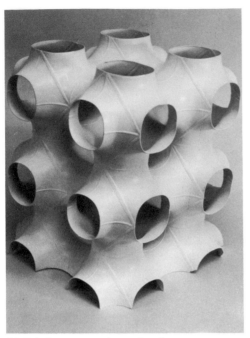

54. Edwin Hauer, *Identical and Complementary Volumes*, 1958.

55. Claes Oldenburg, *Dual Hamburgers*, 1962.

stripped the efforts of sculptors to use it meaningfully. This stasis will eventually confront all attempts to imitate scientific reality on the iconic level.

In the last few years the tendency has been to forsake the *appearances* of mathematical models in favor of mathematical *principles* applied to neutral objects. As a result, ideas on sculptural symmetry have been broadened. One way is through three-dimensional lattice structures. The Austrian-American sculptor Erwin Hauer pioneered the use of industrial molding techniques in plastics. His *Identical and Complementary Volumes* (FIG. 54) utilizes the properties of the mathematical "supercircle," which he discovered for himself. Besides being continuous, the spaces on both sides of the partitioning surface are homologous—that is, they are identical and fit inside each other. More obvious uses of the lattice, relying on binocular eye traversal, are Morellet's sphere of aluminum rods (see Chapter Six, FIG. 95) and Sol Lewitt's (see Chapter Four, FIG. 75).

Ever since the beginning of this decade, a "cool" bilateral symmetry has invaded both Pop and Object sculpture, resulting in an aggressive iconicism of dual but not absolutely congruent images. Claes Oldenburg's *Dual Hamburgers* (FIG. 55) is one example; irregularities in Oldenburg's repeated form soften and humanize an otherwise sterile duplication.

56. Donald Judd, *Untitled*, 1965.

More than anything else, the efforts of the Minimal or Object sculptors characterize the mathematical intentions of this decade. At first glance these formalists appear to have navigated a full-circle return to Cubist and non-objective sculpture with their reliance on the shapes of solid geometry. However, the meaning of Object sculpture revealingly intimates much about the destinity of three-dimensional art. The cones, pyramids, cubes, rectangular solids, regular polyhedrons, and spheres of Object sculpture are an implicit admission that the eternal verities of Pythagorean solids *are* the stuff from which sculpture is made—and always will be. With Object sculpture come no conscious, rational attempts to borrow the formal sensuality of the un-exploited mathematical model; rather, it offers tacit admission that the mathematical model can no longer solve the iconic problems of sculpture. Nevertheless, a number of stripped-down, present-generation Object sculptures utilize formal principles employed by the Constructivists of the 1920's. One reused device is the three-dimensional optical illusion produced by various continuous knot-figures of interlocking symmetry. Again, attempts to use more complex knot figures for sculptural purposes are likely to degenerate into configurations both cumbersome and unpleasing.

What is happening completely realizes Spengler's analysis of modern geometry—"the liberation of geometry from the visual." The regular solids of Object sculpture are Platonic essences which could be termed manipulatable n values—their proportions, both physical dimensions and the spaces between them, are the results of mathematical functions. These disembodied means of handling mathematical reality (not measurable forms) are free of the effects of measured magnitude and sensually definable space. For instance, Donald Judd in the past three or four years has employed set theory in positioning the modular units of his wall reliefs (FIG. 56). Here sets, defined as numerical values, have nothing to do with dimension or finite proportion generated through Euclidean space perception, but transcend the intuitive-concrete to become extensions of pure process and transformation. Sculp-

147

ture becomes "thingified" by means which cannot be perceived except through the rules for ordering finite or infinite sets of abstract points in a given continuum.

Spengler prophesied this very event as it happened in mathematics and is happening in sculpture (1918, p. 65): "Geometry *became* analytical and dissolved all concrete forms, replacing the mathematical bodies from which the rigid geometrical values had been obtained, by abstract spatial relations which in the end ceased to have any application at all to sense-present phenomena."

Space, Scale, and Structure

One lesson the modern sculptor has learned, which is implicit in the sculpture of the last sixty years, is that considerations of scale, proportion, space, and structure are largely irrelevant—in any case, very personal. Scale and proportion are mainly remnants left over from classical formalism; space is a fiction which derives topicality from painting theory, while the most that can be claimed for structure is that it is not a literal, physical problem, but a multilayered theoretical concern which may or may not fit into a sculptor's intentions.

This may be difficult to accept at face value, since in sculpture criticism such terms appear with some regularity. These references to physical qualities are vestigial remainders of an earlier vocabulary, one devised to cope with an art form that took up space as did architecture and received rational consideration in terms of mass and physical presence. The analyses of space, scale, and structure were probably relevant to a form of sculpture that we thought of as a pre-Renaissance storytelling medium and as an adjunct to architecture. In the present era, when sculpture often serves as a model for purely conceptual purposes—admitting no precise relationship to either man or environs—the qualitative and quantitative factors for appraising sculpture must rest on another set of criteria.

Until a few years ago nonobjective sculpture was entitled to the imprecision of allowing us to assign it hypothetical characteristics as if these were physical-perceptual properties of the work. Epistemologically, the scientist is trained to accept properties of the models he uses as being *symbolic* of other physical attributes. As to the limitations of his models, he accepts them with a certain amount of good will and resignation. No one denies the sculptor his freedom to talk about the space he feels he has constructed, except that there is the danger that he constructs an invisible fantasy world for himself, one with little or no relation to the objects he makes. The scientist can do this because the models he constructs are abstractions with assigned values. For the sculptor, though, there seemed to be a growing discrepancy between his conceptual understanding of what, for instance, constitutes space and his resources for fashioning *sensually* adequate paradigms of these spaces.

Space as an active plastic concern of the sculptor grew out of the Post-Impressionist and Cubist realization that pictorial space could be reordered at will; that is, local distortions and depth compression could affect a painting just as could changes of color.

In nineteenth-century sculpture, space, if it had any meaning at all, embodied characteristics assigned by the physicists of Classical Greece. These were localizing assumptions based on the dominance of objects over surrounding but invisible space. One theory held that space formed the inner boundary of containing structures; space in this case only existed inside of objects, hence, space could be defined by the dimensions of objects—this is Aristotle's theory of "place." Another theory defined space only in the immediate area of objects—for practical purposes an accurate description of how space and sculpture are still conceived today. Another spatial notion, that of betweenness—which has so influenced architectural theory—has a relatively short history of thirty or forty years in modern sculpture.

Very little thinking—even in modern sculpture—embodies the common-sense absolutes of Newtonian space: isotropism, infinite extension in all directions, and point definition in terms of a three-dimensional coordinate system. These ideas have been mainly restricted to Neo-Plastic theory. In the nineteenth century non-Euclidean geometry first attempted to question the priority of a three-dimensional continuum; it went on to hypothesize spaces and objects with both greater and lesser dimensions. The invention of mathematics capable of handling continuums of more than three dimensions made twentieth-century theoretical physics a possibility. And if four- or five-dimensional continuums have consistently appealed to the sculptor's sense of plastic involvement, of spatial fantasy, the translation of such an idea into an object with any palpable meaning has so far been impossible.

Archipenko deserves credit for the first systematic rethinking of the function of space in sculpture. He helped to change the sculptural awareness of space from something totally taken for granted to a prime concern, one quite abused by many sculptors. This misuse was hardly Archipenko's fault, but very much like the mystical concern for an *élan vital;* space too was invisible and consequently fair game for the concoction of aesthetic fairy tales. Helpful journalists saw all kinds of "spaces" that never did and never could exist. There were also concrete contributions to the sensing of sculptural space.

According to Archipenko, sculpture had been thought of as shape embedded in space. Moreover, space proper *began* at the outer limits of an object—very much as the Greek physicists had thought of it. This was common-sense perception. Archipenko's contribution was to reverse this relationship, surrounding, as it were, space with sculpture (all other twentieth-century exploitations of space and "open sculpture" stem from this discovery). Archipenko accomplished this in two ways: by complete penetration of his sculptures, in *Woman Combing Her Hair* (FIG. 57), and by hollowed-out negative surfaces in sculptures, as in the *Concaves*. Some of Archipenko's early works are masterpieces in both forms.

Barbara Hepworth has mentioned the intense feeling of achievement that came with carving a hole directly *through* a sculpture (FIG. 58), which she attempted first in 1931. Not intending to create a negative silhouette, she rather intended in making these penetrations to make an *inside* to her carvings. Often she seductively emphasized this *insideness* with the use of brilliant yellow and white paint. The viewer is very much lured by the inviting brightness of these lightened spaces. One is reminded of Gaston Bachelard's essay, "The Dialectics of Outside and Inside" (1958, pp. 211–231), where he writes of the "interior immensity" and spatial dizziness that can result even from small spaces that lend themselves to sudden accessibility.

Very frequently Naum Gabo's "Realist Manifesto" (1920) has been quoted as one of the first affirmations in sculpture of space as a primary concern. Gabo saw, quite correctly, the old concept of monolithic sculpture as a denial of the presence of space. In an interview with the artists Ilya Bolotowsky and Lassaw in 1956, Gabo speaks of the absence of a conscious awareness of space in earlier art. At the time of his "Manifesto" educated members of Gabo's generation were just becoming aware of the role of space in scientific theory. "It was in the air," according to Gabo, and it was the task of the sensitive artist to pick up its implications. In another essay written for *Circle* in 1937 Gabo affirms the perceptual properties of space and the fact that one could be made conscious of space in the same manner as one is conscious of sound or light impinging on the senses. He states (1957, p. 168):

Up to now, the sculptors have preferred the mass and neglected or paid very little attention to such an important component of mass as space. Space interested them only insofar as it was a spot in which volumes could be placed or projected. It had to surround masses. We consider space from an entirely different point of view. We consider it as an absolute sculptural element, released from any closed volume, and we represent it from inside with its own specific properties.

150

57. Alexander Archipenko, *Woman Combing
Her Hair*, 1915.

58. Barbara Hepworth, *Hollow Form (Penwith)*, 1955–1956.

Following the Constructivists and Picasso, Giacometti, Calder, Uhlmann, Smith, Lippold, Lardera, Kricke and Lassaw were but the best-known sculptors working before 1960 who conceived of space as a point of departure for their designs. In regard to space, one thing must be kept in mind. The material reductivism which had been so important as a trend had its limits. Beyond the fine wire constructions of Lippold and the empty glass boxes of Larry Bell (FIG. 59) *nothing* exists which can be called sculpture. Whatever is beyond consists of space undisturbed by visible material form. Even the modern rhetoric surrounding spatial plasticism was largely limited and experimentally exhausted by the end of the 1930's; what has continued for the most part is improvisation on ideas generated by Archipenko, Picasso, and the Constructivists.

Space, as a source of expression, has become a dead issue for the present generation. Even when pressed into service, the challenge of space has been a latent concern, an aesthetic afterthought. Sculpture, moreover, has always been dominated by image makers—and the more immaterial sculpture became, the more important seemed the concept of the iconic "image." Pure spatial expression is one of the unrequited longings of our age. This desire to embody space without matter—like music—fulfills a profound striving of Western technology. This is to produce effect without the hindrance or fallibility of *objects*. With all the theories of four-, five-, and *n*-dimensional space, sculpture remains bound by Newton's rectilinear coordinate system—fixed, uncurved, absolute—and a prisoner of this earthly continuum. Ways may arise which change this condition, but likely it will not be the province of sculpture to find them.

To accept a scale or a theory of proportions for constructional purposes seems to be a need of the past. The so-called rules for visual judgment have become casualties of modern art as Euclidean geometry and Aristotelian logic have been bypassed by developments in mathematics. What *is* human scale—if this is our criterion for building? We can take our choice, and they grow daily, from a four-mat Japanese teahouse, the Parthenon, the Palazzo Farnese, the Crystal Palace, to the Seagram's Building.

Even those few sculptors who have employed formal rules of proportion have not met with results discernibly superior to those of sculptors working from a basis of sensitive intuition. Mathematics, whatever its success in sculpture, has flourished because of the allure of physical images, not through techniques. Mathematical incantation may have helped the morale of a sculptor but not the work itself. And the phrase "good proportions," which we hear less today, usually means that the speaker is more familiar with one set of proportions than another.

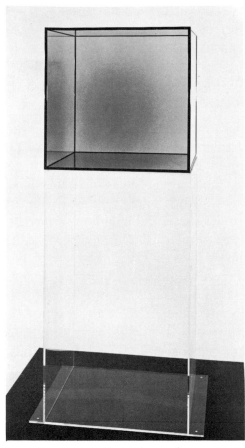

59. Larry Bell, *Untitled*, 1966.

However, there is an important basis for proportional systems in the history of sculpture. When Lysippus, late in the fourth century B.C., improvised a new system that helped to outmode the canons of Polyclitus, he was in effect altering his contemporaries' view of the human body. Sculpture as an idealization of the human form has always had some kind of ultimate goal, and constant, but slight, proportional shifts have been one means of realization. No such biological basis of measurement exists presently. In the 1920's Vantongerloo's mathematical proportioning for his sculpture met with ridicule. Le Corbusier's *Le Modulor* was an ambitious attempt to implement such a standard for architecture, though too little is yet known about biological organization on all levels to make such a scale valid, much less to use it properly. Presently ominous, more than the lack of a metric system of proportions, is the possibility that with continued technological exploitation of materials (organic and nonorganic) no scale is within range. Sculpture with its present fluctuations between miniaturization and giantism seems to reflect that apprehension.

153

All sculpture cannot help but be structural though its *raison d'être* is never structure. This applies to structure as a connected system of forces enabling sculpture to stand erect (i.e., physical structure), and it applies to structure as visual metaphor simulating patterns which mirror our understanding of absolute reality. Unlike painting, sculpture has the added complexity of somehow unalterably combining the two.

In scientific circles structure as a means of interpreting all phenomena has gradually replaced the old Aristotelian notion of *form*. In the past, visual indexes, biological and nonorganic, were set up according to form templates proscribed by the various sciences. Yet, the analytic forces of science have more and more replaced the old templates, which were essentially patterns of visual identification, with more thorough studies in underlying *structure*. Fifty years ago Fry's study in "significant form" opened new vistas for the contemplation of sculpture, but as yet no study in "significant structure" has made an appearance. The place of structure in modern sculpture is one of the most ambiguous and unanalyzed relationships in the entire area of aesthetic analysis. Structure, if it exists in any concrete form in sculpture, is probably a multilayered concept that includes at least three or four definitions: structure as a material-structural analysis of how sculpture stands, or as mirrored in a specific scientific-constructive idea, or as an aspect of the historical stylistic continuum of sculpture, or as a part of the communicative potential of sculpture.

One fact seems to be emerging about the nature of structure. The feeling for it is such an integral part of the scientific apparatus, and so important for our grasp of physical and conceptual patterns, that any fundamental change in the scientific approach to structure does affect our apprehension and valuation of structure in art. As Margit Staber has pointed out in an excellent essay on concrete painting (Kepes, 1965, pp. 165–185), this has been happening throughout the twentieth century. It refers back to the problem of models and the necessarily invisible nature of many models of structure. Also perceivable about structure is its emotive power: often appearing rational and cold—but just as often illogical and unsure through a kind of artistic perversity.

Perhaps because the concept of homogeneous structure is regarded as one of the more powerful symbols of rationality, most sculptors dealing with abstraction choose structured formats with an element of chaos. Moreover, the dialectics of art seem to demand that a sculptor make irrational structures seem rational and vice versa. In addition, structural irrationality was a part of sculpture before this century. But then it had more to do with using materials improperly, especially overextending the tensile strength of stone, than with structure as theory.

As evident from some of the recovered pieces of full-size standing statuary, Greek sculptors were not at all troubled about the propriety of using carved tree stumps or draped forms in support of their thin-ankled figures. The shot hip pose used in Praxiteles's *Hermes and the Infant Dionysus*, with its connecting stone link, is an example of a literal structural support. On the other hand, Canova's *Cupid and Psyche*—with Cupid's extended wings—graphically demonstrates the nineteenth-century mania for extending marble to its breaking point.

With the modern English reaction to nineteenth-century flamboyant carving, massive hunks of wood and marble denoted the need for structural security in the vitalistic and geometric-abstract idiom. "Truth to material," more than being an honest and analytical approach to the use of sculpture materials, was an overreaction to earlier excesses. In retrospect, it appears that the dictum "truth to material" was invoked by a sculptor only when it served his particular stylistic preferences—regardless of moral considerations.

The problem of separating a sculpture from its resting place gradually developed into a chief concern of relating structure to form. Moreover, there seemed to be a variable compromise between the amount of stability and rigidity which any sculptor was willing to sacrifice for a given amount of structural daring. In this respect it is interesting that a sculptor like Gabo, who had pioneered the uses of several engineering principles in his treatment of planar surfaces, should be so plagued with the problem of fragility and breakage in his plastic constructions. Though a high correlation between visual and structural logic may exist in civil engineering, surprisingly little attempt has been made to establish such a logic in sculpture—and when an effort has been made, it has usually been a pseudo-attempt, rather than one which is strictly consistent with the properties of materials. Engineering in sculpture—with very few exceptions—has been a matter of visual assimilation, not function.

The comparatively simple task of making a sculpture stand with a certain amount of confidence has been the sculptor's main physical consideration—one in which engineering needs have usually been minimal. Of note in this respect, one of the first large-scale constructions proposed as a model was Vladimir Tatlin's *Monument to the Third International* (FIG. 60). This was constructed as a laminated wooden spiral and supported by two-by-fours. Translated into steel on a larger scale, it would have resulted in certain disaster. The inability to enlarge a form from one size to another in the same

155

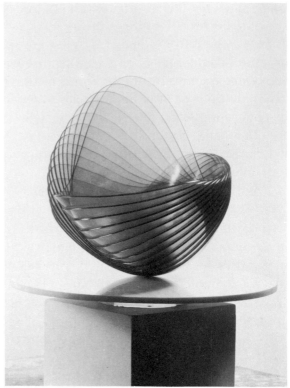

60. Vladimir Tatlin, *Monument to the Third International*, 1920.

61. Deborah de Moulpied, *Form No. 4*, 1960.

material has been one of the few engineering problems which has seriously concerned sculptors.

The purity of an "organic" structure wedded to highly sculptural form has almost totally been taken over by engineers and architects. As building shapes have become visually more dynamic and sculptural, the sculptor has withdrawn from any commitment to create logical structures; rather, he has recognized the value of creating illogically, leaving engineering competency to the experts. This has not resulted in an altogether happy division of charges. Some sculptors have envied the power of engineers, while many critics have blamed architects for trying to create sculpture instead of architecture.

In the past fifteen years shell forms have come into their own as part of the new architecture. Improvements in ferro-concrete techniques and calculating have made practically any stable form in single or double curvature an engineering possibility. Both in design and in the workmanship of constructing concrete forms shells demand the utmost precision. For a smaller, nonfunctional shell it is instructive to look at a form created in heat-molded

156

vinyl. *Form No. 4* (FIG. 61) by Deborah de Moulpied is a series of thirteen transparent plastic shells nested into one another. Loosely parabolic in form, their semiflexibility permits shape retention while producing none of the stress problems produced by inverted, large-scale shells. This plastic sculpture embodies no "form follows function" maxim; if it makes sense, it does so strictly for visual reasons. The contrast is obvious between the analytical-minimal solutions of architecture and sculpture which produces metaphors that are most frequently anti- or a-structural.

One important device could be termed *enjambment*. First used by the English romantic poets, enjambment is a metrical device for destroying the one-line one-idea fixation of the rhymed couplet. Thoughts were designed to end in the middle of a line instead of at the end. Ideas thus employed were interlocked with the metric structure of the poem.

Enjambment in sculpture, by which the eye picks up the disjointed path of a line, functions more erratically than in literature. Julio Gonzalez's masterful use of wrought iron included the continual break and juxtaposition of linear elements in ever-changing relationships. For instance, *Maternity* (FIG. 62) presents an abrupt right-angle break at its heavy center bar. As the eye moves from there, it is confronted at the breast with an overlapping break that continues to the head. The head in turn is a thin curved wire welded, not on top, but tangential to the neck.

A more sensational example of enjambment appears with Isamu Noguchi's *The Cry* (FIG. 63). The attempt is made to relate three forms by seemingly repealing the laws of gravity, along with the idea of structural connectivity. A different form of enjambment is indicated by David von Schlegell's *Needle* (FIG. 64). In this instance, the great thirty-six-foot-long needle form is contained and its momentum slowed by two shieldlike disks which are deftly held in place by hinges and braces.

Visually insecure and illogical connections have become the stock in trade of the sculptor—and an important part of the vernacular of the new formalism, termed by some critics "Concrete Expressionism." What typifies this vein is that it is scaleless, imposing in mass, industrially finished, room-oriented, and adapted from a structural idiom which could be termed "formalism of the absurd." Some of the best exponents of this are Robert Grosvenor (see Chapter One, FIG. 19), Mark Di Suvero, Ronald Bladen, Robert Murray, David Weinrib, and Kenneth Snelson (FIG. 65). In the case of Snelson, where the artist has actually invented a new engineering principle (discontinuous compression and continuous tension structures), it is not so much irrationality that characterizes his constructions as a type of rational approach to building space frames which is so divergent from all previously

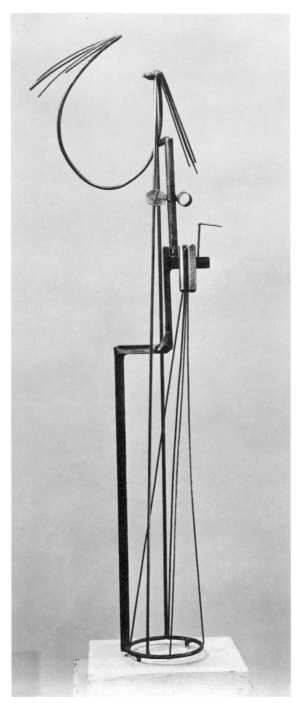

62. Julio Gonzalez, *Maternity*, 1933.

63. Isamu Noguchi, *The Cry*, 1962.

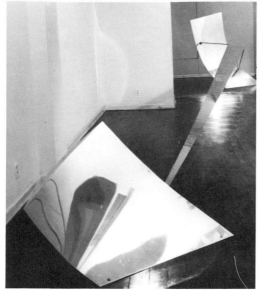

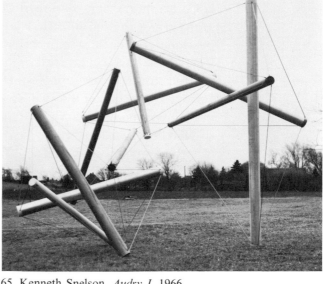

64. David von Schlegell, *Needle*, 1967.

65. Kenneth Snelson, *Audry I*, 1966.

known types of construction—even after twenty years of use—that it still seems illogical.

Except for the matter of stability, structure is not the province of sculpture. While it may flirt with structural theory, sculpture becomes overtly literal and loses its validity once it merely interprets structure. Also, it would seem, irrational devices for joining sculpture together become by constant repetition "rational." So-called irrationality is mainly a matter of timing and infrequency. Sculpture which is principally antistructural, and which demonstrates extreme effort to provide more drastic antistructural solutions, suggests that it may be the fundamental nature of sculpture to mirror its man-made-ness in erratic and wayward forms.

Optical Properties of Sculpture

While many of the older formal attributes of sculpture have declined in usefulness, one means of visual ordering has not. In the past decade the tacit conviction has arisen that light—not form—determines our perception of sculpture.

Just ten years ago, writing about the "optical properties" of sculpture would have seemed a very curious, if not oblique, approach to an art based primarily on the ordering of physical mass. Yet it no longer does. This underlines the great discrepancy between the way individual sculptors actually conceived of and *saw* their works, and their bits of poetic effusion dropped

159

into the ears of favored critics for public consumption. With some of the latest sculptural innovations it is now apparent that many of the greatest sculptors of the recent past saw their works quite analytically, in fact dispassionately, for their optical effects created *purely as light-reflecting sources*. Finally we have begun to look at older sculpture with a new appreciation derived from recent conclusions. Those outlooks which crystallized in Europe by the end of the 1950's as New Tendency rationalism, were elevated into the oversimplification of Op Art by the critical and curatorial powers of New York in 1964.

Students of sculpture could look toward Constructivist, Neo-Plastic, and other visual-technical experimentation as the embryo for these precise, controlled attempts to create reasonably detached optical experiences. However, the movement toward an optical sculpture, as opposed to one defined mainly by volume, has been in progress for the better part of a century and in practically all styles: Cubist, Dada organic, geometric, Surrealist organic, Expressionist, etc. Its impetus has been a slowly growing realization that light, controlled by color, transparency, or reflection—or a combination of the three—is one of the sculptor's most evocative stimuli. As the need to control light (for we perceive forms in terms of their light-emitting properties) gained priority, the tendency grew to construct works *solely designed as modulators of light*. Moholy-Nagy to the contrary, until the 1960's not many sculptors perceived the problem that directly.

Beginning with the plight of Narcissus, reflectivity has been one of the most primitive and hypnotic transmitters of light. Reflection is a consciousness-expanding phenomenon which holds its sacred fire in the bodies of jewels, water splashes, polished metals, ice formations, and, of course, the moon. In his notebooks Baudelaire often seemed aware of the transcendent emotions conveyed by brilliant reflections (1956, p. 179): "What I have always liked in the theatre, from my childhood to the present time, is the *chandelier*—a beautiful object, luminous, crystalline, complicated, circular and symmetrical."

If the chandelier was the nineteenth-century symbol of perfect, inviolate being, the same presence has made Brancusi's *Bird in Space* (see Chapter One, FIG. 8) an arch image of our century. Designed for the natural lighting of Brancusi's studio clerestory windows, the *Bird* seems to distend and then contract narrow bands of light along its vertical surfaces. The sharp-angled truncation at the top of the *Bird*, a vestigial indication of an opened beak, is really more than a decisive termination; its flat surface is a planar reflector, catching the full force of the sun above. The eye moves up the sculpture to a climax of downward reflected light. Brancusi also used reflective light as a workman's tool. As he polished his bronze forms by hand, every tiny surface imperfection was revealed, far better than by any mechanical device.

Early reflectivity, from artists such as Archipenko, Epstein, and Rudolf Belling, was a ramification of the mechanistic aesthetic used in its most obvious form. There were exceptions. Oskar Schlemmer's work as director of the Bauhaus stage came to an aesthetic and technical climax with his *Metall-Tanz* production in 1929. A single dancer, Karle Grosch, held polished metal spheres as the semimechanical choreography of her dance was reflected in the "house of mirrors" surrounding her. While not sculpture in the narrow sense, it was the first systematic use by a sculptor of reflection as a moving phenomenon.

In the late 1930's Jean Arp made the initial bronze castings for his plaster *Concretions.* When polished, the forms resulted in soft, undulant, shifting reflections, a perfect implementation of the vitalist viewpoint. From slight head or body movements, an observer could pick up dozens of minute light pulsations. The round gradual surfaces, then sudden points and knife edges give Arp's convex-concave surfaces a very real elusiveness (see Chapter Two, FIG. 29).

Some postwar American sculpture (beginning in the late 1940's and moving through the 1950's) has used what Herbert Read has termed the "glitter principle." Instead of deriving reflection from a continuous, coherent mass of metal, the sculptor conceived of a fragmented sculpture through semi-random, reflective surfaces positioned in spatial configurations. Lippold, Lassaw, and Bertoia have used this idea in open wire and sheet-metal constructions. Harry Bertoia's altar construction (1954) for the Massachusetts Institute of Technology's Interdenominational Chapel consists of many small steel squares covered with brazing brass, pitched at odd angles and attached to taut wires suspended from ceiling to floor.

Around 1954 José de Rivera began a series of tubular steel constructions mounted on flat disks and turned by low-revolution motors. Purely as linear outline *Brussels Construction* (FIG. 66) presents many configurations in turning. All too often this sculpture is displayed under diffused light, rendering the reflections of polished stainless-steel meaningless. In dim illumination with one or two spotlights it assumes a very different character. Tiny spots of light move along the nearly invisible surface of the steel tube. These swell and diminish as they glide from heavy to thin sections of the tube. Almost like an electron quantum jump, these points of light seem to disappear only to reappear instantly on another surface of the construction.

Over forty years ago the painter Picabia posed a physical notion of the absolute in the following arrangement: two identical mirrors separated a foot or two from each other would be placed face to face. For Picabia they

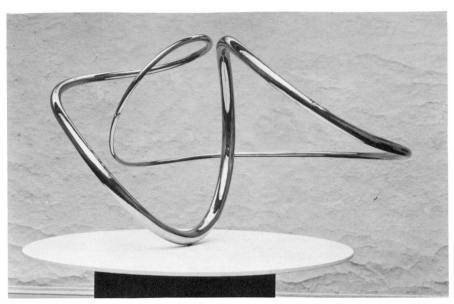

66. José de Rivera, *Brussels Construction*, 1958.

expressed—because of reciprocal and infinite reflection—the unity of noth-ingness. Mirrors, the beguiling toys of artists for hundreds of years, have become less objects of metaphysical speculation and more recently devices for breaking down spatial perception.

Distorted reflectivity as a mode of expression has in the past ten years become a widespread space-expanding technique. Some who have used mir-ror surfaces to effect are the Swiss sculptor Christian Megert, who in 1961 constructed some eighteen models of space with no beginning or end; Heinz Mack, who began reliefs of slotted, creased, and punched aluminum in the late 1950's; H. C. Westermann, who invented (1962) a type of construction housing many panes of partially mirrored glass endlessly reflecting the in-terior spaces; Lucas Samaras, with the (1966) *Mirror Room;* Larry Bell, with glass box constructions which nearly dissolve into invisibility in the feat of optical titillation (FIG. 59); and Hans Breder, with hand-manipulated alumi-num cube constructions (FIG. 67).

Many years have passed since Rodin put his hand to his breast and al-legedly uttered, "I know it here that they did not color it," in reference to the ancient Greek practice of painting their marble sculpture. Until a half-dozen years ago the inhibition against polychromed sculpture was all but unbreakable. Precisely because their work was not in the tradition of Classi-

67. Hans Breder, *Untitled*, 1966.

cal sculpture, groups like the Dadaists, Constructivists, and various Cubists had the option of coloring their work, and did so.

In general, polychromy has returned to sculpture not by frontal assault on the taboos against coloring stone or metal, but by the gradual adoption of painting techniques already accepted on everyday commercial objects. Moreover, as painting reached out after an actual third dimension the result was inevitable. Polychromy has steadily developed as sculptors have appropriated materials in which painted surfaces are standard treatment. The trend has been away from the "hot" involvement of natural bronze and marble and toward the impervious "coolness" of synthetic coverings. As the use of cosmetics has become not just an industrial strategy, but a way of viewing life, assemblage and pop values have unquestionably helped to undermine the aesthetic prejudices of the sculptor. In an incredibly short time the question has changed from "Do I dare paint sculpture?" to "Do I dare not paint it?" As Sidney Geist points out (1966, p. 93), the sculptor ends by asking the rhetorical but reasonable question, What is more "colored," a blue-painted figure in stone or a figure sculpture in natural white marble?

Color seems to have made its entrance into modern sculpture according to a pattern of conservative acceptance with patinas winning approval before other more obvious forms of coloring. Oswald Spengler in *The Decline of the*

West provides an intriguing function for the patina. When men of the Renaissance uncovered statues of Classical Greece and found them green and black with a scale of oxide residue, they did not clean or polish the metal sculpture; in time, reaction to the tones became a mixture of awe and longing. Left in their natural state, these sculptures represented to Faustian (modern Western) man some few remaining fragments of a past which was gone forever. For Spengler, the chemical action of patina represented *mortality*, a remembrance that death had taken ideas and objects once vital. Unlike the gleam of polished metal or stone, the darkened surfaces produced by patina emanate a form world of splendid decay.

Gradually through the twentieth century patina became less identified with classicism and more attached to the idea of "natural coloring"—coloring that was not offensive because it did not "cover" a natural surface but was the chemical reaction of acids applied to bare metal. The vitalist-biotic idiom was especially susceptible to this line of reasoning. Steadily through the 1950's both Roszak and Lassaw took full advantage of the fact that chemical patinas could produce a vast array of colors. When Shakespeare speaks in one poem of the magic of "sea-changes" he refers to the natural reaction of salt water on all objects immersed over a period of time; the results are often surprisingly vivid. Instead of the somber blacks, browns, and blue-greens characteristic of Classical and Neoclassical sculpture, the modern biotic idiom used chemical patinas almost like paint, simulating the vivid contrasts of botanical and undersea coloring. Roszak especially has produced some striking polychrome sculpture looking as if just dredged up from out of the sea.

In quite another sense patina has been more subtly used in the vitalistic idiom to simulate the characteristics of growth. Though it is not apparent from the accompanying photograph, one example is Will Horwitt's bronze *Growth* (FIG. 68). This work consists of a double form patined black; a biotic and irregular "soft cube" rests on top of a slightly swelled but more regular cube shape. Some of the corners of the upper form are aggressively pointed —similar to Arp's metaphor of young tissue or bud emerging from a rounded cellular mass. To clarify the idea, Horwitt has removed some patina from the sharpened corners so that they stand naked and bright—more or less like the tender shoots of a plant. Paint on sculpture now runs the gamut from sedate, mat plastic finishes to rather nasty coatings of orange lead chromate. Paint as an expressive dimension now appears much more at ease than half a century ago on the self-conscious polychromed sculptures of Archipenko. Though certainly few later attempts at polychromy match the dignity and

68. Will Horwitt, *Growth*, 1959.

elegance of Archipenko's *Seated Figure* (1913), this remains one of his rare successes in the fusion of form and color.

The Constructivists, and in general most formally-oriented sculptors, used color with the abandon of industrial designers. Color is a way of discriminating one part of a system from another. The idea of color coding in factory interiors and for electronic components has caught on in the new "formal expressionism," so that there are literally no rules, no present restrictions on polychromy. Stylistics oscillate wildly between monochrome (i.e., all black, all gray, or all white shows) and technicolor fantasy. The fact remains that where color has no boundaries it ceases to have meaning.

It was the destiny of polychromy that the sculpture would draw its chief sustenance from the folk arts. This is apparent in Gerald Laing's *Tunnel* (FIG. 69). Laing, working mostly in aluminum plate, has appropriated the entire *Weltanschauung* of the California custom-car designer. His works are not so much sculptures as totemic homages to "technique" for its own sake:

69. Gerald Laing, *Tunnel*, 1966.

chrome plate and mirror-polished aluminum, iridescent baked-enamel finishes, bronze "flake" glass finishes with metal chips embedded in clear vinyl, etc. Laing represents the other end of the spectrum: where form becomes the means of implementing finish. Even more clearly, *form becomes finish.*

If the trend has increased toward more color and reflectivity, the result has been the development of a cult devoted to optical deception and excitation. This, rightly or wrongly, has been interpreted as the salvation of sculpture. In the broadest sense it is a reaction against the vitalist myth that the psyche of sculpture is buried within the object itself. Furthermore, it suggests that what is important about sculpture lies on its surface for optical examination. In a very special way the desire to refute the vitalistic myths lingers, and even grows, making form and matter lose their substantiality. Form, in effect, *is* what we make it *appear* to be.

CHAPTER FOUR

Form Exhaustion and the Rise of Phenomenalism

A Résumé

One could suggest as Hegel did that the plastic arts have been dying since the end of the Renaissance, and that the spirit behind the newer forms is merely the effluvium of an overriding technical materialism. Or again, as some of the formalist aestheticians (Bell, Fry, and Osborne) were to maintain, perhaps sculpture was just beginning to show its true potentialities. Undeniably, the connection between sculpture and the new technology was, and is, critical. Sculpture has moved from material idealization of human form in Classical Greece to the construction of images which are, according to one's point of view, either the residual remains or the guiding aesthetic of a radically developing scientific technology.

The characteristics of sculpture can be summarized in the fixed attributes of the Classical world: place, position, immobility, parts, proportion, and static homage to the human condition—in a word, the creation of immutable ideals through *objects*. Sculpture increasingly has forsaken its anthropomorphic ideal to become a continuum of steadily changing ideas about the world. Sculpture's status as object continues to be deceptive because it leads us to believe that its substantial attributes—in spite of so many losses—are inert materiality: weight, mass, and form. This too has vanished and *the dialectical tension within twentieth-century sculpture remains its steady gravitation toward seeming immateriality (through forms of attenuated and unstable materiality), while at the same time resisting this trend.*

With more than half a century of nonrepresentational sculpture behind us, Hegel's indication that great sculpture was the highest synthesis of the human spirit embodied in concrete objects may still hold—if we are willing to agree that such an aim can be realized without imitating the human figure. The connection is by no means clear at this time, but there are still many implications that vital (not vitalistic) sculpture is linked to an expression of biological life. One of the underlying meanings of early abstract sculpture was the concept that life could no longer be characterized or idealized according to the disciplines of mimeticism, and that perhaps a more "analytical" approach to form held the key to biological duplication. The swift emergence of the machine as *the* prime object embracing dynamic values was an alternative to biological sources that very few sculptors cared to face. For those who did, their connections with the machine ranged from silent worship to overt animosity.

As a philosophical strategy, the vitalist sculptors insisted on the presence of "essential" spirits dwelling within their works; they reiterated that it was not the *shape* of a sculpture that counted, but some undefined "inner life" buried within a sculpture's psychic and material being. Vitalism provided the empathetic underpinnings of a faith verging on religiosity for those craving belief in a transcendent art form. And for a not inconsiderable and sophisticated laity, vitalism did become a partial surrogate for traditional religious values.

Sculpture analysis in the present century has been achieved through formalism. More self-consciously than previous cultures, we have learned through the visual apprehension of form to penetrate some of the psychical secrets of our culture; we have learned, as Paul Klee observed, "the prehistory of the visible."

This has hardly been the only function of formalism. This technique is not just the prehistory of the visible, it is the prehistory of scientific technique itself—that part made possible by visual study. As in the case of vitalism, advances in scientific conceptualization have nullified the continued vigor of formalism. In a world of invisible values formalism has quickly become a language with a gradually contracting spectrum of possibilities and variations. We observed that the precipitate collapse of classical formal values was succeeded by a less materially substantial "optical" formalism. Even this formalism of light plasticity and surface finish seemed to have exploitable limitations. As a result, *invention*, the creative force which has propelled formalism, has succeeded in pushing "sculpture" further and further out of the scope of its original domain.

Academicism in Modern Sculpture

At present it is difficult for anyone to imagine the state of three-dimensional art just prior to the Second World War. It was certainly not what books published in the past ten years would have us believe. When Carola Giedion-Welcker's *Contemporary Sculpture* first appeared in 1937, her thesis was definitely a minority opinion. However, the text and photographs for this book were an incredibly valid and accurate estimation of significant twentieth-century sculpture as we see it today.

By comparison, a typical anthology was Stanley Casson's *Sculpture of Today* (1939). This is an above average presentation of the more tasteful and popular modes of stylized realism, along with a handful of the more well-known abstractionists—though, on the whole, what passed for modern sculpture in 1939, and what found its way into innumerable studies under the guise of "modern," now seems beyond comprehension. Digging these volumes out of the library stacks composes a salutary exercise in discovering the brainwashing effects of official taste change. Strangely, we have a fairly good idea of how people dressed, their furniture, and their automobiles from the 1930's; but, almost as if a political decree were in effect, sculpture of the era has been banished indefinitely to the cellars. What actually prevailed in the 1930's was, at best, a fairly lifeless and antiseptic realism cleaned up a bit with streamlining; at worst, it deserved a title later awarded by John Canaday, "Fascist Louis XVI." This was a time when Paul Manship, Ivan Meštrović, Frank Dobson, Jacob Epstein, Carl Milles, Lee Laurie, and William Zorach represented the most proficient, or at least the most pyrotechnically ambitious, talents of a generation that, frankly, was at a loss to explain the modern idiom; the modernists *were* strange and hopefully they would soon go away or die out. Yet, from the vantage point of the present, what we now call "modern" resembled then only the visible peak of an iceberg. Today it seems as if that superabundance of figurative carving and casting that filled the reputable museums and collections never existed at all.

Modern sculpture has profoundly unsettled art historians oriented toward stylistics and stylistic cycles—not because of its radicalism, but because it has managed to give so few clues to its direction. Even fifty-five years later, sculpture outside the circle of twentieth-century representationalism still does not lend itself to the cyclical criteria of Wölfflinian stylistics; rather, it seems to move completely beyond the ken of style consciousness. Style no longer relates to the epoch, but serves the collective whim of an ever-shifting design consciousness. Style has become meaningless as the way of explaining what are essentially a series of technological reifications. Hildebrand's claim that sculpture was concerned with the engagement of matter and space was prophetic in its day—truly an illumination—though one that has already outlived its fulfillment by more than twenty years. For artists it is a very human form of self-deception to see continued progress in an art movement by a kind of *post-facto* recognition of once valid aesthetics. However, in the past thirty years there have been virtually no new sculpture advances concerning the interpenetration of space and matter. Until a short time ago, the cant about spatial awareness, spatial counterpoise, spatial ambiguity and spatial integration continued to fill the catalogues of every gallery. Space as a subject constituted half the rhetoric of modern sculpture plasticism. Yet for the generations following the 1930's, and until a very few years ago, it was impossible to admit that gradual stagnation has finally overcome a once brave and fertile idea. Presently we exist on what now seem to be ancient verities, sculptural axioms formulated about sculpture only two generations ago but already on the brink of exhaustion. A little over thirty-five years ago the art historian R. H. Wilenski stated (1932, p. 163): "Essential sculpture is sculpture which has the same kind of meaning as the sphere, cube and cylinder."

Wilenski, among others, thought that the limits of sculpture reductivism had to end with a dependence on Euclidean realities. The sphere, cube, and cylinder *were* the natural reductive essentials of sculpture. These seemed to contain properties that could not be transposed or made congruent with other properties. Later truths concerning topological flexibility, and the plasticity of the painted surface, have only marginally affected Wilenski's original premise. He drove at a more than obvious and literal truth. Wilenski's target aimed at the universal ideal that has concerned every abstract sculptor: namely, each sculptor hopes to see in his work a form so irreducible, so logical and new in conception, that it would seem implausible to another observer that it had not always existed. This is the "image" magic of Brancusi's and Moore's best work. Not surprisingly, young sculptors have followed in the reductivist footsteps of the modern masters—hoping futilely to reduce their forms to even more elementary dimensions. What seemed to have been overlooked is that the number of unique solutions expressing minimal or elementary three-dimensional form is, by the nature of classical solid geometry, quite small. Nonetheless, it has been the reflex of all art movements that followers try to solve formal problems *only after* optimal solutions are self-evident in the work of innovators.

The new postwar academy of modern sculpture has had no center, no Royal School of Art, no Beaux Arts, no Art Student's League. Instead, it has functioned completely as a correspondence school where a dozen elaborately illustrated and comprehensively written art magazines detail precisely what is being thought, bought, and shown all over the world. Admission to this school costs the price of subscription. Graduation and honors vary, but usually rest on an artist's work favorably appearing in one of the select periodicals.

Until just two or three years ago the modern academy of sculpture consisted of the mass production of varieties of "hard" and "soft" geometry and modes of vitalistic sculpture. In a review of American sculpture in 1964 the critic Max Kozloff dismissed the biotic school with the following remark (May–June, 1964, p. 24): "Over-all though, the once pervasive and boring totemistic or insectile clichés are waning in favor of a muscular and physically or chromatically adventurous kind of statement."

Possibly this is being inordinately hard on a second- and third-generation movement that, not so long ago, boasted representatives like César Baldaccini, Seymour Lipton, and Germaine Richier. Kozloff's reaction, though, is directed toward the hordes of imitative admirers. Doubtless he, like many others, began to realize that there was something absurd about walking into a group show and being confronted with whole nests of giant bronze and welded steel bugs, a fusion of Walt Disney and Kafka via some apprenticeship course in welding.

The biomorphic-mineral influence reached a peak during the early 1960's, and with this plethora came the *reductio ad absurdum* of the vitalistic idiom. Thumbing through one of the recent "young sculptors under (specify any age up to fifty) shows," this author was struck by the universal tenacity of the biomorphic mannerist tendency. Pictured in the catalogue were the same cactuslike wire constructions, bubbly cast bronzes with pock-marked openings, open sheet-metal structures with sheathlike leaf forms, brazed rod structures with nobby root endings, bulbous potatolike carvings locked together like crossbreeding gone astray, cleaved rock totems jutting up from minimal footings, relics of informalism as coal slag on polished mahogany, archaic bronze flowers chemically polychromed, metallic seed pods banded together over elegant bud shapes in veined marble, organic "space frames" of woven wire and burnt steel tendons, vegetal-animal conglomerates in fiber and hydrocalcite, limestone randomly caressed to resemble enlarged beach pebbles, bronze-coated driftwood and, as they say in show business, "a host of other favorites."

All this is Klee's prophecy fulfilled with a vengeance after his observation (1961, p. 453): "To achieve the same as nature, though only in parallel. Not to compete with nature but to produce something that says: it is as nature." The result of this proliferation of vitalism is a semi-official academicism as deeply entrenched as that of Gérôme or Falguière. There is one exception: instantaneous communication has made any hint of a school a signal for revolution. Simply public consciousness of biomorphic academicism is a sign of impending change.

It was said that Abstract Expressionism died at 12 A.M., January 1, 1960. No such precise dating has been suggested for vitalism but one suspects that the *coup de grâce* may have been delivered with the Gallery Gertrude

Stein's exhibition of *No-Sculptures* during the spring of 1964. These *No-Sculptures* by Sam Goodman were literally the end result of the biomorphic vocabulary. The show featured twenty-three stone castings of excretions, ranging from small, perhaps human size, samples to a five-foot offering worthy of an unwell pachyderm. As tactile, organic counterparts, these elemental offerings were a succinct reply to Wilenski's dictum that (1932, p. 163) "Essential sculpture is sculpture which has the same kind of meaning as the sphere, cube and cylinder."

Pure Form Becomes Pure Experience

Stated earlier, one of the chief dilemmas confronting sculpture has been the gradual annihilation of scientific vitalism. One need not possess a Hegelian discernment for cultural parallelism to sense the intimate chronology and the need for a metaphysical bias that lingered between vitalism in science and in sculpture. At the height of its scientific respectability and poetic eloquence, vitalism gave an ideal solution for an iconic dilemma—one constantly revived by scientific and philosophical criticism. Vitalism, the ancient way of maintaining psychical contact with objects both animate and inanimate, was too delicate an instrument of faith to withstand the scrutiny of modern rationalism. In a like manner, modern scientific analysis has precipitated a decline in classical scientific idealism. Such a situation has revealed a universe which appears to be sensually irrational calling for the suspension of our normal space-time sensibilities, but, nevertheless, is understandable only through scientific symbolism and computation.

Some critics speak of a sculpture renaissance based on color, new materials, and a synthesis of present formalistic principles. The previous chapter shows the unfounded optimism of a formalism continued along those lines. The decline of formalism is the decline of a world fashioned to operate on a strictly visual-geometrical level. For the doubtful, compare the inside of a pocket-sized transistor radio with the workings of a spring-wound watch. The geometry inside the radio is the orderly assembly of electronic coding and circuit miniaturization, not causal, coherent relationships as in the watch.

In an essay, "Einstein and the Crisis of Reason," the philosopher Maurice Merleau-Ponty (1960, p. 196) touches upon the stability of the Cartesian rationalist's outlook and Einstein's inability to reconcile his own classical sympathies with the sensory irrationality of modern wave mechanics. Einstein is depicted as being philosophically at odds with the scientific generation following him; Merleau-Ponty, toward the end of the essay, reveals his own desire for a world where an all-powerful science does not exclude other essential forms of analytical perception: "If only we were willing to regain the concrete world of our perception with its horizons, and to situate the constructions of physics in it, physics could freely develop its paradoxes without authorizing unreason."

Merleau-Ponty's suggestion postdates an awareness that had its start at the beginning of the present century with Edmund Husserl's *Logical Investigations*. To that philosopher, as with others, a "crisis in European science" was already evident. Objectivity appeared to be the highest epistemological goal of science and Husserl saw the need for studying the mechanisms of consciousness by which objectivity was reached. The raw materials of phenomenology became the modes of consciousness itself. Husserl observed (as we have in relation to formalism) that science tended to produce an increasingly abstract, if not artificial, picture of reality for itself, derived less and less from sensory data and more by systems of formal logic. Husserl did not question the validity of the scientist's techniques or his results, although he did find cause to presage the possibility that an unchallenged scientific reality could be harmful to the culture as a whole.

As an antidote, Husserl formulated his *absolute consciousness*, a state of mind whereupon "pure" conscious experience could be distilled unhindered by all previous experiences, abstractions, or presuppositions. This process Husserl called *phenomenological reduction*. Consciousness, as defined by *intention*, could be taken increment by increment and inspected for its own sake. Reaching beyond the domain of empirical psychology, *transcendental phenomenology* is an analytical method that, on its own terms, could be used to investigate dreams, memories, obsessions, sensual impressions of all kinds—in fact, anything that registered *intentionally* in human consciousness. *Reduction*, by which these processes are observed, becomes a bewildering process for anyone but a philosopher trained in the phenomenological method. In part, this involves a rejection of the *natural attitude* of cognition, which serves, according to the phenomenologist, to obscure the perceiver from the true nature of his perceptions.

In the years during and following the Second World War, Merleau-Ponty's writings reflected some of the most important elements of Husserl's thinking. Moreover, because of his fundamental questions concerning the everyday modes of perception, Merleau-Ponty has had a special and growing relevance for writers and painters—and very recently, with the rise of Object Art, for sculptors also. As indicated by the title of this chapter, this has resulted in a shift of emphasis: away from a basis concern for form reduction and formal relationships and toward the varieties of experience which surround the perception of form. Thus Merleau-Ponty has written at length on problems of phenomenology that deal with the arts as alterations of the visual process.

Traditionally the sculptor has concerned himself with the making of objects—even when those objects served only to objectify theories or non-concrete expressions of reality. In general, the sculptor has given little thought to the fact that the viewer not only is free to but must reconstruct the sculpture for himself. In this respect, the act of perception and bodily gesture while standing among objects—and in turn being perceived by other beings—forms the locus from which Merleau-Ponty has developed his phenomenology. The perceiving person constantly interacts with objects, others, and self to create a closed conceptual unity. Given a limited number of perceptual experiences, how does our world picture manage to transcend our actual knowledge of reality? This is a question which acts as a leitmotif through much of Merleau-Ponty's philosophy.

He seemed to suggest that logical analysis is fine for directing and understanding the processes of a computer, but complex organic minds need a more supple method for the inspection of perceptual activities. Regarding perception, list structures might adequately define an "object" for a computer. Yet Merleau-Ponty continually stressed the fact that perception allows us to know far more about things than we realize, or than we are given by inductive analysis. Therefore, a phenomenology of perception intends (1960, p. xiii) "to give to organisms their own manner of handling the world...." Merleau-Ponty's classic illustration of an artist relying on a fragmented "real" perception instead of abstract conceptualization from which to paint his pictures is Paul Cézanne. But in spite of Cézanne's compositional idiosyncrasies, most of the short history of nonrepresentational sculpture has revolved around the mechanics of *seeing* according to the logic of formal analysis. Perhaps a special crisis had to appear before sculptors would begin to consider *seeing* as essentially an existential act by the observer. This special type of seeing is more attuned to situations than the construction of idealistic images. Through this approach the sculpted form is not an end in itself, but only the means—the vehicle—by which perceptual experiences are made possible.

It is no secret that since 1960 the vitalist and formal-reductivist tendencies of sculpture have approached exhaustion. Sculptors who chose not to investigate kinetics or some kind of representationalism were in search of a new post-formalist aesthetic. The urge to create "objects," that is, three-dimensional entities that did not resemble sculpture—that were even a-sculptural—had been building up for some time. In London this was best expressed by the enigmatic polychromed constructions of Phillip King (FIG. 70) and

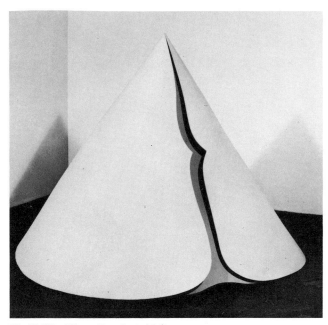

70. Phillip King, *Rosebud*, 1962.

William Tucker. These artists created free-wheeling, polychromed affairs which, on the surface at least, seemed to have little to do with the much more restricted and self-conscious sculpture that first made an appearance in New York City during the 1963–1964 season. American names connected with what shortly became known as "Object" or "Minimal" sculpture were Donald Judd (FIG. 71), Robert Morris, Ann Truitt, Lyman Kipp, Robert Murray, Tony Smith (FIG. 72), and Dan Flavin. The works of the first two of these artists have stood out in quality, uniqueness, and because of their occasional theoretical pronouncements.

Object or Minimal sculpture, if nothing else, is a rejection of "open" sculpture, pseudo-mechanistic sculpture, organically-derived sculpture, Neo-Plastic sculpture, "dynamically" poised sculpture—or any of the other forms of latent kineticism that have characterized three-dimensional conceptualization. Object sculpture admits to being itself—nothing else. Similar to other forms of nonobjective sculpture, it seeks a separate identity unattached to all influences except the space in which it stands. However, this was the claim of the Constructivists. The aura of scientific idealism that pervades their work gives it an iconic identity, an "image" flavor that denies all claims of independence.

If one looks at Object sculpture with all the preconceptions of the modern idiom, one might very likely reject it out of hand as a celebration of

175

71. Donald Judd, View of exhibition at Green Gallery,
December 17, 1963–January 11, 1964, New York.

the "aesthetics of sterility"—a term used (1965) by Max Kozloff. All the
words attached at various times to the Object idiom: sterile, cool, stillborn,
massive, clumsy, space-devouring, antiseptic, and minimal—to name the few
that come to mind—imply some deliberate attempt to shun emotional
challenge and retinal involvement—to produce instead one more stage in the
formal-reductivist syndrome. Reductive canvases by Barnett Newman,
Clyfford Still, and Ad Reinhardt produce a pregnant expansiveness that wills
the viewer to observe and scan whether he expects to find something or not.
The trick is to leave enough clues, making perception seductive but not satisfying enough to cause the resolution of a precise image. Object sculpture
abandons overt imagery by a different route. Conceived intellectually, Object

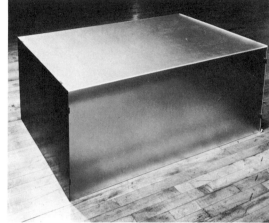

72. Tony Smith, *Amaryllis*, 1965.

73. Donald Judd, *Untitled*, 1964.

sculpture depends upon its lack of associated meanings and trivialized format
for an identity. It does attempt to present meaning as a series of perceptual
experiences. Many of these are triggered by inconsistencies and slight ambiguities which put in question the harmony of *all* the physical attributes which
make up the object. These include weight, color, texture, mass density,
materials, and *Gestalt* complexity. As suggested by Merleau-Ponty in his
essay "The Film and the New Psychology" (1948, pp. 48–59), the meaning of
an object lies not in the sum-total record of shots devoted to it (a list structure
of attributes), but in the concretion of a temporal *Gestalt*, an aggregate of
sequential views that distort each other like the inconsistencies in a Cézanne
painting.

Take Judd's stainless-steel and pink-orange plexiglas box, *Untitled*
(FIG. 73). The two stainless-steel ends are held against the plastic edges of the
sides by five tension tie-wires inside. Because of the internal reflections, a
number of mirror illusions are made possible, but the purpose of this box
is not to evoke the fragmented interior spaces of Bell, Westermann, or Lucas
Samaras. On the contrary, the simplicity of this rectangular-shaped object
induces the viewer to become involved with the properties of the box as a
rectangular container. No clue makes any other approach possible. In fact,

the more minimal an object, the less opportunity for an observer to play the game of admiration, so much a part of the image fixation of traditional sculpture. Stripped bare of all "artistic" complexity and ideal accretions, one is confronted with the box's real geometry as opposed to its given appearances. Merleau-Ponty speaks of watching a cube in perspective while *knowing intellectually* that ideally it has six sides and twelve edges; he states, (1960, p. 50), "I cannot *see* a cube as its geometrical definition presents it: I can only *think* it" (Italics added).

But seeing something *intellectually* as a mental construct with all of its geometry intact is a perceptual habit acquired by every person educated in the Western tradition. Judd, perhaps, forces us to see ourselves seeing objects unencumbered by the analytical games and value judgments promoted through art education. The perception of the box develops and we have the option of sensing that development. As with all aesthetic approaches, aligning Object sculpture to a phenomenalist point of view has its pitfalls. Placing such an immense burden on the observer eventually allows the sculptor to present an empty gallery space for inspection (which has already been tried several times). Or he can simply ask gallery goers to observe each other or ask them to bring an object to be observed. None of these are out of the question. Probably Object sculpture which has a chance to endure combines the phenomenalist approach with more traditional criteria.

Vitalist- and Constructivist-derived sculpture, it became apparent by the end of the 1950's, had become so absorbed with the problem of transcendent imagery that the *idée fixe* of all the makers of maimed birds and lunar apparitions became the "image" itself. Most sculptors no longer produced an *objet d'art* but sought a transcendent icon for the veneration and edification of collectors and museum officials. The problem became one of dwindling efficacy and exhausted means. Who continued to believe in the "bandaged women," the brazed totems, and shimmering apparitions that tried more and more to deny their presence as lumpish objects? Was not sculpture, as the Greeks had insisted, "*palpable* delight"? To look at Object sculpture of the 1960's as a retreat to hyperformalism is to miss its reason for being made. Classical scientific formalism, as Husserl had insisted, had rapidly become a dated picture of provisional reality. Sculpture that tried to hold on to artistic formalism had the same chance of survival as its scientific counterpart in a world ruled by invisible energy and statistical formulae.

The Object sculptors, consciously and unconsciously, were acutely aware of this crisis. Hence much of their work appears to be a blanket retreat from many of the earlier hard-won values of modern sculpture. One attempt to untie the art object from the ideal imagery of biology worship and scientific rationalism is reflected in the gallery "environments" devised by these sculptors. After the clumsy and futile attempts of a few years ago to build crawl-in and walk-in sculpture environments, the work of Judd, Morris and Flavin (FIGS. 71, 74 and Chapter Seven, FIG. 112), radiated a different sense of experiential purpose. Their work contains the implicit realization that sculptural "spaces" are meaningless unless some reason exists for physically penetrating them. Most gallery pedestals for sculpture until a few years ago were on a level with department-window display—if that. Viewers went from sculpture to sculpture like shoppers at a sale; the goal of the viewer was always the next sculpture. In contrast, *ambience* became the word that defined one's relationship to Object sculpture. To use Merleau-Ponty's term, each object "arose" through the viewer's perceptual ordering.

As the viewer walks between sculptures, he may find two or three pieces positioned so as to engage him at the same time. This is not an inspection tour with an ideal vantage point—each view has its contradictions and illuminations taken as they come. What arises from the first glance is what Merleau-Ponty called "carnal intersubjectivity." Thus, the viewer becomes aware of a set of latent and primordial truths concerning his habits of perception through the nature of the objects involved.

In the most elementary fashion Object sculpture is Optical Art—though stripped of the childish ambiguity of graphic illusionism. The object, once again we are reminded, remains at a distance giving signs of its presence. Its coldness, its impenetrability exerts the same raw presence as any other object; it makes no attempt to be understood or to come to us. We learn to appease such objects as we do the implacability of the statues of the Greek gods, in terms of their silence and inflexibility. In the present decade an evident shift is in process. Static sculpture has emerged from millenniums of transcendent idealism and now moves toward transcendent phenomenalism.

In vitalist and earlier formalist art, attraction to a given sculpture depended on what could be called a complexity-ambiguity index. All sculpture aimed at producing, not only a degree of presence, but a degree of doubt concerning its presence. This was manifested through the ambiguity of relationships. Works could easily be made ambiguous by making them complicated; but part of the success of the reductivist syndrome was that *simple* formalist works could be imbued with strong elements of visual ambiguity. And these were satisfying. Much of the rationale of Object sculpture lies in a firm grasp of this fact, hence the use of the simplest possible forms. In one article (1966, p. 44), Robert Morris has discussed the existing visual hierarchy between forms with simple and complex relationships. He

179

74. Robert Morris, View of exhibition at Dwan Gallery, Los Angeles, 1966.

gives an example in which regularity and a minimum number of qualities make the *Gestalt* of a structure conceptually graspable. However, even the most elementary of Morris's sculptures (FIG. 74) evade total and precise recall by any viewer. This unknowable aspect of even the simplest objects has been a point repeatedly stressed by the sculptors of primary forms. Beyond this, Robert Morris in his series, "Notes on Sculpture," has defined what he has termed the infrastructure of the forming and handling of objects in our culture. This he has done with a precision and insight unrivaled by all other critics of contemporary art. His main contribution has been to define the borderline between the old aesthetic ideals of illusionism and the tacit set of concerns by which we apprehend all objects fabricated and designed by modern industrial technology. This shifting set of values accounts for the severe simplicity, forced modular aspect (FIG. 75), and tendency away from anthropomorphism which defines so much abstract sculpture.

As with other sculptors sharing his concerns, Morris relies upon an abbreviated notion of phenomenalism. Through the mechanism of reflecting

75. Sol Lewitt, *Untitled*, 1966.

upon our habits of visual perception, his theory intimates that even the simplest object harbors mysteries that remain locked within its presence. Yet in all candor, beyond the domain of scientific analysis, phenomenalism cannot imbue an object with attributes which are not there. It can only force us to be aware of the chaos and multi-layered nature of our visual habits.

To summarize: Object sculpture has come in conflict with three ideas dominating modern sculpture. For one, the tacit concerns of abstract illusionism based on model theory have been challenged, if not already discarded. These have been supplanted by idealistic notions of phenomenal perception. Running closely parallel to this is a strict materialism, based on art criticism, and achieved through listing techniques and the properties of industrially produced materials. Secondly, the attempt to construct obviously static and inert objects represents an aesthetic rejection of the kinetic impulse. Finally, much of the obligation to "vitalize" sculpture—make it come to life before the viewer—has been shifted to the viewer's capacity for analyzing his private methods of seeing. It remains to be known if viewers will accept such a responsibility.

181

PART TWO

SCULPTURE AS SYSTEM

CHAPTER FIVE

Sculpture and Automata

A Continuum of Images

We are just beginning to understand the great latitude of purpose detectable in the human and animal replicas created by man in the past ten thousand years. Fetishes, idols, amulets, funeral images, dolls, waxworks, manikins, puppets, and, most dramatically, automata, all play their part in the vast substratum of figures which historians used to rank far below sculpture as a fine art. Many of these artifacts have a basis rooted, not in any Western concept of beauty, but in some very practical purpose. And only recently have the liberalizing tendencies of modern art and the discoveries of archaeology finally compelled historians to consider the aesthetic merits of thcsc and an increasing range of other anthropomorphic forms. A "history of human images," free of what the art historian Wilenski refers to as "the Greek prejudice," has yet to be written. This section does not attempt to provide that history; rather, it follows the Western development of one particular branch of subsculpture: automata.

The term subsculpture refers here to types of images aesthetically ranked below sculpture and not included in the fine arts. Already some of this subsculpture has crossed the boundary line of scholarship into the category of major art. In time the psychological motives behind the drive to create human images will assume greater importance than the supposed hierarchical levels of beauty which separate those images into minor and major art.

Automata may be defined as all seemingly self-propelled or self-animated images of animals or men. The history of automata has always run close to that of technology. Both the feats of automata and the progression of outward forms assumed by automata indicate a parallel pulse in modern art and technology. Therefore, this chapter will contain considerable mention of those assumed forms as well as other types of subsculpture, such as dolls and manikins. What must be scrutinized, and what characterizes Western culture beyond these other forms of subsculpture, is the progressive mechanization of automata. Here the aesthetic core of the Faustian urge shows itself; Western man unknowingly converges art with a universal desire to re-create life nonbiologically.

This last is an assumption which may be disputed. Nevertheless, it cannot be denied that the ultimate concern of the maker of anthropomorphic images is to "bring to life" the human-shaped entity, though not through natural biological creation. In the past this has been achieved by the metaphorical subtlety of art, by attempts at precise mimetic representation, through supposed magical properties, or, as in the case of automata, by literal movement and animation. Generally, this last embodies the fewest psychical reverberations. While it denies aesthetic-religious sensitivity, it has become the most expedient.

There is great poignancy in the fact that so many of the images fashioned are attempts to reproduce man. To some extent these invariably fail to match the qualities of higher living organisms. As the male gender plays only a brief role in procreation, the drive to create images (also technical inventions) is, in part, a sublimation of the act of birth. A reproduction of self, or of beings friendly to one's species, by nonbiological means must also be viewed as an attempt to bring ideal life into one's midst; this would be company or a presence—in an age before accelerated invention—capable of swaying fortune in the image maker's favor. Such is the psychology of fetish images, of idols, and sometimes even of puppets or dolls. It is only a step from fashioning a figure, expected to affect an owner's life, to desire for a potent image possessing the power of movement, one which can alter the convictions of an entire people. In myths and legends a recurrent theme is the turning of inert material into living tissue; there is also the converse: solidifying humans into statues. With this last goes the knowledge that flesh is transitory and painful, while static being is eternal security—yet, as with the Greek *kouroi*, touchingly in need of protection.

The story of Pygmalion begins with the sculptor's disgust with female carnality and ends with the blessings of Venus. Pygmalion fashions an ideal female figure of ivory but is not content with admiration. He becomes progressively infatuated with his creation, Galatea, which miraculously comes to life. This short tale, as told by Ovid in his *Metamorphoses*, foretells the mystical equation of all art: that with hard work and faith in divine results a creation may magically become more than the sum of the artist's energies. Though, as Ovid is careful to observe, elephant bone into lovely female flesh is not an altogether happy exchange. Deterioration and death through decay are the ultimate ends even after successful love-making.

The psychic reality of a body and mind coming alive because of sexual love was linked by Ovid to the act of sculpturing. However, the ancient methods of animating images falls somewhat short of Pygmalion's transference of passion. There were two methods for providing inert figures with a semblance of free will and autonomy. Direct human manipulation is probably the oldest, while within the history of automata proper are the gradual refinements of mechanical techniques. As for realism, waxworks and funeral images come closer to mimetic perfection than even the best classical sculpture or automata. Something else draws sculpture and automata toward one another—the joint religious and magical functions which they both shared until modern times.

As Spengler would concede, sculpture, in its quietude and static order, remains Apollonian while automata possess a Faustian drive to transcend natural limitations. Both forms of image making play with divine madness: sculpture coolly, with a sense of well-defined limit and a knowledge of probable success; but not automata, where the soul of the artist is tied to mechanical fallibility and madness lies in the indefinite possibilities of technology. Thus the machine radiates an impertinence for everything that stands still about it. It revels in drastic change.

Like the illusions of a magician, the pathos of automata lies in that they are doomed to failure, not only by physical disintegration, but in the mind of the beholder, by a final sense of inconviction. This sculpture would never tolerate. But suppose automata had been raised to the level of a fine art thousands of years ago, would we today have an aesthetic of moving statuary? Or would it have been an impossibility; for, as Arnold Toynbee maintains, mechanics cannot help but erode the soul of art? Automata since the sixteenth century have intrigued the public without frightening or intimidating them. The average person craves "safe" magic, the titillation and tiny ecstasy afforded by the occult kept securely in its cage. Gradually automata lost their divinity and were regarded as base creatures; they did what they were constructed to do and, unlike sculpture, made no seductive promises. Only an occasional philosopher, and those few scientifically curious souls who wondered about the ultimate structure of life, sought profound meaning in the making of mechanical men. It must be remembered that the most talented androids found serious acceptance as scientific marvels in an age which did not trifle with distinctions between science and technology—or for that matter with distinctions between science and art! Partially this explains the happy circumstance between sculpture and automata in the eighteenth century, a period just prior to the full effects of the technological onslaught. It was a situation in which the arts freely admitted and encouraged scientific aid. No paralytic fear of creative impedimentation yet existed. For the human intellect automata have always been a source of compelling fascination; though in terms of the emotional resonances generated automata have assumed a very secondary role to sculpture.

Egyptian Proto-Automata

Egyptian servant figures, while they might remain fixed in their poses for thousands of years, should be regarded as fledgling automata. The historian James Breasted has placed the height of the tradition of the servant sculptures in the Middle Kingdom. There, in chambers adjacent to the tombs, or sometimes next to the sarcophagus, were placed whole tableaus of retainers working at various tasks. These wooden models, at first crudely made in the Pre-Dynastic era, became literally the entourage which accompanied a rich man or powerful ruler into the next world.

The tradition for these sculptures most probably originated in the custom of mass human sacrifice carried out following the death of an important person. With the decease of the head of a large household, or a kingdom, favorite concubines and valued servants were chosen to follow their master directly to the grave. The tragic custom of consigning members of a household to the same fate as their master had severely destructive consequences for the remaining society. Providing company and assistance into the next world proved rather hard on the chosen victims. Servant images became the logical form of substitution.

Tableaus of laboring servants often unfolded within a specially constructed complex of scale-model rooms and courtyards. Many such structures still exist. In addition to showing other than the most rudimentary gestures needed for the performance of a craft, servant figures also offered the valuable function of preserving the lives of those represented. The first substitute images for servants were nearly shapeless terra-cotta forms. Painted wood became the most commonly used material for more elaborate models. Often the arms of these wood figures were pegged so they could be manipulated from the shoulders. The variety and subtlety of these work gestures give a far clearer indication of the daily lives of the Egyptian people than the stiff, hieratic portraiture of the upper classes. One could consider these wooden figures proto-automata. While not self-propelled, they do possess the option of alternate positions.

More actively, automata were used by ruling factions for magical-religious purposes. The priesthood controlled the masses, and often even the royal family. This control was accomplished through the adroit manipulation of large and small animated statues. Since priests were the only ones who could invest images with an animus or soul (called Ka), they could create either good or evil. Supernatural prediction determined a good deal of the political policy of Egypt, so that certain stone images, transformed into speaking oracles, became all-important in the politics of formulating attitudes and desires. The mechanics of making a statue speak were quite simple. A priest would secrete himself behind the image. As he spoke into a depression hollowed in the back of the figure, his voice was transmitted through a tube-like passage to a hidden opening in back of the ear of the statue. At Thebes, reportedly, there existed images capable of making gestures as they spoke. For a considerable stage in the development of religion, the dividing line between magician and priest was nonexistent.

Greek Ritual: Orgiastic and Mechanical

In Greece movable play dolls and articulate votive figures have been found that date from as early as the eighth century B.C. One bell-shaped figure with swinging legs dates from the Proto-Geometric period. This Boeotian doll has painted black-figure dancers ringing its exterior. The famous scholars of automata, Chapuis and Droz, (1958, pp. 16–17) also depict a small seated Aphrodite of the Hellenistic era. On this figure the arms swing free by means of metal pins. Some of the dolls unearthed most probably served as the consecrated offerings of adolescent girls ready to exchange their playthings for marriage. None of these are strictly automata, or even sculpture, but they do anticipate the technical facility, if not functionalism, that would mark the decline of Classical culture with the beginning of the Hellenistic era.

In all the civilizations which have come and gone, perhaps no more dramatically than in Greece could we witness the fatal interaction between religion and technology through the medium of art. The fate of Classical expression was marked long before Alexandria stood as the hub of scientific endeavor, and long before Hero became its master inventor with numerous moving marvels and automatic theatres. The ancients may have looked upon Hero's *Apotheosis of Dionysus* as a clever entertainment, but we possess the perspective to view it as something more. Reviewing the origins of Greek art and religious ritual, the mechanical *Dionysus* looms up, not as cultural progress, but as an omen of the exhaustion of spiritual and physical vitality.

Greek mythology was guided in its characterizations of the gods by the intuition that they, like mortals, were neither all good nor all bad. Even in sculpted form such pragmatism toward the deportment of the deities can be seen. This resulted from a one-way relationship. The Greeks felt that the gods' power over mortals was unlimited and constant, yet human intervention into the affairs of the gods was impossible. Also statues could not communicate with their human creators. Thus relationships which arose between mortals and the gods—deities who remained motionless, implacably serene in marble and precious metal—avoided direct confrontation. This separation between the Greek citizen and his world of god images, between everyday existence and transcendent life, represented not only an aesthetic attitude but a form of practical metaphysics.

"Born of pressing human needs and desires, images projected by active and even anxious ritual, they pass into the upper air and dwell aloof, specta- torlike and all but spectral." In this concise description (1913, p. 203), the historian Jane Harrison designated the protocol which existed between ancient Athenian and the inanimate image. Miss Harrison sets out a vivid theory for the common origin and branching connections between the cycles of active life and art, with ritual as the catalyst between the two. Ritual through dance is an immediate form of activity that provides a practical way for circumscribing all the activities of life. Art, somehow, is still one step further from this *re-representation* of life. For Miss Harrison the word *mimesis* has a basic function in explaining this *re-representation*. More than the making of a literal representation which is closer to the modern defini- tion, mimesis was the action or doings of a mime; that is, the acting out or *re-creation* (even the word *recreation* finds its origins in the joy of making anew) of an event through feelings or gestures. Through symbolic actions it generated, not the event or thing itself, but a certain emotional state sur- rounding it. In either theatre or sculpture, then, realism is only a subsidiary means for achieving emotional effect. Ritual is primary, and from the object of ritual, sculpture may evolve; while from the codified actions and circum- stantial variations of ritual springs drama. The fusion existing between sacred statuary and sacred drama has been lost to us in the secular segregation of the arts. Yet this fusion was not uncommon and Pausanias describes (A.D. 2, p. 203) a situation in which the wooden figure of Orthian Artemis was involved in a ritual of blood sacrifice.

[*To avert further deaths resulting from quarrels over the ownership of a small wooden statue, the oracle commands the towns of Cynosura, Mesoa and Pitane in Sparta to let blood on the altar housing the statue of the goddess Artemis.*] And instead of a person drawn by lot being sacrificed, Lycurgus changed it to flogging the young men there, and so the altar got sprinkled with human blood. And the priestess stands by during the operation, holding the wooden statue, which is generally light from its smallness, but if the scourgers spare any young man at all in his flogging whether on account of his beauty or rank then this wooden statue in the priestess' hand becomes heavy and no longer easy to hold, and she makes complaint of the scourgers and says it is so heavy owing to them. So innate is it with this statue, in consequence of the sacrifices at the Tauric Chersonese, to delight in human blood. And they not only call the goddess Orthia, but also Bound-with-willow-twigs, because the statue was found in a willow bush, and the willows so tenaciously twined round it that they kept it in an upright position.

From this passage we can speculate that the wooden Artemis was either sculpture confused with life, i.e., proto-automaton, or a kind of embodied spirit impelling ritual to a point of frenzy. Either way it planted the seeds for a later development. More than statuary, these proto-automata were almost liturgical instruments, working hand-in-hand with the keepers of the cult.

Although later automata certainly appeared more realistic than statuary, they were never meant to transcend or take the place of the statue. Automata remained inferior, but in some respects miraculous, drama that moved independent of human interference. Ironically though, sculpture, once willed to move, becomes the symbol of ennui and spiritual fatigue. In part, the decay of religious participation and the cool conceit of technological virtuosity spawned secular and religious automata after the death of Alexander the Great. Drive-in churches and television services typify contemporary counterparts.

The place of automata in the scheme of Greek religious practice and aesthetics is by no means self-evident. The Greek decay of cultural values may ultimately have had more to do with loss of spiritual fervor than any advance in technology. Intensity lies at the core of ritual. As intensity disappeared from ritual it regathered in the sublimated form of religious drama. When intensity wanes in human actors it is only a step to seek it further in mechanical means. Jane Harrison's illustration of the stages of the Dionysian drama is relevant.

The festival was originally an agrarian rite of thanksgiving, born of the tragic joy that came with experiencing the death of Winter and the birth of Spring. Dionysus incarnate was a god of extreme contrasts in both human greatness and fallibility. His offering of the wine cup during the rite presages unlimited inspiration and a capacity for creating great harm. Unlike other gods, Dionysus gained his power through wine, and to a lesser degree through drama, so as to enter directly into the spirit and body of all human beings.

The earliest *dromenon* (meaning *rite done* or pre-drama) was a joyous celebration set in the market places of Attica and lasting five days. Such a ritual debut, by coaxing the emergence of spring, had passion and psychical meaning only as long as the country people involved harbored not the slightest doubt that it would bring fertility back to the soil. When doubt finally crept in and men began to reflect, the question arose, why should we take part in the proceedings? What is their meaning? Slowly the dance circle became a stage, and as the section devoted to seating grew the rituals passed from mass participation to organized observation. The drama became an act of watching and marble seats the symbol of inaction. "To understand and still more to contemplate life you must come out from the choral dance of life and stand apart," (1913, p. 165). Such, according to Miss Harrison, was the birth of art and the death of ritual—and also, one might add, the beginning of philosophy in ancient Greece. With the separation of actors and spectators the greatest tragedies were written and an observer could afford to become critical, or even bored.

Still, drama lacks emotional distance, the quietude necessary for aesthetic contemplation so natural to sculpture. If sophisticated automata have their roots in Greek drama rather than in sculpture, then this same loss of the capacity for uninterrupted meditation might typically be found in the hubbub of moving machinery. The machine, like the actor on the stage, engages the mind on immediate terms; both are devoid of that aloofness and serenity which surround the static object.

Yet as early as the third century B.C., the Egyptians under Ptolemy Philadelphus constructed a Dionysus capable of pouring wine from a golden goblet. The treatise *Automata* by Hero of Alexandria dates five centuries later and one of its chief topics is mechanical theatres. A series of relatively simple cisterns, syphons, hydraulic conduits and counterweights explains the functioning of the theatre of Dionysus. After the apparatus was set and the water vessels filled, the ritual proceeded. The altar of Dionysus turned and positioned itself in back of the cult figure. As the altar burst into light Dionysus came to life. Refreshing liquids poured from his thyrsus and cup. With a clash of cymbals the frenzied Bacchantes danced around his perch. This dance of the follower of Dionysus was repeated as the altar automatically moved in front of the viewers (Chapuis and Droz, p. 33).

Alexandria, already under Roman jurisdiction for three hundred years, was by the time of Hero considered the southern capital of Greek learning and science. Technical exotica and penchant for architectural splendor made it the Los Angeles of the second century. These Alexandrian automata with their infusion of Eastern ideas and spectacular elaborateness presented the very death pangs of religious sensibility. By this time, the dithyramb dance no longer encouraged spring with wild leaps and song by rural participants. Instead, the great turntable under Dionysus groaned as the mechanical cymbals paced the tempo of the treadmilled Bacchantes.

We can look in vain for any fragments of the Alexandrian automata and precious little exists of the early Greek moving doll figures. According to the rates of decay inherent in each material, the maker of automata has always dealt with an ephemeral art, one far outdistanced by the life span of stone. Just as the human body steadily decays through life unto death, then drastically decomposes once it is interred in the ground, the fugitive life of the Greek automata must be regarded in the same sense, a fleeting procession of technical achievements, a nonliving, proto-art seen in retrospect.

Clockwork Men Before the Enlightenment

Medieval attempts to reproduce semblances of life through automata were alternately condemned and encouraged by the Church. Mechanical figures recreating biblical scenes obviously furthered Church doctrine and were regarded as part of God's handiwork. This was not the case with the alchemical creation of *homunculi*, or synthetic flesh-and-blood reconstructions considered the work of the devil. Medieval strictures against magic, alchemy, and early science were never precisely defined by the hierarchy; thus some monks practiced in all three fields at the same time.

The early church scholar and scientist Albertus Magnus was reputed to have made a working life-size servant from wood, metal, leather, and thread. Pious and somber Thomas Aquinas destroyed another android, an automata in human form, the creation of his teacher Albertus, because its babbling incensed Aquinas. He declared it the work of evil spirits. Actually the use of holy water, consecrated instruments, images and exorcisms by the Church differed only in intention (and perhaps slightly in means) from the modes of magic practiced by secular sorcerers. In the case of Albertus, even his primitive scientific experiments were regarded by the Church with some suspicion. This, to no small degree, accounts for the conservative reservations of Thomas Aquinas against meddling with nature. Therefore, he was canonized shortly after his death while Albertus Magnus was not elevated until 1931.

Yet the Church sought out ingenious mechanics to make automata for processions, religious cults, and cathedral tableaus. The use of machines at that time was a most impressive form of doctrinal instruction. Small stages controlled by a single driving mechanism remain as evidence in a few places of worship. Here, involved tableaus of figures moved in different directions and displayed a variety of individual actions.

The Church took full advantage of deeply rooted folk customs of the European peoples and encouraged the making and displaying of religious dolls and votive manikins. Today, for example, one can see the richly costumed "Virgin of the Pilar" which stands in a side chapel of Chartres Cathedral. The profusion of these saint images in the form of dolls with real hair, silk raiments, and costly ornaments was no doubt a creative release, being a favorite pastime of nuns who had not forsaken their maternal instincts. Highly naturalistic votive images made of wax came into popularity during the Middle Ages. These were often clothed self-replicas donated by affluent parishioners.

With the flowering of the Renaissance the ideal of a lifelike approximation of the human form became an obsession for the Western European artist. Mechanical and aerial perspective, methodical anatomical study, the unearthing of Classical sculptures and the development of oil painting all contributed to a form of mimetic representation, increasing, thereby, the difficulty of creating believable mechanized automata. Renaissance successes in sculpture and painting produced an enduring cleavage between the fine arts and the *ars mechanica*. The biographies of Vasari constantly reveal the author's awe of the power of realism. A Giovanni Bellini painting completed by Titian was said by Vasari (1550, p. 267) to have "... one nude figure of a sleeping woman which is very beautiful, and appears living as indeed do the other figures." Michelangelo criticizes the drawing in a painting by Titian with these words (Vasari, 1550, p. 286): "...for if this artist had been aided by Art and knowledge of design, as he is by nature, he would have produced works which none could surpass, *more especially in imitating life....*" And Vasari agrees. Further, Vasari marvels (p. 55) at the "perfection of research" to be found in a dead Christ by Michelangelo: "...every muscle, vein, and nerve, nor could any corpse more completely resemble the dead than does this." Or there is Soderini's remark (Vasari, 1550, p. 59) at a supposed improvement by Michelangelo of his great *David*—"You have given it life." Even Michelangelo, fearfully proud of the stark realism of his works, struck a groove in the knee of his *Moses* to signify its man-made and not heavenly origins.

As the total Renaissance designer and inventor, Leonardo da Vinci was probably not the only artist to attempt a simulation of life in painting, sculpture, *and* mechanics. In depicting the variations of skin tones, no artist surpassed da Vinci. Occasionally he was asked to design spectacles of amusing automata for official pageants. His "tame lion" for Louis XII's entry into Milan was one such effort. This mechanical animal, upon being presented, walked toward the King, opened the furry costume covering its chest and revealed the French royal coat-of-arms. Leonardo's simulations of life were also carried out in private experiments. One description recounts Leonardo playing with air-filled sheep's intestines. These produced giant balloons that nearly filled the studio. Under his manipulation model birds were sent through the air powered by these inflated bladders.

If religious rites and semireligious plays were the chief stimuli for fashioning ancient automata, then the development of the mechanical clock must be regarded as the guiding spirit behind early modern automata. Several reasons exist for this. The mechanical clock, more at first than the book, produced an atmosphere that made possible modern rhythms of living. No longer did men mark time in the day by a series of fluctuating periods, such as the seven canonical hours used to call the members of the monasteries to prayers. Their lives were ordered by the regularity of hours and minutes. This precise periodicity and fragmentation, found only in mechanically regulated time, was a major step in breaking down the organic work pattern of the hand artisan, replacing it with the beginnings of piecework mass production. The idea of "clockwork" gradually gave man a physical conception of the universe which lasted until the present century.

The earliest clocks in the modern sense of the word originated in about the eleventh or twelfth century. These clocks were not regulated by water or sunlight, but were activated by a slowly unrolling weight attached to a rope wound around a spindle. The weight reached the ground hourly so that a "keeper of the clock" was responsible for striking a bell marking the end of an hour, then rewinding the weight to the top of the tower. The clock as a semi-autonomous mechanism grew very gradually with the application of various controlling and transmitting mechanisms. Thus, temporal precision, until the twentieth century, was the systematic application of new mechanical improvements—wheels, balances, springs, and escapements. Of prime interest is the early (mid-fourteenth century) substitution of "jacks" or jointed figures for the human "keeper of the clock." Jack may be a shortening of the word *Jaccomarchiadus*, or man in a suit of armor. Actually the first clocks were made by metal workers and armorers; thus the jacks represented soldiers. By means of secondary controls the jacks rang a bell hourly or in fractions of an hour just as its human counterpart had done. From the fourteenth century onward the jacks became more complex; not only did they announce the time, they evolved into a series of animated vignettes portraying medieval and biblical life.

In the annals of clockwork automata the great Strasbourg Cathedral clock stands as the most elaborate masterpiece of the art form. This construction, several floors high, is not only a clock and many-tiered panoply of automatic pageantry, but it includes many vividly portrayed astronomical functions and an ecclesiastical perpetual calendar. The original clock dates from 1352 and the Schwilgué clock (1842) is a reconstruction with added features. Even now the clock is being rebuilt for a third time.

Actually, there is nothing comparable in our day to this Renaissance universal timepiece. These machines set the living pattern for an entire vicinity. They also acted as vital recorders for every conceivable sacred and secular cycle. By no accident the figure of Death and the stages of human life from infancy to senility became stark motifs used repeatedly to denote the passage of time. The Christian outlook concerning man's duration on earth was that life could be taken away at any moment. Imminent judgment faced the departed. A culture acutely aware of the transient nature of mortality was bound to be impressed by the linear relentlessness of the clock. Being God's timekeeper, the automata clocks repeated cycle after cycle of man's stay upon Earth and, naturally, the cycles of both Earth's and heaven's movements.

More significantly than their religious function, the clocks' automata helped to describe the world in terms of a series of multileveled, interconnected time structures. They gave a sense of orientation to Renaissance man in a way that no other device had ever done before. For the sixteenth and seventeenth centuries these planetary and local timekeepers, with astrolabe, astrological recorder, history index, perpetual calendar, and an allegorical world of mundane and heavenly figures were all the stratifications of theological, philosophical, and scientific thinking compressed into one mechanical, miniature cosmos. For any culture, this represented a monumental concession to technology.

In its day the great clocks, such as the one at Strasbourg, were more than just important scientific instruments; they were mechanical models representing the subtle array of correspondences which stood between the celestial and terrestrial worlds. The great clocks of that age were working models depicting a man-interpreted universe controlled by God. As a picture of the Renaissance time scale they had important implications for future generations of scientists, men who would fit geological durations and organic life spans into a single rational, universal frame of reference. Automata at this point became part of the Age of Reason.

Mechanistic Aspirations in the Age of Reason

Ample evidence points to the eighteenth century as the golden age of automata. Indicative of the new age of precisionism is the connection between music-box players and the structure of evolving classical musical forms. The morphology of music had several directions: one lay in the expansion of tonal ranges and harmonic intervals; another was generally aimed at symmetry, precision, and clarity of idea. In no marginal way, the music boxes, with their porcelain-faced, silk-clothed figures above and precision-programmed cylinders below, personified the regulated, balanced framework of musical composition. Like perfectly cut crystal, shimmering in completeness, classical musical expression was logically extended, not only through human interpretation, but by the crisp fidelity of the music box.

How close this lay to the prevailing intellectual temper of the day can best be examined by going back to the seventeenth-century rationalistic constructions of René Descartes. For all the brilliant, if often wayward, fantasy involved in Descartes's explanations of natural phenomena, he remains the first scientist-philosopher capable of logically circumscribing all the aspects of Nature, sweeping away both the fog of scholasticism and the interventions of a Higher Being, except of course as a prime mover. The subtlety of Descartes's theories of physiology enabled him to establish his own independent existence as a thinking being, along with the existence of God, which decisively cleared the way for rational explanations of the material world.

Of significance are Descartes's mechanical similes to all the animal functions: sleeping, digestion, breathing, heartbeat, formation of ideas and emotion, etc. At times these parallels were grossly unfaithful to the model, similar to comparing a mule to a steam engine because they both could be set to the same task. But in terms of understanding the human optical system, the circulatory system and the nervous system the initial insights are there for the modern physiologist. Humans, according to Descartes, were invested with a soul while animals were not, and in his *Discourse on Method* he made the supposition that a machine constructed perfectly enough could duplicate any of the lower animals. In contrast, he reasoned, a synthetic man could not be so built. First, because of the powers of speech, and second, because of the ability to reason autonomously, man was beyond the power of the machine makers to recreate. Descartes, it should be remembered, had a theological position to protect. Yet it is interesting that, with the development of the Enlightenment, both speech and the simulation of intelligence became prime goals of the inventors of automata.

The Cartesian concept of mechanism was a very problematic beginning for defining a rationally ordered universe. What gave the idea substance and authority beyond doubt was the *Principia* (1687) of Newton. In a single intellectual effort many loose bits of scientific conjecture came tied together in one neat package. If a mathematical-mechanical system based on the idea of universal gravitation could explain the orbits of the planets and their satellites, the paths of celestial projectories, the regularity of tides, comets, eclipses and pendulum motion, then what could prevent the inquiring man from understanding all earthly phenomena in terms of a series of mechanical models? The world for all earthly intentions was a great clock, operating cycle after cycle, imperturbably, always in order, and probably never running down. The winder of this clock of course was God, and from this point onward what could be more pious than studying the beauty of God's mechanism?

By the eighteenth century the influence of the mechanistic conception had pervaded every area of thought. Given balanced constitutions and generally elected law-making bodies, men could keep themselves in a constant state of law and order. The arts perfected new degrees of regularity in the extended use of the rhymed couplet and the sonata. John Locke's philosophy and the economics of Adam Smith displayed Newtonian influences in an attempt to set up self-sustaining mechanisms of government and commerce. Though widely divergent, all this had profound implications for the young ladies of the courts of Berlin or Versailles who desired to be amused by the latest mechanical toys.

Before examining a few of these automatic devices, it is well to note that there arose in Descartes's century a new classification of works—nonanthropomorphic and autonomous—which had significance for the later development of automata and, oddly enough, for the sculpture of today.

The dim premonition that a mechanism could have some autonomy over its own actions was sensed by the philosopher Blaise Pascal. His invention (1642) of the arithmetical calculating machine was the forerunner of the modern computer. With its goal of "thinking through" certain types of basic mathematical problems, it possibly represents the first nonanthropomorphic automata. In a sense, while it performed the human act of abstract problem solving, it did so without looking human. What Pascal's calculator simulated to a limited degree was the logic of the Arabic number system. And, though this was not conscious thinking, it was the beginning of the automation of thought processes.

Pascal's work was carried forward in the next century by the philosopher and mathematician Gottfried Wilhelm von Leibniz. A cogwheel machine by Leibniz not only multiplied, but could be preset to carry out a given program. His intuitive grasp of how the senses function, instead of more scientific cause-effect relationships, has subsequently become important for pattern-recognition techniques in artificial intelligence. With his pioneering work in symbolic logic, Leibniz may deserve designation as the spiritual father of modern cybernetics. Since the work of Pascal and Leibniz, the problem of designing automata, if one discounts industrial machinery, has been divided into two branches: the traditional objective of constructing amusing facsimiles of men and animals; the other, progressively more important for modern automata, the designing of logic systems and programming techniques for the solution of problems put into mathematical form. The implications for both will be set forth in the last chapter of this book.

No better example of an eighteenth-century mechanical genius could be found than Jacques de Vaucanson. Born in Grenoble in 1709, Vaucanson showed an early aptitude for the designing of machinery. Finishing his studies in Lyon, the young inventor went to Paris to perfect himself in the diciplines of anatomy, art, music, and mechanics—seemingly a strange combination, yet one that embodies the talents and flavor of the century.

A statue of *The Flutist* in the garden of the Tuileries inspired Vaucanson to construct an automaton capable of moving its fingers over the stops of a flute while actually playing tunes. When introducing two other mechanical musicians, the inventor displayed his flutist before the French Academy of Sciences in 1738. The flute player entailed great patience and analytical ability in dissecting all the hand motions and breath control needed for playing the instrument. Vaucanson was even willing to allow an incredulous audience to inspect all the springs and inner movements controlling his piece (this was due more to Vaucanson's pride in his work than to the practices of the day, which sought to maintain anthropomorphic illusionism at all costs). Looking at the diagram provided by Chapuis and Droz from the descriptions by Vaucanson, one must marvel even today at the thoughtful complexity of this realer-than-life construction (1958, p. 276).

Some years before his election to the Academy of Sciences in 1746, Vaucanson's genius was recognized by Cardinal Fleury, who made him the state inspector of silk manufacturing; Vaucanson's lesser-known fame rests on a series of mechanical improvements made in that industry. Later, he was persecuted by the silk weavers in Lyon, who felt that his talent for production efficiency was taking the bread out of their mouths. Aggravated to the point of revenge, Vaucanson threatened to replace the weavers with donkeys. Then he set about perfecting a machine regulated by punch cards which produced flowered silk and was driven by such an animal.

Probably the most famous automaton of all time was Vaucanson's *Canard*. This animal possessed a fidelity in the imitation of organic functions which surpassed any machine built to that time. Descriptions of the duck give it the ability of moving its body, flexing its wings so that all the feathers work in unison, quacking, drinking water, eating grain, and excreting the results— all in perfect mimicry of the living animal. Situated on a great pedestal housing an imposing mechanism, Vaucanson's creation actually underwent some of the cruder processes of digestion. The *Canard* was an attempt to produce more than the outward features of an organism. If, like Descartes, Vaucanson applied mechanical principles to the internal organs of the body by crude analogy, at least his was a step in the direction of modern physiological analysis. After Vaucanson's efforts no longer were automata abrupt, uncoordinated, and "mechanical" in their gestures; instead, with the development of coordinated cam systems, smaller flexible spring mechanisms and tiny chain drives, automata assumed the grace of living beings. Records show that Vaucanson was secretly occupied with a project sponsored by Louis XV: the duplication of a complete man with functioning internal organs, including blood circulation. But the King's slowness in paying for the android finally made Vaucanson abandon this work. In all, the making of automata was now a matter of popular technology. If these mechanisms were secular, surely the minds behind them were even more so.

The variety of automata devised in the seventeenth and eighteenth centuries is only surpassed by the excellent quality of the workmanship involved. Not until the nineteenth century were watches inexpensively mass produced. Before this all mechanisms were precious, and the least utilitarian machines were playthings of the rich. Most treasured were table clocks, mechanical oil paintings, jewelry with automata, snuff boxes, singing birds, and other mechanical toys. By the middle of the nineteenth century inexpensive mechanical toys were produced in large quantities.

The Sociology of Modern Automata

Certainly the level of genius which went into designing automata in the nineteenth century was considerable. If anything, the entrepreneurs, whose task it was to think up new mechanical novelties for an increasingly jaded public, outdid themselves with the production of chess players, conjurers, singers, and acrobats. The spirit in which these androids were conceived made them inferior to those of the eighteenth century. Consider, for instance, some of the classical Dresden clocks with their displays of mythology, or the small, precious *objets d'art* by Jaquet-Droz, or the incredibly dainty porcelains mounted on music boxes, all fashioned by the greatest artists of the day. Before the nineteenth century a sympathetic fusion had existed between the mechanical and fine arts. Yet certainly automata made after the eighteenth century had and still have their share of fine artisans, men who take exceptional pride in luxury handicraft—though the breed, as any antique collector knows, is nearly extinct.

A parallel can be drawn between the declining stature of nineteenth-century automata and rising signs of human alienation. When not used to instill religious awe, automata have often provoked a kind of childlike joy, an elemental delight in the nature of moving objects for their own sake. This delight started to become alien with nineteenth-century sensibilities. In its place arose a modern craving for the impossible. Automata no longer merely danced or played tunes. They were expected to improvise well, win chess games from expert players, or perform feats of magic—in fact, they were presumed, in certain ways, to be the equals of men. An element of despair accompanied these new mechanical writers and calculators. In essence, an undercurrent of the machine's real potential vis-à-vis man was felt for the first time. Perhaps a tinge of bad faith was also involved. Vaucanson's threat to replace skilled silk workers with donkeys formed a sustained nightmare for many craftsmen of the last century.

In the genre of science fiction a recurring theme is the invisible line between humans and pseudo-human androids. A secret delight is attached to guessing if a human actor acting as a mechanical man has not in some unknown way assumed the identity of his role. We experience a *frisson* when some author convinces us that we would be better off as a race of regulated automata than remaining chaotic humans. The danger is that as the public becomes bored and reconciled to the possibility of an automaton existence it acquiesces to government by technological expediency. This is not to say that society is doomed to mass robotry, but that the first step toward accepting robotic values is appreciating the logic and ease of robot life.

One might ask, how has the robot invaded and replaced human-looking automata? Similar to the androids of previous centuries, the robot is also a mechanical man. Its difference lies in its non-human characteristics, that is a lack of skin coloring, hair, clothing, and natural movements. Rather, the robot is an attempt to produce a mechanical servant in the spirit of the modern, ultra-functional machine.

By the end of the nineteenth century machine designers had decided that machinery was more than period furniture with moving insides. At the time Frank Lloyd Wright spoke out for the use of the machine as a means for design simplification (1960, pp. 55–73). Certainly within Wright's romantic and idealistic philosophy making way for machines was not the same as capitulating to them. In 1908 Adolf Loos wrote *Ornament and Crime*, while in the same year H. P. Berlage in *Basis and Development of Architecture* denied the essentiality of decoration and ornament in architecture. A year before, Picasso had painted the first full-fledged Cubist composition, and just five years later Mondrian and Malevich would begin their first purely geometric paintings. All the arts seemed to clamor for a new, nonrepresentational precision, a spiritual cleanliness which would manifest itself in the geo-mechanistic simplicity of the forms used. The feeling spread that man was living *with* and *by* machines. If the machine was precise, economical, and geometric in its inner workings, why should the culture that depends on these devices not express this condition externally?

The First World War was a "war of machines," and, as such, brought home the ghastly complications of machines' double-edged nature in a way never before fully appreciated. As an aftermath to the war, plays and stories about "mechanical men" began to appear with some regularity. This was certainly not in the genre of the Gothic horror tale, and Mary Shelley's *Frankenstein* (1817) is nearly a pastoral devoted to a biological accident, a novel that never anticipated the widespread hopelessness of the new literature. Perhaps the most enduring example of the new vision of automata is Karel Capek's play *R.U.R.* (1921). The letters stand for "Rossum's Universal Robots" and the play hinges on the old scientist Rossum's discovery of how to fashion artificial beings in human form. Prophetically, Capek realized the many implications of near-human artificial life and how these would eventually affect the race of man. Moreover, through later literature and science, many of the dilemmas which Capek advanced have already begun to have surprising counterparts. Underlying all else in the play is a kind of Faustian fatalism which precludes the exchange of robots for men on this planet. The science popularizer and science-fiction writer Isaac Asimov totally rejects this fatalism as a kind of "Frankenstein complex" (Frankenstein in the sense that tampering with organic creation could have nothing but a tragic end). One of the earliest writers to reflect intelligently on the role of robots, Asimov views these creatures as basically harmless machines which, sensibly enough, should first be programmed not to harm or outwit their creators. According to Asimov, all technology is potentially dangerous, and it is up to the technician or user to control its results, rendering it harmless. Easier said than done. Most specifically, the resulting fear of the mechanical unknown has been burlesqued by the robot—an often threatening creature clad in polished stainless steel, possessing abrupt motorized motions, metallic voice, and flashing lights for eyes.

The term *robot*, first coined by Capek, comes from the Czech word meaning "forced labor," and implies a lack of autonomy and free will. In Capek's play (Lewis, 1963, p. 13) his robots were not metallic imitations of men but *androids*, machines constructed to appear human. In a factory these were shaped from materials which could simulate the consistency of the body's organs.

Gradually Capek's original conception of the word *robot* has undergone debasement until it implies either a fearsome, cartoon-style, clanking mechanical man, or a person who insensitively follows orders with rigid efficiency regardless of their implications. Both in their own way are fearsome prospects, hostile to some of the most valuable human qualities. With slivers of irony, Capek touches upon the second popular meaning, which directly implies the totalitarian mentality, and indirectly an attitude of alienation where machines prevail, producing a decay of social, moral, and vocational ideals. In spite of these serious implications, the electromechanical robots have produced a kind of Disney-like folklore for the automatic age.

As motion pictures were perfected, a new type of human image far surpassed the mechanical automata. The automata had had their day; they became museum curiosities. The public adopted a common-sense attitude toward the mechanized task. Machines *were* normal; they should look like machines, doing no more and meaning no more than their function prescribed. There was no outward mystery about the new breed of industrial automata; people not only expected them to work like machines, but thought of them as complicated extensions of the many electrical utilities in use daily. No longer the brain children of lonely inventors or side-show entrepreneurs, industrially produced robots were the advertising creations of large electrical-appliance corporations—to be demonstrated at stores, trade fairs, and conventions.

Such a robot, described by the historian of dolls, Max von Boehn, was used at a London model engine exhibition in 1928 to give the opening address. It walked to the speaker's platform, where it addressed the audience in a loud clear voice, referring to the many displays as a preview of the future of engineering. A similar robot, displayed in London in 1932, looked very much like a medieval knight in full armor except for a cylindrical head mounted with acoustical pickups and light-sensitive resistors. In the 1930's the differences between unconscious automata and automata considered to possess some degree of consciousness became apparent. Engineers no longer felt satisfied to create the illusion of a "seeing" robot; but in the sense that it did respond to a given stimulus, a light beam, it did "see." The Westinghouse Company used the new development of sound film for their talking robot, "Televox." The names of other such creatures, "Electro, the Man of Steel," "Vocalite," "Monsurus," and "Sabor" suggest a certain lack of aesthetic sensitivity in their creators, and an attempt to provoke an aura of monstrous other-worldliness. These steel-clad machines with electrodes projecting from their temples, are pathetic titans, more helpless and powerful than any human being. Science fiction abounds with humans who eventually penetrate the outer casings of their robot enemies, revealing their internal organs, smashing diodes and ripping out intricate wiring by the handful.

Since the war, a new sort of apparatus has followed on the heels of the cumbersome machine man. For too long the robot personified a Luddite fear of the conscious machine without ever really being conscious. After 1945 experimental research in man-machine relationships was coordinated under the title of cybernetics, resulting in electronic pseudo-organisms quite unlike robots in appearance. Grey Walter's "tortoises," Ross Ashby's "homeostat," the maze-running "mice" of Claude Shannon are all attempts by scientists to construct paradigms of organic behavior; these are not clever copies of flute playing or poetry writing, but working models, generally analogues of various aspects of the nervous system found in simple organisms. These pseudo-organisms constructed by psychologists, neuro-physiologists, and communication engineers are, in conception and intention, far more sophisticated than all automata preceding them; no longer complex mechanical toys, they are tenuously linked with life itself.

The theory of automata—which has nothing to do with mechanical men —has become one of the most fascinating and vital branches of communication and cybernetic study. From the visual standpoint, the English writer P. E. Cleator recalls that, just as the first automobiles looked like and were called "horseless carriages," the first industrially devised robots were clumsy caricatures of the human form; hence there is no reason why the coming generation of industrial robots should resemble men. Already "power amplifiers" have been designed that are electronically sensitive to neural-muscular activity. These "power amplifiers" look nothing like human beings but enable a man to perform the work of ten or twenty men. Like the factory machines of the nineteenth century, the new adaptive, complex, role-playing automata will be regarded as machines, first and foremost, with no attempt to preserve anthropomorphic appearances. A glance at any pictorial history of machines shows that whenever a new machine is invented to replace either an older machine or an animal the tendency is to preserve the appearances of the obsolete object: hence there were "clock watchers" that struck the time, steamboats with sails, and trains that looked like stagecoaches.

As sociology and psychology analyze the viciousness of alienation toward work, literature grows on the phenomena of human beings gearing, or refusing to gear, themselves to the rhythm and communication style of machines. In terms of interaction and sensitivity to human needs, a machine may be more effective than *another person*. Witness the situation in which teaching machines are so hotly debated. In the long run machines may win out because it is cheaper and more efficient to mass produce teaching machines with effective programs than to train sufficient quantities of good teachers.

In a gentler vein, we have come *à la* Disney to regard the robot almost as a house pet (in derision we may refer to someone with a strong sense of loyalty to his organization as a "cheerful robot"). Some relatively inexpensive children's robot toys use feedback principles that are just out of the design-research department. Antonioni, the director whose movies personify modern purposelessness and ennui, has used automata powerfully. In *The Red Desert* (1964) an opening scene shows a series of lingering shots of a nursery. Against the soft shadows of the room a repetitious mechanical sound can be heard. It stops and starts, stops and starts. Finally we see a small battery-powered toy robot; it repeatedly drives into a wall, stops, then backs up and turns, only to crash into the wall again.

One of the most pathetic cases of machine behavior has been recorded by Bruno Bettelheim in his essay "Joey, the Mechanical Boy" (Josephson, pp. 437–446). This is a study of a nine-year-old who believed himself a machine, rid of the humanity which he finds unbearable. Bettelheim first reminds us that there is something innately fascinating and frightening about a machine turned human—but still more ghastly is the human who finds security in actually becoming a robot.

The acting out of Joey's machine existence was so emotionally intense and thorough that even the attendants and nurses in the school for the mentally disturbed where he stayed had a difficult time remembering that this thin little boy was not a machine. For long periods his "machinery" might not "work" and he would sit stark, rigidly still. Or perhaps his machinery would idle, and he would make low, gentle noises, rhythmically rocking back and forth. Other times he would shift gears toward a higher speed, until shouts of "crash, crash!" would warn all nearby that the mechanism was out of control. Radio tubes, bits of machinery or stray objects would be hurled by the child, signifying the final breakdown of the machine. Joey plugged himself in to run his eating apparatus. At night "machinery" made of wire, masking tape, cardboard, and other bits of material had to be reassembled next to his bed so that it could "live" him, keeping him running during sleep. Awake, all of Joey's human functions and interests were guided by practical necessities of maintaining the machine. When he was engaged in play, the machine would be "turned off." He demonstrated the frailty of his body by hurting himself on a jungle gym, thereby showing the superiority of machines over humans: "…they don't break; they're much harder and stronger."

Bettelheim recounts the first painful steps of Joey trying to enter the human world from that of machines. Joey's condition was the result of an extreme reaction to parental rejection, and his recovery meant regaining the ability to trust people around him. Bettelheim observes that probably only in our time and culture could such a situation have arisen. As machines, with enormous commercial sponsorship and methods of enticement, become the accepted surrogate for human attention and affection, what better escape route is there for the unprotected?

Subsculpture in Modern Art

The theme of the pseudo-man, as manikin or robot, became a central issue of art after 1910, but not until the next decade did it dominate the subject matter for any one artist. An early forerunner in the use of this theme, Giovanni Battista Bracelli in 1624 began a series of *Bizarreries* or mechanical men in the mode of Analytical Cubism. Not until 1910 when Cubism became firmly established in Paris was there any acceptance of mechanized anatomy, and very soon this kind of geometricism became the lever for graphic criticism of the automobile era.

As for Cubism, its development and popularity among artists have been much explained. They grow out of an increasing sense of urban dynamism and the inability of the painter to register the relativity of object-observer movements with the traditional tools of representation. Similarly, the relativity of space and objects could not be captured with the Impressionist's optical breakdown of light and color; the same was true for the Fauvist magnification of color relationships. The need was for a new form of analysis serially depicting multiple views of a set of objects. The basis for this lies in Cézanne's approaches to fragmented and simplified modeling. Broken planes resulting from this treatment gradually assumed a separate life and, rather than the subject matter, they became the structural basis of Cubist painting. In the hands of Picasso and Braque this treatment of subject and space tended toward depth ambiguity, monochromatization, and multi-view images.

Picasso's few early Cubist sculptures are less spatial explorations than elucidations to his painting problems. As for plane geometry, its loose employment by Cubist painters was a semi-intentional gesture (vaguely that of analyzing), rather than an end in itself. Nevertheless, Cubist sculpture owes a considerable debt to Cubist painting; most of its plastic devices are founded on the discoveries of painters. One exception is the early sculpture of the Russian émigré to Paris Alexander Archipenko. Probably Archipenko has some justification in proclaiming himself the prime innovator of modern sculpture. Much of the vocabulary of modern sculpture first appeared in his work between 1910 and 1920. Paris then was such a hotbed of avant-garde eclecticism that works were copied in principle even before they found their way out of the studio. As yet, no full and fair assessment of Archipenko's sculpture has ever been made.

Much of Archipenko's talent stemmed from his father, an inventor and mechanical engineer in the city of Kiev. Early in his education the sculptor sensed a strong affinity between mathematics and art, in itself not unusual for an artist, but in Archipenko's case the inventive and analytical portion of his mind often outstripped the ability to unify discoveries into a body of

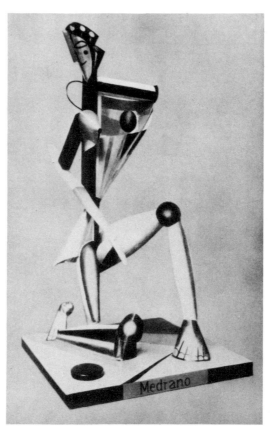

76. Alexander Archipenko, *Medrano I (Juggler)*, 1912.

works of consistent artistic merit. For most artists, later work is a refinement of earlier ideas, but in Archipenko's case refinement meant weakened contours and a barrage of unfortunate materials and color choices. The irony of Archipenko's efforts lies in the disparity of its quality. If we were carefully to pick fifty pieces from his output of over a thousand works, he unquestionably would stand as one of the seminal masters of our century; on the other hand, another choice of fifty of the worst sculptures puts him in a category with industrial designers producing lamp bases and knick-knack ceramics of the most banal taste.

Part of Archipenko's greatness, as he insisted, was that his early sculptures were not based primarily on Cubist painting but upon his investigation of geometric relationships. Thus many of his innovations look clumsy in their first stages because of his concern for formalism and use of material. Aesthetic propriety became a subsequent consideration. No work demonstrates this more graphically than *Medrano I (Juggler)* (FIG. 76). Archipenko claims this as the first three-dimensional construction; if not, it certainly is one of the earliest.

207

Altogether, *Medrano I* represents a strange assembly of anatomical dislocations which statically portray bodily movements rather than the body itself. Constructed of wood, sheet metal, wire, and glass, it may be the first intimation of the modern robot in art. The head, parts of the trunk and some of the limbs are curved metal forms; the knees represent mechanical joints while the right arm actually moves from the shoulder. A wire form at neck level symbolizes the trajectory of body movement. Archipenko's anticipation of kinetic sculpture is further shown by a series of disks in *Medrano I* tracing a path of movement. His use of mixed media for constructed sculptures was limited until about 1920, when reflective metals in various textures and colors precipitated the trend toward polychrome sculpture. Doubtless these early sheet-metal constructions made an impression on the Russian Constructivists (FIG. 77).

Before reviewing the mechanistic tendencies of other sculptors under the Cubist influence, it would help to clarify Archipenko's relation to Cubism. Whatever validity his statements have in regard to his independence from Cubism, it would have been hard for any artist then working in Paris to stay aloof from ideas which were common currency. The Section d'Or group considered higher mathematics and the vocabulary of machine images to be "in." However, Archipenko did produce an anthropomorphic idiom of metallic, geometrical forms which expressly moved beyond the needs of Cubism and became both the basis of the first anthropomorphic images of Constructivism, and the industrial designer's conception of the modern robot. Moreover, Archipenko never discouraged critics and art historians from seeing parallels between his work and the developments of modern science.

Most other admittedly Cubist sculptors remain on the periphery of the mechanized man theme. Raymond Duchamp-Villon's *Great Horse* (FIG. 78) nearly submerges the recognizable animal into an aggregate of compact forms of organic and mechanical parts. The simplifications of his *Seated Woman* (1914), its faceless head and mechanical knee-joint insertions, suggest a manikin more than anatomical improvisation.

Jacques Lipchitz eschewed the mechanistic propensities of his Cubist friends. One of the ironies of Lipchitz is that much of his finest work, the severe, linear, Cubist sculpture of 1914 to 1920, runs completely counter to his natural inclination for baroque globosity. His rectilinear Cubism (FIG. 79) derives from a three-dimensional adaptation of the collage Cubism of Picasso and Braque. In no way does this detract from its being one of the finest products of Cubist thought, yet it does imply a direct contrast between Archipenko and Lipchitz. Archipenko produced sculpture for the sake of experimentation, often at the expense of art; a careful sensitivity toward

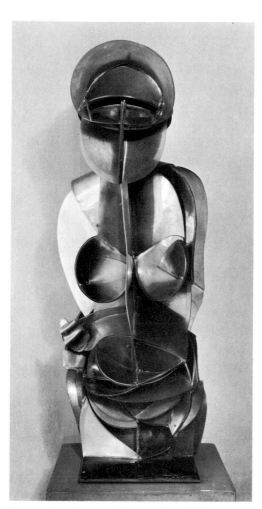

77. Antoine Pevsner, *Torso*, 1924–1926.

78. Raymond Duchamp-Villon, *The Great Horse*, 1914.

79. Jacques Lipchitz, *Man with Mandolin*, 1917.
Yale University Art Gallery. Gift of the Société Anonyme.

80. Fernand Léger, *The Card Players*, 1917.

avant-garde vogue and a need to make, above all else, "Art," led Lipchitz
into safer waters.

The robot made its full-dress appearance in Cubist painting. During a
two-year period before his first nonobjective drawings, Kasimir Malevich
composed Cubist paintings with metallic cylindrical figures—to some extent
the result of Rayonnist painting theories in Russia. Fernand Léger explored
a related style, in France, during the same years before the First World War.
The feeling for machine forms was undoubtedly there as attested by Léger's
observation that the sight of a gleaming cannon barrel changed his outlook
on painting thereafterward.

Léger's painting *The Card Players* (FIG. 80) most precisely defines the
robot in its modern form; the figures are drawn as polished tubular men.
The entire picture makes a multifaceted display of cylindrical steel surfaces;
all hints of organic matter have been omitted. In the 1920's Léger redefined
his mechanical world to include not only cams, valves, conduits, and steel
structures, but a number of objects, organic and household, which do not fit
precisely into the industrial landscape. This is reinforced by his film *Ballet
Mécanique* (1923), which through montage executes a symphony of parallels
between everyday human activity and the rhythmic drive of the machine in
overlapping proximity. Léger's pose was that of uncomplicated survival in
an age of machine values, rather than the intellectual's ironic resignation.

Certainly this last could not be said for the pseudo-machine creations of Francis Picabia and Marcel Duchamp. The second decade of the twentieth century was the period in which the machine overtly entered the iconography of art. It seemed hard to believe, mentions Mme. Buffet-Picabia (Motherwell, 1951, p. 257), that artists had turned their back for so long on the presence of the machine, as if they had some secret pact with the muses to deny its existence. Almost until Delaunay's use of the motif, the Eiffel Tower remained a source of derision for even the avant-garde of Paris. Moreover, Picabia laid bare psychical hostilities toward the machine age. He implied that because the artist uses the machine does not mean that he sympathizes with the value system which it tacitly erects. In an oblique manner Picabia suggested a certain merging of interests and physical characteristics between machines and future human beings. The essence of this can be found in his *Portrait of a Young Girl in a State of Nudity* (1915), an enlarged, proto-pop, commercial line drawing of a spark plug with the inscription "FOR EVER." Occasionally this drawing also appears as *The American Girl*, pointing out, rightly enough, that America represented the fountainhead of pragmatism and the mechanistic rationale. More obscure, and more subtle, are the dozens of drawings and gouache paintings devoted to improbably coupled machines. These Rube Goldberg creations with their punning nomenclature are not definable as robot humans so much as organizational diagrams for social and interpersonal relationships. Picabia, long before other artists, realized that the higher power of the machine lay in its ability to be united with other machines into feeling relationships, and to assume some of the social interaction of organisms living together.

As a painter Giorgio de Chirico stands by himself, the fabricator of a private imagery classified as a forerunner of Surrealism. About 1914 his arid cityscapes were succeeded by groups of manikins, often partially dismembered and faceless like dressmakers' dummies, strangely human in their gestures, and placed among buildings. It is a credit to the painter's poetry that these stuffed and sewn men seem more at home in their environment of sun-bleached buildings and arcades than were the robot figures of the Cubists. Robots are robots—they lack focus and subjectivity.

The art historian James Thrall Soby submits the possibility that a play, *Les chants de la mi-mort*, the concoction of de Chirico's brother, gave the artist the idea for his invention of metaphysical actors. The voiceless and faceless hero of *Les chants de la mi-mort* seems a perfect foil for the painter's settings, where all drama is performed with an exactitude of silence and gesture. Often de Chirico's manikins give hints of either mechanical or organic insides; their torsos sometimes merge with almost human limbs or their pelvises sprout from stone columns. Rather maddening is all this symbolism out in the clear Italian sunlight. The inferences are there to be read, but somehow the situation remains eternally vague.

A common stereotype of the Bauhaus depicts it as a gleaming workshop which produced tubular furniture, gas-pipe lettering, and highly geometrical silverware. In truth the most ardently romantic and informal sensibilities continually clashed with this kind of formalistic utilitarianism. This image of the Bauhaus is due to the selectivity and preferences of the people who have written books about it. That Oskar Schlemmer was one of these romantics can never be said. No other Bauhaus theorist, not even Moholy-Nagy, was as acutely cognizant of the limitations and potentials of the totally mechanized stage, nor did anyone desire to create such a stage more than Schlemmer. Schlemmer's stage in theory can be envisioned as a kind of metaphysical microcosm that attempts to reflect the psychic evolution of man. One of his more specific theories deals with the theatre as an organism (or complete mechanism) capable of engulfing the audience, thereby becoming the means for the total preoccupation of man's sensory equipment, Schlemmer's virtual "feast for the eyes."

Long before the present generation of Kinetic artists, Schlemmer uncovered a major doubt which has beset every designer desiring to invent an "art of movement" by mechanical means—the problem of keeping such an operation from becoming routine and boring. In his notes for the Bauhaus stage Schlemmer reminds the reader that he is not speaking of the automatic control panel, which has become a progressive reality in the past forty years, but the possibility of pseudo-actors or mobile machines capable of conveying their messages through light, electronic music, and the mechanical equivalents of dance. Sadly and realistically he realizes the limitations of mechanical kinematic motion—except as an instrument of human parody (in his diary he cites the greatness of Chaplin, as the movie actor juxtaposed the consummate unnaturalness of the machine with his own artistic perfection). Schlemmer was one of the first modern artists to recognize the interlocking triangle which exists between the artist's urge to produce an autonomous mechanical fine art, the limited public appeal for such an expensive undertaking, and the financial interests, who see little profit or ideological purpose from such a venture.

How in practical terms did the automaton enter Schlemmer's conception of the stage? As with artists before, Schlemmer was stimulated by literary precedents which accepted the mechanical person as potentially superior to the human being. He also understood the implications for control and freedom as manifested between operator and puppet in Heinrich von Kleist's essay "Über das Marionettentheater." Schlemmer was keenly aware of its Faustian implications: first, the ability of perfected mechanical performers to transcend human capabilities (he uses, as an example, freedom from gravity, thinking mainly in terms of dance), and secondly, the attendant dangers for man of such power uncontrolled. Certainly the second consideration remains fairly hazy and his uppermost feeling is expressed when he writes in his diary (1958, p. 199): "Not distress over mechanization, but gladness for precision."

Of the absolute visual stage he writes (1957, p. 22): "Man, the animated being, would be banned from view in this mechanistic organism. He would stand as 'the perfect engineer' at the central switch-board, from where he would direct this feast for the eyes."

Schlemmer obviously envisioned his optimum stage as a sort of giant organism, with man, the spectator nested in its bowels, getting his sensory fill while standing outside directing the feast. Of course, today, when automatic preset lighting consoles are a fairly common part of the theatre, there is relatively little reason why even control should be a human matter.

The fact that building robots flexible enough for the stage was an impossibility left Schlemmer with the alternative of designing stylized robot and geometric costumes for his human dancers. These costumes, and often *constructions* is a better word, were derived from a number of sources—the masks of the Classical Greek theatre, the sculpture of Archipenko, the stuffed figures of de Chirico, the medieval knight in full armor, the machine and mechanical doll. Schlemmer directed the dancer toward an awareness of his body as a machine producing patterns of motion expressly designed to intersect and fill the plenum of the stage space. As in machine design, the dancer, rather than being an actor in a choreographic routine, plotted a precise series of kinematic sequences. According to costume and assigned function, each dancer was wedded to certain "laws" of motion and spatial attack—like a piece on a chessboard.

In the area of static sculpture Schlemmer's output gives only a slight indication of his obsession for animated form. Compared with his painting and reliefs, his sculpture production remains rather slight. *Abstract Figure* (FIG. 81) exemplifies whatever progress Schlemmer did make. Its masses undoubtedly owe something to Archipenko, especially the Russian's discovery of the interchangeability of negative and positive (concave and convex) contours. More nearly unique is Schlemmer's handling of the penetration of forms in a manner reminiscent of the way modern machine designers began to assemble the cowlings which housed the various parts of machines. They only hinted at what was happening under the metal covering. The asymmetry

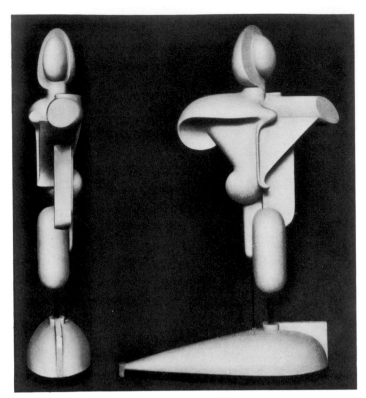

81. Oskar Schlemmer, *Abstract Figure*, 1921.

of *Abstract Figure* owes more to Schlemmer's curious conception of how the body invades space and is shown in cutaway fashion than to any natural pose. In fact, Schlemmer found his real medium for sculpture only when he was able to create choreography and costumes for his dancers.

With scant exception before the late 1950's, the demarcation line between sculpture and all other forms of anthropomorphic imagery remained intact. If primitive fetish images inspired the Cubists and robot sculpture found its stimulus in the machine, in all, sculpture remained sculpture and outside influences were assimilated into the art without destroying the chain of tradition. Except for the theorizing of a handful of Dadaists and Surrealists, very few artists contemplated producing a "fine art" exclusively from the domain of fetishes, automata, dolls, or other subsculptural forms. The dignity of the base, compositional considerations, the tradition of permanent materials: all conspired to prevent something as trifling as a wind-up doll from consideration as an art object. However, in German-speaking countries during the First World War there was a great vogue for puppetry; this pastime, as for instance in the geometric marionettes of Sophie Taeuber-Arp, became the springboard for several postwar experiments of the Dadaists.

Oskar Kokoschka's fetish, a doll which he lovingly planned in his letters to its maker in Stuttgart, is probably the most famous instance of an artist developing a passion for an ideal woman constructed of cloth and wood. The doll had to have certain tactile qualities besides specified visual charms. With its final arrival at Kokoschka's studio early in 1919, it proved to be a monster: the sum total of the painter's dreams, lifelike, but grotesque in its lack of animation. It was buried after a mock murder, then later unearthed. Kokoschka was reported to have escorted the doll on occasion to the opera in Dresden.

The German Surrealist Hans Bellmer has built his life around the evocative qualities of the doll. The crude vitality of some long-forgotten childhood toys awoke Bellmer to the realization that both his life as an advertising executive and his attempts at art were more pose than not. Bellmer, like Schlemmer, felt influenced by the phantasy of mechanical life. The beautiful automaton Olympia in *The Tales of Hoffman* excited the artist into creating his own manipulable dummies. Where Schlemmer chose costumed actors, Bellmer built and dissected his own doll anatomies—mechanical yet appearing softly human.

The first version of Bellmer's doll appears skeletal, a skull and torso structure with broomstick limbs and metallic joints. Soon he enhanced *The Doll* (1934) with flesh and skin in the manner of a little girl's doll; only Bellmer reassembled these legs, torso, and hands into suggestive combinations. Posed to tease, it explores, in compliment to Freud's mental unconscious, the *physical unconscious*. In its more grotesque and erotic forms *The Doll* becomes the plaything of a "Peeping Tom" or voyeur, twisted about with false hair and clothing, half coy Lolita. In its most analytical form "She" is spread out on a blanket, totally dismembered, like the components of a weapon during military field inspection. In later versions he made his own humanoid creations, all legs or oval anatomical forms fastened together. Bellmer literally sundered the corporeality of his female dummy, penetrating the psyche that lay within the cavity of its wooden frame.

The doll, the manikin, and the robot precariously began to find their place in the fine arts. However, another artist must be considered because of his profound insight into the man-machine relationship. Marcel Duchamp's metamorphosis as an artist concerned with facts of machine life cannot be described here, except to say that no work in our century better crystallizes the themes of alienation (environmental, vocational, male-female), than his *The Bride Stripped Bare by Her Bachelors, Even* (FIG. 82), known also as *The Large Glass*. *The Large Glass* has an overwhelmingly complex iconography which can only be touched upon in reference to the "Nine Malic Molds," those images inhabiting a section of the lower, or male portion of the *Glass*. The "Malic Molds" appear to be metallic hooded forms, almost robotic, resembling a cross between the hoods of automobiles and the pieces of a chessboard—the last, of course, being quite likely in the light of Duchamp's preoccupation with the game. In *The Green Box* (1960), Duchamp's collection of notes for *The Large Glass*, he identifies each of the molds by occupation: *gendarme*, *cuirassier*, delivery boy, busboy, priest, policeman, undertaker's mute, flunkey, and station master—all male, uniformed types in good standing, solid citizens who are actually hollow containers for the Bride's *lighting gas*.

In defining the shallow and self-deluding role of the "Malic Molds" Duchamp, as Lebel comments, makes one of his few unhappy observations concerning the meaning of the work. He drops his guise as cheerful meta-ironist to hint at the essential servility of the male types portrayed. It should be remembered that Duchamp, obsessed with the need for his own personal freedom, has scant respect for the psychic subordination of most practicing artists, and even less for that of the man in the street. By envisioning his fellow men as a body of unthinking, unfeeling functionaries in the power structure, Duchamp only modernized a sensibility which Charles Baudelaire expressed three-quarters of a century earlier. The poet, in his essay on "The Salon of 1846," gave his views on the possibilities and debilities of heroism in modern life by comparing sartorial modes (1955, p. 128):

Is it not the necessary garb of our suffering age, which wears the symbol of a perpetual mourning even upon its thin black shoulders? Note, too, that the dress-coat and the frock-coat not only possess their political beauty, which is an expression of universal equality, but also their poetic beauty, which is an expression of the public soul—an immense cortège of undertakers' mutes (mutes in love, political mutes, bourgeois mutes…). We are each of us celebrating some funeral.

A uniform livery of affliction bears witness to equality; and as for the eccentrics, whose violent and contrasting colours used easily to betray them to the eye, today they are satisfied with slight nuances in design in cut, much more than in colour.

Baudelaire's comments, of course, referred to the use of dark colors for men's clothing. These had been in the process of becoming standard business wearing apparel since the 1830's. In France then there was talk that continual wearing of dark clothing endangered health, and that such clothing also represented the soul-deadening invasion of English styles and ideas. Baudelaire noted the lack of individualism in dress, especially in colors, and implied that this was only symptomatic of a greater malignancy: this universal business uniform that withstood only minor variations so as to signal the status of each man. Parallel is a note from Duchamp's *The Green Box* which reads

82. Marcel Duchamp, *The Large Glass* ("Nine Malic Molds,"
lower left center), 1915–1923.

(1960, no page number): "—Provisional color = The malic forms. They are provisionally painted with red lead *while waiting* for each one to receive its color, like croquet mallets."

Alluding to the small colored bands that make a set of croquet mallets distinctive, Duchamp also refers to the standard coating of red lead applied to metallic surfaces to prevent corrosion. Thus the connection between the poet and artist is clear: if the dark business suit is a badge of conformity for Baudelaire, then the metallic robot uniform seized upon by Duchamp only helps to show the critical nature of the situation less than a century later.

CHAPTER SIX

Kineticism:
The Unrequited Art

Mechanization and the Artistic Sensibility

"For me, the machine is above all an instrument that permits me to be poetic. If you respect the machine, if you enter into a game with the machine, then perhaps you can make a truly joyous machine—by joyous, I mean free" (quoted in Tomkins, 1965, p. 146).

Thus speaks the arch-sculptor of mechanical perversity, Jean Tinguely. He brings to light what has always been suspect concerning the artistic use of machines: namely, that it is extremely difficult to produce a physical system which strives toward psychic ambiguity and liberation and, at the same time, remains a device conceived upon the precepts of physical restraint (i.e., conceived as a mechanical artifact).

In the previous chapter on automata we have investigated what could be called the prehistory of Kinetic sculpture. Yet it is curious that what were considered *automata* in the age of statuary should become *Kinetic Art* and *robotry* during the twentieth-century reemergence of abstract geometricism. It has been implied throughout the chapter on formalism that geometric formalism applied to modern art is proto-mechanization; it attempts to introduce directly machine values into art. As such, the entire trend toward the mechanization of modern art contains elements of psychic disharmony, something already witnessed with the steam-propelled Dionysian rituals of Hero. Furthermore, at its roots Kinetic Art represents the contemporary artistic recognition of the drive toward total mechanization; it is the celebration of what Franz Reuleaux, in defining the machine, called the "closed kinematic chain"—the ability of man to control motion and power in a determinate fashion.

Compared to automata, what is Kinetic Art? Most specifically, Kinetic Art has been a gradual attempt throughout this century to produce non-representational art using the parameters of real time and motion. Unlike automata development, it has not been an art rooted in traditional crafts-manship and mechanical competence. Instead, Kinetic Art has been a prod-uct of makeshift necessity, stemming from deeply felt needs of avant-garde painters and sculptors. Besides an unwillingness to produce realistic facsimi-les of men and animals, the short history of Kinetic Art has been marked by the comparative mechanical incompetence of its champions. What slight technical facility Kinetic artists have demonstrated has usually been the re-sult of technical assistance contributed by sympathetic technicians. Often these two facts have been used by the critics of Kinetic Art to launch attacks on the entire movement. Yet the relative aesthetic failure of Kinetic Art is significant in itself since the desire to make art kinetic is one of the prime ar-tistic urges of the present century; to misinterpret this is to reject the direction to which Western art has committed itself. The technician has consistent-ly failed to make machinery conform to the older aesthetic precepts of our culture; instead, it has been the artist who was forced to try to make his art relevant to the prevailing technology. The Kinetic artist, along with his ene-mies, has often sensed that he has united his art with forces inherently at odds with artistic endeavor. Even the engineer with his superior training has so far not produced superior Kinetic Art, usually the opposite. Successful Kinetic Art until now has either defied or trivialized the principles of me-chanical invention.

It appears that Kineticism has its roots in a philosophy which controlled the first industrial revolution. Thus the machine was and still is viewed as a discrete, closed unintelligent system for producing work. Kineticism has had its basis in the recognition that *motion* is the present center of artistic interest. The word *kinetic* is important because it decidedly places the empha-sis for this new art on motion and its effects—not intelligence, anthropo-morphism, temporal sequence, or coordination, all aspects of the older art of automata. In this respect it is interesting that the young American art his-torian Willoughby Sharp has been responsible for coining the words *Kine-ticism* and *Kineticist* to distinguish interest in the artistic effects of motion. The scientific study of controlled motion is really the first phase of modern machine design and consequently the source for much of the thinking which has pervaded the practical side of kinetic effort in the past fifty years.

For some time before the middle of the nineteenth century much ma-chine design was a matter of nearly random trial-and-error adjustment of given mechanical components. Only in the year 1830 did André Ampère de-fine the nature of machine relationships so that they could be subjected to mathematical analysis and planning. In his "Essay on the Philosophy of Sciences" he concluded that the direction and velocity of *motions*, not *forces*, was the core of machine study. This enabled the designer to propose the translation of forces primarily on the strength of visually apparent geometric relationships. Kinematics (or *cinématique* as Ampère called his new science) consequently became the study of motion unattached to forces or objects; applied to machinery, it dealt with ideal situations in which motion was derived from surface contacts made by pairs of machine elements. Essentially kinematics has remained the geometry of touching surfaces.

Kinetics, on the other hand, is concerned with motions resulting from forces directly connected to physical systems. For that reason, perhaps, it is interesting that an art of visual motion became connected with the more materially orientated word *kinetic*, instead of the theoretical *kinematic*. Most probably Moholy-Nagy's *The New Vision* first brought *Kinetic sculpture* to public attention in the early 1930's. Since the concept of *Kinetic* was necessarily attached to sculpture, because of its tangible properties, perhaps it was inevitable that the physical side of motion would be stressed over the ideal. Kinetic Art's connection with sculpture is both an accident of classification and a natural consequence of there being only two dominant fine arts in the twentieth century: painting and sculpture. Being neither illusional nor two-dimensional, three-dimensional machine principles of Kinetic Art have thrust the art form provisionally into the realm of sculpture. Whether it belongs there or not is not so important as the realization that sculpture has become a reservoir of mechanical artistic activity in our century.

As ensemble, with a mechanism that drives and regulates it, Kinetic sculpture remains three-dimensional, though often essentially flat in presentation. For the first time in art, outside the area of pure automata, Kinetic Art presents the baffling problem of an art form in which essential parts of its working order are purposely hidden from the observer. Often produced are effects without visible cause.

In reviewing the theory of classical machines, the German professor of kinematics, Franz Reuleaux (1829–1905), stood as the pivotal intellect who first presented a comprehensive analysis of mechanical parts and their underlying relationships. He developed the schematic picture of precisely how individual elements of a machine engage or come in contact with each other so as to insure the most economical and frictionless work advantage. This was reduced to the principle of what Reuleaux called "pair closure." One of his important discoveries historically was the observation that machinery developed as designers reduced the freedom between pair-closure elements. In other words, the gradual improvements in the meshing of machine components progressively resulted in more efficient movements.

Reuleaux's contribution to the understanding of machines was that of an analyst with a universal grasp of the physical aspects of his subject. In an area such as machine design, already the epitomization of Western rationality, he completed the process of rationalization. It would take a new order of physical principles (automation made possible through electronics) to render his essentially Newtonian world of geometric relationships of secondary importance for the coming era of mechanical invention. *Art still feels the effects of Reuleaux's systematizing of mechanical invention.*

Beyond the local properties of individual machines, Reuleaux realized that mechanization contained an inherently new philosophy of life, one that had grown into the universal realization that mankind possesses seemingly infinite capacities for mechanical invention. This embraced more than the optimism of the eighteenth century; it provoked the conclusion that machines could be studied and created with scientific thoroughness.

The fact, as Reuleaux has insisted, that the machine was "a faultlessly constrained and closed system of bodies" bothered many nineteenth-century poets and thinkers. What would happen to the more autonomous and ephemeral values of life if the unstoppable rationality of this new breed of objects were to proliferate into all areas of life? Was man actually a tool of his tools as Thoreau had pondered? Buried under the enlightened reasoning of nineteenth-century inventors and mechanical theorists like Reuleaux were the seeds of an implacable bourgeois totalitarianism, the despair of the most sentient souls of the era. Yet we possess evidence of Reuleaux's sensitivity to the arts and to the cause of human freedom, and perhaps this is a harsh judgment. But, on the other hand, Reuleaux was capable of seeing the machine as *the* model for the well-run society. And nothing would further implement this than more machines (1876, pp. 241–242).

Small wonder that most artists working today with machinery use it primarily as a power source and as a "randomizing" device, a means for producing unstable and unsuspected results. Tinguely speaks of making a "joyous machine"—one that is, in fact, *free*. This freedom is actually an attempt to divert the essential restrictive nature of the machine. Artists have been all too conscious of the machine's propensity to *restrict* change and their desire has been to allow the machine new degrees of freedom—even, on occasion, by destroying it.

Compared with Reuleaux's implicit faith in the beneficial effects of the machine are the less optimistic pronouncements of his contemporary the French poet Baudelaire (1955, p. 173): "Typical victims of the inexorable moral laws, we shall perish by the thing by which we thought to live. Machinery will have so much Americanized us, progress will have so much atrophied our spiritual element, that nothing in the sanguinary, blasphemous or unnatural dreams of the Utopians can be compared to what will actually happen."

There exists almost a pattern among great intellects and perceptive poets in the nineteenth century of prophetic pronouncements concerning the future of a culture dominated by machines. Yet few of these men brought themselves to embrace mechanistic culture as anything more than a sad joke on humanity. For the most part, these were the leaders of sensitive reaction and pioneers of the literature of alienation. To varying extents Goethe, Kierkegaard, Schopenhauer, Emerson, Thoreau, Dostoievski, Mark Twain, Henry Adams, Samuel Butler, and Baudelaire belong to the ranks.

Surely the most prophetic, if satirically directed, attack on the machine came from the pen of Samuel Butler. Following Darwin's suggestion that machines obey something like evolutionary theory in which complex organisms evolve from simpler ones, Butler pushed the point to its limit by proposing that man was unknowingly preparing his own successor. Realizing the futile absurdity of his proposal, he advocated instant destruction of *all* machines as the only means of protecting the human race from eventual extermination. Butler envisioned machines as superior organisms—though still in a stage of infancy—and man as a kind of nursemaid whose purpose in life would disappear once the machine gained the ability to take care of itself and reproduce its own kind.

As droll as this might have seemed in the 1860's, it was an uneasy foreboding of what would be theoretically possible by the 1930's. In 1937 the young English logician A. M. Turing devised a theorem on the computability of numbers. One of its aspects deals with the capacity of computers to handle problems concerning their own limits. From there, the question arose of automata's ability for self-reproduction. Obviously, as the physicist-mathematician John von Neumann pointed out, it should be no problem since organisms produce young as complicated as themselves. Turing's theorem seemed to imply that, given the proper program and materials, there was no reason why an automaton might not reproduce itself—just as well as an organism.

Samuel Butler was by no means a Luddite—an uneducated smasher of industrial engines for their ability to throw men out of work. With many contemporaries, Butler understood that the machine had the means, through its ability to short-circuit human participation, to systematically destroy many human interrelationships. The machine may not have directly reduced sensitivity, but it seemed to diffuse aesthetic focus by a meaningless repetition of the same stimuli. Art, to survive, demanded a certain degree of psychic involvement, an autonomous capitulation to a not always rational visual order—and the machine, as Reuleaux made clear, could not allow that to happen. Consequently, there was little reason for the twentieth century to welcome with open arms an "art of machines." The term itself was a self-contradiction, like an "art of advertising" or an "art of scientific optics." It seemed to deny the very spiritual concern it was designed to support.

For any understanding of the prehistory of Kinetic Art, one other source of activity, also connected with the machine, is of great significance. To physiologists, kinematics suggested the following intriguing question: if order in machines can be determined by plotting their motions in sequence, then what is to prevent us from learning more about muscle structure and coordination from plotting the paths of living organisms in motion?

The revolutionary attempts by the physiologist E. J. Marey and the photographer E. Muybridge, both born in 1830 and living until 1904, produced the first scientific records of organic motion. A craving by the nineteenth-century public for moving illusions of humans and animals has already been well documented by the archaeologist C. W. Ceram. According to Ceram, the panoramas and dioramas of the larger European cities equaled in number the movie houses of today. Marey and Muybridge succeeded in transforming the recording of motion phenomena from entertainment into scientifically useful information. As Sigfried Giedion has stated (1948, p. 31), the "mechanization" or analytical reduction of motion has been for our era "the end product of a rationalistic view of the world," one in which the visual appearances of motion took a precedence over objects at rest for the first time in world history. Nevertheless, the task of capturing the trajectories of birds in flight, trotting horses, and humans descending stairs, all very common forms of locomotion, proved to be deceptively complex when compared to plotting the profiles of pairs of machine elements.

It is easy to understand why these pioneers of organic kinematics were interested in motion itself. Motion has become the basis for understanding phenomena in the natural sciences. Medicine, for one, has become increasingly concerned with organic processes. As we have observed with modern mathematics, variable functions overwhelmed the idea of static proportion; in physics the need to deal with dynamic systems led to the invention of statistical mechanics. Finally, matter itself was increasingly regarded as energy in motion. Motion and motion process became the elusive *Gestalten* for viewing the world in its true prospective.

Marey first recorded the movements of life by directly graphing the muscular spasms of various live organs under stimuli. For this he invented the Spymograph, a device for inscribing pulsations on a smoke-blackened cylinder. Later, in the 1880's, Marey turned to the rapidly maturing art of photography in an attempt to capture bird flight in three dimensions with three cameras positioned at right angles to one another. Muybridge, on the other hand, was interested in a two-dimensional succession of images. His famous book *The Human Figure in Motion* (1880) not only spurred the development of motion pictures, but with Marey's work it inspired Duchamp to depict motion through a succession of overlapping forms. The three-dimensional concoctions of Marey quite possibly relate to Futurist attempts to simulate motion in sculpture through a series of fused images. Yet, while there were immense incentives for the avant-garde to become involved in motion effects, there were equally strong aesthetic and human reasons for rejecting any such adventure.

Kinetic artists, until recently, have not considered the construction of machines by themselves as representing sculpture. There have been some mock machines in static form, spanning attempts from Jacob Epstein to Eduardo Paolozzi, but Duchamp's use of the bicycle wheel in 1913 was the first use of a working mechanical principle. The tendency then, and to a lesser degree now, was for artists to use machines furtively and obliquely. The determinate relationships of machines were considered confining and counter-artistic. Therefore, most of the early modern attempts to use actual mechanics have resulted in parodies of machines: this would include Man Ray's metronome entitled *Destructible Object*, Duchamp's *Roto-Relief* display at a Paris Exposition for industrial products, Calder's early motor-driven spoofs of medieval celestial automata, Bruno Munari's "useless machines" and Tinguely's motorized wire sculptures which reminded his wife of pastiches of precision-made Swiss watches.

Kinetic sculpture has most often been merely motorized sculpture—with the motor tucked away and well out of view, inobviously attached by a shaft or belt drive. The machine, like Milton's *Samson Agonistes*, was thought to have been rendered harmless, forced to labor far in the recesses of the work of art.

Early Stages of Kineticism

Ideas have a way of seeming unthinkably *passé* and then, all at once, remarkably relevant, even to the casual observer. Such a reversal describes the brief history of Kinetic Art. It came and went, only to come again searching for artistic fulfillment. Motion, a passion of twentieth-century artists, does not die easily and remains as illusive as ever.

The fact that dreams can be revived is typified by what the sculptor George Rickey has called "the morphology of movement." In 1963 the plan of this book called for a single chapter on Kinetic Art; this at a time when

224

literature on early Kinetic Art was relatively scarce and the European Kinetic revival was just being publicized. The outstanding piece of literature on the subject then was K. G. Hulten's catalogue for the "International Exhibition of Art in Motion," which opened at the Stedelijk Museum in Amsterdam, March, 1961. Now, more than six years after that exhibition, the literature on the subject has expanded considerably. Presently, all the iconology which previously symbolized movement and speed has played out of sculpture; we are left with a curious duality between inert *object* sculpture and sculpture that moves—both attempting to shed their status as sculpture.

Until 1961 in Europe (and three or four years later in the United States) remarkably little attention was directed toward Kinetic activity by critics and curators. Aesthetic hierarchies in New York City, not particularly conservative, still debate full acceptance of the Kinetic trend. In spite of official doubt, however, exhibitions and retrospectives have sprung up here and in Europe. The reason for this is evident: either critics have begun to suspect that they have neglected an important faction of modern art, or this was only a spurious attempt to produce a "history" for a recent fad. The author is inclined toward the first view.

From the standpoint of statistical distribution, Kinetic Art chronologies draw a revealing profile. The interest in Kinetics has been scattered and relatively small since the first decade of the present century. Two clusters of activity emerge from assorted names and works. Beginning for practical purposes with Duchamp's first effort in 1913, Kinetic interest mounted and came to a focus about 1925; from there, a steady decline of activity was evident which, aside from Calder's, Thomas Wilfred's, and Moholy-Nagy's work, resulted in near stagnation during the 1930's and 1940's. By the mid-1950's a renaissance had begun to take place, and by the early 1960's Kinetic activity, especially in Europe, was attracting some of the best young talent.

Many of the early names peripherally connected with Kinetic Art were interested in the aesthetics of dynamic situations—not in the far more complicated task of making moving art. These men—Boccioni, Luigi Russolo, Malevich, and Alexander Rodchenko—were literary prophets of future Kinetic Art—not mechanics of the possible. For instance, Umberto Boccioni's "Technical Manifesto of Sculpture" (1912) bombards the reader with hints of sculpture's impending dynamism, yet not once does it fasten on the practical problems of real movement. Significantly, Boccioni attacked the "nobility" of bronze and marble—the inherent pomposity of so much monumental sculpture—and laid the way for the use of many materials which would make Kineticism possible. His conception of motion is classically bound to the forms and means of the first industrial revolution as these sentences from the "Manifesto" illustrate (Herbert, 1964, p. 55).

One must not forget that the tick-tock and the movement of the hands of a clock, the rise and fall of a piston in its cylinder, the meshing and unmeshing of two gears with the continual disappearance and reappearance of their little steel rectangles, the frenzy of a fly-wheel, the whirl of a propeller, all these are plastic and pictorial elements of which Futurist sculptural work must make use. For example: a valve opening and closing creates a rhythm as beautiful but infinitely newer than that of a living eyelid.

The men pivotal in determining the practical aesthetic of future Kinetic Art were few in number—Marcel Duchamp, Naum Gabo, Alexander Calder, and László Moholy-Nagy. Significantly, the reputations of three of these artists are based primarily on their fixed works, not their Kinetic output. If nonmoving art has dominated the nonobjective trend of the past fifty years, to a large extent this has been due to the overwhelming technical and financial difficulties attending all Kinetic experiments. The Kinetic Art produced has simply not compared in creative stature with other works by the best painters and sculptors. Even for these four artists, a course from involvement to disillusionment and withdrawal from Kinetic activities (or at least from motor-driven Kinetics as in the case of Calder) can be traced. These artists, at a point fairly early in their careers, recognized the potential of an art of motion, but each made a few experiments, and finally abandoned the Kinetic direction.

The artists named first challenged but did not destroy the aesthetic partition between Kinetic constructions and static sculpture. Therefore it is profitable to review some of these early "failures"—failures in the limited sense that, while most of these men did not achieve a viable Kinetic Art, they did make definite contributions to the present Kinetic movement. Importantly, each produced *objects*—objects which could move—yet material entities more affiliated with the traditional sense of sculptural presence than with motion as a prime consideration.

Marcel Duchamp's forays into Kinetics remain difficult experiments to evaluate because their metaphysical and aesthetic implications run far deeper than their success as art in motion. Ever present in Duchamp's efforts is the intimation that nothing is gained in art without losing something of equal or greater value. As prophetic as his efforts were, they shared none of the enthusiastic idealism of Gabo and Moholy-Nagy.

The *Bicycle Wheel* (FIG. 83) by Duchamp cannot be regarded primarily as a mobile object although it is the first modern Kinetic work. Both its liter-

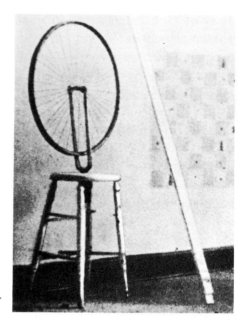

83. Marcel Duchamp, *Bicycle Wheel*, 1913.

al reproduction of the stroboscopic effect, simulated in Duchamp's earlier mechano-morphic paintings, and its reiteration of rotative energy, a wheel-of-life fatalism that becomes an integral element of Duchamp's iconology, barely touch the tangled web of metaphysical speculation ever present in the mind of its creator.

From a practical standpoint, the Readymade bicycle wheel was an apt choice. Only a few years before Duchamp's appropriation it had been mechanically perfected. The ball-bearing-mounted axle and tension-wire spokes made the bicycle wheel one of the lightest and most elegant devices then commonly in use. Free of the friction of the ground, the wheel keeps turning for minutes from any small push of the hand. The lightweight wheel, the chain drive, and tubular frame construction made the bicycle, along with the automobile, revolutionary forms of personal transportation.

Inverted on a kitchen stool, only the rim turns, fixed in space, invisibly attached to its hub and the inverted Y-frame. It would be misleading to suggest that Duchamp regarded the *Bicycle Wheel*, thus propelled, as an ideal solution to Kinetic Art. While beautiful in itself, the utilitarian wheel has been rendered functionally immobile—like a turtle on its back. It is motion that goes nowhere and a machine that does not "work" in the accepted sense. Yet, by aesthetic inversion, Duchamp had transformed the wheel into an optical device. As in the glass paintings that he was shortly to create, the viewer was given the options of looking through the moving wheel or catching the reflective patterns of its glinting spokes. This ambiguity of motion intention—of seen and unseen effects—continued with the hidden objects inside *A Bruit Secret* (1916), and the thermometer thrust into the sugar cubes of *Why Not Sneeze?* (1921).

The kinetic-optical intention of Duchamp's post-painterly investigations is first self-evident in the *Rotating Glass Plates* (1920). Constructed with the help of another early Kineticist, Man Ray, this optical machine consists of five glass plates clamped to a spindle and turned by a small fan belt connected to an electric motor. Some have speculated on the frequent use of mechanical rotative motion by Duchamp and later Kineticists. No aesthetic or metaphysical justification seems necessary. The answer, both circumstantial and physical, is due essentially to the fact that the motion generated by electrical motors is rotational. Since the electric motor forms the basis for a good deal of Kinetic Art, an artist may either convert its torque drive into linear or eccentric trajectories or leave it rotary. Since motion conversion demands some proficiency in mechanical engineering, artists often have been obliged to leave it rotary—or to employ the most basic conversion mechanisms. Duchamp, for one, was fascinated with the hypnotic potential of rotary motion. But even with his simple devices he constantly resorted to technical expertise.

The *Rotating Glass Plates* presents a form of inverse illusionism. Rather than making an object immaterial, as do the wire spokes on the *Bicycle Wheel*, the rotating glass plates, actually just strips of glass, fill in a pattern of concentric lines, forming a whirling cone of movement. This fabrication of *virtual volumes* was for Moholy-Nagy the artistic realization of the physicist's notion of mass and volume: namely, that volumes were constructed of coordinated events in space-time. Although Duchamp has observed that several of his works contain ideas analogous to later scientific discoveries, it seems doubtful that he had anything more in mind concerning the *Revolving Glass Plates* than an artistic experiment in perception.

More optical in the sense of producing an unexpected or ambiguous image was Duchamp's *Rotary Demi-Sphere* (FIG. 84). Its illusionary quality is based on two sets of eccentrically-centered, concentric circles. Lebel has likened it to the eye of a gigantic Cyclops and there is little doubt that one of its purposes was to induce hypnotic reveries. As a form of power-driven beguilement, it was the prototype for the *Rotoreliefs* (1935), Duchamp's last serious experiment in Kinetics. These mainly are linear drawings on cardboard disks which, when revolved at high speed, produced graphic illusions in depth.

It is more than likely that Duchamp gave up the pursuit of art when the psychic and practical problems of a mechanical technology began to over-

84. Marcel Duchamp, *Rotary Demi-Sphere*, 1925.

power his vision. The author had this impression in 1960 when he had the privilege of asking Duchamp a few questions about his intentions. One question was about the "electric disrobing mechanism" which he had planned to fit halfway between the two sections of *The Large Glass* (Duchamp's last painting, his *magnum opus*, worked on between 1915 and 1923). Was this to have operated on actual electrical-mechanical principles?

He answered no. The mechanical nature of the device was purely metaphorical, and furthermore, he insisted, he did not believe in the use of mechanics in art. Duchamp maintained that the physical possibilities of mechanics had been falsified in their practical artistic value. In a word, they were "unartistic"—a strange sobriquet from such an iconoclast. By this, he alluded to the direct application of machines to art so that the machines could "produce" art—as they might be set to work producing goods for a manufacturer. The machine, he seemed to imply, was only an object worthy of philosophical speculation, not a philosopher or creator in its own right. Certainly Duchamp has affixed his blessing to machine art, as his approval of Tinguely's endeavors indicate. His stipulation appears to be that the artist must establish a relationship with his mechanisms whereby they are tamed or humanized, thus rendered incapable of upsetting the balance of cause and effect.

Perhaps inconsistent with this was a speculation which Duchamp made concerning the future of art. Art is an underground phenomenon—this has been his contention for some time. He speculated that art may come from a person or people who do not even consider themselves artists. This has happened in the past. More surprising at that date was the prediction that a future art could come about from the manipulation of light. Probably this would only happen with a technology more sophisticated than the mechanicalism which he had earlier rejected as "unartistic."

More than any artist previously, Duchamp confronted the psychic and practical difficulties of realizing a viable motorized art. A Kinetic Art, somehow, presented a contradiction in terms. As a sculpture totem, the machine remains unassailable. Yet to function in actuality—and artistically—it had to be injected with elements of imprecision and irrationality. Then, perhaps, it could begin to live, in doubt and indecision, as human beings do. Most revealing is the fact that Duchamp, according to Lebel, regarded himself as an "unfrocked artist" after his art became centered around the *Rotoreliefs*. No longer dealing with the gentle illusionism of painting, nor even the leverage of Dada's tools (irony, fallibility, and repetition), Duchamp realized that he had placed himself on the brink of raw technology. Such a situation demanded that one either draw back or plunge into a rational world of impersonally controlled effects. He chose to do the former.

"The Realist Manifesto," written and distributed in Moscow in 1920 by Naum Gabo, is a curious document. Half the writing devotes itself to denigrating the role of the Cubists and Futurists—condemning the works of the Paris- and Milan-based artists as a superficial glorification of contemporary reality. Gabo's attack possesses the vehemence and moral indignation of someone who feels within himself a superior truth. His truth was, in fact, a mixture of scientific idealism and some relatively new plastic conceptions: these included the use of planar, linear, and transparent surfaces for structural solutions which radically departed from the monolithic tradition of sculpture. In particular, Gabo attacked the Futurist notion of speed as a vapid abstraction with no basis in painting or sculpture. He reaffirmed the supremacy of the space-time continuum as the single logical basis upon which to construct an art form.

"*We affirm in these arts a new element, the kinetic rhythms as the basic forms of our perception of real time*" (1957, p. 152). This is the only sentence in the document which gives serious indication that Gabo is concerned with real motion in his constructions. In that same year Gabo produced his only three-dimensional Kinetic work, *Kinetic Construction* (FIG. 85).

Technically, the construction is utter simplicity, which accounts in part for its importance. At the base of the work a vibrating electrical motor is attached to a vertically erect length of flat spring steel weighted slightly

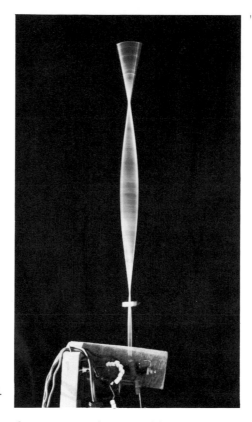

85. Naum Gabo, *Kinetic Construction*, 1920.

on the upper end. In motion its outer form strangely resembles the mass-defining contours of Brancusi's *Bird in Flight* (1919)—of which Gabo could have had no knowledge. In the same way as Duchamp's revolving glass construction, the *Kinetic Construction* presents a virtual volume, a volume described by the speeding trajectories of an object. It has already been noted that the harmonic wave-form pattern which Gabo's construction creates is, in spirit, if not in physical principle, a visual echo of then recent theories of wave mechanics as the basis of matter. It announced on the macroscopic level—to the few capable of understanding the message—the essential immateriality of matter. And, like Duchamp's *Three Standard Stoppages* (1913), it remains one of the supreme artistic interpretations of the sensually indefinable core of solid matter.

Except for some rotating Kinetic paintings, Gabo never attempted more constructions in real motion. In the 1937 *Circle* essay he had this to say about the future of Kinetics (1957, p. 169):

Closely related to the space problem in sculpture is the problem of Time. There is an affinity between them although the satisfactory solution of the latter still remains unsolved, being complex and obstructed by many obstacles. The definite solution is still handicapped by its technical difficulties. Nevertheless, the idea and the way for its solution is already traced in its main outlines by the constructive art. I find it essential for the completion of the discussion of the whole problem of our sculpture to sketch here in general terms the question of Time.

Gabo goes on to insist that the illusion of motion in such works as *The Victory of Samothrace* (ca. 200 B.C.) does not substitute for real motion. It is evident, he states, that the human mind responds to motion presented artistically, but as far as sculpture is concerned (1957, p. 169): "Mechanics have not yet reached that stage of absolute perfection where it can produce motion in a sculptural work without killing, through the mechanical parts, the pure sculptural content; because the motion is of importance and not the mechanism which produces it. Thus the solution of this problem becomes a task for future generations."

Concerning Gabo's statement on the visual competition between motion and motion-producing mechanisms, his viewpoint succinctly defines the dilemma of early mechanistic Kinetics. Somehow the motor "interfered" with the motion it produced and had to be made small and inobvious enough not to cause competition with the sculpture itself. To an extent, this problem was solved by Calder and others by considering the machine and any motion-translating mechanism as part of the sculpture itself, thereby putting sculpture to the "truth to material" test! There is almost something pathetic about an unadorned machine set up as a work of art. So it is not surprising that most "machine" sculptures have been presented as comic or Neo-Dada episodes—rarely as purist constructions.

In 1956, during an interview with the artists Ibram Lassaw and Ilya Bolotowsky, Gabo reiterated that his views about time and kinetic rhythms had not changed. In a talk with Gabo in this same year, the author remembers his emphatic denial that kinetic rhythms had to be incorporations of real motion. He insisted that the work that he and his brother had been doing since the Russian Revolution was based on temporal principles in which the viewer's eye apprehended linear rhythms of a construction *in succession*. He tried to distinguish this from the way the eye fastens on the surfaces of a monolithic sculpture all at once. For some time this has been his justification for attaching the word *kinetic* to his constructions.

One of the legendary events in the annals of modern sculpture, a meeting with fruitful repercussions, was Alexander Calder's visit to Mondrian's studio in 1930. After this visit Calder reputedly dropped his representational wire constructions. Briefly he turned to painting, and then proceeded with a series of geometric constructions fashioned from wood, wire, and sheet metal. By 1932 he had begun the first of a number of motorized constructions. Mondrian's ideas on the use of simple, primary-colored forms in dynamic equilibrium had solidly taken shape.

Anyone fortunate enough to see Calder's total output could not but be amazed at his wealth of ideas in kinetics; in particular, the early 1930's saw both the beginning of the mobiles and a number of experiments with motor-driven sculpture. However, Calder was dissatisfied with his machine art and he received little encouragement in that direction. Gradually he moved out of the Constructivist idiom toward the more sprightly shapes of Surrealism via the influences of Miró and Arp.

During this Surrealist metamorphosis Calder consolidated his mechanical technique into a simple vocabulary of point balances and catenated counterbalanced linear elements. In both matters of mechanics and metal finish Calder's thinking became—the simpler the better! Temperamentally he has consistently rejected the precisionist finishes of the Constructivists.

The fact that Calder did not develop the mobile mechanically seems to bother one advocate and practitioner of Kinetic Art, George Rickey. In Rickey's view the present generation of Kinetic Art owes its impetus to the Constructivists—and to some extent he is right. Nonetheless, it is unfortunate that Rickey continues to vastly underrate Calder's influence on recent Kinetic efforts.

Calder in all seriousness explored a considerable area of present Kinetic activity before settling on the hanging mobiles. In the process of exploration, as Rickey has pointed out (Kepes, p. 113), Calder touched upon many ideas in Kinetics, but developed few. Yet certain types of constructions by Tinguely, Jesus-Raphael Soto, Walter Linck, Harry Kramer, Julio Le Parc, Yaacov Agam, Takis, and Rickey—a good portion of the front-rank Kineticists—have in common elements explored by Calder in the period between 1931 and 1936. It may be helpful to name a few of the devices very much in vogue which Calder used in principle: in Kinetics some of these are sticklike and unstable objects hung in front of a panel producing random shadow effects, sculptures propelled by pumped liquids, belt and wheel systems as an integral part of a sculpture, constructions in which elements are interchangeable by hand, the use of hand-driven cams and crank trains plus motorized animation of coiled springs.

Quite obviously Calder's particular temperament demanded a physical configuration more sensuous and free-wheeling than any producible with machines. Calder chose to explore *sculptural* means, in the traditional sense, more than mechanical potentialities. It is erroneous to regard this election as a failure of nerve or as essentially noninventive. Calder's uses of plate steel through welding and bolting large structures proved to be important technical realizations for, among others, David Smith and Anthony Caro.

Calder's motorized construction *A Universe* (FIG. 86) may serve as a pastiche of the Newtonian concept of cosmic bodies in a mechanized void. It would seem originally, according to his remarks to the art critic Michel Seuphor, that Calder had a much more serious intention: to transform the celestial aura of moving bodies into something which could be witnessed in miniature. Mechanical Constructivism gave the answer. Yet, if we compare the amateur crudeness of his little spool-and-belt-driven contraptions with the consummate precision of eighteenth-century astronomical clocks, we grasp what must have occurred to Calder also as an absurd situation. His talents for parody, unintentional or otherwise, were never so subversive as Duchamp's, nor pleasurably masochistic as Tinguely's.

As Rickey has observed, perhaps in years to come Calder's stunning success with the mobile (FIG. 87), coupled with a dearth of research by younger artists into the possibilities of mechanical motion, will appear as some curious breach in the plastic evolution of this century. One might ask, where were the kinetic explorers between 1925 and 1955? There are several answers: this absence was due in part to the continued vitality of abstract painting and sculpture through the 1950's; also Calder's early overwhelming success with quasi-random motion convinced almost all observers that attempts to produce a machine-driven deterministic art would be clumsy by comparison; finally, considerable financial and technical backing was absolutely necessary for further Kinetic experimentation. Calder had not set out to solve the tangled psychological problems of motion perception and temporal organization. Instead he chose to limit himself to the problems of balance, form, and motion, almost as a primitive or an intuitive sensualist. The basic problems of making a mobile—determining the position of joints, degrees of rotational freedom, and length and curvature of the balance arms—became a matter of determining physical equilibrium after an initial compositional conception. Knowing that the elements of a mobile naturally follow a Markovian chain of cause and effect—a series of connected trajectories—proved to be the first step in the investigation of time-space aesthetics.

That any system—biological, musical, or mechanical—seeks equilibrium, and after various diversions finds it, becomes a psychological goal in the perception of organized activity. When at rest, Calder's mobile constructions show the security of static sculpture. Wind or human interference destroys this self-containment. Given the opportunity to seek equilibrium

234

 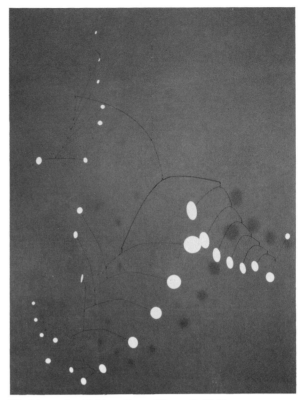

86. Alexander Calder, *A Universe*, 1934.   87. Alexander Calder, *Snow Flurry I*, 1948.

again, the mobile engenders a series of thrusts and counter-thrusts—which become smaller and smaller—and eventually end in stillness.

László Moholy-Nagy's contribution to nonobjective art has been often deprecated since his death in 1946. However, as a teacher and thinker Moholy was responsible for a good share of the methodology which survived the closing of the Bauhaus. He had a genius for understanding the potential of collective visual phenomena (not to be confused with the creation of startling icons—private images were not Moholy's forte) and, in particular, the phenomenology of motion. While a creator of ambitious Kinetic devices, his real talent lay in showing young people, with brilliant clarity, the promise of Kineticism.

It would be fitting in a historical review of Kinetic Art to begin with Moholy's famous *Light-Space Modulator*, a device perfected between 1922 and 1931. However, this will be saved for a later examination of light as an art form. As a theorist, though, Moholy's ideas on Kinetic Art deserve to be examined more fully than they have been up to now.

235

In 1930 his *The New Vision: From Material to Architecture* was translated into English from German and published in New York. The book offers two things: a description of the *Vorkurs*, the Bauhaus basic design course which Moholy along with Johannes Itten and Josef Albers helped form, and an outline of the visual potentials of materials and structures then available. Significant is Moholy's method of categorizing sculpture into evolutionary stages. These five developments of sculpture are: the blocked-out form, the modeled (hollowed-out) form, the perforated form, (also assembled constructions are in this category), the form in equipoise, and Kinetic sculpture. He lists these steps of sculptural development—"not in the individual, but in the history of culture as a whole"—implying, one assumes, that the stages cover more than just the modern Western tradition. If this is true, then it has been only in this century that his evolutionary theory of sculpture has realized its potential. Previously, kinetic devices may have reflected technical, religious, or recreational values, but hardly ever artistic. His list is more an artistic imperative for this century than a historical survey. Moholy's analysis is essentially a technical morphology. He says, in effect, that the sensual apprehension of form has been overtaken by an intellectual grasp of form, that cultural stylistics are giving way to a burgeoning technology.

Interestingly enough, Moholy inserts *equipoised* sculpture between *perforated* (also called *open*) sculpture and *Kinetic* sculpture. Ten years before Calder realized his first mobiles Moholy's students constructed works based on the principle of equilibrium. These student efforts, or at least those photos of them published, never achieved the flexibility or grace of Calder's mobiles. Most of the Bauhaus solutions were rigid Constructivist attempts to balance unequal weights on uneven arms. Moholy recognized that the great obstacle to equipoise sculpture lay in finding a power source not obviously visible. He considered magnetic force and remote electrical control as possible solutions. It was left to Calder to harness random currents of air.

While rest remained the natural state for equipoise sculpture, Moholy felt that motion belonged primarily to Kinetics. The intellectual conception of Kinetics in the 1920's very much revolved around his idea of *virtual volumes*—the outline or trajectory presented by an object in motion. With this in mind, he sought to represent the transformation of sculptural qualities with the following equation (1938, p. 129): "sculpture = material + mass relationships, changes to the dematerialized and highly intellectualized formula: sculpture = volume relationships...."

As with Gabo's planar constructions, mass was transformed into volume, weight was reduced, thus the space-filling capacity of sculpture was maintained. *Thingness* continued to be an important consideration to the Kineticists of the 1920's. It still is for the present generation of Kinetic artists, though their *theoretical* concerns are less a space-object duality. The emphasis presently seems to be on the *qualities of motion* and on *time sequences*. As a result, the immateriality or de-emphasis of form which has taken place seems extreme compared to Moholy's equation, though not far from a later concern of his with musical time.

In his book Moholy includes a thumbnail sketch entitled "The History of Kinetic Sculpture." It is a tribute to Moholy's intellect and visionary powers that the outlines of Kinetic histories to date have pretty much followed his pattern. He quotes from Gabo's "Realist Manifesto" and refers to it as a model for the manifesto which he published with Alfred Kemény in 1922, "The Kinetic-Constructive System of Force." In an excerpt from his own manifesto he quotes the usual doctrinaire ambitions of constructive art about exchanging static for dynamic values. The last paragraph quoted, though, contains a singularly important and speculative statement about the future of Kinetic Art (1938, p. 138): "The first projects looking toward the dynamic-constructive system of forces can only be experimental, demonstrating devices for the testing of the relations between man, material, power and space. Next comes the *utilization of the experimental results for the creation of freely moving (free from mechanical and technical movement) works of art.*" (Italics added.)

This paragraph implies two things. As a later, expanded version of his *New Vision* would indicate (*Vision in Motion*, 1947), Moholy was well aware that the artistic deficiencies of mechanical motion made it less than a perfect medium, even in its most realized form. Nevertheless, he spoke of the need by artists to continue the Kinetic investigation—even with failure as a strong possibility. He surmised that experience in the Kinetic medium plus a new acclimatization to time-motion perceptual patterns would be indispensable for the ultimate success of the Kinetic cause.

Moholy spoke from experience. He produced one work, *Kinetic Sculpture* (1930–1936), that could well have emerged from the Kinetic vanguard studios of Milan, Paris or Düsseldorf during the 1960's. This construction consists of two square forms rotatable from gyroscopic axes, and extended from a plate of polished steel. Inside the two kernel forms are networks of glass tubing partially filled with mercury. It appears that these mercury receptacles are set in motion by hand. The total effect, one would guess, is not overpowering—the movement of the mercury and the turning of the kernel forms do not seem to justify the complexity of the apparatus. Conquently, it is prophetic that in 1922 Moholy saw the necessity of a "freely moving" sculpture (free from mechanical and technical movement), a form of locomotion without the cumbersomeness of classical machines.

Precisely what form this could take he does not specify. Yet he spoke of there being more to the evolution of sculpture than technological development, and insisted that all the experimentation of artists must have "significance for the biological 'nourishment' of man." Moholy had been one of the few artists to recognize the biological relevance of motion phenomena. He perceptively saw that much of the motion produced by technology, while perhaps outwardly impressive, was injurious to the human nervous system. It was not Moholy's purpose, nor that of Gabo, simply to reproduce the environmental chaos of urban technology.

What is the alternative? Certainly Moholy never strove to parody the machine. He was at once too optimistic and temperamentally attuned to the future to be caught in such a dead end. He sensed a greater truth than lamentation for the decline of age-old perceptual sensibilities. He understood that Kineticism would be viewed as more than another stylistic innovation. It would mean probing a concern which sat at the very apex of Western desire: breaking the bounds of Classical tradition. In Spengler's words (1918, p. 228):

The problem of motion touches, at once and immediately, the secrets of existence, which are alien to the waking-consciousness and yet inexorably press upon it. In posing motion as a problem we affirm our will to comprehend the incomprehensible, the when and the wherefore, Destiny, blood, all that our intuitive processes touch in our depths. Born to see, we strive to set it before our eyes in the light, so that we may in a literal sense grasp it, assure ourselves of it as of something tangible.

Precursors of the New Tendency

Between 1956 and 1965 young artists in Western Europe reacted to Tachist painting (gestural abstraction). The New Tendency in art somehow went beyond preoccupation with the painterly gesture; it went into the dynamic *apart-from-thingness* characterized by scientific concern with fields of energy. Artistically, this awareness found expression through the following question: what material aspects of a work of art influence its appearance besides obvious considerations of how mediums are individually manipulated? By the late 1940's a small group of artists had sensed that "circumstantial events"—the shadows created by the raised surface of a painting, the reflective glass protecting a drawing, or the diffusion properties of emitted light—might be the key to a new mode of artistic perception. Beyond this lay a slowly growing awareness that art was not bound by frame or pedestal, but, in terms of its effective control of surrounding space, enjoyed considerable power to expand into its immediate environment. That quality of aesthetic isolation which had so long characterized both the art work and its subject was in the process of vanishing. A growing desire was to extend phenomenal appearances as far as the eye could see. Hence the repetitive surfaces of the Atlantic Ocean were viewed as perfect New Tendency painting or sculpture. As mutually exclusive mediums even the terms painting and sculpture began to lose their importance.

In 1946 a small volume appeared on the Italian sculptor Lucio Fontana (Zocchi, 1946). The book reveals a profusion of styles by Fontana: late Roman Classicism, early Renaissance, Italian Impressionism, French post-Cubism, Modern Neo-Realism, and even elements of a particular brute Concretism. This last mentioned emerged as the nearest approximation to Fontana's mature style, having within it an imperviousness to accepted principles of plastic abstraction. Yet the book gives little intimation that its subject was also the author of the "White Manifesto" *(Spazialisimo)*, written in the same year.

Within the next few years the "White Manifesto" became an aesthetic focusing point for various artists centered around Fontana in Milan. In one sense the group Spazialisimo attempted to reaccept the challenge of Kineticism after the Constructivists of the 1920's and 1930's had lost their impetus. However, the influences of Tachism and informalism were too pervasive at that time not to dominate all tendencies toward the reabsorption of machine values. The strength of the manifesto lies in its realization that motion and plastic art are inseparable goals; it recognizes also that such a merger is far from being achieved. Fontana begins by stating (1962, no page number):

Art is passing through a latent period. A force exists which man is unable to express. We shall express it in a literal form in this manifesto.

It is for this reason that we are asking all the men of science throughout the world, who are conscious of the fact that art is a vital necessity for the human race, to orient a part of their research towards the discovery of the luminous and malleable substances and the sound-producing instruments which will make possible the development of tetradimensional art.

Just as many others before Fontana realized that a good portion of the evolution of temporal or Kinetic Art depended upon technological advancements. And long before Marshall McLuhan, Fontana grasped the fact that technology radically reorganized man's perceptual capabilities: the psychic response of man becomes blunted in an age of mechanics.

Like the Futurists and Constructivists before him, Fontana reconstructs, historically, the fundamental dynamism of the world. He reiterates the inability of artists to match this dynamism technically and testifies to the impotence of contemporary art.

After acknowledging a temporary inability of technics to provide the physical means for a space-time art, Fontana states the principles of a methodology leading toward, if not uniting with, Kinetics.

Our intention is to unite the entire life of man in a synthesis which linked to the function of his natural conditions, constitutes a true manifestation of his being.

...Sensation was everything with the primitive man; sensation in the face of misunderstood nature, musical sensations, rhythmic sensations. It is our intention to develop this original condition of man.

Since he lacked the desire to produce meaningful Kinetic Art, much of Fontana's subsequent work hinged on an uncovering of primeval sensation to which he refers. The dry, earthlike surfaces, punched holes in pattern, mixtures of raised and reflected surfaces all attest to his desire to reveal the origins of phenomenal perception—beyond the canvas with its techniques of symbolic differentiation. The primitive handling of Fontana's canvases is still generally mistaken for a variety of Tachism. And, since so many of Fontana's Milan followers were painting in the vogue of Tachism (1946–1959), this is not surprising. Nevertheless, in his own work he extended the principles of his manifesto to where his original intentions could not be mistaken by younger artists north of Italy.

Fontana's spatial ceilings, his plastic use of neon light and his grotesque "nonsculptures" eventually convinced important younger European artists that his direction was aesthetically and perceptually unique. Toward the end of the 1950's artists from France, Holland, Germany, and other nearby countries began to make periodic pilgrimages to his studio in Milan. Fontana's example had generated much new thinking about the random nature of light and dark and its ever-changing potential to show where space begins and extends, and particularly to exploit the natural sources of optical stimulation. He is the precursor of a Kineticism not constrained by studied mechanical relationships, but as natural as the changing patterns of sunlight filtering through the leaves of a tree to the ground beneath.

Another important mentor of the New Tendency is the French geometrical painter Victor Vasarely. On the surface at least Vasarely represents all the rationalism that Fontana would eschew. More systematically than the older generation of geometric painters, Vasarely has pushed the idea of methodical investigation. As with Albers in America, this has taken the form of a search for what has lately become known as the "optical" principle. While Vasarely's progress has been primarily two-dimensional, his glass and aluminum reliefs, gaining effects by overlapping perforated planes, have influenced sculptors. These are kinetic inasmuch as an ambient viewer produces his own change of patterns.

Possibly Vasarely's influence, aside from the structured uses of positive-negative figures, has been best manifested by his private writings. These were first made available by the École des Beaux-Arts in Paris in 1962. To some extent their impact was already evident before their publication because of Vasarely's many conversations with younger artists. From their beginnings in the early 1950's, these notes anticipate many of the attitudes toward the control of machine art soon endemic to the New Tendency. Many of his philosophical positions concerning mutability and instability helped to trigger some Kinetic Art. These positions contain a strongly analytical and objective flavor in the face of an expanding desire for simplification in the arts. However, this level-headedness inspired numbers of young artists to make investigations where progress appeared hopeless and technically out of reach. As with Gabo and others peripherally involved with the scientific ethos, Vasarely has maintained a fast line between "art" and the results of scientific research. From the notes and reflections for the year 1959 (1962, p. 49):

There exists groups of young artists in whose midst everything occurs as if feverish inventory of all plastic possibilities was being carried out. Here, to be sure, is the material for an electric brain, and for the future storage center (banque plastique) of plastic devices. Perhaps you will say that this plasticity, which is now running into debit, is not capable of being anything but mediocre quality. Nevertheless, let us begin. We will see what follows. In any case, if the product of art does not go beyond the ranks of the elite "connoisseur," then the art will die of suffocation. (Translated from the French by Barbara Stafford.)

Vasarely's observations include an attitude toward plasticity (as a sort of artistic complement to mechanical invention) which appears now far more realistic than the duplicity of thousands of Tachists and Abstract Expressionists running in circles coveting microscopic ideas. He realized, as many have, the essential social nature of art—not only in its dissemination but in the making of it. Consequently, sharing results toward small but real increments of plastic "progress" became a legitimate posture for the New Tendency artist. The very human need for artistic signature was not discouraged—though that too was to be questioned by the younger generation.

Vasarely realized as early as 1954 (and only Moholy-Nagy seemed to see the same implications) that Kinetic Art would demand a mode of cognition capable of grasping the visual complexity of kinematic motion. It was more than a matter of developing "moving pictures." It took a practical turn with Vasarely's participation in the "Le Mouvement" show (1955) at the Galerie Denise René. His work appeared with works of art by Yaacov Agam, Pol Bury, Calder, Duchamp, Robert Jacobson, Jesus-Raphael Soto, and Tinguely. In the catalogue for the exhibition are his "Notes for a Manifesto," which include some brief explanations about his own particular development of positive-negative and form-color ideas. His statement summarized postwar awareness toward the integration of kinetics with artistic activity—rather than polemicized for innovational works of the future. His view of the kinetic spectrum is orthodox enough: kinetic situations can be generated through architectural synthesis where the ambient spectator produces his own optical motion via a fixed relief, or Kinetics can resort to automatic constructions (the venerable idea of automatons), or thirdly, motion art can develop through abstract cinema. Vasarely attacked the concept of "the unique work of art" as a myth, helping further to clear the way practically for an art, not only of machine values, but *by* machine. The idea of "multiples" or editions of factory-made art has, moreover, become commonplace following his insistence that *quality* was never affected by repetition in literature or music.

As the champion of monochrome painting, Yves Klein, after his initial direction had been exhausted, had little choice within the range of traditional art. Thus, in the last few years of his life (d. 1962), everything attempted reached intentionally beyond the scope of the canvas. Rather, the canvas became the residue of poetic ambition turned away from painting. Each work implied activities and undertakings which were directed toward the stream of life. Even the electric blue sponge reliefs gave off a pungent, if not offensive, odor in a warm gallery. Moreover, nudes smeared with "International Klein Blue" were "living brushes" only in the sense that Klein was a "living" painter. Certainly the scene of Klein in evening clothes directing his "brushes" with a background of strings was more a work of art than the framed result.

This attempt to carry art work into the void was climaxed with the exhibition "Le Vide" at Iris Clert. Presenting himself in an immaculate room in pure white *sans* paintings, sculpture, or works of any kind, Klein represented the artist returned to innocence. What effulgences he gave off were due to earlier works in the minds of his admirers. Klein, perhaps better than any practitioner before, realized that consummate Kinetic works of art would somehow overspill into the catch basin of ordinary activities—eating, breathing, playing, existing.

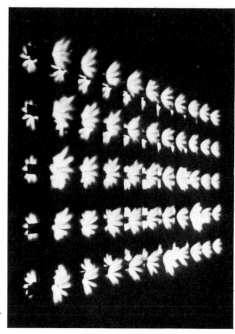

88. Yves Klein, *Double Sided Wall of Fire*, 1961.

But for a few exceptions, Klein's Kinetic projects remained unrealized. One suspects that his plans for air-conditioned cities in the tropics stationed on Buck Rodgers "space platforms" were destined never to leave the drawing board. The same is mostly true of his fire-and-water fountains with the important exception of the Krefeld exhibition (FIG. 88). Klein wielding an automatic blowtorch in front of a canvas was infinitely more dramatic than the resulting *La Marque du Feu*. What Klein was able to do was to promise unexplored continents to others at a time when iconoclast avant-gardism was dying on its feet.

"Immateriality" was Yves Klein's rallying cry, and immateriality, manifested in barely revealed signs, became the standard of the New Tendency. He was the nucleus of a new art reality—not in bronze, steel, stone, or even plastic—but in the gaseous and liquid elements, and their residue. The sky itself became an extensionless pristine canvas waiting for some enterprising draftsman. At the Hotel Chelsea in 1961 Klein wrote (1961, p. 3): "I think of those words that I was inspired to write one evening. Wouldn't the future artist be he who expressed through silence, but eternally, an immense painting lacking any sense of dimension?"

Can the world ever accommodate such spirits of the "possible"? The "immaterial sensitivity" that Klein spoke of was not fully realized in his art and is not yet any artist's personal conquest as something captured in the tyranny of the *objet d'art*. Rather, Klein's desire for immateriality was like some unrequited "Romantic Agony" unliberated from its Shelleyan grave of blue sky and blue water.

By now it should be apparent that the artists who propelled the New Tendency into life were for the most part painters. The flexibility of the New Tendency was its concern only for visual effect. Its disregard for the objective status of works of art was complemented by a will to realize motion in new forms—not in the clattering machines and watch escapements of Boccioni, but in the fluid traces of completely ethereal phenomena.

Much of what has been described as "Optical Art" did not originate as retinal gymnastics but, as Jesus-Raphael Soto insists (quoted in Fox, June–July, 1965, p. 15), "to get rid of all the problems of form, to have a work without history or composition in which the elements are anonymous and can be repeated *ad infinitum*."

Perhaps the kinetic sensibility in Optical Art owes its origins more to Soto than to any other artist. His work in Paris since 1950 on the interference patterns produced by lined surfaces goes beyond both two- and three-dimensional considerations. As he says (Fox, p. 15), "The elements describe nothing. It is an art detached from any language of expression." Soto's work with various *Vibration Structures* and overlapping patterns are profoundly important. They attest to the constant recurrence of immateriality in modern art.

Jean Tinguely serves as a symbol of activity, not a formal model for the New Tendency—providing, as it were, comic relief from the ultra-seriousness of Op and "programmed" Kinetics. Tinguely has succeeded psychologically because he has exploited the underlying human hostility to mechanization. A Kineticist employing a strictly determinate program for a luminous screen device *tries* to sustain the attention and interest of an observer. Sometimes he succeeds—but mostly not. Tinguely, by proclaiming the boring and repetitious nature of the machine, insulates his creations against the attacks of frustrated observers. Small "surprises" and breakdowns often disrupt the repetition of Tinguely's devices. In concert his machines produce a peculiar kind of feedback and group psychology. Rhythms of mechanical alliteration and lassitude connected with incessant nonorganic activity begin to pervade the viewer's mind.

Tinguely's forays into world politics perversely avoid orthodox social protest. Similar to Aldous Huxley's Gammas assisting with their own nullification, he is bent on making self-annihilation an inglorious aesthetic act. On March 21, 1962, in the desert south of Las Vegas, *Study No. 2 for an*

End of the World was detonated. Stationed behind the control panel, equipped with safety helmets and all the paraphernalia of ICBM experts around their rocket silos, Tinguely and crew made the countdown. He explained later (September, 1964, p. 14):

After all, we're living in an age when the wildest fantasies become daily truths. Anything is possible. Dematerialization, for example, that will enable people to travel by becoming sound waves or something. Why not?

I'm trying to meet the scientist a little beyond the frontier of the possible, even to get there a little ahead of him.

Tinguely's ritual on the infinite expanses of the desert is insignificant compared to the technology mustered by the world's great nations. However, this mock world-suicide spectacle objectifies the despair and inevitability of the present situation in a way left untouched by painting.

More so than Klein's "living brushes," Tinguely's "metamatic" painting machine helped to reduce Tachism to a silent shambles. Instead of the artist's isolated raw emotion in paint, the spastic palpitations of the machine questioned the entire gestural psychology of the "living" action painter. In his place Tinguely inhabits the world with colonies of machines—machines "creating" their like, "devouring" each other, machines "working" or "going on strike," machines "creating" works of art, "committing" suicide, "singing" *a capriccio*, "having nervous breakdowns."

Without the advantages of cybernetics Tinguely has come closest to "humanizing" the machine. A precise definition of "human" is illusive. It is not an extension of that anthropomorphic precision which characterizes the automata collection at Neuchâtel. Rather to be "human" is to expose oneself through animal vulnerability and fallibility. Standing alone in a room, one of Tinguely's metamechanical works appears nakedly subject to the whims of the gods—like the standing male nudes of archaic Greece, the *kouroi*.

In 1962 Tinguely held a show of radio constructions in New York City (FIG. 89). These constructions were anatomical studies. Their cabinets were taken off, their parts detached from the chassis, dismembered and linked together by wire on transparent plastic reliefs; they possessed the pathetic uniqueness of biological specimens such as frogs with their muscles separated and pinned down to a dissecting table. The tuner and volume control of each *Radio Drawing* was motorized by an eccentric cam-and-rod system. At times when an observer generalized his listening attention, they seemed to communicate with each other—by whisper, hiccup, or a news report transformed into an eerie howl. These sculptures and reliefs were probably

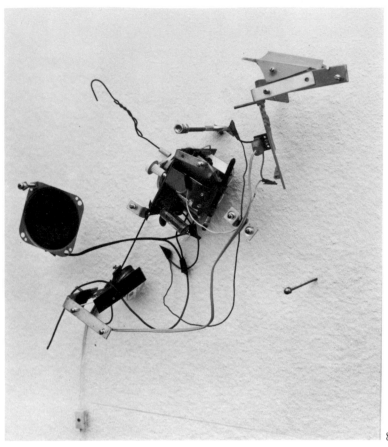

89. Jean Tinguely, *Radio Drawing*, 1962.

unhappy, but like the sad creatures on the upper circles of Dante's *Inferno*, they at least had each other.

The author has tried to circumscribe with thumbnail descriptions of a few artists a European-wide artistic ideology that evades precise naming and style categorization. This is due to the history of New Tendency shows, alliances, splits, and antagonisms. Viewpoints are very important. According to where one stood at a given time, important names have been left out or some names included that may not belong. With the first general New Tendency exhibition at the Museum of Contemporary Art at Zagreb (1961), many diverse groups of young artists were thrown together for the first time. By 1963 at a second show in Zagreb of the same title these same groups of artists were engaged in fierce ideological discussions that resulted in permanent schisms. In fact, a study of the "grand old men and respected contemporaries" of each of these groups puts their differences in perspective and accounts for their antagonisms.

These individual groups of young European artists will be introduced in the section below, but roughly their adherences could be described as follows: Geography accounts for some of the factionalism since groups from Germany, Italy, Yugoslavia, Bulgaria, France, Holland participated in the first shows—along with separate individuals from these and other countries. The split came between those groups and individuals who stressed experimental objectivity, anonymity, perceptual psychology, and socialism, and those who stood for individual research, recognition, poetry, idealism, immateriality, luminosity, and nature. Into the first fell the French Groupe de Recherche d'Art Visuel, the Italian Group N and Group T, some Munich artists, and various artists of the Communist countries. Those embracing the second set of values were the German Group Zero, the Dutch NUL, other Munich artists, and sundry individuals. This division was not firmly drawn up. Ideological alliances shifted from year to year between 1958 and 1966. Generally, Group Zero and NUL venerated Fontana, Yves Klein, and Soto, while they had little feeling for Vasarely. The Italian New Tendency artists have all felt the guiding influence of Fontana and Piero Dorazio. The Groupe de Recherche d'Art Visuel was, of course, strongly influenced by Vasarely. Soto was overlooked by those more scientifically oriented for personal art-political reasons, though he was initially important to all. Also, because of their Dada bent, Tinguely, Armando, and Yves Klein were scorned by those allied to scientism. Other artists that should be mentioned as precursors of New Tendency are Marcel Duchamp and the Israeli Optical and Kinetic artist, Yaacov Agam.

The New Tendency and Field Kinetics

Among artists providing the climate which brought the New Tendency to life was a common quest for the physically sensed but insubstantial. This quest embraced infinite spatial extension, immateriality, control through invisible forces, and the use in art of the temporal dimension. The efforts of Fontana, Klein, and others in this direction already have been noted.

Still earlier, attitudes of the first formalist and Constructivist sculptors were considered; here the unseen was sought through scientific idealism and Neo-Platonism connected with regular geometrical figures; all was analyzable, first metrically and then as function. We have observed that as early as the 1920's a crisis in visual realization confronted the model-making scientist. Yet it has only been since the end of the 1950's that the potency of scientific idealism declined in favor of absolute realism or Object sculpture—sculpture which in many cases possesses a family resemblance to the Constructivist idiom, though really a reaction to the immaterial iconic tendencies of the Constructivist-formalist position.

As the New Tendency crystallized in Europe toward the end of the 1950's, it became a reasonable aesthetic alternative to both Constructivism and later Object Art. This field formalism could not be presented in terms of Euclidean verities, Newtonian mechanics, or even physics as conceived before the 1920's. Umbro Apollonio, the Italian historian, explains this in an essay which appeared in conjunction with a "Neue Tendenzen" exhibition at the Municipal Museum at Leverkusen, West Germany, in the spring of 1964 (Kultermann, March–May, 1964, p. 6).

Man may "test" the organization of perceivable reality. Yet today we do not feel disturbed if he does not intuitively grasp in empirical form a "plenum" of accessible sequences: every body is a mass of energy, a planetary system, something that constantly moves within very elastic limits, is easily transgressed and otherwise quickly ruptured. Consequently nature is no longer an idealized essence of certainty, but a provisional appearance of the universal harmony that rules over everything. (Translated from the German by Ingeborg Burnham.)

If formalism had been rendered impotent by invisible principles, the result of scientific investigation, then the New Tendency sought to recover some of this lost power. It was, as we shall see, a temporary theoretical advance over the Constructivist position of scientific idealism. Apollonio's statement above begins to explain why. The New Tendency undertook to represent problems of physical order that, while they might have been anticipated by the formalists of the 1920's, were then considered irrelevant.

What has been generally termed "visual research" in Europe reached focal consciousness with the "Nove Tendencije" exhibition in Zagreb in 1961. This exhibition grew out of the recognition that a common set of plastic sensibilities had taken root among many European artists almost concurrently. The feeling persisted that lyricism was passé if not dead. Groups of young artists believed the role of the artist as an individual was a thing of the past, along with "art for art's sake." A new plastic means had to be invented, though science had set an example of how wasteful and redundant individual experimentation was. In some instances research was collectivized and the results pressed into group projects where no one was considered the prime creator. Some viewed this as an attempt to communize art; however, the real aim was not ideological conversion but technical expediency. Moreover, the entire ritual of seeing which presupposes a codified viewer-object relationship was seriously questioned for the first time. Various theoreticians among New Tendency artists sought, in the eternal parlance of the avant-garde, to bring "art and life closer together." As a result, exhibitions included labyrinthine "environments," hand-manipulated works, night-time *vernissages*, and various spectaculars where the sky or walls of a studio were transformed through lighting effects. This refound freedom (like that of the "happenings") was made possible partly because many of these works were not easily sold through the gallery system. Lofts and abandoned store fronts were the first showplaces of the New Tendency. Complicated ensembles were created less to be sold than to be seen and experienced.

The rising generation of the New Tendency had its premier with some one-night exhibitions (1957) held by Otto Piene and Heinz Mack of Düsseldorf. In the following year both artists opened more exhibitions to artists of all nationalities working in a similar direction. For the seventh of these, "The Red Picture" exhibition, a catalogue was issued explaining the paintings as a post-Tachist "beginning," an attempt to purify and reestablish the ties between human nature and the fields of energy which emanate from the painted surface. This idea was more fully defined in a less-inclusive exhibition, "Vibration," in which the grid paintings or "Rasterbilder" of Mack, Almir Mavignier, and Piene were shown. Here, with paintings, actually low reliefs, light was "articulated and vibrated" in shifting field patterns. In one sense this began the New Tendency's drive to escape the confines of painting and sculpture by bringing them together into relief form via field dynamics.

By 1958 this desire was crystallized in West Germany as Group Zero. Most of Zero's early projects and philosophical positions were outlined by one of its three leaders, Otto Piene. Subsequently Piene wrote of his fascination with reflecting water, wind-swept grain fields and wartime searchlights playing over cloud banks. These nonmechanical and very ordinary phenomena became the more lyrical basis of New Tendency perceptualism. Stimulating conversations with Yves Klein and Jean Tinguely in Paris strengthened these feelings. Heinz Mack in particular used the rippled and cut surface of sheet aluminum as great sparkling, ever-changing landscapes of reflection. A nature-oriented synthesis with uncomplicated technology typifies the work of Piene, Mack, and Günther Uecker, the inner circle of Group Zero. Increasingly their work became concerned with light play. Color was reduced to white, silver, or other monochromatic applications.

During the early 1960's rival groups formed in Holland, France, and Italy; isolated artists working in the New Tendency direction became known through group shows and communication among themselves. Ideas were exchanged freely until the dynamics of gallery competition and rivalry for reputations made individuals more circumspect. By 1963 various factions of the New Tendency had begun to dissolve. Eventually personalities became more important.

In 1960 the Paris-based artists Horacio Garcia-Rossi, Julio Le Parc, François Morellet, Francisco Sobrino, Joël Stein, and Yvaral rented an empty store for a central studio and formed the Groupe de Recherche d'Art Visuel. The following year they exhibited as a group at the Galerie Denise René in Paris. During this period two statements were published: "Propositions on Movement" and "Enough of Mystification." Both statements were issued to clear the air of much implicit idealism which pervaded painting and sculpture at the time. In the same year the group held a public debate in their studio, with the artists Nicolas Schöffer and Vasarely participating, along with the critic Guy Habasque—all sympathetic to the aims of the G.R.A.V. Certainly what was proposed offered a sharp alternative to the painterly lyricism and informalism prevailing in the galleries and museums. During the same year the G.R.A.V. also published the text of their "General Propositions." Because this statement figures so heavily in the thesis of this book, it has been translated and set down in its entirety. Many of these ideas already have a formidable history in connection with Constructivist-Concrete art. Therefore they are unexpected only in the forcefulness and precision with which they are stated (G.R.A.V., April, 1962, p. 2).

General Propositions of the "Group for Research in the Visual Arts" (1961)

Relationship of the artist with society
This relationship is presently based upon:
  The unique and isolated artist
  The cult of the personality
  The myth of creation
  The overestimation of aesthetic and anti-aesthetic conceptions
  Elaboration for the elite
  The production of unique works of art
  The dependence of art on the marketplace

Propositions to transform this relationship:
  To strip the conception and the realization of works of art of all mystification and
    to reduce them to simple human activity
  To seek new means of public contact with the works produced
  To eliminate the category "Work of Art" and its myths
  To develop new appreciations
  To create reproducible works
  To seek new categories of realization beyond painting and sculpture
  To liberate the public from the inhibitions and warping of appreciation produced
    by traditional aestheticism, by creating a new social-artistic situation

Relationship of the work to the eye
This relationship is presently based upon:
  The eye considered as an intermediary
  Extra-visual attractions (subjective or rational)
  The dependence of the eye on a cultural and aesthetic level

Propositions to transform this relationship:
To totally eliminate the intrinsic values of the stable and recognizable form be it:
  Form idealizing nature (classic art)
  Form representing nature (naturalistic art)
  Form synthesizing nature (cubist art)
  Geometrizing form (constructivist art)
  Rationalized form (concrete art)
  Free form (informal art, tachism, etc.)
  To eliminate the arbitrary relationships between forms (relationships of dimension, placement, color, meanings, depths, etc.)
  To displace the habitual function of the eye (taking cognizance through form and its relationships) toward a new visual situation based on peripheral vision and instability
  To create an appreciation-time based on the relation of the eye and the work transforming the usual quality of time

Traditional plastic values
These values are presently based on the work which is:
  unique
  stable
  definitive
  subjective
  obedient to aesthetic or anti-aesthetic laws

Propositions to transform these values:
  To limit the work to a strictly visual situation
  To establish a more precise relationship between the work and the human eye
  Anonymity and homogeneity of form and relationships between forms
  To stress visual instability and perception time
  To search for a nondefinitive work which at the same time is exact, precise, and desired
  To direct interest toward new variable visual situations based on constant results of the eye-art rapport
  To state the existence of indeterminate phenomena in the structure and visual reality of the work, and from there to conceive of new possibilities which will open up a new field of investigation

(Translated from the French by Davida Fineman.)

Essentially the above proposal forms a methodological basis for what has been misleadingly called Op Art. Although the bulk of the work of

G.R.A.V. consisted of paintings at the time the statement was written, much of the activity cited by the group as a goal is by nature and necessity three-dimensional. Not alone, the group has sought to destroy conventions which separate painting from sculpture—art thus becomes a matter of accommodating perception. Moreover, revealing the limits of perception meant an increased use of kinetics. And, as with Group Zero, their conception of movement (perhaps because the most easily managed) soon became based on unstable, random happenings given a statistical appearance of semi-order through field structuring.

With the inception of the G.R.A.V. in 1960 similarly oriented groups were started in Milan and Padua by young Italian artists. However, the Italian groups neither produced the theoretical conjecture nor established a vogue for anti-lyrical values with as much public success or drama as the G.R.A.V. As the values of the G.R.A.V. reflected Vasarely's notions of a no-nonsense, salable, mass-produced art, so the Italian groups attempted to fulfill Fontana's hopes via the "White Manifesto" for an art of kinetic values. As with other New Tendency groups throughout Europe, the Italians embraced an ambiguous moral position which fought the cults of egoism and commercialism while ardently working for recognition—first as groups, then as individuals.

Alberto Biasi, Ennio Chiggio, Edoardo Landi, Manfredo Massironi, and Toni Costa were the founders of Group N in Padua. Their philosophy represented the nearest thing to a scientific approach undertaken by any group. Specific experimental projects were set up, conferences held, and results examined and shown publicly, though not signed by the members themselves. Group N disbanded after 1964, perhaps split by the inherent artistic tendency toward personal recognition. Group T in Milan at this writing continues and its members, Giovanni Anceschi, Davide Boriani, Gianni Colombo, Gabriele de Vecchi, and Grazia Varisco, have not tried to maintain anonymity.

The New Tendency has had early advocates in Holland with Henk Peeters, Jan Schoonhoven, and Armando in the form of NUL. Spain has contributed Equipo 57. In cities all over Europe independent artists have worked and exhibited in New Tendency exhibitions periodically: these include Yaacov Agam, Carlos Cruz-Diez, Martha Boto, Bruno Munari, Piero Dorazio, Luis Tomasello, Gregorio Vardanega, Pol Bury, Karl Gerstner, Diter Rot, Gerhard von Graevenitz, Christian Megert, Uli Pol, and Yayoi Kusama.

Plastically—both in static and Kinetic art—the compositional device that has overwhelmingly united New Tendency artists is the format of the repetitive field structure. This, of course, appeared as early as 1917 in

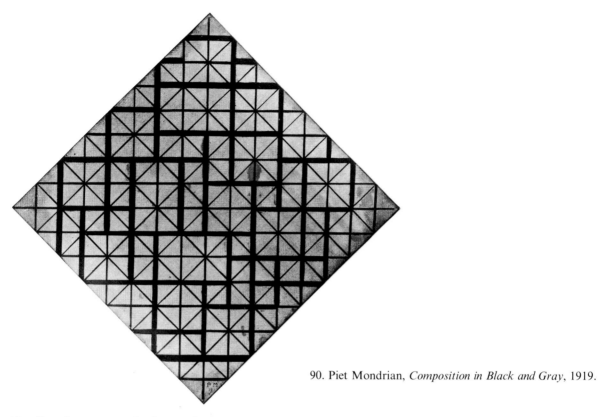

90. Piet Mondrian, *Composition in Black and Gray*, 1919.

the first lozenge paintings of Piet Mondrian (FIG. 90). In the early 1950's Soto was to use it in unilinear form in his Kinetic reliefs, as did Boris Kleint in his glass reliefs, while Victor Vasarely used it consistently in paintings and sculptures. Toward the last half of the decade it appeared in the screen-controlled relief paintings of Piene, the periodic drop paintings of Almir Mavignier, the lined grids of Piero Dorazio, and in some of Yves Klein's monochromatic works. In the early 1960's lattice constructions were built by G.R.A.V. members Garcia-Rossi, Morellet, Sobrino, and Stein. Variations of field constructions were built at one time or other by nearly all the artists associated with the New Tendency.

These works may all have echoed Mondrian's checkerboard paintings of forty years earlier, but, unlike Mondrian's first efforts in Neo-Plasticism, the rasters of the New Tendency were made visually connective by the incremental transformation of adjacent elements. In some cases nothing more than the plasticity of shadowed surfaces permitted this. In other instances the tendency was to fuse figure-ground relationships into a nearly homologous field. Generally the incorporation of relief elements means locking them into adjacent positions so as to define the field structure.

253

In striving to overcome the influence of the dominating motif and the "gesture" of Tachism, the New Tendency sacrificed the personal image or mark for what could be called "the personal field format." Primarily a dynamical concept, the optically controlled field did almost inevitably give way to motion by mechanical means. In many cases where mechanics have been used to generate field changes, the connection between the kinematics of the machines used and the impression of field movement have been unrelated. Yet the field concept did become the means by which the impasse of stagnant, deterministic mechanical motion was given new life and meaning.

The idea of a field as a plenum of kinetic effects has been extremely useful to the physicist for the last one hundred years. The willingness of artists to accept a current scientific concept as the most convincing description of reality, even a very tentative one, is born out by New Tendency adoption of field dynamics. There has been the predisposition of apologists for the New Tendency to stress the transitional and provisional character of all scientific theory. This should not be interpreted as a disclaimer, but as a means to prepare a viewer for art works which are fluid and inconstant in their structuring. Of sociological import is the fact that New Tendency mannerisms have been interpreted as being effective to the degree in which they depersonalized, made "cool," and objectively structured "subject matter," so that they approached the impartiality of graphed data in a laboratory. Only the most original artistic personalities survived such subjugation. The point is sometimes made that such depersonalization is unavoidable in order to arrive at new aesthetic "truths." In reality the "truths" proclaimed by the New Tendency were modes for perceiving patterns of energy long in theoretical and practical use in physics. These insights involved ways of handling events in no way determinable through classic mechanics. Implicit in New Tendency sensibilities are a set of questions already asked and to some extent answered by the physical sciences. How does one grasp the effects of invisible quantities of energy spread over great areas of space? How are deterministic or statistical relationships shown between such forces? Are visual models possible for spaces charged with energy fields?

It is well to keep in mind that what has been discussed in relation to New Tendency field dynamics relates to notions of theoretical mechanics which postdate and supersede Newtonian physics. These go well beyond the intuitions about space and the relationships of bodies implied by classical Newtonian mechanics. Thus the term *mechanics*, as it is presently used in high-energy physics, does not refer to classical machine theory, but to ideas about the behavior of matter which give a more comprehensive, if still incomplete, picture of physical activity in the universe.

Nineteenth-century physics was increasingly drawn toward understanding the underlying consistency of light, radiant heat, electricity, magnetism, and gravity—all bodiless forms of energy. Earlier Newtonian mechanics might have explained the rough operational laws of these non-material agencies, but at the same time classical mechanics contributed little to their "how" and "why." Particularly obscure were the structure and means of transmission of quantities of energy. However, a pattern emerged which showed that the physical nature of energy was not a vacuum nor was it structured as solid matter.

Working in the 1820's and 1830's Michael Faraday, with little formal education, produced the first experiments which gave some visible idea of the field effects of electricity. With the aid of apparatus devised by the experimenter, Faraday graphically mapped "lines" or "tubes" of magnetic force as they seemed to present themselves while surrounding an electrical circuit. Thirty years later James Clerk Maxwell took Faraday's diagrams and proved them mathematically—thus making them scientifically respectable. He did this by setting them to equations devised by Leonhard Euler for solving problems in hydrodynamics. Thus, the consistency of one fluid field in three dimensions, water, was used to explain another field in three dimensions. Ultimately, the partial differential equations used by Maxwell proved so successful and elegant in explaining Faraday's fields of "lines" that he applied them with success to other forms of radiant energy.

The validity of Maxwell's equations was further strengthened by the discovery of identical velocities for electromagnetic and light waves. Maxwell deduced that both phenomena could be viewed as manifestations of the same set of laws. A larger importance for Maxwell's mathematical expression of electromagnetic fields was realized in 1915 when Einstein published his General Theory of Relativity.

Until this century an unspoken agreement existed between physicists and mathematicians as to who would have priority over certain phenomena within the investigation of physical reality. It was accepted that the mathematician was to define the laws of space and time while physicists were responsible for physical activities within the space-time matrix. Einstein fundamentally challenged this approach. He declared that the elements and various forms of spectral energy acting as point-events in space-time influenced and shaped the space-time continuum and the continuum conversely affected matter and energy. Hence the properties of space were directly contingent on what was inside it. No longer was space-time conceived as an inert, unchanging void: a passive stage for internal activities. Newton had viewed gravitation as a set of forces exerted on each other by bodies at a distance. Einstein deduced that the gravitational field was actually shaped or curved space and that systems of forces throughout the universe were, by the nature of field effects, continuous.

For the layman or even the conservative scientist with a yearning for Newtonian mechanical models, the mathematician-physicist's new conception of wave packets and/or particles of energy embedded in a variable field where all parameters were inconstant had virtually nothing to do with the world of sense perception. As field theory found a larger place in physics, it became evident that three-dimensional models of this new spatial plenum were out of the question. Thus the epistemological transition in physics during the 1920's was a shift from discrete, geometrical models of the atom as an array of points in space to the use of field configurations to show stable and unstable energy states.

In many ways the conception of a field as a repetitive set of elements had already begun to dominate environmental design. This can be perceived in the redundant array of solid-state components fitted into switching circuits in electronic equipment, the sameness that prevails over glass and steel façades of curtain-wall office buildings, the grill patterns which appear on electrical appliances and the raster structure of light display boards for computers. Thus the discrete element, implacably regimented with identical members to its right and left, to the front and back, has become the format of the New Tendency. Crude and distant though this image is from the theories of gravitation constructed by Einstein, it served to bring the invisible world of energy dynamics—those forces which make technological society a reality—back to the level of visual comprehension.

The two- and three-dimensional grate has become important for other reasons. In theory the field structure could be extended infinitely; like Yves Klein's plans to make an art work of the sky, the boundless raster became a symbol of infinity. It provided both a visual convention for fluid activities, and dispelled the impression that Kinetic Art was solely tied to the activity of machine kinematics. Though, if not obviously, machines were to remain the controlling forces.

As intoxicating as it is to tie New Tendency field configurations to Einsteinian mechanics, the analogy stops short of physical reality and rests upon visual correspondences. There are many artists today who will deny any psychical or physical connection between the two. Precisely how these correspondences come about is difficult to say. In most instances it would seem that the innovators of an art style—usually extraordinarily perceptive beings

—pull them from the air, but in any case do not borrow them from scientific sources as a matter of rational decision. After a period of incubation a style becomes contagious, spreading to many artists who add to its fulfillment.

Vasarely in a brief essay written in 1963 (1965, p. 74) speaks of an early fascination with all kinds of visual networks and grids, both natural and as scientific diagrams. He speaks of "devouring" works on relativity, wave mechanics, cybernetics—and then suddenly for him pure physics emerged as a profound source of poetry in the early 1950's. He saw in his own paintings a tendency discovered earlier in quantum physics: the peculiar behavior of atomic matter in possessing both the properties of particles and waves. In similar fashion, embedded in Vasarely's "networks" are geometric modules (particles) that are unified optically into pulsating compositional fields (waves). Noticing these similarities did not bring an immediate sense of assurance to the artist (1965, p. 158): "This meeting of two disciplines apparently opposed... disturbed me... for I have never consciously found my inspiration in the exact sciences. It is after the plastic accomplishment that I noted the existence of certain analogies, which have become dominent facts in the plastic arts in our day."

Another artist who early recognized the value of the grid and the kinetic implications of lined interference patterns is Jesus-Raphael Soto. Soto's remarks on his work reveal that he perfectly understood the laws and visual implications of field effects (November–December 1965). And very early he introduced actual movement, replacing or superseding the previous virtual movement (viewer's change of position) pioneered by Vasarely. Not that Soto has ever appropriated any of the physicist's methodology, but his thought processes for apprehending certain visual phenomena correspond very closely to that of the atomic scientist for his area of study (p. 4):

The World of Relations exists before and beyond elements. The value of the elements is only a descriptive reference of the relations. The element is a secondary factor which I utilize to communicate my idea of relations. Relations exclude the idea of the void. Relations have an autonomous existence. My works are executed with this in mind.

Another, perhaps more direct, antecedent for New Tendency field composition was the Bauhaus and Bauhaus-related pedagogy concerned with the manipulation of two- and three-dimensional modular systems. Strangely, these had been introduced in the 1920's as first-year design problems, but few if any artists until the 1960's thought of adopting their properties for personal expression.

The field illusions used by the Bauhaus have their origin in part in some of the experiments conducted by the early *Gestalt* psychologists. One in particular was developed around patterns of dots. Here, spacing of the dots, their proximity to one another, decided whether a viewer saw them in horizontal or vertical rows. *Gestalt* theory and early abstraction were mainly concerned with figure-ground relationships where there was a high degree of differentiation between the figures and figure and ground—just the opposite of the New Tendency where the attempt has been to produce the illusion of fluid patterns (either fixed or moving) by making only incremental differences between the units in a field or network. One important set of field illusions, that of the progressive change of regularly spaced elements producing an impression of field depth or field change, has been thoroughly documented by the psychologist James Gibson. In his *The Perception of the Visual World* (1950) one can find many graphic examples of field transformations which were to become the stock-in-trade of the New Tendency.

The materials and techniques for producing interactive fields are very numerous. But in terms of the optical principles employed, two categories of field effects stand out: those that are static but provide an optical sensation of movement between units, and those that use machine principles to produce real motion. In some cases, such as de Vecchi's screened constructions of moving fabric, both real motion and its illusion are produced together.

In a fixed situation where viewer ambience produces the illusion of motion, the *textural gradient* or consistency of the field alters itself automatically. This brings about changes in configuration orientation, shadow and light, color, and, most subtly, in texture. Agam, along with Soto and Vasarely, have all made pioneering use of these types of changes in their vibrational reliefs. Tomasello has produced alterations in reflected color and shadow through the location changes of the viewer. Lengths of wire have been employed for textural and shadow alterations by Yvaral and Biasi. Nails have been used in this context by Uecker, but the work illustrated uses a spotlight and a moving turntable platform (FIG. 91). Costa (FIG. 92) and Cruz-Diez alter colors and provisional shapes with the use of overlapping plastic strips. Form and shadows of extreme immateriality are ordered by Peeters with the aid of rows of cotton held in place by a fine gauze cover. Enrico Castellani obtains repetitional shadows with shaped canvases (FIG. 93). Sobrino's structures read ambiguously as shifting, transparent plastic units fitted together (FIG. 94). One of François Morellet's most imposing structures is a giant lattice sphere of aluminum rods, (FIG. 95). This alters in consistency as a viewer moves around it.

Pseudo-random movement (movement which appears completely inde-

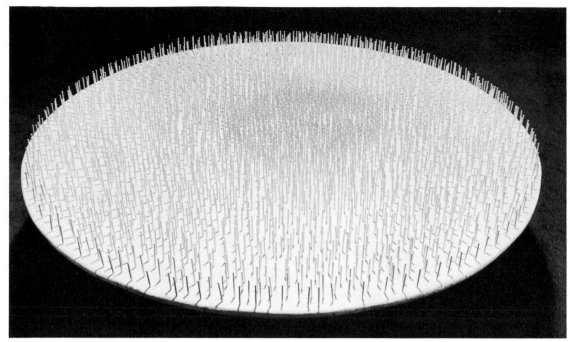

91. Günther Uecker, *Moving Light*, 1960.

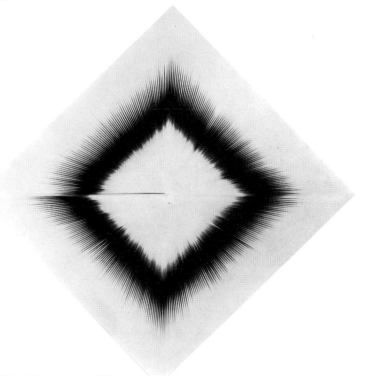

92. Toni Costa, *Visual Dynamics*, 1965.

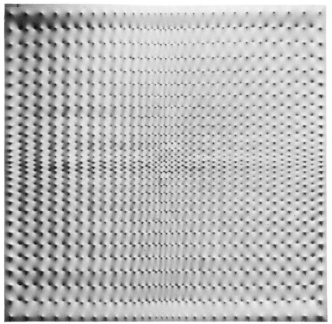

93. Enrico Castellani, *Convergent Structure*, 1966.

94. Francisco Sobrino, *Juxtaposition Superimposition C*, 1962–1963.

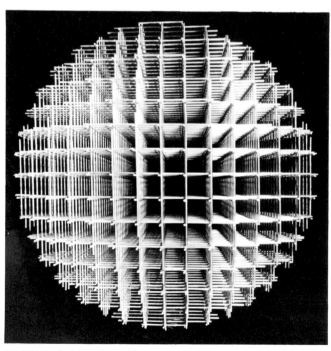

95. François Morellet, *Sphere-Web*, 1962.

96. Joël Stein, *Trihedral: With Manipulatable Elements*, 1964.

terminate but still has some statistical foundation) has also figured heavily in field kinetics. Soto's *Vibrations* depend on moving wire, augmented by hand or wind, in front of a lined grid. In the same respect, redundant rows of loosely hanging transparent plastic squares are the visual basis for some of Le Parc's constructions. A purer version of random field effects is found in *Unstable Bi-Spaces* of Group N. Here an aggregate collection of black and white spheres are endlessly rearranged within a container through hand manipulation. Other hand-manipulated works have been constructed by Agam, Joël Stein (FIG 96), Munari, Rot, Armando, Biasi, and Gerstner—to name but a few. Actual alterations in field configurations are more usually generated by motors than by spectator intervention. Electrically illuminated raster constructions have been built by Morellet, Boto, Enzo Mari, Varisco, Stein, Le Parc, Garcia-Rossi, and Mack. Those by Mack are both illuminated and left as external light reflectors; these employ a glass-ribbed face with a corrugated aluminum disk turning behind it (FIG. 97). The patterns generated are on the moiré principle, also used by many purely Optical artists. Von Graevenitz has constructed fields of turning blades controlled by a single belt and motor arrangement. Working on a somewhat different principle are reliefs of hundreds of pegs and wires constructed by Pol Bury (see FIG. 101).

261

97. Heinz Mack, *Light Dynamo No. 2*, 1966.

In all the examples listed above, the principle of field structuring departs from older concepts for making sculpture or sculptural reliefs. As Soto suggested, it is the *relationships* between these elements, *not the elements themselves* which produces a new kind of optical situation. The field, even within the borders of the Kinetic relief, was the plastic beginning for a new sense of artistic extension; it became the symbol of an artistic yearning for immateriality, though only achieved so far on the most provisional and iconic terms.

Theory and Practice in the Kinetic Revival

The point has been made that most Constructivist sculpture could have been fabricated before the Industrial Revolution, that it was the conditioned willingness of society to accept the images influenced by scientific idealism which constituted the real artistic transformation. In a similar sense, a good deal of contemporary Kinetic Art could have been constructed by an ingenious eighteenth-century toy maker. This is not meant to depreciate the Kinetic movement but to stress that in an open society art mainly stems from the psychic drives of individual artists. When numbers of artists move into an area where tremendous technical and aesthetic difficulties remain, it indicates that a sense of manifest destiny may, in the long run, be more important to art than technical limitations. As critics have observed, except in the field of light programming, new Kinetic works have not relied on the most recent technology. They have been helped by it; but advances in programming, environmentally sensitive switches, miniature relay devices, compact long-lasting batteries, variable-speed motors, in fact, the entire trend toward miniaturization and diversification in electronics have so far played only the most marginal part in the recent growth of Kineticism. This is changing rapidly.

In most instances the contemporary Kineticist is confronted by identical problems which discouraged his counterpart forty years ago. Many of today's Kinetic artists harbor the same conservative fears of decay and breakdown that have always disturbed the makers of art objects. The ideas attempted by contemporary Kineticists constantly face compromise between relative permanence, or at least the desire for it, and the need to realize an idea although its physical life may not extend beyond the duration of a single exhibition. This is a pressing and continued issue for the artist involved in motion. In many instances he does not possess the technical knowledge or the facilities to create what for industry would be a relatively minor technical project.

Breakdown and resupply of parts is a major problem for the Kineticist, one only occasionally faced by the traditional artist. Tinguely created many of his anthropomorphic constructions with the thought in mind that they would not be smoothly functioning machines but cripples, or machines with a physical flaw. Many of these issue noises due to mechanical imperfections, such as bits of metal tied into a pully or fan belt. Where a machine is designed with built-in defects, a self-augmented malfunction is the inevitable result, leading to sure breakdown. For gallery display and sales the young Kineticist is in no position to promote such disasters. They come easily enough without the artist's intervention. The sale of Kinetic Art is difficult for just this reason. Purchasers bring back broken machines expecting the artist to fulfill a lifetime guarantee. While post-sale services and stocked parts remain an indispensable aspect of the commercial appliance business, neither artists nor customers have adapted themselves to the realities of machines as art. It becomes apparent that the Kinetic construction is not an *objet d'art* in the conventional sense, but a *système d'art*. It is a system in the sense that any series of interacting components may need repair and adjustment from time to time. This hardly fits the description of the traditional inert painting or sculpture.

Kineticists have reacted to this predicament in several ways. The most common is to ignore it. Some regard Kinetic Art as an experimental and provisional form of expression. They reject the Kinetic construction as an object but regard it as the matrix for a possible event or "happening." Some artists see in Kinetics a need to restructure the commercial gallery system: this means either taking the artist off the market and supporting his work noncommercially, or creating new alliances between Kinetic artists and manufacturers so that successful constructions can be put into serial production. In many respects scientists working on independent projects or free-lance industrial designers command much of the autonomy which a Kineticist might envy. For any of these to happen on a sizable scale remains improbable for the foreseeable future.

Postwar affluence has been largely responsible for the Kinetic revival. Industrial improvements and a relative abundance of money have made Kineticism almost a mass movement. While advanced mechanics and electronics are still out of range of most artists, welding and brazing, stock timing motors, animation devices, varieties of lighting fixtures and sound equipment have made the motion potential of artists with scant engineering knowledge formidable. However, few artists have the support of industry or laboratories for real investigation into movement; as a result the level of engineering prowess remains generally low. A significant exception to this situation and one which will later be discussed in a general essay on systems is the formation in 1966 in New York City of the foundation Experiments in Art and Technology, Inc. Supported by generous patrons and staffed by enthusiastic engineers and artists, it remains to be seen whether this foundation ultimately expires as the passing whim of the New York avant-garde or actually contributes to the needs of artists with ideas outside the clique. Critics of Kinetic Art, such as Philip Leider (editor of *Artforum* magazine, now based in New York), have been quick to detect Kineticism's weakest spot (May, 1966, p. 42):

The heavy atmosphere of TECHNOLOGY that seems to dominate so many kinetic exhibitions, sets up, quite naturally, expectations of an art which has been able to put to its own uses the most sophisticated mechanical, electronic or magnetic advances of the technological age. In such an atmosphere, the puniness of the actual technology employed becomes emphasized to the point of hilarity.

When it is remembered that two electromechanical mediums (motion pictures and television) took many millions of dollars to perfect into profit-making mediums, it seems unfair to expect the same results from individual artists using very limited, private funds. Society is structured neither ideologically nor economically to finance Kinetic adventures, much less serious research, on anything like a level needed to turn Kinetics into major art form. Many Kineticists give the impression of being impressed with theoretical and practical developments in the sciences. Here lies a discrepancy between desire and realization. This is not a contradiction, but a great unspanned void between what artists feel they could do given the material means, and the actual importance which society designates for its artists who can only realize their visions through technological means.

Many Kineticists have no concern for technology outside the immediate aims of constructing their works; for these, interest resides strictly in the quality of movement itself. Many Kineticists also lack enthusiasm for technological complexity. They are aware that, unless complexity is accompanied with a corresponding amount of precision, intricacy will only lead to a much higher rate of breakdown. As a rule, they are more concerned with the "life-giving" qualities and functioning capability of a mechanism than with how contemporary it is. If an artist is interested in motion more than nonsense effect, he tends to view any physical bulk of undisplayed technology as a detraction from the directness of his work.

Until 1965 most Kinetic experimentation in the United States was sporadic and isolated. Shielding younger American artists from the pitfalls of European Kineticism, in 1966 Philip Leider had his own ideas about the dearth of American talent in this direction (May, 1966, p. 40): "One would suspect the reasons for this indifference might be a considerably more sophisticated awareness by the Americans both of technology and of the esthetic difficulties which modern sculpture has so long faced."

Leider is correct on one count. With the exception of a handful of first-rank Kinetic artists—Alexander Calder, George Rickey, Len Lye, Thomas Wilfred, and Robert Breer—Kinetic Art is a European rediscovery. That in itself has deterred batches of young American artists from following in the wake of the New Tendency. This is not to say that European Kineticism does not have elements of the old tendency, namely attitudes and plastic techniques borrowed from the Bauhaus and *de Stijl*. But the most important reasons for the American official rejection of Kineticism are aesthetic-ideological. Static sculpture thrived and flourished up to a few years ago in postwar America; curators, dealers, owners, and particularly artists have nothing to gain from encouraging Kinetic experimentation. In most cases Kinetic sculpture is difficult to exhibit; hard to sell, with a very few exceptions; even harder to maintain; and usually for the artist, in terms of work, very time consuming. Beyond the *Realpolitik* of this situation, the fact remains that goodly numbers of the American vanguard have become involved in the problems of Kineticism. For many young artists at present sculpture means either choosing static abstraction in which aesthetic issues and plastic inventions have already been fairly well defined and accepted, therefore dead for creative purposes, or choosing an art form which has a long history of aesthetic, technical, and financial failure—but which also promises hope of open-ended discovery.

Stated categorically and given the standards set by past art, the present Kinetic revival is with very few exceptions a failure. It has not even solved the technical obstacles elaborated by Gabo and Moholy-Nagy forty years ago. In fact, it has sought to minimize inherent physical problems. Yet unrealized art has its heroic aspects, certainly much more than sculpture which flabbily accepts its "thingness" and giantism almost as a signal of defeat. Within the limitations of the first age of machines, the Kinetic revival reveals certain determinations which perhaps at this point are more important than "good art"; Kineticism represents a willingness to attempt the logically inevitable though at present this may be technologically unrealizable.

Philip Leider is correct about some of the failings of the Kineticists. Some still see their contributions as fantastically original—as if motion had never rightfully occurred before they recognized its existence. There is a great deal of vagueness about roots and the origins of principles, as if obfuscation, not honesty, were the best policy in experimentation. Writing about Optical artists—but it could be Kineticists just as well—Sibyl Moholy-Nagy has this to say about the cyclical character of art movements (June, 1966, p. 24):

It is the privilege of young people to see their contributions as unique. Measured on historical rather than on individual time, 40 years are a mere beginning in any cultural development with a claim to lasting continuity.... The antecedents from which this new phase (optical and kinetic art) developed are largely unknown to the Second Generation; yet it is by their subconscious absorption of the earlier solutions through the teaching of art and design, through photography, film, stage lighting, advertising and product design, that their optical art developed.

George Rickey, an important participant and literary prophet of the Kinetic revival, has rightly defined *motion* as the essential medium of the movement. More adamantly than any other writer, Rickey has conveyed the message of New Tendency Kineticism to the English-speaking public. Not surprisingly, his thinking about his own sculpture changed, at least partially, owing to his contact with the nature-oriented NUL and Zero groups in Europe. In 1956 Rickey could write (1956, p. 174): "My medium is so removed from nature and, really, from "art" that even the most unschooled public does not raise the question of verisimilitude. Imitation of nature

98. George Rickey, *Two Lines-Temporal I*, 1964.

would be so difficult in my métier and look so awful (the automaton with waving arms outside the gas station?) that I am spared the whole question."

By 1963 Rickey not only recognized himself as an artist but was compelled to state (Kepes, 1965, p. 110): "The artist finds waiting for him, as subject, not the trees, not the flowers, not the landscape, but the *waving* of branches and the *trembling* of stems, the piling up or scudding of clouds, the rising and setting and waxing and waning of heavenly bodies; the creeping of spilled water on the floor; the repertory of the sea—from ripple and wavelet to tide and torrent...."

The real lyricism of Rickey's work began to appear in the early 1960's after his substitution of natural forms of motion phenomena for the anecdotal motion of sailing ships and garden parties. His aim has been to carry the principle of mechanical equilibrium beyond the range of activities staked out by Alexander Calder. Kinematically this has demanded a fairly sensitive and complex array of mechanical relationships. While much of Calder's emphasis has been placed on the cutout shapes of his mobiles, Rickey has sublimated form through geometric reduction and concentrated on the *quality* of movement generated by his constructions.

As with many Kinetic sculptures, Rickey's require a sympathetic environment. In 1964 the outdoor sculpture plaza of the West German Kassel Documenta exhibition featured one of his "Line" constructions, consisting of two thirty-five-foot, vertical, stainless-steel "needles" balanced, on a pedestal, on knife-edge fulcrums (FIG. 98). Set in slight motion on a summer evening against the outline of the moon they remain a memorable fragment of poetry.

Most succinctly, Rickey has grasped the meaning of Kinetic Art for the First Age of Machines. The machine, although the artist may choose to hide evidences of it, remains the wellspring of Kinetic sculpture (1956, p. 172).

A machine is not a projection of anything. The crank-shaft exists in its own right; it *is* the image. It is many other things, too. The paradox of the machine is that the projection from it—the mechanical drawing or the blue print—exists before the machine does. The concreteness of machines is heartening. They do not depend on a rush of feeling or embellishment of surface or nervousness of execution or tragic renunciation of all that interferes with "process." Yet they can, without being "images of…," evoke and suggest comment. They can be figurative in the sense of suggesting living forms.

As a prognosticator of Kineticism's future, Rickey's views are worth considering. In his essay "The Morphology of Movement" (Kepes, 1965, pp. 81–114) he lists eight forms of "unexplored kinetic territory," including water-driven sculpture, sculpture suspended in magnetic fields, works held in mid-air by jets of air or water, synthetic membranes distorted by mechanical forces, color and motion produced by polarized light, "feelies," more integral use of spectators in Kinetic environments and architectural-scale Kinetics in which time becomes a function of distance. Although that list was drawn up in 1963, even at that time every one of these techniques was being investigated and used by more than one artist. In many cases the implementation of these ideas, beyond the necessary talent, is a matter involving scale beyond gallery dimensions. To be effective at all, these mediums need money and more technology than most artists can summon. Many of the ideas which he mentions were first suggested by Moholy-Nagy more than thirty-five years ago. The point is that these ideas represent a certain plateau of conceptualization about the artistic use of abstract motion, a plateau which has been fully conceived, but hardly reached to any significant degree.

During the evening of April 5, 1961, Len Lye presented at the Museum of Modern Art in New York a variety of "Tangible Motion Sculpture." On the surface, Lye's sculptures are reminiscent of the "virtual volumes" of Gabo and Moholy-Nagy—with the important difference that they realized, conceptually and mechanically, considerations that had only been outlined by these pioneers. In this show of manipulated spinning forms, Lye produced the first successful type of motor-driven Kinetic sculpture in the United States.

His *Revolving Harmonic* was, in the words of the critic John Canaday (April 6, 1961): "...a four-foot length of polished nickel rod one-eighth of an inch in diameter of the kind that could be bought in any supply house. It stands straight on its platform but it is footed in a motor that can rotate at varying speeds, causing it to bend into an arc (and occasionally to whip back and forth) so that it becomes for the eye a transparent shimmering lozenge struck through with lights that glitter, weave and waver within and around the core."

A feeling of barely harnessed physical power—half material and half pure energy—pervades Lye's work, demanding greater scale for a more complete expression. Many of his best pieces have moved in this direction in the intervening six years. In 1961 Lye suggested that his *Revolving Harmonic* could be transformed from a four-foot rod to a thirty-foot tube with perforations every three feet acting as outlets for a high-pressure jet of water. Lye has finally completed a project similar to this one.

The important feature of Lye's work is the incorporation of a temporal program into the presentation. The "Tangible Motion Sculptures" employ their own cycles of audio and visual tempo change. These are mechanically controlled but violent enough so that they constantly generate a sense of surprise and expectation. Where ephemeral form was the end product of Gabo's and Moholy-Nagy's moving wire constructions, form is only a manifestation of shifting events for Lye.

In the late winter of 1965 the Albright-Knox Gallery in Buffalo installed one of the most impressive productions of Lye's work: seven major pieces automatically programmed. The artist gave his intentions by insisting (Selz, March–May, 1966, p. 43): "From conception to death some form of motion is part of life; every waking moment is directed to enacting behavorial patterns of motion...." On another occasion Lye described one piece which appeared in the Buffalo exhibition (FIG. 99) as follows (March–April, 1965, no page number):

269

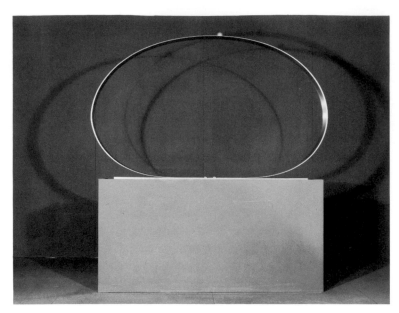

99. Len Lye, *Loop* (still), 1963.

The Loop, a twenty-two foot strip of polished steel, is formed into a band, which rests on its back on a magnetized bed. The action starts when the charged magnets pull the loop of steel downwards, and then release it suddenly. As it struggles to resume its natural shape, the steel band bounds upwards and lurches from end to end with simultaneous leaping and rocking motions, orbiting powerful reflections at the viewer and emitting fanciful musical tones which pulsate in rhythm with *The Loop*. Occasionally, as the boundless Loop reaches its greatest height, it strikes a suspended ball, causing it to emit a different yet harmonious musical note, and so it dances to a weird quavering composition of its own making.

The vicissitudes of experienced motion raise the question of "the gay laborer of magnetic fields" the Paris-based Greek artist Takis. The *Telemagnetic* constructions of Takis, once current is applied to them, like the steel bands of Len Lye assume their own dynamic trajectory. Electrical magnets first attract, then go dead, producing uncontrolled spasms among the wire-harnessed metal objects of Takis's choosing. The vitality of the *Telemagnetics* varies greatly (FIG. 100). Some pieces are lethargic while others, because of their switching arrangement, number of objects in the air, strength of the field, or the geometry of the construction itself, produce endless quantities of useless but aggressive energy. Their wires sing and something blatantly sexual takes place as the space-bound objects strain toward the magnetic core.

In a sense the art of Takis is either pure Zen or totemic homage to the instruments of technology (Selz, March–May, 1966, p. 59):

100. Takis, Installation photo of 1967 exhibition at Howard Wise Gallery, New York.

I follow the indications of the materials, I do not dominate them, I hardly ever create. You must understand that. When I use a found object, a piece of some machine, it is to get away from art and nearer invisible forces.

This philosophy is similar to that of some Kineticists, whose goal is to create a "situation" in which things can happen, rather than an object *per se*. In a statement of purpose Takis has stated (Takis, Oct.–Nov., 1964, p. 2): "*The good way of using metal must consist of following its profound spontaneity*, for man, despite all his inventions and his machines, has not completely succeeded in dominating nature. *Metal resists man whenever it can... it is constantly sabotaging the plans of man....*"

Takis, obviously more than the many artists connected with the New Tendency, has dramatically utilized field effects without having made the field itself visually evident—except for its effects upon steel objects. A primitive streak of animism runs through the rationalizations of Takis; his investigations with electrical and magnetic currents has more the taste of camp science fiction than orthodox Constructivist Kinetics. The London-based *Signals* magazine (which owed its name to a series of work by Takis) showed in its October–November, 1964, issue several pictures of the *Telephoto* sculptures. Employing mercury-vapor lamps activated by a variable magnetic field, the *Telephoto* sculptures were pictured side by side with a replica of Marconi's first wireless telegraphic apparatus. A strange unity, a kind of wayward poetry of the barely tangible and antiquated, exists between the two divergent objects. One senses that Takis tries to objectify the invisible with emphasis on electricity instead of mechanics. This does not result in the sleekness and self-sustained order of solid-state electronics, but in a desire to capture the palpability of electricity itself with hand-wound coils and now ancient discoveries.

Between the immobile and mobility, a certain quality of slowness reveals to us a field of "actions" in which the eye is no longer able to trace an object's journey....

Journeys avoid "programmization" in the degree that they are endowed with a quality of slowness; they finally achieve a real or fictional liberty, a liberty acting on its own account and for its own pleasure....

Extracted from an essay, "Time Dialates" (Selz, p. 27), the statements above by Pol Bury characterize one of the most peculiar and compelling types of motion to come out of the Kinetic revival. If most motions associated with Kineticism generate patterns of immateriality or are macroscopically visible in their effects, it would be correct to construe the activity of Bury's moving sculptures as microscopic. Motion becomes, in this case, minute and trembling patterns of animation; it modifies but does not significantly alter the form of the actual relief. Bury's wire and peg reliefs have given way in the past four years to large sculptured volumes of cabinet-fitted plywood to which lightly textured balls of various diameters are affixed (FIG. 101). One could make a good case that these are not Kinetic sculpture at all. They suggest that much attention has been bestowed on formal outlines and surface finishes, to fixed compositions rather than the trajectories of moving elements. From time to time even Bury has questioned his own inclusion as a Kineticist. With the "ball" sculptures cords lead to a random activating device; the "moving sculptures" stir almost imperceptibly. Each ball observed for its particular animation does not make much sense. Viewing one of Bury's constructions demands that one see and feel peripherally. The eyes, the ears and the sense of kinesthesis are not directly engaged, though one becomes aware of the meaning of the activity almost as an aftereffect.

Witnessing a single Bury sculpture or relief in a room is not dramatic. One is interested, perhaps even fascinated, then turns to another work. The experience of a whole roomful of Bury's is something else. Through silence, one *feels* the creaking of cords, spools, and linked shapes from all directions. Out of the corners of the eyes hundreds of multisensual movements take place imperceptibly. As in the hull of a sailing ship, wood strains against

101. Pol Bury, *18 Superimposed Balls*. 1965.

wood as the elements press against the live shell of doweled beams and planks. Without the interference of other human visitors, a room of Bury sculptures rocks with subliminal activity.

To view Kinetic Art as a collection of isolated events, toys with assigned activities, is a natural but unfortunate mistake. Painting and sculpture have produced a tradition of separate marketable objects and it is understandable if artists try to carry this over to Kinetics. But Kinetics presents a different métier. The effects of motion depend on environmental conditions and spatial planning much more than static works.

In January, 1966, *Time* magazine ran an article entitled "The Movement Movement," which placed the emphasis for today's Kinetic Art on the great rushing vehicles and noisy events heralded by the Futurists at the beginning of this century. Further, it regarded motion as mechanization at its most Chaplinesque; whereas the silent fleeting beams of light used by Gabo in his "Realist Manifesto" of 1920 come much closer to meaningful Kinetic expression in this generation. There exists an evolution of concerns among Kineticists, and the earlier preoccupation with form realized through motion has given way to visions of immateriality and a concern for the dimension of time itself. Time becomes the medium of expression, the means of measuring the dynamics of an event so that, beyond the problem of sculptural presentation, interest is sustained in kinetic activity itself. One truism of art is that motion produces lassitude more quickly than complete stillness. Few Kineticists come to the problem of temporal expression with any preparation. Certainly thinking in this area is ingenuous and unsophisticated compared to the investigations into the dynamics of time which have become an integral part of avant-garde music theory.

Philip Leider, critically analyzing the activity pattern of a certain Kineticist's sculptures, justifiably points to one of the profound weaknesses in the Kinetic position (May, 1966, p. 41):

The cycle stops and begins when the viewer steps on the starter button. The structure of this event is basically the literary, or dramatic structure of beginning-middle-end, and weds awkwardly to an art form which we ordinarily contemplate in no such sequence. The literary structure assumes, and is designed for, repetition, and beginnings, middles and ends of books, movies and plays are filled out with a rich complexity of incident to assure not only that boredom will not result from this repetition, but that, on the contrary, the work will reveal itself even more richly upon repeated viewings. Most kinetic sculpture which is structured in this fashion, is so simplistic, however, that we are never tempted to "see it again" (in the sense in which we "see a movie again"). Its content is quite exhausted after one or two "performances."

It might be well to add that the dynamic cycle of beginning-middle-end which Leider speaks of has been a fundamental pattern for all Western art, including music, since the Renaissance. In essence, it repeats the path of birth-life-death which affects every living organism. Many a music or literary critic has analyzed this life cycle in terms of specific works of art. It has been the avant-garde intention in all fields concerned with the effects of duration (literature, plays, movies, and music) to interrupt and in some cases completely destroy the natural life-cycle pattern, hopefully substituting in its place a more dynamic and meaningful sequential structure. This has been especially true in the twentieth century, with the school of Schoenberg, bop and some "cool" jazz, the Theatre of the Absurd, the stream-of-consciousness novel, and "field" poetry techniques. For the majority of Kinetic artists the issue of controlling time is so recent that it is to be expected that most artists fall back on sequential forms which reached their zenith in the nineteenth century. These repetitive sequences are not unlike the programs that controlled the movements of eighteenth-century automatons. Probably the Classical and Romantic symphony are their fullest expression.

With a few Kineticists such as Len Lye, the program of their work is generally controlled by the dynamical properties of the materials used.

Some artists use precisely controlled programs. Yet, for a great many, the idea of "programmed art" is more wish fulfillment than visual reality. Such diverse attitudes toward temporal control of the medium has not been too important for Kinetic artists, though it has generated a much more heated schism in musical composition. This dispute actually entails a spectrum of positions and runs from those advocating strict *aleatoric* processes (where the course of a work is generally determined but separate details depend on chance alternatives), to serial techniques where as many musical parameters as possible are mathematically determined, and finally through varying degrees of traditional tonal composition.

It is immediately apparent that a fully deterministic control, in fact any kind of detailed and precise programming, demands more engineering ability from artists than a decision to let randomness run its course. It is not surprising then that much New Tendency Kineticism has placed both a practical and theoretical reliance on random or aleatoric techniques. This is to be expected if one considers the limited technical capacity of most Kineticists, plus the great vogue in the past ten years for the use of aleatoric techniques in the musical avant-garde. The reasons for using random or pseudo-random Kinetic techniques are subtle and compelling and we should look at them. Moreover, the arguments against the cumbersomeness of real programmatic Kinetics makes sense—within certain limits. These arguments revolve around the recognized primitive state of three-dimensional Kineticism and its technical inability to produce rich determinate programs which are not too cumbersome mechanically. When the word *programmed* has been used, as for the Olivetti-sponsored "Programmed Art" traveling exhibition (1962–1965), it has been devoted mainly to aleatoric techniques.

To do this, a little bit of word juggling has been necessary. In an introduction to the "Programmed Art" exhibition (1962, pp. 2–3), which included large elements of both the Italian and French visual research groups, the historian Umberto Eco defined the word *programmed* so that we can accept the statistical laws of nature as a legitimate "programmer." For Eco the "linear purity" of a mathematically statistical program suffices. Needless to say, such a program may be easily employed for the artist's purposes.

In Kinetic circles there has been much talk of "free-play" effects, randomization, instability, "shattered motion" and other pseudonyms for statistically controlled events. Dadaism and "*l'art informal*" have been quite important in forming the psychological habits necessary for accepting the casualness of statistical events. Perhaps the acceptance of instability (which is really the result of looking at many small random motions representing

275

a homogeneous field of activity) is best put forward as an aesthetic philosophy by Le Parc. This stems out of a series of mobiles (FIG. 102), *Determinism and Indeterminism* begun by Le Parc in 1960. These consist of rows of hanging plastic squares sometimes illuminated by moving light sources and projected on to a flat curved backdrop. Le Parc's ideas on the equivalency of field events are very close to the wheatfields, surface phenomena on bodies of water, and other unified flickerings so important to artists in Group Zero. In an essay written in 1962 and entitled "A propos of: spectacle art, the active spectator, instability and programming in the visual arts" Le Parc writes:

These ensembles [his own and others created by the G.R.A.V.] are capable of creating unstable structures perceived in the field of peripheral vision, creating an indeterminate perception-time in which the physiologically activated viewer senses the unstable work. (Translated from the French by Davida Fineman.)

Speaking of a related form of Kinetic experience (perhaps overlapping optical interference patterns), Le Parc notes a type of self-generated time in which the spectator's random movements produce whatever Kinetic effects are to be seen.

These works (volumetric kinetic works) lead us to those which compose themselves (in proportion) as one looks at them. Here the act of "living" the work attains another degree, for the viewer sees the work in a real time. The particular movement of his perception solidifies a measure of time in which the work realizes itself for him. The notions of beginning and of end find themselves swept aside in the same way as the stable and finite quality of traditional works; it is a question here of nondefinitive works, movable to multiple positions and constant variations. (Translated from the French by Davida Fineman.)

Inadvertently Le Parc touches on an important issue: the degree to which the programmatic content of a Kinetic work can be determined by the viewer alone. The motion forms which he describes produce motion without the morphological consideration of beginning and end. In a word, they are the phenomena of infinitely random activity, probably the least causal and directed motion for any observer. Consequently, it is important for the vitality of Le Parc's art that he suggest active ways in which a viewer can engage the work. The fact that many of the patterns which he suggests produce the same statistical leveling-off as the random noise on an unused television channel means that perceptual variations generated by the viewer are the only way to maintain and stimulate interest. Much of the programmatics of the New Tendency have been solved in this fashion. Certainly such a "nondefinitive" work does not have the trite beginning-middle-end formula of which Leider complains. But the only thing significant about this form of motion is its relationship to nature-made events. Kinetic sculpture has a problem which only a few sculptors have partially surmounted. Deterministic Kinetics either produce simplistic motion patterns which do not sustain interest—because somehow the nature of mechanical motion is not intrinsically interesting—or they are reduced to a mesmerizing effect such as light dancing across a body of water.

If we were to compare the plight of avant-garde music to the programming of Kinetic works, there exists this similarity: music suffers either from over- or understructuring while visual Kinetics are beset with attempts to impose structures which are meaningless or attempt to produce antistructural situations as suggested by Le Parc.

A few artists, mainly those involved in the Kinetic effects of light, have attempted complex, strictly determinate programs. The majority, though, have employed a semi-program based on the permutations of several combined linear cycles. Nicolas Schöffer has produced some precise and fairly complex light constructions operating this way. A permutational series has the advantage of generating a very long nonrepetitive cycle from a set of much shorter sequences. Schöffer has been hailed by one New York critic

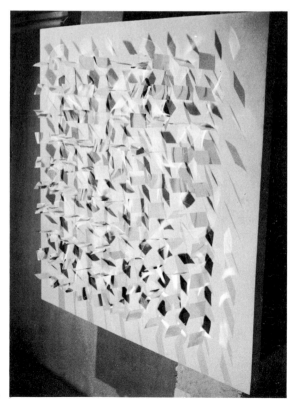

102. Julio Le Parc, *Continuel-Mobile Suspended*, 1962.

(Kramer, November 28, 1966) as a forerunner of the future, using the latest ideas and technology to produce the most daring visual spectacles, while in the same article, Tinguely is dismissed as "a gadgeteer manipulating the materials of accepted esthetic practice." Actually for many projects, the level of technology and the purposes to which it is put are practically the same for both artists. Schöffer uses more apparent precision, more motors, lights, and polish, but neither man, through the programmatics employed, is that much further toward the twenty-first century.

Nevertheless, Schöffer's *Microtemps* series (FIG. 103) are a good illustration of a permutational kinetic sequence. The *Microtemps* are table-sized, open boxes with a curved, polished aluminum backdrop. Inside the resulting proscenium space are a group of projecting spindles fitted with plexiglas blocks and metallic reflective surfaces. The spindles with their hardware revolve at variable speeds and are subjected to changing colors from pinpoint illumination. One witnesses, not so much the virtual volumes of the spinning forms themselves, as a procession of evolving flickering illuminations of the reflective backdrop. Begun in 1961, these constructions were first called *Anamorphosis*, referring to the diffusion of light into patterns of extreme change.

By 1964 Schöffer called this same series by their present name. The author had the opportunity at Schöffer's studio in Paris to ask if this name had anything to do with the concept of *micro-time* and *macro-time* as defined by the *Kölner Rundfunk* electronic composers. Schöffer's answer was that he had suggested the idea of *micro-time* to Karlheinz Stockhausen of that group early in the 1950's. Musically, this idea has played a part in serial composition technique and refers to the fact that *duration* or the length of notes in a composition, and *pitch* or the tonal frequency of musical sounds, exist in the same continuum. In other words, *micro-time* is a sequence of sound vibrations which occur so fast that we perceive them as a single tone; *macro-time* refers to the perceivable duration of tones and of the intervals between tones. Serial composition has on some occasions tried to break down the *perceptual* division between the pitch of a note and its duration. Schöffer has attempted a related feat with light and its speed in intervals. The frequency of revolution of the revolving reflections on his *Microtemps* constructions sometimes becomes so great that a solid pattern of light results. At other times the light-reflecting spindles turn quite slowly, producing the impression of a series of single moving lights. The result is a sense of constantly shifting tangibility and intangibility; light and material substance constantly fuse in this awe-provoking matrix of motion. The dramatic and sometimes abrupt changes which are effected in the *Microtemps* program lead

103. Nicolas Schöffer, *Microtemps 10*, 1964.

onc to bclieve that one is observing a strictly determined sequence, and
possibly this is true for some of the later models in the series; for the most
part, events seem to be unsynchronized happenings between several sub-
programs.

There is a type of semistructured program in Kinetics which is perceptually random in Le Parc's sense, but is also statistically definable.
With the *water boxes* of Hans Haacke, gravity becomes a means of simulating control and a sense of purposefulness. The *water boxes* are completely
sealed containers divided into two or more compartments. Water or other
fluids move from one compartment to another by means of gravity and
through tiny holes in the partitions separating each compartment. Natural
movement is seen in Haacke's work with condensation (FIG. 104). Here the
sequences of evaporation, condensation, and moisture collection are even
more subtle.

Haacke's use of nonmechanical motion (if we speak of "mechanical"
strictly in terms of rigid body relationships) and natural time has an interesting implication. Long before Lewis Mumford, writers were commenting
on the inhuman rhythms of the machine. In an exhibition of the sculpture

279

104. Hans Haacke, *Weather Cube*, 1965.

of Tinguely or Schöffer one's sensory capacity is alternately attacked or lulled by the staccato and humming noises issuing from machines. Noises and motions have a kind of spastic abruptness with very little relation to the pace of the human nervous system. This ability to lull the viewer pleasantly through natural temporal rhythms is equally a part of the constructions of Calder and Rickey. In both instances, where the sources of power are gentle pushes or breezes, one senses the undulant effects of swaying branches and rocking boats. Tinguely and Schöffer envision an electro-mechanical world from which there is no escape—for this Tinguely has regret, it haunts him, while Schöffer is compulsively optimistic.

Time is of the essence to the Kineticist, but except on the most elementary terms it continues to escape meaningfulness in three dimensions. Visually, we are still far from the programmatics of the nineteenth-century symphony. And until the dynamics of visual happenings are better understood probably latent time, what Le Parc calls in one respect "living the work," will determine how we see the aesthetics of motion.

If Kineticism has been designated "The Unrequited Art," the cause is its close ties to the methods and attitudes of the first age of machines. To be satisfied with the state of Kinetic Art as it exists is to ignore the technical, aesthetic, and commercial problems still perplexing the artist. The nature of Kinetics is such a radical departure from all past forms of sculpture that it can hardly be called sculpture, nor can we expect it to find its place as an art form in the accepted tradition of painting or sculpture. Means and persons will arise to dispel the dilemma of Kinetics which will be temporarily unacceptable to critics and other artists. Yet, no matter how violent artistic solutions have been in the past, consistently art has met impasses with different ways of *seeing*—technical solutions have always been secondary, a means to an end. Signs indicate this may no longer be true. Present obstacles to motion as a viable art form will demand primarily technical solutions. It can be expected that artists, many at least, will resist such a development.

During the winter of 1964 in New York City, the Cordier & Ekstrom Gallery conducted an exhibition entitled "For Eyes and Ears." Fully twenty-seven artists participated, though not more than a third would be considered Kinetic artists. All produced sounds and motions of a sort—some attached to or hidden inside static painting or sculpture. For a number of these non-Kinetic works the mathematician and electronics engineer Billy Klüver designed the sound or Kinetic capacity. This event plus a number of similar exhibitions suggests two conclusions. Obviously it is more "in" to be Kinetic. But perhaps more important in the long run, as art accepts the technological scale of values, as it looks toward electronic know-how to solve its present inadequacy, the more outside help it will require.

A new and growing symbiosis is happening. At a meeting of the College Art Association of America in January, 1966, Billy Klüver noted the inevitability of a closer relationship between artists and engineers. Already most Kinetic artists use the services of technical specialists, some constantly. Klüver further suggested that engineers are not visionaries. Therefore, it will always be the artist who determines what must be done—although the artist will find it increasingly difficult to realize his visions without the aid of his practical advisers. However there are already indications that the engineer may become more than an equal partner with the artist, depending upon the technical complexity of the projects under consideration.

Jacques Ellul in *The Technological Society* has analyzed "technique," or what Lewis Mumford has called "technics," in terms of its property of "self-augmentation." Worded another way: there is no such thing as introducing "a little technology." Beyond a certain plateau, technology breeds technology. Each generation we speak of a doubled number of scientists in certain fields, or we say that ninety percent of all the scientists who ever lived are presently alive. Not only does technique engender more technique, our capacity to resist technology, or, phrased more positively, our reluctance to accept the fruits and methodology of technology, becomes fainter and fainter each passing decade.

For the future of a mechanized art form Ellul raises an even more decisive question. He notes the power of technical apparatus to replace traditional symbolism in the human mind. Moreover, the coupling of the human being to the machine is an accepted theme of modern art. The machine by itself needs a strong antidote and Klee, de Chirico, Duchamp, and Picabia have all mixed extremes of deranged fantasy with the materiality of technology. Ellul strongly doubts whether any art as we know it can stem from the ultra-rationality of technics. Consequently, the artist finds only one hiding place from technological proliferation (1954, p. 404).

A major section of modern art and poetry unconsciously guides us in the direction of machines; and, indeed, for the modern man there is no other way. Only madness is inaccessible to the machine. Every other "art" form can be reduced to technique; note the utilitarian art of the Soviets.

When the idea is stressed by Ellul in such antipodean terms, it is no wonder that the Kinetic revival maintains its internal contradictions. Many Kineticists readily see the danger signals. Yet there are those like Schöffer who see no incompatibility between art and advanced technology. Their view is that the artist has always used what technical facilities were at hand and that it is nonsense to interpret the new technology as anti-artistic. Another view sees that art has always been a subtle balance between irrational and rational human characteristics. Probably in the past irrationality was a much more integrated and culturally compatible force in the lives of men. The compelling logic and almost authoritarian ethos of science and technics has changed that. Technics either tends to undermine the psychic structure of irrationality, therefore destroying it, or forces it into a position where it must manifest itself in stronger and more antithetical terms. The madness which Ellul speaks of is a case in point. If humanity means maintaining a balance between the rational and irrational, it makes sense that Dadaism should be regarded by artists as a breath of sanity while those who attempt to apply ultra-rational technology to areas which have always defied rational explanation should be looked upon as being largely perverse, if not insane.

Even within the groups perpetuating an aura of scientific examination there exists a great amount of semipublic soul searching. In a statement first published by the G.R.A.V. in 1962, Yvaral clarified the group's relationship to science (April, 1962, p. 14).

In many points our method of work and our research technique corresponds to the method and technique of the scientist. Indeed, we take as our point of departure given results already acquired and we exploit them in an experimental manner, forcing ourselves to control all possibilities and all issues. From these studies are born new bits of knowledge no longer disparate, but codified. They will thus constitute new bases for new research which will make us progress towards our goal: the knowledge of the "visual phenomenon."

The comparison between our research and scientific work makes us conscious of an insufficiency which we desire to repair: it concerns technology. While that of science is well defined and leaves no room for misunderstanding ours was not.... Towards this purpose contacts already have been made and will multiply in the future with representatives of all disciplines of scientific research. (Translated from the French by Davida Fineman.)

Although the quote above is a fairly precise disclaimer, the G.R.A.V. has had to face accusations of pseudo-scientism. It is difficult for most critics to discern the difference between scientific ends and means. Here certainly is a case where only means have been employed, and then only to a limited and well-defined extent. Other than that, the G.R.A.V. has tried to make the best of two possible worlds. As scientists do—sometimes—its members share their information with their colleagues, yet at the same time there is a certain amount of individuality and autonomy among them. They reject the implication that their group represents a "super-individual" where six men produce a collective or aggregate style. Nevertheless elements within the group have attempted to play down a magnification of individuality. At the present time the G.R.A.V. has not disbanded (it remains together for group shows and the power of its name) but the recent fame of some of its members has substantially diminished its former cohesion.

Whether an artist is interested in producing a controlled visual experiment or a work of art is immaterial. The ultimate fate of a created object depends upon its commercial acceptance. This is the nature of our society and this is how the artist establishes his identity in society. For galleries, almost as an act of metaphysical transubstantiation, there is a private to public passage for the art object. With a "cold" experimental object, such as produced by the G.R.A.V. according to its private ideological considerations, it is only a matter of time, publicity, and taste before it is transformed into a desirable artifact sought by a public greedy for the innovational. Few artists can or want to withstand the temptation and recognition that follow creation of such work; to paraphrase a response by Takis: poverty does not allow me [the artist] the luxury of remaining unknown.

As was shown previously, there have been any number of attempts since the beginning of the twentieth century toward a collective anonymity among artists. All have failed for reasons not too different from the ones presented above. Not before 1960 did artists concertedly set out to use scientific methodology in solving artistic problems. This represents an evolution of a sort, and one can only speculate on the next step. At this point Gabo's attitude about the limitations of science in art are very much shared by the G.R.A.V. Moreover, while the G.R.A.V. does not feel in competition with scientific discovery, its members grasp the meaning of the word "scientist" in a much older sense—that is, the scientist as an amateur interested in everything, rather than specialist involved in a prescribed research program. Artists who do involve themselves in the complexities of science tend to view science as a humanistic endeavor and not as Ellul's treadmill toward oblivion.

There remains, nonetheless, an almost frantic fear that typifies the reactions of the nonmoving avant-garde. This fear takes the form of ridicule and champions anything stationary, accepting an increasingly overt technology only when it does not move. Kineticism is boring, they say; its values are false; its technological capacity is puny; and, worst of all, it does not attempt to solve the "real" problems of sculpture (May, 1966, p. 43):

The nature of progress in science and in art is not a parallel one, nor are developments in one area reflected on a simple one-to-one basis in the other.... To the extent that the rhetoric of motion sculpture attempts to justify itself esthetically with portentous references to quantum mechanics, to that extent does it deserve little more than to be dismissed out of hand. The tragedy of so specious an emphasis on a kind of bogus scientism is that it tends to deflect the attention of practicing artists from esthetic problems no less complex and sophisticated than the technology they so breathlessly admire and so dismally fail to reflect.

This book attempts to put into perspective many serious critics' doubts concerning the place of science and technology in modern sculpture. Admittedly it is a difficult relationship, one in which sculptors often hesitate to make parallels. Yet they do state their interests. If they do not grasp science as well as the scientist, if they do not possess the wherewithal to compete with the fully equipped and trained engineer, that should hardly be surprising. The important thing is that the Kineticist is trying to make himself relevant in a world which is continually being recreated. He has refused to become an anachronism painting or making vapid gestures with larger and larger surfaces. In an art world of "cool" stances and exploding values a dialectical tension continues to build around Kineticism. The very fact that it is unrealized art should remain a sign of encouragement for future artists, even though Philip Leider suggests (1966, p. 42) that Kinetic artists should enlarge upon the stance of Tinguely and create more self-destroying machines. Actually, even with the desire attached to that death wish, it is, at best, only a Luddite solution. The real way to kill an art movement is for it to realize its goals—an objective which Kineticism has yet to achieve.

CHAPTER SEVEN

Light as Sculpture Medium

Emitted Light in Art

The controlled use of light is the most flexible visual art form yet devised and its enormous variety of uses is far from exhausted. At its present stage emitted light best demonstrates one of the primary qualities of *systems:* the tendency to fuse art object and environment into a perceptual whole. In fact, the trend of Light Art is to eliminate the specific art object and to transform the environment into a light-modulating system sensitive to responses from organisms which invade its presence.

What defines emitted light, light directly discharged from the art object or system, is the relative quality of *luminosity*. Equally the product of sun, moon, fire, electric lamps, luminescent chemicals, and various electrical aerial phenomenon, luminosity is the visual impression received when an area of light exceeds a threshold of brilliance relative to its surroundings. To an observer this glowing quality appears to be the result of internal energy in the source itself. Possibly this explains why luminosity acts as an emotional stimulant: primeval man's response was to be drawn toward the life-giving energy sources of heat and light.

Systems devised from various types of electric light and its control apparatus are the means for the recent and successful entrance of direct light in the plastic arts. Until the 1920's—without exception—attempts to use emitted light were aesthetically misconceived, without a perceptual basis, and technologically primitive. This is not said to disparage the pioneers of Light Art. If anything, Light Art's recent successes are mainly circumstantial: this is due to the diminishing vitality of traditional art forms and to newer, more flexible means of electrical illumination. As previously mentioned, the rise of Kinetic sculpture offers a parallel: formerly forgotten artists working in an unsuccessful medium suddenly became heroes and pioneers only *after* the medium began to make progress and receive public approval. For those working in Light Art before 1965 it was a lonely and financially unrewarding task.

For hundreds of years painters have been most sensitive to the effects of reflected and radiant light. With growing sophistication, artists have analyzed and reinterpreted every aspect of indoor and outdoor illumination for the canvas. However, in the eighteenth and nineteenth centuries music, not painting, was the theoretical basis for most compositions employing emitted light. In 1734 the Jesuit priest and mathematician Louis-Bertrand Castel presented the first color organ, this being a series of transparent colored tapes illuminated from behind by candles and controlled by a person playing the keys of a clavier. The results were not appreciated by Castel's contemporaries, a situation that would become familiar to Light artists.

For those interested in the development of Light Art to 1925, no book is more complete or exhaustively documented than Adrian Bernard Klein's *Colour-Music: The Art of Light* (1927). Klein gives a detailed account of what he calls "correspondences," or the relations between musical tones and colors. Dozens of painters, musicians, scientists, and inventors are cited as being for or against any quantitative physical analogy between sound and light. This debate continued for many centuries and Klein takes the presently accepted stand that no correspondence exists.

Aside from writing countless papers on theories of color music, some serious experimenters of the nineteenth century actually made instruments for the purpose of closing the gap between music and painting. D. D. Jameson, Frederic Kastner, and A. W. Rimington made organs for the manipulation of light. These experiments with gas and electric illumination were unfortunately premature.

One of these experimenters, A. W. Rimington, professor of fine arts at Queen's College in London, on June 6, 1895 gave his first concert on a color organ. According to reports, it was an artistic failure. Fourteen arc lamps projected a series of juxtaposed colors on an undulating curtain of white silk. While light and color were controlled by Rimington, their programming had little to do with the musical accompaniment. Spectators complained of indecisive, flickering illumination. Musically based color abstraction has had a long history of technical unfulfillment and public apathy.

Yet it seems that where light as a medium of expression has had a remunerative commercial outlet it has matured technically. Klein devotes a chapter in his book to the art of stage lighting and mentions Gordon Craig, Max Reinhardt, Adrian Samoiloff, Matthew Luckish, and Norman Bel Geddes as being pioneers in creating, not only more versatile lighting consoles, but a theatre in which light becomes a powerful emotional factor. The immense sophistication of today's automated lighting-control boards owes more to the ability of the theatre to pay its own way than to a desire for an art of light.

In 1921 Mary Hallock-Greenwalt demonstrated a color organ in New York City after fifteen years of experimentation. She based her system too on a theory of musical notation and included the control of seven colored lights focused on a stage screen. In reference to Hallock-Greenwald, Klein made the observation (p. 21) that "...it is an odd fact that almost everyone who develops a colour-organ is under the misapprehension that he, or she, is the first mortal to attempt to do so."

Adrian Klein designed a color projector built in 1921. The sizable cost of the instrument and financial difficulties with the theatrical company underwriting the cost of the projector prevented Klein from further building to test his theories of Light Art. The brilliance of the arc lamp employed by the inventor and the size of its lenses made it the most powerful and flexible light-control apparatus then in use. Moreover, Klein was perceptive in his conviction that an "Art of Light" would have to cover large areas of the viewer's visual range before its success or effects would be assured.

In general, a dichotomy has evolved in Light Art between those favoring patterns of light confined to a screen and those artists interested in light's prime property of spatial dispersion from a source which may or may not be considered an art object. The former might be called "painters," those artists involved in projecting a series of colored configurations onto a flat translucent surface, while the latter are "sculptors" or environmentalists constructing with sculpture-like light sources.

Before considering the uses of light in a three-dimensional context, it might be well to mention one light "painter." Thomas Wilfred has been the most consistent pioneer in the "Art of Light" or what he has called *Lumia*. Beginning serious work in 1919, Wilfred constructed an organ-like instrument with hand-manipulated rheostats to control light intensities. This lay hidden behind a curtain and translucent screen; here the inventor-composer "played" a series of programs. In 1922 Wilfred gave his first public performance and soon became something of a minor sensation. *Lumia* was the rage for several seasons and people accepted it more as a novelty than as what Wilfred would have preferred, a new art form. Critics found fault with *Lumia* and complained of muddy colors and a lack of musical accompaniment—a standard feature of previous color organs. One of Wilfred's firm tenets has been that *Lumia* must develop as an independent art form free of all the usual comparisons with music. Through the years Wilfred has built many versions of *Lumia* and has perfected his compositional techniques toward a purer and wider range of colors and shapes. In the 1930's he formed an institute for research in programmed light with a studio in the Grand Central Palace in New York City. The war prevented further work, but afterward research with a group of assistants was resumed in West Nyack, New York. Here

287

during the late 1940's Wilfred attempted a stereoscopic *Lumia* that worked without a screen. This failed primarily for lack of funds. While the best of the *Lumia* constructions do not reproduce an illusion of parallax vision, the brilliance of the images and the limpid, deep quality of the backgrounds are suggestively three-dimensional, and Wilfred composes his programs in terms of a projected space that tends to come out of the screen toward the viewer.

As an innovator, Wilfred occupies a curious and solitary place in American art. After his public successes in the 1920's and 1930's the vogue for *Lumia* receded, owing as much to the technical perfection of motion pictures as to audiences' impatience with the slow-moving, unearthly silence of the *Lumia* programs. Wilfred deserves credit for resisting many commercial offers to exploit the eye-catching advertising value of his medium. However, his attempts to have *Lumia* accepted as an art form have met with limited success—particularly among painters. This is not surprising, since painters have always regarded the use of pure light as a threat to their own medium. Beyond that, they have regarded Wilfred's use of colored light as overly sweet and vulgar. Wilfred, nevertheless, has received grants and the New York Museum of Modern Art through the years has commissioned him to construct several pieces for their collection. The successes of American informal painting through the 1950's probably did much to throw *Lumia* into eclipse as an art form. Wilfred has taken this lack of artistic recognition with some bitterness, and only since the trend toward Light Art in the 1960's has his position as an innovator been partially restored.

Lumia can now best be seen in a small theatre set up (FIG. 105) for the purpose in the basement of the New York Museum of Modern Art. Here the viewer sits in relative silence. A heavily curtained room contains about twenty seats with a luminous, almost transparent screen in front as an only source of light. The changing forms for this program take on the wispy quality of high-altitude clouds. The resultant hues illustrate both the strengths and weaknesses of color as it usually appears in Light Art; while often very pure and penetrating, they are frequently diluted into a milky whiteness. Overtones of shadows and reflected lights in normal environmental situations are never present. It is a transcendent but unnatural presentation of color where vivid blue-purples, glowing yellow-greens, and deeply saturated reds make up a fraction of an unforgettable spectrum. These are not painterly colors, nor are they like the stained glass of the great Gothic cathedrals. They comprise a range of hues which many artists have been unable to accept, labeling them candy-box pastel. In Wilfred's defense, such criticism has more to do with prevailing artistic taste than with a lack of sensitivity on his part toward the use of luminescent colors. Moreover, *Lumia* bears favorable comparison to other contemporary examples of programs using light screens. Ironically, it may be that Pop Art and the new-found appreciation for neon light has made *Lumia* almost quaintly respectable.

The intensely slow and deliberate unfolding of Wilfred's compositions disturbs some viewers. Wilfred has claimed that *Lumia* is an art unaffected by the problems of musical time; syncopation or periodic suspensions of movement, he claims, would only detract from its effect. He insists that the gradual unfolding of *Lumia's* luminescent shapes happens at an ideal speed: rather like nearly frozen honey running out of a jar. By making programs without clear sequential intersections, durational structuring, or tempo changes, he has, in effect, destroyed the experience of temporal duration. Time is rendered completely homogeneous, becoming formless and extinct.

The future of *Lumia* as an adjunct of the mass media is doubtful. Not only does the cost of constructing such a system remain quite high, but the medium itself stands too far removed from the perceptual expectancies of today's general public. Nevertheless, Wilfred must be appreciated for what he is: a pioneer who has consistently moved counter to the popular trends of modern art.

105. Thomas Wilfred, *Lumia Suite, Opus 158*, 1963–1964.

Often the Bauhaus of Weimar and Dessau, Germany, has been cited as one of the gestation places for light's first entrance into modern art, and an earlier chapter reviewed the stage experiments and manipulation of reflected light by Oskar Schlemmer. The Bauhaus painters, Lyonel Feininger, Paul Klee, and Wassily Kandinsky, took a profound interest in the effects of light as a plastic element of composition. Moreover, the stained-glass workshop under the direction of Josef Albers attempted to reestablish the glory of medieval window design, yet with more emphasis on the abstract and sculptural qualities of glass itself as a medium.

In a privately printed paper, "Colored-light Play—Nature—Goals—Criticisms" (1925), an associate of the Bauhaus, Ludwig Hirschfeld-Mack, describes his investigation of kinetic light sequences. Unlike Wilfred, he eagerly sought to establish a relationship between acoustical and visual rhythms. He also notes the first attempts (1922) in the Bauhaus workshops by Joseph Hartwig and Kurt Schwerdtfeger to produce multiple shadow images on a translucent surface. Entitled *Reflective Lightplays*, these configurations quite possibly provided prototypes for some of Paul Klee's most successful watercolors of overlapping transparent forms. Hirschfeld-Mack describes his apparatus as a translucent light screen set in front of a stencil which masks the images projected upon it. The illuminated forms resulting could be vibrated, transformed in shape or color, or altered in terms of brightness. An operator situated in back of the mechanism improvised his own program. Photographs of the rear of this boxlike structure indicate the technology in use as rather unsophisticated compared to Wilfred's *Lumia*. From Hirschfeld-Mack's remarks about abstract painting and the effects of transparency by the Constructivists, it is likely that he viewed his own efforts as another step toward an art of total immateriality. Indirectly this desire for immateriality has always been an aspect of the Light artist's program. The *Reflective Lightplays*, however, were to remain stillborn and undeveloped, simply one more premature venture during the short but vital history of the Bauhaus.

The most important uses of light as an art form were made by another member of the Bauhaus. László Moholy-Nagy was one of the first moderns to regard the cityscape at night as pure pulsating light sculpture. Car headlights could be frozen into paths of luminous tracery and illuminated advertisements would in time become the basis for an environmental art of darkness. It is perhaps well that Moholy-Nagy never lived to see the overripe fulfillment of his prophesies. His visions of turning outdoor advertising into a nighttime art form were truly overoptimistic. In his basic design course he devised several problems for showing how sculpture in the round could be transformed by alterations of its lighting. In the New Bauhaus in Chicago this

106. László Moholy-Nagy, *Light-Space Modulator*, 1922–1930.

emphasis on form through light became the impetus for "Light Modulator" problems. Students were taught not only to see form, but form as it could be created by beams of light and the resulting shadows.

Between 1922 and 1930 Moholy-Nagy, with the aid of an expert mechanic, designed and built his famous *Light-Space Modulator* (FIG. 106), a six-foot-high apparatus of moving aluminum and chrome-plated surfaces driven by an electric motor and a series of chain belts. To achieve its full effect the machine must be experienced in a room darkened, with spotlights alternately thrown upon its turning members. The result: a myriad of dissolving shadows passing over walls and ceiling. Shortly after its completion Moholy-Nagy and his future wife, Sibyl, made a film, "Light Display: Black and White and Grey." In her biography of the artist, his wife recreates some of Moholy-Nagy's remarks about the planning of the film (1950, p. 69):

I'm not thinking in chronological terms...at least not in the accepted sense. The rhythm of this film has to come from the light—it has to have a light-chronology.

Light beams overlap as they cross through dense air; they're blocked, diffracted, condensed. The different angles of the entering light indicate time. The rotation of light from east to west modulates the visible world. Shadows and reflexes register a constantly changing relationship of solids and perforations.

For several reasons the *Light-Space Modulator* (or *Lichtrequisit*, as it was referred to in Germany) was an important prototype for later light sculpture. Its purpose was not to project but to exist as a three-dimensional object appreciated for itself. Through the use of moving shadows, it permeated the surrounding room. It did not use, as so much earlier Light Art had, Wilfred's "focal stage technique" of backlighting a screen. Instead, the modulator created both shadow and substance; it supported Moholy's feeling that light, if rendered into art, must first be *transmitted* and *transformed* through materials—not projected directly at the viewer. The *Modulator* now stands inactive at Harvard's Busch-Reisinger Museum, where on special occasion it can be operated.

Gyorgy Kepes traveled from London to Chicago in 1937 to assist Moholy-Nagy at the new Institute of Design. There Kepes headed the Light and Color Department. In 1946 Kepes assumed the directorship of the Visual Design Department at the Massachusetts Institute of Technology. Since then his solitary voice has proclaimed the potentials of light as a new art medium. Kepes has directed many seminars and courses on the nature and uses of light (particularly in photographing shapes and field formations under varying light conditions). Kepes has continued to work mainly as a writer, painter, and design adviser—and infrequently as an artist using light as a medium. In 1959 he completed a light mural for the KLM office in New York City. This immense wall of stenciled shapes in light anticipates the poetry of a cityscape as seen from an airplane at night. Superimposed over these thousands of tiny points of light are colored arabesques illuminated at different tempos.

In contrast to the KLM mural, Kepes had a decade before designed a large neon and incandescent light sign for The Radio Shack, an electronics supply store in Boston. This structure consists of a belt sign in textured steel with an abstract painted background and electronic symbols superimposed in neon; above rests a tall stick-out sign with the letters of the store backlighted against a vertical row of concave hemispheres. This effort by Kepes—directly using the technology of light—was one of the most imaginative commercial displays of the period. In many ways this strictly commercial venture is much better "art" than the noncommercial KLM light mural.

Until the present decade Light Art has remained a stillborn affair. It is informative to compare its progress with the projection and animation of realistic images, that is, by the motion pictures. Even in its infancy this medium satisfied the story-telling needs of a large, semi-educated public. "Color music"—perhaps because it never fulfilled any profound need—remained financially destitute, while, because of its vast commercial potential, many millions of dollars were spent to perfect cinema photography.

In this respect the archaeologist C. W. Ceram makes a more fundamental point in his brief but excellent treatise on the development of the early cinema. In reference to the alleged beginnings of motion pictures through Hero of Alexandria, Claudius Ptolemy, the serial cave paintings of Altamira, the friezes of the Parthenon, baroque automata, and magic lantern shows, Ceram states (1965, p. 16): "What matters in history is not whether certain chance discoveries take place, but whether they take effect."

Ceram gives some key inventions without which the motion pictures would never have evolved to their modern form. And further (p. 17): "...there is no question of 'evolution'.... Between inventions a mutation intervened, the change from mechanical to technical thinking."

Ceram's opinion suggests several facts about Light Art. The results of much Light Art, even contemporary, suggest that most artists try to accommodate light to already existing art. Two breakthroughs have occurred in the present decade: one is that a few successful artists have tried to strip "art" from their uses of light; the other is that an aesthetic based on "cool" values, Minimal Art, the industrialized use of plastics and metal, has allowed various types of emitted light to become artistically acceptable. This is Ceram's change from mechanical to technical thinking put into practice.

Moreover, one wonders about the "mutation" which Ceram mentions. What great inventions during the last forty years now make Light Art popular? Very few in fact. Neon was available forty years ago, as were switching mechanisms, incandescent light, lenses, colored glass, etc. What have changed are public sensibilities. As the last part of this chapter will suggest, Light Art is still in its infancy and its prime inventions have yet to come.

Postwar European Exploration of Light

Few if any examples of architecture before the Second World War show an awareness for the uses of light which matches that given to problems in mural painting and sculpture. There were "artistically" designed lighting displays for stores and commercial buildings, but hardly any art as such. Not until 1946 did Lucio Fontana, in drafting his "White Manifesto," define the conditions under which artists could surmount the static qualities of pigment and stone. In subsequent writings and works Fontana demonstrated that art does not remain in an environmental vacuum, but is continually changed by the light engulfing it.

In 1949 Fontana created a "spatial environment" of hung wooden sculpture illuminated by black-light lamps in the Galleria del Navigilio in Milan. In the following year, using the raised and depressed holes of his puncture paintings, Fontana designed a seventy-six-foot-long ceiling with integrated lighting, acoustics, and air-conditioning. One of Fontana's outstanding projects was a design (1951) for the ceiling of the entrance hall of the Ninth Triennale in Milan. Here lines of small, circular holes were arranged in the polished ceiling; out of some of these strips of neon were suspended at angles. These were positioned to point in different directions so that the reflected image of the neon seemed to change as an observer moved through the hall. Here Fontana used his light sources quite directly—not masking their naked light behind plastic or metal shields, or hiding the electrodes at the end of the neon tubes. Even more spectacular was his use of six thousand feet of neon vertically suspended for Italy's exposition hall at Turin in 1961. It is safe to say that no artist has been more influential on this generation in the handling of light media than Lucio Fontana.

Before 1960 there were other European artists using light, though none totally committed to its exploitation. One should mention the collage projections of Bruno Munari shown in coordination with electronic music. Also the Argentine Martha Boto, now living in Paris, began to explore the possibilities of illuminated liquids in 1957. Since 1961 Miss Boto has worked with the reflective properties of moving light in field reliefs of highly polished metal. These are highly seductive and tend to entrance the viewer as does water reflected on the smooth bottom of a pool. In respect to light, the liberating influence of Yves Klein must not be forgotten. Klein's first fire painting (1957) of International Klein Blue contained a row of Bengal lights which gave off an intense blue arc of light (Sharp, April–May, 1967, p. 7). In 1961 Klein repeated his "La Vide" at the Krefeld Museum, this time with a single fluorescent tube in the empty room.

Much that has recently passed in the United States for so-called "psychedelic art"—using environmental light projectors—has its modern beginnings in the *Light Ballet* of the German artist Otto Piene. In Düsseldorf (1958) the eighth evening exhibition by Piene and Heinz Mack took place with the publication of the first issue of *Zero Magazine*. Toward the end of the 1950's, Piene, working out a philosophical and plastic basis for the use of light, conducted a series of nighttime exhibitions with Mack that attempted to move beyond the thinking of Fontana and Moholy-Nagy. Piene attempted to mix the outdoor phenomenalism of his wartime experiences—searchlights against the clouds, arcs of tracer bullets, the sun on the changing North Sea, moving reflections of windswept fields of grain—with the peaceful means of the lighting expert, in his words: "a synthesis of the technological, urban world and the world of natural forces."

The *Light Ballet* (FIG. 107) demonstrations were first held in Piene's studio and then moved to various indoor locations, where the contours of the walls became as important as light dispersion itself. The gradual developments of the *Light Ballet* are best explained by the artist (1965, pp. 3–4):

At first I used hand-operated lamps whose light I directed through the stencils I had used for stencil paintings. Controlled by my hands, the light appeared in manifold projections around entire rooms—that is, not only on a limited plane such as a movie screen or standard stage. The light choreography was determined by jazz or by accompanying sound which I produced myself.

The solo turned into a group performance, with each member of the ensemble holding individual lamps and contributing different shapes and colors to the overall rhythm of the projection. Feelings of tranquility, suspension of normal balance and

107. Otto Piene, *Light Ballet*, 1961.

an increased sensation of space were reactions that viewers volunteered to me after finding themselves in the center of the event. That their everyday fearful nervosity diminished was a sensual effect that I welcomed.

The light ballet lost spontaneity and gained steadiness when I mechanized it. Motors caused the steady flow of unfurling and dimming, reappearing and vanishing light forms which metaphorically described the continuous change from day to night. A light ballet continues as long as one likes. He who wants it switches it on. He who has had enough switches it off. I like the possibility that it may last, without beginning or end.

In 1959 I played the light ballet with hand lamps, in 1960 I built the first machines, in 1961 they appeared in large darkened rooms at exhibits and in museums; one object, two objects in a large hall, a waste of space, an elimination of conventional attitudes about quantity. The farther the distance between the projecting device and the light-catching confines of a room, the larger are the light forms. And when they are large, the claustrophobia caused by the ordinary cubicity of our interior spaces recedes.

Mechanized, Piene's programs consisted of searchlights which produced overlapping light patterns by being shown through revolving perforated disks; another version consisted of three- or four-foot-diameter canvas spheres perforated and turning with concealed light sources inside. A certain richness of combination was gained by having several of these machines in operation at the same time in a room. In a short essay, "Lichtballett" (1961), Piene gives his idea of an ideal situation for a light presentation: the first would be a hemisphere into which any person could wander and sink into a reclining chair, ready to receive the changing light pattern that flooded the space, completely free of the feeling of being closed in by a dimensioned space; the second plan was a recurrent obsession of Piene's—that of illuminating the night sky with specially constructed projectors.

Piene's past few years have been preoccupied with a more technically demanding use of light, usually as an architectural installation. Pictures of his earlier *vernissages* show the artist surrounded with dozens of yards of cables, transformers, and theatre lights. Piene has held to the goal of using light as directly and flexibly as possible, and this undoubtedly was one of several reasons that prompted him to seek out the technology of the United States in 1964. Here he has found a range of lamps, lenses, and power supplies that are unknown or difficult to come by in his native Germany. He has given considerable thought to the problem of colored light and, as a result, his sculptures do not employ any kind of artificial coloring, either gelatin or painted lamps. Piene prefers the natural color of the burning filament and he explains that even this, depending on the current running through the lamp, produces its own spectrum of color—from the blue-white of high-intensity light, through the range of yellows and orange-yellows to the dull red of the

108. Otto Piene, *Corona Borealis*, 1965.   109. Nicolas Schöffer, *Lux I*, 1957.

nearly extinct filament. The result has been a recent series of works (FIG. 108) —some very elegant—where the naked, transparent lamp with a visible filament becomes the unit for a cluster or field of lights programmed to go on and off in sequence.

In 1957 the Hungarian-French sculptor Nicolas Schöffer created his first *ensemble luminodynamique*, entitled *Lux I* (FIG. 109). This was a variation of Schöffer's earlier spatiodynamic constructions of aluminum structural members bolted together and decorated with perforated plates of brass and chrome-plated steel. This was mounted on a slow turntable, spotlighted with rotating color filters, and the resulting shadows and colors were cast on a translucent screen. Fundamentally, the luminodynamic idea resembles the *Light-Space Modulator* of Moholy-Nagy.

Schöffer's *Microtemps* series (see Chapter Six, FIG. 103), which have already been described in the previous chapter, are coloristically and kinetically more interesting than the luminodynamic series. Here the light sources and their color changes are less obvious. They fuse in a hypnotic web through a spinning array of plastic and chrome elements.

The artist has used colored light much more serenely in his *Musiscope* of the *Chronos* series (1960). This employs a keyboard console and a large translucent screen backlighted by diffused and diffracted light sources which produce forms comparable to Wilfred's *Lumia*. Superimposed on this are revolving geometric images derived from the spatiodynamic sculptures. Schöffer has made a further extension of this in *Chronos 6, Wall of Light* (1962) which uses a bank of light-modulating units. These units, Schöffer relates, have since been put into production for architectural use by the Phillips Corporation. This is proof to Schöffer that a working relationship can exist between the businessman and the artist.

In his writings (Joray, 1963, pp. 62, 132–137), the artist has cited colored light as being only one of many parameters of expression open to temporal control. As with many New Tendency artists (though Schöffer is hardly New Tendency), his vision of space-time aesthetics is based on the statistical leveling-off of random phenomena. Here the indeterminacy of unstructured light sequences merged with revolving sculptures is regarded by the artist as being superior to a repetitive determinate program. Schöffer's light programs go on indefinitely, never quite the same but always appearing the same; this he designates as *continuous discontinuity*.

Schöffer's skill with light resides more on the environmental level than with small gallery works. His display (1961) at Liège, Belgium, was a spectacular triumph. Inside the Palais du Congrès an electronic console controlled a number of projectors which cast images on plastic screens hung in front of the façade of windows which line the building. Outside and at some distance stood one of the artist's *Cybernetic Towers*, its polished metal parts spinning at variable speeds, while the whole structure was bathed in white light from spots positioned on the ground (Nan Piene, May–June, 1967, pp. 40–41).

Probably the most painterly of all Light Artists is an American who has lived in Paris for the past fifteen years. Frank Malina, a geophysicist and aeronautics engineer, made his first optical reliefs in 1954 and had his first show of kinetic light reliefs in Paris in 1955. Malina's constructions, or what he calls *lumidynes* are rectangular boxes faced on a single side with translucent material and containing a mechanical-electric or electronic program. Some of Malina's effects resemble the results of Wilfred's *Lumia* and Schöffer's *Musiscope*, but the most unusual have a fixed composition of illuminated forms that pulsate in brightness and change color. The construction of the *Lumidyne* includes layers of opaque and translucent material which when set in motion or illuminated let light project through certain portions of the glass face. (The result is a composition of forms which seems to move in place.)

This is done through a relatively simple mechanism. Behind the glass pane is a stationary plane of negative shapes, or the *stator*; in back of this is a series of rotating disks with strips of color and polaroid material adhering to them; this is the *rotor*. Behind these lie the motor, lights, and reflecting surfaces. In principle, the motions of Malina's *Lumidynes* are obtained by duplicating the various "Technamation" ideas used in motion displays to represent fluids, gases, combustion, etc. At first the stationary shapes of some of his works may be disappointing until the viewer realizes that Malina is primarily interested in the interpenetration of rhythms through specific time cycles. This is sometimes akin to watching the internal organs of the body at work. There is a kind of slow, deliberate steadiness to these configurations, and often the cycles employed are mechanically linked to each other. In the past few years, Malina's compositions have become more and more exotic as they take their clues from both real and imaginary visions of outer space.

In England since the late 1950's John Healy has worked on what he calls "luminous pictures." These are encased in boxlike constructions ranging from two to ten feet in width. As with most artists using a hidden mechanical system, Healy is quite reticent about divulging technical explanations of his work. These have taken some years to perfect and it is obvious from their variety that they function on several principles. Considering Healy's technical background and facilities—also the flexibility and complexity of the images themselves—the "luminous pictures" probably employ some of the more sophisticated engineering used today. Healy, working at considerable expense with a paid crew of technicians, feels that eventual mass production of his light constructions is the only reasonable answer to continued experimentation. In general, Healy's luminous pictures appear to be composites of symmetrical images which expand, mutate, overlap, and completely transform themselves from one structure to another.

Most Light artists who have worked for industry, including Healy, who claims no training as an artist, envision their Light Art as a sort of visual sedative for urban masses beset by a multitude of nerve-racking experiences. Schöffer sees his light walls installed in each house and sold like television. Healy wants his luminous pictures in airport terminals, hospital waiting rooms, and psychiatric wards. Perhaps there is a tinge of irony to the fact that in order to pacify the human nervous system—so fragmented and rubbed raw by mechanical and electronic devices—the artist must rely on more electronics.

Increasingly since 1960, the Groupe de Recherche d'Art Visuel has shifted from paintings and light-reflecting reliefs to the use of emitted light. As a group and individually they have experimented with light in so many contexts that only the most unusual can be described. From the inception of the group Julio Le Parc has manipulated light sources cast on hanging squares of plastic and reflective metal—his "continual mobiles." Le Parc has also made many variations of his "continuel-lumière": reliefs with polished, projecting, parabolic surfaces which defract light in many directions from a hidden source below.

Another member, François Morellet, has since 1963 worked with both grids of incandescent lamps (FIG. 110) and crossed lengths of neon tubing; these are automatically or spectator controlled. Horacio Garcia-Rossi's experiments have been mainly with luminous boxes inside of which fields of forms are mechanically made to flutter. Through a translucent screen these forms take on an "immaterial realism" and "instability" which is the artist's goal.

Possibly the most interesting group project of the G.R.A.V. is their series of *Labyrinths*. These began in 1963 at the Paris Bienial. A small one was created for the "Kassel Documenta" exhibition in 1964; a more involved one for The Contemporaries Gallery, New York, 1965. And the most controlled one to date took place at the "Kunst-Licht-Kunst" exhibition at Eindhoven, Holland, in 1966. Generally the labyrinths have taken the form of narrow ambient spaces where darkness and viewer traffic control the path of the spectator. In many cases individual works by the G.R.A.V. members are placed in unexpected and always changing contexts: against a blank barrier, a large plexiglas construction with shifting shadows, a wall of vibrating nylon cords, a black winding passage with exploding grids of white neon light, a cul-de-sac with an illuminated construction reflected on three sides, a table of spinning optical disks, a visual barrier of polished metal squares, then variable heights and textures for the head and feet, etc. The group has stated that it is not their intention to create a super spectacle by these effects, but to provoke spectators into acts of participation. If one can sensually disorganize a viewer by darkness, then surprise him with flashing light or unexpected situations, public reactions tend to be much more genuine. Play and aesthetic discovery, so hope the group, thus become the natural mode of public involvement, instead of artificial gallery manners.

The younger generation of Italian artists under the influence of Fontana, particularly those of the now disbanded Group N in Padua, have been particularly sensitive to light as a kinetic medium. Under the sponsorship of the Olivetti Company the works of Group T in Milan and Group N have traveled all over Europe and America. With this initial experience of a much-moved kinetic show, the problems of displaying Light Art became at once apparent. Shipped from Europe to the United States, the plugs, cords, motors, and transformers for the "Programmed Art" kinetic light constructions had to be altered to fit American power sources. After a month or so in each gallery half the light constructions were out of order and needed repair. This is not particularly a reflection on the young artists of the two groups. But it becomes obvious with Kinetic Art that unless an artist has the technical competence and means to work with electricity the job of construction could probably be better done by any specialty display company. For the most part, the light constructions of Group N do not rely on involved electronics or complex programming, but on the structuring of visual situations which can be activated by reasonably simple light controls. Some of these are blinking colored lights behind metal grids and frosted plastic, indirect light slowly moving over reflective metal mazes, "piped" light coloring the edges of plastic sheets, the spectrum cast on a white field by slowly turning prisms and the many uses of polarizing plastic. Considering the relative simplicity of many of these light reliefs, one has the feeling that the inventors did not become bogged down in elaborate technical setups and, indeed, many of these works are more successful as art than the early "color music" efforts. It must be added that the works in light of Group T have grown in sophistication with the "Kunst-Licht-Kunst" show in 1966.

In Copenhagen a surprising amount of light sculpture has arisen in the past ten years. Both William Soya and Knud Hvidberg have worked extensively in electronics: Soya has devised some radio circuit reliefs that light up or make sounds according to the manipulations of the viewer, while Hvidberg has worked with sound-light walls and free-standing sound-light sculptures. Ib Geertsen has made spinning fluorescent mobiles; Per Lütken has con-

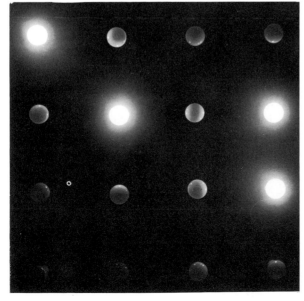

110. François Morellet, *Successive Illuminations*, 1963.

structed lens reliefs; and Børge Jørgensen has constructed lamplike sculptures somewhat reminiscent of the stained-glass constructions of Josef Albers in the Bauhaus. Examples of Danish Light Art show a remarkable range of individualism with no stylistic concessions to the New Tendency. These Danish avant-garde artists have a fair idea of what is happening in the art centers of Europe, but for the most part they do not take the opportunities occasionally to compare ideas as other Western European artists do. To a certain extent this is true of English artists also, and it may be the psychic distance created by geographical water barriers which is responsible. Some Scandinavian artists sense this lack of contact quite strongly and feel that perhaps internationally they have been by-passed. Quite recently, in bringing Danish artists before a larger public, the H. Folsgaard Electro A/S of Copenhagen (electrical wholesalers, importers, agents, and manufacturers of lighting fixtures) has commissioned some of the above-named artists to design Light sculptures—not lamps—to be put into limited production. A number of these were exhibited at the Georg Jensen showroom, New York City, in the spring of 1966.

Recent Use of Light in American Art

Certainly most of the early Light Art in the United States stems from European-born artists: Wilfred, Moholy-Nagy, and Kepes. One must also include Archipenko, with his series of edge-lighted plexiglas carvings of the late 1940's. Except in the theatre and outdoor commercial advertising, electric illumination has played a negligible role in American art until the present decade.

In 1954 the author began to use incandescent light as back lighting for various wood and cardboard reliefs. The author's first experiments with neon light were begun in 1955, partly as a result of Gyorgy Kepes's example. These were followed by a number of neon and plexiglas constructions. Subsequent works, beginning in 1959, have included various experiments in *photo-kinetics*, or light-motion phenomena. Early attempts used the principle of apparent motion on large-scale "light walls." The work shown (FIG. 111) is a recent environmental effort consisting of aluminum channels and electroluminescent Tape-Lite. One advantage of this material is its excellent response to electronic programming, with none of the lag, flicker, or color change found in other light sources.

Not surprisingly, a few American painters have successfully come to grips with standard forms of electrical illumination, attempting to define light so that it is no longer derivative of either painting or sculpture. Since 1961 a

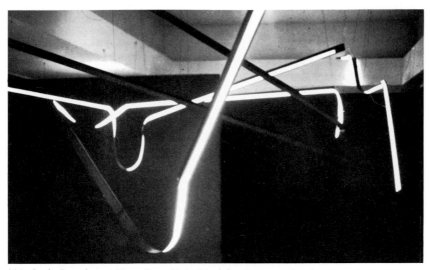

111. Jack Burnham, *Two Four-Unit Modular Tapes*, (aluminum and electroluminescent tape), 1968.

New York artist, Dan Flavin, has used fluorescent fixtures and incandescent bulbs for painting reliefs, and in the past several years for environmental compositions (FIG. 112). Flavin's thinking has steadily matured until he is probably the most accomplished American working in this medium. These works have a directness and purity which are partly due to the fact that their creator does not hide their mundane origins. He relies on context and juxtaposition. Where before this meant the painted background of his reliefs, increasingly it includes all spaces and surfaces near or distant from the lights. Unlike many exhibitions by Light artists, Flavin's constructions work together, and if they impinge upon one another they are meant to do so. Flavin takes very much a phenomenalist position in regard to seeing one of his environments; there is no ideal viewpoint, but many, some distant, from which to see each work and several at the same time. Corners, ceilings, floors and the ends of walls come alive in the context of a Flavin composition. This back lighting and reflection is very much a part of the piece. The artist's room at the "Kunst-Licht-Kunst" exhibition, Eindhoven, Holland (1966), entitled *Greens Crossing Greens* is probably the most successful environment using light yet devised.

What has separated American Light Art from most European experiments is its uninhibited adoption of commercial and advertising technique. Particularly in the use of neon and fluorescent lighting, American experiments have displayed a purity of means that is probably a more accurate statement of *what light is*, at our stage of technology, than all the lyrical Neo-

112. Dan Flavin, Installation photo of 1964 exhibition at the Green Gallery, New York.

Constructivist attitudes left over from the 1920's. This degree of aesthetic success, ironically, is due to the use of formulas devastatingly effective in advertising media. These artists (and not a few are Europeans living in New York) are not so much inventors as discoverers and reconstructors in miniature of the urban landscape.

The work of the Greek-American Chryssa has moved from a concern for letterist reliefs and type-font assemblages to use of neon and neon letter troughs for reliefs and free-standing sculpture. To date some of the most successful works in neon have been her *Ampersand* series (FIG. 113). In the past, artists have been inhibited in the use of light because of the electrical devices which must be used. Transformers, glass tubing, high-voltage wire, all seemed to detract from the light sources themselves. But, rather than hiding the glass housings and rubber insulation in a metal box, Chryssa incorporates these into the visible superstructure of the *Ampersand* constructions. These become a coolly literal part of the total design. Some of Chryssa's newest constructions use high-voltage rheostats which allow the viewer to control the current through the neon tubing. At some levels a pulsating thin light results.

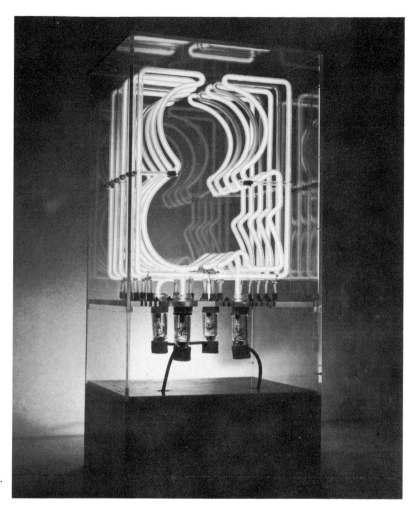

113. Chryssa, *Ampersand IV*, 1965.

Martial Raysse, living both in France and in New York, produces some of the cruelest and most satirical neon art (FIG. 114). These are blatant take-offs on sign techniques, billboards, and the other evidences of giantism in commercial America. Raysse's neon is not pure visual irritant. While impaling the eye, some of his best pieces have coloristically a raw but painterly quality. One viewer compared this to what sunlight does to objects along the Riviera. The artist in his use of automatic sign programming devices reveals the most wit and attention to cultural overtones of any artist working in light.

In 1964 the St. Louis painter Howard Jones began to construct reliefs of miniature bulbs mounted on masonite panels. Soon these became connected panels with human silhouettes in Dada-Pop assemblages. In the past two years, though, Jones's work has found a purity of means in which the only images employed are lights and reflective surfaces. *Skylight Two* (FIG. 115)

114. Martial Raysse, *Proposition to Escape: Heart Garden*, 1966.

115. Howard W. Jones, *Skylight Two*, 1966.

presents a concentrically spun aluminum surface with 161 three-watt pilot lamps. The work contains six circuits which function independently through variously timed thermal relays. Altogether, *Skylight Two* has a random program with eighty possible states.

Ted Kraynik is a Milwaukee artist who for the past four years has experimented with light-sound constructions. *Video Luminar No. 3* (FIG. 116) is the model for a light wall to be installed at a television station. The wall is a thirty-foot length of translucent plastic. Behind this, and positioned at various depths, is a grid of three-color light units. These are brightened and dimmed by a sensing device composed of a battery of photo-cells. These last pick up changing light intensities as they are relayed on a television screen by the station's program.

Two European-born artists who live in New York and use neon with total authority are Stephen Antonakos and Ben Berns. Both artists tend toward object-oriented constructions possessing strong symmetry and formalism. Antonakos uses much neon; Berns uses less and to greater effect. Thomas Tadlock of New York has been working since 1963 on programmed constructions faced with ribbed glass. These pulsate and change with kaleidoscopic frequency. Programmed edge lighting is used with unusual

116. Ted Kraynik, *Video Luminar No. 3*, 1967.

beauty in the *Cloverleaf* series of Preston McClanahan. Another artist of great technical skill in the use of edge-lighted plastics is Boyd Mefferd of Whitewater, Wisconsin.

It is apparent that flexibility in Light Art—but not quality—depends on new technology. The trend in technology is toward compactness, control, and operational elegance, if not added cost. Thus light—along with linear open sculpture, transparent materials, and attempts to set sculpture free of the ground plane—must be viewed as a further step in the "ephemeralization" of the art object. Equally true, light as it exists in today's art is a relatively inflexible and fragile medium. It is still wedded to glass tubing and cumbersome electrical equipment; it has neither the compactness nor durability that made painting an ideal art for display and collection. As will be shown more fully in the last chapter, the Light sculptor is dealing with a *system* of variable life expectancy. Though he may desire to do without electrical appendages and place his work on a pedestal as he would other works of art, light and its modern mother, electricity, want to be treated in ways that often clash with the aesthetic intentions of the creative mind.

In the fall of 1966 in a noncommercial exhibition, the neon sculptor Billy Apple came to grief with the electrical codes of the City of New York. Apple is a lyrical user of neon (FIG. 117) with a very personal sense of color. For reasons of effect, he rejects the highly protective plastic cases of Chryssa

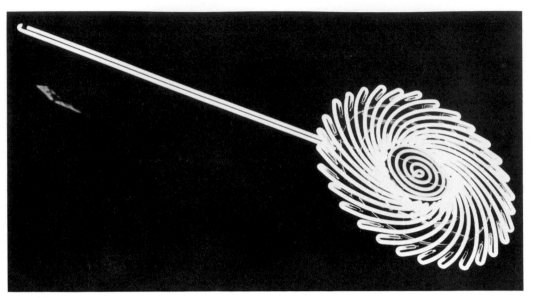

117. Billy Apple, *Solar 15*, 1966.

and some of the standard neon safety devices used by commercial electricians. The stands and supports of some of Apple's works are simply steel rods holding up impressive amounts of glass tubing. However, the city inspector for such installations claimed that Apple had not insulated all of his connections, grounded his circuits, or had his wiring done by a licensed electrician. A fragment of Apple's letter of petition has significance (Canby, October 8, 1966): "I wish respectfully sir, to point out that I am not making electric toasters, lamps or signs. I am an artist dealing in my own medium."

Apple readily admits that he should not be held exempt from the electrical codes of New York City. Yet a problem presents itself which is liable to grow rather than diminish as more artists become involved with the precarious technology of their environment.

The Future of Light as an Art Form

One of the persistent platitudes of Light Art is that it is in its infancy and must be given time to reach maturity. For over forty years Light Art has remained the child of future technology. However, it is clear that soon we must look back upon the glowing patterns of neon with the same nostalgia that we reserve for Impressionist painting today. Light Art must solve its practical problems not only to progress but to survive as an art form. Such devices as color-corrected fluorescent tubing, high-intensity mercury-vapor lamps and electroluminescent tape are only the first steps toward a much-needed flexibility.

308

Billy Apple has within the past year written on the possibilities of the laser image in art (February, 1967, pp. 46–47). Much research has been accomplished since 1947 when Denis Gabor in London invented the first hologram, or glass-plate positive for viewing pictures in three-dimensional space. Dr. Ali Javan at MIT made the hologram practical through the development of the gas laser light beam projector; this produces a coherent light source and can be set up anywhere. When projected through a hologram the light images show depth and seem real enough to touch. The problem of making a commercially feasible three-dimensional motion-picture film with laser light is yet to be solved, though in the areas of color and the aligning of laser beams there has been progress since the first two films were made at Stanford University, California, in 1965.

Apple has suggested the eventuality of laser images with an exterior and interior. A viewer could literally step through an image to better inspect its internal contents. Such a revolution in the reproduction of three-dimensional images—still and moving—has another implication. Allon Schoener (Schoener, March–April, 1966, p. 43), assistant director of the Jewish Museum in New York, predicts that the laser image could become the basis for museum collections. Museums still tend toward acquiring objects; the perfected laser image, though, may lead institutions to reduce their physical holdings in return for larger collections of micro-records which can be reproduced in normal three-dimensional form.

Thus far, the only artist to successfully use optical lasers is the New York environmentalist Robert Whitman. In October, 1967, he defined a series of spaces in a Manhattan gallery with the aid of a ruby-red laser projector and two mercury-vapor lamps. Each apparatus was housed in a formica box in the center of each room. Their beams of light were reflected horizontally through turning glass cylinders. These controlled the timing and pattern of the emitted line of light as it projected onto the walls of the room. An entering spectator received and carried the imprint of the laser light on his body. The ruby-red lines seemed to have a life of their own as they darted from corner to corner, then back to their source. Though none of these laser light projectors sold, or were expected to sell, Whitman's gallery financed the project because of its experimental and aesthetic significance. Also, it was made possible by another circumstance: as a key member of Experiments in Art and Technology, Inc., Whitman received the expert assistance of two Bell Telephone engineers.

An area which may prove fruitful to artists of the future is surveillance systems and their display techniques. These are designed in both two and three dimensions to keep military commands graphically aware of events in any specific situation. The number of laboratories, both private and governmental, devising these systems is staggering—as is the cost in most instances. Compendiums of these devices have been issued semi-officially from time to time. The range of techniques used and the visual effects gained are truly phenomenal from the artist's point of view; but as yet most of these computer-display devices are far beyond the technical and financial range of the artist.

It might be well to describe briefly one nonmilitary graphic communication system. This is the plasma display panel used in conjunction with PLATO, a computer-based teaching system. The plasma display panel derives its name from the excitation of gas which is pumped into a raster of cells between two micro-thin plates of glass. Two sets of orthogonally placed transparent conductors will illuminate any point on the panel when the current at any set of coordinates exceeds a certain threshold. In other words, a screen of almost any needed size and mesh will produce a televisionlike picture. The further advantages of this system are that it has an innate memory and images remain until erased; also the viewer may selectively erase all or any part of the plasma display panel. Eventually, when perfected, such a system may replace the cathode ray tubes now in use for this purpose.

The mysteries of controlling plasma phenomena could provide the ultimate field of exploration for the Light artist. Plasma, itself, is the fourth state of matter: being neither solid, liquid, or gas, but the state that certain gases reach when they are "ionized" or given a negative electrical charge. Fluorescent lighting, neon, and arc welding are forms of low-temperature plasma. While attempts to control high-temperature plasma have not yet succeeded, important industrial uses have been found for low-temperature plasma through interaction with electromagnetic fields.

Plasma may be responsible for one of the most baffling of all phenomena: this being the question of unidentified flying objects. Recently the author talked with an astronomer-mathematician who has written several books on the scientific implications of the U.F.O. data gathered and correlated. According to this scientist, official agencies which deal with the U.F.O. phenomena pay insufficient attention to witnesses who see objects making fantastic changes of color and shape in the sky. Such witnesses challenge the limits of physical credibility, and are therefore ruled out. However, the idea of a body of coherent plasma, charged with energy, highly mobile and plastic, and even possessing some form of intelligence, is not out of the question. Such a theory has been accepted as reasonable by a few reputable scientists; yet, according to this U.F.O. expert, such acceptance is not very significant since the properties of plasma, particularly at very high temperatures, are so little understood. He did go on to speculate that already there is talk among computer designers of fifth- or sixth-generation computers which build and rearrange their own circuits of plasma.

Vincent H. Gaddis, in his book *Mysterious Fires and Lights*, recounts dozens of cases of globular lights and luminous flying objects in which witnesses consider the antics of objects to be like those of "atmospheric animals." Gaddis contends that these space organisms may grow and flourish according to rules completely different from our own. Sustained possibly by energy taken from space beyond our atmosphere, they would be composed of plasma and appear as gaseous jellyfish glowing luminously in the night, changing color and shape according to speed and energy expended. Infrequently one of these creatures may become trapped or move purposely into our atmosphere.

Such a theory certainly lacks—as yet—scientific substantiality, though the entire development of plasma technology, even in its present primitive state, points in a curious way toward the unrecognized ambitions of many Light artists: which is to grasp the barely understood. As Jung specified, the U.F.O. ranks as a prime phenomena, real or imagined, in the collective unconscious of contemporary man. For the artist, the core of the phenomena resides in the word "Unidentified." What is sensed as some terrible or beautiful truth—through remaining unknown and fantastic—is the artist's objective. Hence once "Flying Objects" are identifed, their value for the artist will be reduced to the task of illustration.

Perhaps a more primary concern is the cultural trend toward intangibility. Light, as Otto Piene has pointed out, is the incarnation of visible energy. Also the writer remembers back a few years when during a lecture Marshall McLuhan pointed to a glowing light bulb and remarked that it radiated pure information—at least to those who understood its signal. Increasingly pure energy and information seem to be the essences of art; all else is being dropped methodically by the wayside.

CHAPTER EIGHT

Robot and Cyborg Art

To indicate the role of the message in man, let us compare human activity with activity of a very different sort; namely, the activity of the little figures which dance on top of a music box. These figures dance in accordance with a pattern, but it is a pattern which is set in advance, and in which the past activity of the figures has practically nothing to do with the pattern of their future activity. There is a message, indeed [one way] but it goes from the machinery of the music box to the figures, and stops there. The figures themselves have not a trace of any communication with the outer world, except this one-way stage of communication with the music box. They are blind, deaf, and dumb, and cannot vary their activity in the least from the conventionalized pattern.

—Norbert Wiener (1950, p. 9)

The Cybernetic Changeover

The plight of Wiener's music-box automata has not been an isolated situation; in principle, it has in common all free-standing sculpture beginning with the paleolithic age. An inherent defect, psychical and physical, in sculpture and automata—and even today's Kinetic Art—is that they do not *respond* to man in any intelligent fashion. They are dead souls made alive through "art" and prearranged mechanized motion.

Reaching back into prehistory, the artist-magician was faced with the challenge of fabricating images which would not only, to use the art historian Arnold Hauser's words (1951, p. 10), "...indicate, imitate, simulate, but literally replace..." the animal which was painted or carved to resemble it. As we observed in an earlier section on sculpture and automata, little changed in sculpture in this respect until the second half of the twentieth century. Thus, behind much art extending through the Western tradition exists a yearning to break down the psychic and physical barriers between art and living reality—not only to make an art form that is believably real, but to go beyond and to furnish images capable of intelligent intercourse with their creators.

Wiener's illustration makes the point that, unlike insensate automata, all living creatures communicate with their environments and other beings within it—if only on the most elementary levels of food gathering, survival by combat, and sexual reproduction. Wiener also suggests that the reciprocated message is the prime means by which intelligent beings communicate with one another. In this respect, a blow on the head, a caress, a look, or a lecture on philosophy can serve, within the proper context, as communication between two beings. In a like sense, the painterly handling of a Rubens nude, the texture of a Henry Moore bronze, the noisy dissonance of a Tinguely exhibition, or the flashing red bulb on a Robert Rauschenberg combine painting may serve as part of the "message" for the receptive observer. However, these are all one-way messages, and as we have observed in the case of New Tendency aesthetics the attempt is to try to make communication between the work of art and the observer a sustained two-way experience.

In the past such an interaction was impossible—or at best a very one-sided affair. It was, to place it within a cybernetic context, a relationship between a complex, self-stabilizing, goal-seeking system (man) and an inert object (a stone statue perhaps)—or man and a work of art designed as a mechanical system seeking stability through pseudo-random motion (a Calder mobile)—or man and an aesthetic system with a determinate but very complex program (motion pictures, symphonic music, Kinetic Art, etc.). Still, the result in every case was not communication but one-way stimulation for the human party involved.

Even Julio Le Parc's novel critique of art-viewer relationships never touches the consideration that art, to engage in a series of interactions with a human observer, must itself possess some degree of intelligence. Le Parc, though, does point out that (September, 1962, no page number): "To cause the active participation of an art work is perhaps more important than passing contemplation and can develop the natural creative instincts within the public." (Translated from the French by Davida Fineman.)

This does not mean that an art work is invested with the power to act, think, or communicate in any meaningful sense. Le Parc only implies, speaking realistically of the present, that a form of interaction does take place—just as a bow interacts harmoniously with the movements of a skilled violinist, but not with the kind of interaction of two men talking. It is this last example which typifies the most exotic, if distant, goal of *Cyborg Art* (i.e., the cybernetic organism as an art form) and which is very gradually becoming the next, and perhaps ultimate stage of sculpture. An early myth prevailed in modern art that somehow "open" sculpture was more spatial than "closed" or monolithic sculpture; a newer myth sees mechanical kinetic sculpture "act" as a spectator participates with it. Yet this sculpture no more "acts" than does a ball of yarn when it is batted and chased by a kitten. To say that sculpture does "act" sets the scene psychologically for the eventuality that it will.

Earlier in a discussion of the biological origins of modern sculpture, the dichotomy between geometric and organic art was brought out, and the point was made that very likely vitalistic sculpture was an attempt to prepare the way for an art more closely approaching the organic ideal, one fusing the geometric propensities of machines with the qualities of living matter. We observed elements of this fusion in vitalist sculpture through the biotic-geometric sculpture of Gaudier-Brzeska, Moore, Brancusi, and Arp.

In Chapter Three *sculptural formalism* was interpreted as a preparation or pre-stage for the literal assembly of machine components and systems in art. With its dependence on geometric and quantitative relationships, modern formalism appeared not to be a return to geometric decoration, but incipient mechanization applied to art. It follows that the reappearance of Kinetic Art can be viewed as a precocious attempt to take a few sizable steps toward the goal of organic integration, albeit by the same process of classical mechanics used by the makers of eighteenth-century automata. The machine, then, becomes the legitimate heir to the sculptural tradition of form creation. The implications of this are bound up in Spengler's comment on the origins and destiny of Faustian technics (1918, p. 411): "They listened for the laws of the cosmic pulse in order to overpower it. And so they created the *idea of the machine* as a small cosmos obeying the will of man alone."

The historian proceeds to link Western culture with an unstoppable craving to wrest the secrets of natural order from God—with the unconscious aim of controlling human destiny, if not in fact becoming God itself. The machine, of course is the key to this transference of power. If it constructs our destiny, it can do no less than become the medium through which our art is realized. As a reflection of the Faustian drama in the twentieth century, it is increasingly impossible for sculpture to hang midway in its present position between the imperfection of the machine and the artistically superior tradition of figure sculpture. Though contemporary Kinetic Art is an offspring of classical mechanism, the step beyond is totally a child of the present century.

On several occasions it has been stated that cybernetics never had a father, but rather a number of uncles, each occupied with a different aspect of the same discipline. Originally, the science or pre-science of cybernetics received its start from two efforts: that of processing information reduced to mathematical form for the purpose of solving problems, and the devising of control mechanisms, machines capable of self-adaptation to variable work situations. Both tasks were being accomplished simultaneously while an interdisciplinary science developed from them. This was made known with the publication in 1948 of Norbert Wiener's *Cybernetics: Or Control and Communication in the Animal and the Machine*. This volume was the scientific inception of a dream which had haunted the makers of automata all through history—that of creating mechanical analogues to the nervous systems of animals, and through this gradually effecting some level of intelligence in the machine.

This goal had its first successes during the Second World War when Wiener and other scientists at the Massachusetts Institute of Technology and Harvard University envisioned the need for cross-disciplinary scientific projects, particularly a project capable of fusing aspects of pure mathematics, electrical engineering, and neurophysiology into a science explaining the organization of complex systems—systems which think and show some degree of environmental adaptability. It seemed probable that while the machines of the first industrial revolution had removed many burdens of physical labor, much more could be transferred to the machine by allowing it to handle constant and variable inputs of information. Wiener, among others, gradually realized that some of the functional models for these new machines already existed through the autonomy of organisms. Wiener's work prior to World War II included the design of a computer for solving differential equations; much of his time during the war was concerned with a related task of inventing an automatic aiming device for anti-aircraft guns. Both involved systems which handled more than one variable at a time—before then, a feat impossible for machines. As Wiener observed (1948, p. 6): "[Twice] I had become engaged in the study of a mechanico-electrical system which was designed to usurp a specifically human function"—that of rapid, complex calculation.

In 1943 Wiener, along with two colleagues, the physiologist Arturo Rosenblueth and the mathematician Julian Bigelow, published a paper entitled "Behavior, Purpose and Teleology." This paper—dealing with a malfunction common to both the nervous system and electromechanical control systems—suggests how purpose could be built into machines. Bigelow and Wiener had earlier come to the conclusion that *negative feedback* (in both animals and machines, this is a fractional return of the energy output of a system in the form of information guiding the system's future activities) was the key concept to control. Wiener, from his work on computers used as control devices, was familiar with the phenomenon of "hunting," in which a control device would send a machine wildly out of order when a feedback impulse "overcompensated" or became locked in a cycle of self-induced oscillations. The two scientists as a result asked Dr. Rosenblueth if a similar pathological condition existed in the human nervous system. Rosenblueth identified such a nervous disorder as "purpose tremor," an involuntary oscillation of the limbs and an inability to function when the mind ordered a motor action such as walking or picking up an object; the result would be a loss of kinesthetic coordination between the nervous system and the muscles.

This was the first of many attempts to establish a connection between the regulated functions of the body and the protocol of electromechanical control. Even before the end of the war other scientists were engaged in parallel researches. Two early investigators of the mathematics of nerve nets were the neurophysiologist Warren McCulloch, and the mathematical logician Walter Pitts; both men laid foundations for the use of logic systems in devising computer languages. Claude Shannon adopted the theory of classes in Boolean algebra to study switching systems in electrical engineering; later, Shannon's and Warren Weaver's creation of communication theory allowed the designer to handle computer fidelity and capacity of transmission mathematically.

In the spring of 1947 Wiener left for Europe to attend a mathematical conference. Various papers presented at this meeting plus discussion with friends in England convinced the mathematician that an extremely useful pattern of machine-animal analogues was emerging. During his stay in Paris Wiener was asked to formulate his ideas on cybernetics in book form for the nonprofessional public. At the urging of social scientists Wiener soon realized that the discipline which was evolving had much more than technical ramifications; developed to its logical capacities, it meant a social, economic, and industrial revolution perhaps more important than the first industrial revolution.

Previously cybernetics had been referred to as a proto-science. It never existed as a science in its own right, but became the theoretical springboard for a number of related activities. Even before the publication of Wiener's book in 1948 cybernetics began to branch off into a number of areas concerned with the regulatory mechanisms of complex systems: presently this includes computer technology, information storage, systems analysis and development, learning theory and the design of teaching machines on feedback principles, pattern recognition, artificial intelligence, and bionics (integration of artificial with living systems). Before going further, it should be made clear that cybernetics is preeminently the science of *organization*. Where in the

1920's or 1930's organicism was a rather lovely if unrealized dream of architects and sculptors, it began to hold real meaning for the cybernetics-affected designer. The underlying role of cybernetics has been the implementation of organic relations through a profound understanding of the patterns of organization in evolving and living systems.

Biology in the early 1940's experienced a new philosophical turn—succeeding both vitalism and mechanism—with the concept that *organization*, complex and multileveled, was responsible for the composition of organisms. As the vitalists have insisted, life surely is greater than the sum of its parts, but only because of an incredible interconnectedness *between* the parts of an organism, which when assembled *seem* to add up to more than the sum of the parts: this was the view of the organic biologist. In *The Wisdom of the Body* (1932) Dr. Walter Cannon of Harvard explained the balanced plumbing of the human body, those ever present involuntary mechanisms maintaining the health of the whole organism. He called this system of automatic valves and thermostats *homeostasis*. Defined, this is the ability of the body to keep its quantities of liquids, solids, and gases in a state of equilibrium. Cannon found that the body is constantly forcing such a balance by various strategies, which include feedback mechanisms.

A few years earlier, the biologist Ludwig von Bertalanffy had grouped the organizational properties of organic entities, both social and biological, into the category of *systems*. Bertalanffy was one of the first scientists to classify biological systems according to abstract principles rather than appearances. Systems, in essence, were the multileveled organizational structures of living forms, and very diverse systems could have very strong similarities according to the way they were *organized*. This was where the independent study of biological and social systems coincided with the aims of cybernetics; cybernetics *is* the analysis of linked and interacting systems— precisely Bertalanffy's view of biological activity. While this sounds less dramatic than Wiener's emphasis on relationships between machines and animals, the implication is just as important: both natural and man-created systems, if equipped with similar organizational properties, elicit related behavioral responses.

It has been the very nature of the machine that it could always be connected with other machines to perform a complex array of work motions. As a machine has had to cope with more difficult operations (activities not strictly repetitional but altered according to input of the machines), the machine has become less simply a set of "power drives" and more a series of "servo systems"; or systems with closed-loop communication regulated as are Cannon's homeostasis functions for biological systems—but certainly with less complexity. As true automation became a reality and information-processing machines grew more flexible, the designer gradually came to think of the hardware involved not as a group of coupled machines but as an assembly of systems.

The concept *system* itself is a pure abstraction, an assembly of isolable properties studied in terms of their transformations, either alone (closed) or in relation to other systems (open). Isolating a system in context is an important part of the cyberneticist's task, since the number of systems inherent in any given situation is theoretically infinite. Ashby has specified that a system can be isolated only if an observer defines the variables involved so that they form a "singleness." This "singleness" is the matching together of transformable values so that they form a closed set of relationships. In this manner highly complicated assemblies can be segregated into finite, observable subgroups. The system is a logical means for handling complex interacting mechanisms in motion. Stated differently, the system becomes the unit by which all levels of fluid organization are analyzed up through and including living organisms.

While the system is a fundamental concept of cybernetics, its value as an artistic idea lies in its power to cope with kinetic situations, and particularly the connecting structures of evolving events. A property of all systems is *stability*, and its counterpart, *instability*. The most stable system, of course, is the inert object having no moving parts and changing only through physical deterioration. The basis of all art in history has been durability, the relatively permanent quality of the fixed art object. In this century, particularly, we have witnessed the technological ascendance of perishable, mass-produced materials—and a growing lack of inhibition on the part of artists to use them. Metallic plastic-based paints, plastics, corrosive metals, electric motors, assembled mechanisms, electric light sources, plaster, rubber, paper are only some of the self-destroying materials and systems used by artists in an attempt to make their creations "dynamic" or relevant.

Systems tend to assume a given purpose depending upon their context, although, quite conceivably, a designer would not see in a system one end result but a number of possibilities. Also, all systems exist in an environment and may or may not interact with their environment. Such an interaction the cyberneticist interprets as communication. For instance, the fixed work motions of a classical machine acting upon materials fed into it is a form of low-level communication. As long as the machine continues to produce the desired results in changing the materials, we are happy with its internal and external messages. As for Kinetic Art, the machine communicates to us merely as we observe its motions. As we are able to steer or program the actions of a machine, and the machine reacts in sundry ways to our guidance, we attain higher levels of communication. In this respect a most important attribute of systems or machines is *input* and *output*. For either the material, energy, or information going in must be emitted in some converted form. A human body takes in food (i.e., energy) and sensory impressions (i.e., information) and in return produces work, heat, information, and waste products. In a sense, all of these are types of messages; thus input and output are the communication within a system.

Another property of systems and a fundamental aspect of organization is that of *coupling*. Machines and their components naturally fit together into larger and more effective systems. The very methodology of cybernetics demands that a researcher be able to "uncouple" a system, that is, break it down into analyzable subsystems so that it can be studied with more precision. Coupled systems may or may not receive the output of other systems, just as some or all of their output may go on to other systems.

Coupled systems evidence a *feedback* relationship when a reciprocal transmission of energy or information between systems affects the process of transmission itself. *Negative feedback* (as was mentioned with Cannon's homeostasis) is the process whereby any number of coupled systems are designed to maintain a relatively constant input-output relationship. This might be the chemical equilibrium of the body or the constant adjustments of a servo-controlled processing mechanism. *Positive feedback* (Wiener's "hunting" symptom in neural pathology being one example) is caused when a mechanical or chemical chain reaction exceeds the boundaries of restraint and each "cause and effect" relationship triggers off a still larger "cause and effect" cycle. An explosion of dynamite is a graphic example of this type of irreversible chain reaction.

Many artists, particularly Kinetic Artists, have expressed a desire for a flexible interrelationship between their work and the viewer. This interrelationship implies the use of negative feedback, and present Kinetic experiments reveal few, if any, significant successes in this direction. While a nonpassive relationship with the work of art is one goal of the Kinetic Artist, another more basic problem exists for all moving systems.

Plainly the problem of stability and instability within a Kinetic Art system confronts the Neo-Dada fatalism of a machine artist such as Jean Tinguely. Sculpture as a category of objects with a provisionally unending life seems to be giving way to the kinetic system with a life and death cycle of its own. The machine with a motor is a stable system which only becomes unstable when the motor fails or a part wears out. Instability lies inherent in all systems and the probability that it will appear rises at an exponential rate as the systems include more moving parts and higher levels of complexity.

In effect, the Kinetic sculptor is no longer building objects with potentially infinite life spans, but systems with a life that in many cases can be predicted. Just as parts must be repaired and constantly replaced in an automobile, the stability of a kinetic system is insured by periodic inspections. Art objects in a museum are also systems in the sense that they are subject to constant deterioration and must be periodically inspected for necessary restoration work. In effect, we are moving toward a systems view of art, and, as the old attributes of the sculpted object are dropped one by one, the sculptor will begin to think about increasing the life duration and stability of his mechanical creations.

In this too brief introduction to the cybernetic viewpoint, we have not stressed the technical elements of information theory, computers or computer programming, but instead those essential aspects of organization which will be responsible for future alterations in three-dimensional sensibilities. We have learned to speak with complete nonchalance about number systems, philosophical systems, data-processing systems, ecological systems, communication systems, political systems, control systems, weapon systems and many others. The suffix "system" was not in nearly such evidence a few years ago. Now, not only the scientist, but everyone lives intermeshed daily with a hierarchy of synthetic systems dominating the quality of life. This in effect is the new biological reality which both man and art must abide by. For the first time the word *organic* ceases to be an unobtainable ideal held out to the artist; following in the wake of cybernetic technology, systems with organic properties will lead to "sculpture"—if it can be called that—rivaling the attributes of intelligent life.

Mock Robots as Sculpture

Well into the 1950's the concept of the *robot* was more a literary convenience than a recognized fixture of utilitarian living. Before the Second World War, books written about freight-yard switching systems, electric refrigerators, and vacuum cleaners used the term "robot servants" to dramatize their place as mechanical aids to man. Plainly these were "robots" with no connection to human anatomy. And until a few years ago the anthropomorphic robot was the brain child of science-fiction writers and publicity-seeking appliance companies, rather than a machine with any practical uses. Now we are confronted daily with classes of machines for which the title *robot* seems every bit appropriate. The new mechanisms are not only capable of physical work and some degree of autonomy, they are to some extent decision-making devices. Cybernetics, the development of the control concept in machines, and rapid advances in electrical engineering have been responsible for much of this. The ability of machines to accomplish more sensitive and demanding tasks, tasks traditionally thought to be human prerogatives, has in a sense diminished the dread of robotry by making it a reality.

There is an inherent fear connected with the term *robot*. For the early mechanical age, the robot was the collective demon in human form, and to give its powers to actual subjugated machines, to realize its potential capabilities, is to undermine the image of the soulless, clanking monster. Our robots—in the sense of machines capable of a variety of seemingly autonomous actions—are becoming more real every day. For some sculptors, the human condition mirrored by the robot, the spineless doll, or the waxen image, has become an *idée fixe*. He sees this in robot or doll-like form because as yet the machine has not been made which mirrors personality to the extent of the human physiognomy.

It is well, though, to look briefly at the contemporary breed of robots. They work, they affect matter and involve man in their doings more every day. Psychically, the sculptor cannot match their influence; he can only suggest certain static parallels to their consequence upon mankind. On March 30, 1966, the *New York Times* announced in a headline: "'Walking' Truck Is Drafted by U.S. Army—Model Developed by General Electric Costs $1-Million—Versatile Robot Can Move Easily Over Rocks and Mud." It is described as four-legged, ten feet high, four feet wide with a human driver housed inside. This "truck," or pedipulator as it is called by its inventors, carries a five-hundred-pound load over all terrain; the controls for moving its "limbs" are hydraulic powering devices capable of responding to any of the normal motions of the driver's body. CAM (cybernetic anthropomorphic machine) uses no electronic controls since repairs and parts replacement would be impractical under battlefield conditions.

Industry has steadily learned the uniqueness of the human hand and how difficult it is to build an automatic hand that duplicates its actions. Ralph S. Mosher (October, 1964, pp. 88–96) considers the case of the clumsy robot who, not possessing the sensitivity to weigh the strength and rigidity of a chair, might easily pull one apart in picking it up. As a result, any mechanical manipulator must have a sense of kinesthesis equivalent to that of a human being; that is, a pressure-detecting sense for judging the force and position exerted on objects by a robot hand. Mosher gives several descriptions of metallic clawlike hands now at use in industrial work. One manipulator is programmed to perform on an assembly line—and can be reprogrammed for any number of routine tasks not involving a human operator.

In this category General Electric's Handyman includes two machine hands with ten forms of motion controlled by an operator. For complex manipulation human control by means of knobs and levers is altogether too imprecise. Since a human being uses his limbs unconsciously, the answer seemed to be to let a person go through the manipulative actions which the machine is to undertake. Since the actions of both man and mechanism are coincident, a master drive strapped to the arm of the operator receives signals of change in position that are transmitted to the machine arm. In turn, a feedback returns signals to the operator informing him of the pressures exerted by the Handyman arm on the real objects being manipulated. Handyman is a perfect example of how disparate systems can be coupled together; in this case, a man-machine relationship is established on a set of highly sensitive feedback loops which extend and amplify the work capacity of a technician.

A month after the Soviet Government landed *Luna 9* on the moon on February 3, 1966, the *Saturday Review* published an article, "The Robot on the Moon." This is an account of the Jodrell Bank interception of the first Soviet television pictures of the moon's surface. Heretofore, the Russian *Lunik* probes had relayed information back to earth, but never close-up pictures of the moon's surface. The Russian descriptions of their miniature television station are revealing. As *Luna 9* landed on the moon, it acted as a "shock absorber" for a two-foot sphere ejected from its surface and landing some feet away. Like a seed pod, the sphere then "flowered" as four petal-like outer forms opened exposing the rotatable television camera and four pistil-like projections used as broadcasting antennae. It is not stretching a point to say that *Luna*'s miniature television station fulfilled the organic analogy of botany's combined womb and spaceship, the seed pod.

In contrast, *American Surveyor I* landed on the moon on June 2, 1966, and resembled a tripodal space frame with landing pads of crushable aluminum. Radar and an on-board programmer calculated the rate of thrust needed by the retro-rockets to accomplish a soft landing. This was a marked contrast to the nonprecision of the Russian robot with its compact, tough exterior.

It is significant that both extremely complicated cybernetic systems were self-adjusting mechanisms but also delicately man-controlled from a distance of thousands of miles. The cybernetic system, unlike Handyman, does not have to be in intimate proximity to its human control source to effect fine and precise alterations in its behavior. It is only limited by its ability to communicate with other systems. In fact, the romantic ideal of landing men on Mars—in the sense that Columbus traversed the Atlantic to the New World—is probably too expensive for its scientific value and could be accomplished for a fraction of the cost by what has been described in the *New York Times* as a (March 29, 1966, p. 4) "robot-like 'automated biological laboratory' designed to be landed on Mars in several years to perform a series of 35 tasks in search of signs of life."

Early in 1966 newspapers carried a story of a "robot teacher" hired in Palo Alto, California. This "teacher" is a computerized teaching machine with four media of contact with the student: a television screen, a typewriter, a movie screen, and a set of earphones over which instructions, commands, corrections, and encouragement are given to children. Of marked advantage over other teaching machines—and in fact most human teachers—is the almost instant response to a pupil's answers; these computer responses are programmed to vary in tone and word pattern so that the child gains no sense of machinelike repetition. The IBM "1500," as this super teaching device is called, is capable of drawing on its facts so as to deduce different sets of logical conclusions. Psychologists have already observed that because of the infinite patience and responsiveness of the machine some children develop a real emotional attachment to it. Very likely "1500" shows signs of warm attention lacking in some parents.

In Disneyland, or what Ray Bradbury refers to as "the machine-tooled happyland," pageants of humanoid robots have reemerged after the eighteenth-century golden age of automata under Vaucanson and Jaquet-Droz. The late Disney's robot factory at Glendale, California, has already produced the first seemingly alive figures for Disney's conception of an "audio-animatronics" museum: General Grant at Appomattox, the Vikings at Vineland, cavemen making fire for the first time—these are a few of the auto-mated, three-dimensional tableaus that Disney had in mind.

For the 1964 New York World's Fair Disney's technicians were com-missioned to build a life-size, talking, walking Abraham Lincoln for the Illinois State exhibition. The carrier of a deeply masculine voice and a statesmanlike manner, Disney's creation would have given the original Emancipator a close race at the polls. The new Lincoln got up, glanced around, cleared his throat, moistened his lips and recited a few passages from his best-known speeches, complete with appropriate histrionics down to the last genial wink. Reported *Science Digest* in an article of December, 1963: "Shake Lincoln's hand; its texture is enough like real flesh to make you cringe. It's moist, for the vinyl plastic skin exudes fine oil over a period of time. The plastic even bruises."

This carnal anthropomorphism of plastic and electronics far surpasses earlier masterpieces of android precision such as the *Writer* (1774) of Jaquet-Droz. Tough but flexible plastics, electronic programming, feedback systems, and refined, work-amplifying hydraulic systems may possibly return the humanoid robot to a place of competition with other visual mass media.

Significantly the robot now functions to interact convincingly and intelligently with human beings—not to frighten them as do apparitions of the Franken-stein variety.

A rather bizarre—though not complete—instance of this coupling of human to robot was reported in newspapers in the spring of 1966. A young lady attending Radcliffe College advertised in the Harvard *Crimson* for a male to contract marriage for one year, this to circumvent the school rule against unmarried students living off campus. Her ad drew two hundred and fifty replies, including one from the owner of a movie-star robot named Dalek. Dalek, in need of publicity, was described as "a cone shaped, 5-foot-6 robot, dressed in silver and red, with one eye scanner, a radiation antenna, a flame-thrower, and red bulbs in his head that light up when he speaks"— a perfect match for a Radcliffe junior. A marriage of sorts was arranged; they spent their honeymoon at the Hotel Americana in New York City.

In collaboration with the Aerojet General Corporation, the University of Southern California School of Medicine has recently developed a 6-foot-2-inch, 195-pound "patient." This is a lifelike plastic dummy used to train medical students. It is controlled by a computer program to exhibit "symptoms" during a student diagnosis. Subsequently, the computer will print a critique of the student's mistakes. According to one of its developers, Dr. Stephen Abramson (quoted in June, 1967, p. 1) "The second generation of Sims [simulators] will be able to bleed and sweat and will be shaped to simulate different ages of each sex. The third generation which we hope to evolve within several years, will be better in many respects than cadavers for training medical students." Even that last act of generosity, leaving one's body to a medical school, will soon be a futile gesture.

A most realistic variation of the robot theme is present scientific experimentation in RHIC or Radio-Hypnotic Intracerebral Control. Control of a subject is effected by the implantation of electrodes in the brain. These may be stimulated by radio signals which do not directly disturb the normal electrical activities of the brain. Such signals can be used to trigger post-hypnotic suggestions at considerable time and distance after they have been made. At its most harmless and beneficial RHIC could be regarded as a very promising teaching tool; more ominously, it foreshadows the possibility of efficient thought control. Progress in RHIC has been under way for many years among the major political powers. As yet, no experimenter admits to using anything but animals for subjects.

What is significant about these examples is their very logicality and inevitability. If we devise robots to do our work for us, both physical and intellectual; if we can invent robot teachers more efficient than humans; if robots provide amusement; and finally, if we have the power to turn ourselves into functional robots, then what hinders the eventual robotization of all humanity? Such a theme has supplied the basis for countless science-fiction stories, and is by no means a dead issue.

At the beginning of this century the robot represented a symbolic threat to human values. As the robot in its multitude of forms has become a reality, our views of man-machine life have grown in sophistication. Almost as a gesture of capitulation, the artist has begun a serious rapprochement with technology. It seems as if the vision of sculptors, attached to anthropomorphic images, has begun to blur. The dividing line between man and robot has become most imprecise. Today, moreover, the robot has become a semi-personal, fallible being—a pensive, twilight figure, an unknowing accomplice to the undermining of once intransigent Western values. *For our generation much significant anthropomorphic sculpture does not imitate man, but imitates robots trying to become human.*

Most sculptors instinctively realize that they lack the technical skills to create functional robots. They continue—as sculptors have with the human model for thousands of years—to produce obsessional figures which simulate machineness. Chief among these creators of pseudo-robots (FIG. 118) is the English sculptor Eduardo Paolozzi. Employing the ancient technique of lost-wax casting in bronze, Paolozzi first began his rusticated machine men in the mid-1950's. Slabs of wax were impressed with machine parts and technical paraphernalia. The castings which resulted were welded into torn, top-heavy figures with cog wheels insides, a far cry from machine sleekness of the 1920's. These works present several iconographic inversions, the chief being a sham pathos which brutally juxtaposes classical idealism with mechanical inadequacy. This sculptor's stylistic progression underlines a point already stressed: the seeming progression away from external anthropomorphic values and toward machine complexes that, while they do not appear human, interact with people at steadily higher levels of control. The imitation robot, nevertheless, remains a piece of sculpture in the traditional sense. Possibly because we identify intelligence with human appearance, Lawrence Alloway (1963, pp. 20, 22) regards Paolozzi's machine men as justified:

Robots, as machines that perform services for men, would, if designed functionally, not be man-like. They could be expected to resemble trollies or cranes or traffic-lights or vacuum-cleaners or juke-boxes or roller-skates. However, they are persistently imagined in human form: the human contour and stance haunt robot iconography, just as persistently as they do the physiognomy of screen monsters. The human body is a structure with very highly adaptive skills, whereas robots, to be of maximum use, need to be specialized, and shaped accordingly. From Capek to Asimov and after,

118. Eduardo Paolozzi, *St. Sebastian, No. 2*, 1957.

however, a basic human schema shapes robots, with side references to suits of armour, diving-suits, tanks and space suits. This aspect of robot-lore is criticized by engineers of servo-mechanisms, but in fact, the anthropomorphizing of the machine, which robots classically demonstrate, has a basic human charm and satisfaction.

Even when Alloway was writing his text, Paolozzi began diverting the form of his sculpture from the human figure toward a machine form without the benefit of arms and legs, a combination gasoline combustion engine and computer display panel. Alloway treats these robots as a more iconic and instrumentlike anthropomorphism, and this has continued in light of recent Object-Optical sculpture by Paolozzi. These last are brittle, mirrorlike metal constructions with erratic undulating edges, exercises in optical ambiguity which have little to do with the misshapen robots of the previous decade.

A very different, mock, robot has been contrived by the American sculptor Ernest Trova. Trova's figures, highly polished bronze manikins, recall the faceless "Oscars," Hollywood's yearly, self-inflicted Academy

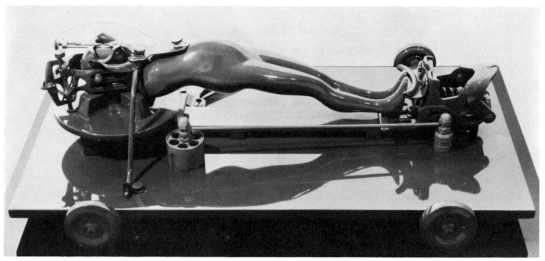

119. Ernest Trova, *Study Falling Man (Landscape on Wheels)*, 1966–1967.

Awards. The bodies of Trova's statues are not idealized physiques, rather they possess spindly legs and distended stomachs; they are biological specimens undergoing some fundamental "processing"—perhaps the paces of space-travel training—with the implacable resignation of cheerful robots (FIG. 119). Trova's best-known series, *Falling Man*, consists of drawings, reliefs, and free-standing sculptures of streamlined bodies in sequential rotation around an axis positioned just under their feet. Breathing or heart-pumping apparatus spring from the breasts of some of these bronze manikins. These men have an inhuman precision, a beyond-conscious resignation to being enmeshed in artificial systems. Somehow this anesthetizes the pain of robot existence conveyed by Paolozzi's metalized demons.

Aside from the pseudo-mechanical man, anthropomorphism in recent sculpture has usually been confined to varieties of subsculpture: the doll, the waxwork curiosity, and the painted, store-window manikin—all proto-robots of everyday life. Shells inhabited by human souls, these subsculptures live tenuously as imitations of human beings. Not a part of modern sculpture's reaction to anatomical classicism, they embrace the values of twentieth-century pop totemism; they take the last step before the automobile kewpie doll inherits the Western tradition of mimetic influences from Praxiteles, Michelangelo, and Rodin.

George Segal's plaster people at once come to mind, just as the *Nanas* of Niki de Saint-Phalle and Claes Oldenburg's *Teddy Bear* park monument strike a similar chord of titillating despair. These "sculptures" are lumpishly

327

morbid, embalmed sensibilities within shrouds of plaster, stiffened cloth, vinyl, wire, and wool yarn. Through many pounds of plaster Segal's people make love, tend store, wend their way through urban traffic, or simply sit straddle-legged in silence; the *Nanas* of Niki de Saint-Phalle cavort about the gallery like three-hundred-pound matrons at an amateur theatrical; Oldenburg's *Teddy Bear* unseats the war memorial tableaus of the urban park and substitutes in gigantic scale the cuddly, floppy imbecility of a child's bed companion.

Not long ago life-size, sophisticated dolls purchased to sit cross-legged at one's rumpus room bar could only be had at chic and expensive novelty shops. Today the art gallery is well established in this direction. Frank Gallo's sculptures are neither dolls, waxwork figures, clothing manikins, nor molded plastic advertising reliefs—they draw on elements from all of these. In a sense they are human bric-a-brac (FIG. 120): leftover party guests, moody teenagers, nymphets at the beach and semi-erotic spinsters posing before the mirror. Each is polychromed to appear uncomfortably real but finished in the unconvincing waxiness of epoxy resin plastic. Some of Gallo's figures, the free-standing reliefs, lack the back side of a sculpture, thus exposing an uncomfortable cavity of plastic technology. *Time* magazine calls these "humanoids" in the sense of beings which inhabit some of Isaac Asimov's robot science-fiction stories. Often these warm personalities prove to be mechanisms with plastic skin described as faultlessly human.

Since the mid-1950's New Yorker Larry Rivers has consistently created fetish figures from manikins. In 1957 Rivers constructed *Iron Maiden*, a sculpture of welded sheet steel from an automobile; it has all the burned, twisted, and sharpened edges of its namesake, the torture device. One writer called it a "robot blasted from all sides by ray guns." A tableau by Rivers *Parts of the Body: English Vocabulary Lesson* (1964) arranges three manikins in varying stages of disassembly, with parts of the body laboriously indicated. Perhaps inspired by *The Doll* (a Swedish film about the sexual fantasies of a department-store watchman who falls in love with a clothing dummy and commits a murder for it), *Murder at B. Altman & Co.* (1964) is a study of the undressed manikin and baroque *putti* made unbearably real through mutilations. As one writer describes this tableau (Berkson, November, 1965, p. 51):

The central figure is a display window St. Theresa with her throat cut. Her head, with its furious leer, hangs back onto something like a chopping block; the torso is cut off at the rib cage, the legs split down the middle like firewood; there is an ochre smudge under the neck. Beside her, to the rear, stands a cupid with steel plates at neck and hips. Above the victim, there is a diving board, with another cupid apparently walking off it.

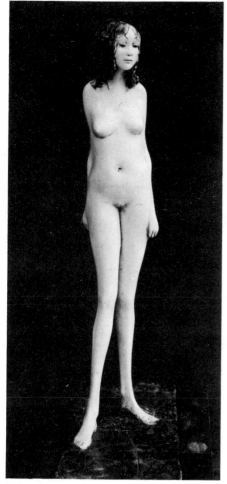

120. Frank Gallo, *Walking Nude*, 1967. 121. Jean-Robert Ipousteguy, *David and Goliath*, 1959.

The French sculptor Jean-Robert Ipousteguy has synthesized both classical and robotic values into his hybrid humanoids (FIG. 121). Ipousteguy's bronzes are orthodox in most respects, except where he adds a third leg to a figure or otherwise destroys its biological symmetry. The artist consistently uses the device of "antiquing." In the nineteenth century new sculpture was often artificially aged to resemble unearthed Classical fragments. Authentic bronzes sometimes had holes and pock marks from chemical corrosion. Ipousteguy duplicates this type of blemish, but one feels that his corpulent bodies are also hollow shells of human beings, in essence, humanoid robots without working mechanisms.

The drawn, cast, carved, painted, assembled manikins of the Venezuelan

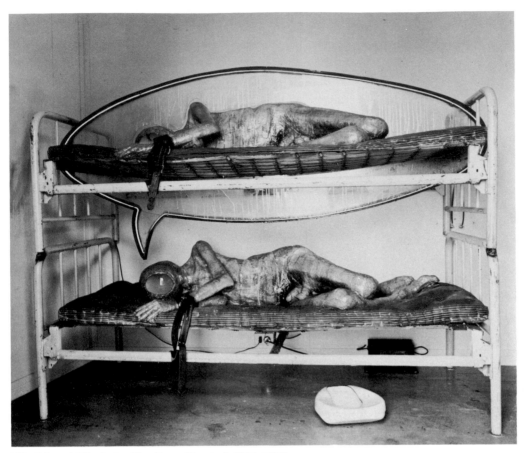

122. Edward Kienholz, *The State Hospital*, 1964–1966.

Marisol are personal portraits with many formal surprises. High among them is the talent of the sculptress for evoking three dimensions by graphic techniques and unexpected projections; formidable slabs of wood are thereby rendered "human" in the sense of *haut monde* fashion models on display— the classic example of the commercial robot!

A few years ago during the apex of Japan's industrial boom, word spread that some enterprising Yokohama businessman had marketed a rubberized replica of a Hollywood star famous for her contours. This "pleasure toy" was anatomically, if passively, complete and could be filled with warm water —for men with need of more than a hot-water bottle. Perhaps related was the environmental construction *El Batacazo* (1965) of Marta Minujin, which included a complement of stuffed rugby players, live rabbits, and a giant, soft vinyl Virna Lisi. Miss Lisi's replica hissed and groaned softly as participants in the environment clambered over mounds of yielding plastic pulchritude.

Rivaling the frightening pathos of the great Counter-Reformation Spanish woodcarvers, the Californian Edward Kienholz has produced some of the strongest and most memorable tableaus of this generation. The moral vantage of Kienholz is keenly evident in *The State Hospital* (FIG. 122). Here the artist has reincarnated memories that reflect his experiences as an attendant in an asylum. These are no longer human beings, but fetid bodies and faces represented by cloudy, translucent containers. Even more eerily pathetic is *Birthday* (1964), in which a young woman lies on a portable operating table in an abortionist's office. Everything vibrates muted whites and grays; all surfaces of the tableau are bathed in a sickly sheen of clear polyester resin plastic. The mouth of the young woman on the table emits a plastic bubble containing a floating toy—signifying perhaps the scream of lost motherhood; from her stomach seven giant plastic arrows protrude; the center arrow carries the soul of the dead fetus back to its place of origin.

It would be wrong to interpret this cruel, mock robotry of the past ten years as a return to metaphysical realism—best illustrated by the German and Spanish wooden polychrome sculpture of the seventeenth and eighteenth centuries. One has the intuition that if this "superrealism," frozen into everyday experience, could move, the sculptor would will it so. Whereas, it is kept still and silent by the knowledge of its makers: that intuition which tells the sculptor that to induce motion forsakes the protective security of sculpture. Spengler understood this when he identified sculpture with the classical virtues of spatial definition and orderliness; thus (1918, p. 139), "the statue is rooted to the ground...."

The Cybernetic Organism as an Art Form

In *The Living Brain* (1953) the English neurophysiologist Grey Walter states that the maker of lifelike images could be a magician, artist, or priest. Further, he asserts, the difficulty rests in persuading the public that the behavior-simulating models created by the experimental scientist are not related to these earlier disciplines dominated by extra-logical concerns. Walter observes something else reiterated in this book—namely, that there is an indefatigable human urge to project life into inanimate substances, to "create" life through artistic and metaphysical means. And while man remains a habitually totem-forming animal, Walter insists that the scientist's motivation for reproducing life springs from a different set of concerns. We can only wonder if they are so different, though Walter does try to make a distinction (1953, p. 115):

There is, however, a well-defined difference between the magical and the scientific imitation of life. The former copies external appearances; the latter is concerned with performance and behavior. Until the scientific era, what seemed most alive to people was what most *looked* like a living being. The vitality accorded to an object was a function primarily of its form. . . .

Moreover, any performance by a sacred image must be magical—a Virgin with an ingenious mechanical smile would get no worship. Again, an image may be only a toy. The technical genius of the Swiss watchmakers was really wasted on their delicate clockwork automata; they arouse only a passing interest because they are neither sacred nor, like life, unpredictable, their performance being limited to a planned series of motions, be it a boy actually writing a letter or a girl playing a real keyboard instrument.

Grey Walter further outlines some of the scientific and technological preparation which has made organic simulation a reality. He mentions such scientists of the nineteenth century as Clerk Maxwell and Claude Bernard for their contributions to the understanding of feedback in both animals and machines. He demonstrates how even the tiniest cell of natural origin would have been impossible to duplicate in principle without the invention of the electron vacuum tube, and later its solid-state equivalent.

Grey Walter's robot toys, which we shall investigate shortly, can be categorized as crude but early cybernetic organisms, mechanically constructed to simulate behavior patterns, the origins of which the psychologist tries to discern through empirical testing. While Walter readily admits that these laboratory toys only approximate animal behavior—being far simpler in construction and neuro-interconnectivity—they represent the first mechanical steps in duplicating the purposiveness of living organisms.

In the deepest sense sculpture has always been anthropomorphic. Whether imitating animals or the god-spirits determining the destinies of men, fashioned images have always been extensions of man's psychic and physical existence. Earlier, in Chapter Three, we have considered modern formalism as a unique stage of anthropomorphism, as a direct prelude to the re-creation of intelligent life by nonbiological means. This drive toward successively more efficacious forms of anthropomorphism seems to be a cultural characteristic of the human organism. A tentative reason for this will be outlined in the last part of this chapter.

It is doubtful if non-anthropomorphic sculpture can exist. Since the creation of the first nonobjective and Constructivist sculptures in the early part of the twentieth century, artists have consistently denied the anthropomorphic and mimetic content of their works. Each successive generation of nonobjective (or to use the most recent term: "literalist") sculptors has accused the previous generation of anthropomorphism. Even the present generation of Object sculptors do not escape this charge (Fried, Summer, 1967, p. 19). What we will examine as Cyborg or Post-Kinetic art is really the first

332

attempt to simulate the structure of life literally. *Thus, sculpture seeks its own obliteration by moving toward integration with the intelligent life forms it has always imitated.*

Less than a decade ago the term *cyborg* (i.e., cybernetic organism) was created to mean a man-machine system in which the human partner functions unaware of his connection with the machine component; the machine behaves automatically through feedback connections with the muscular or nervous system of the human component—just as the pupils of the eyes, connected to the autonomic nervous system, contract automatically when subjected to bright light. Unlike an automobile and driver, the sense of physical and perhaps psychic separation between man and machine is eliminated. A cyborg, then, is any artificial system connected through reciprocal feedback to an organism. Handyman, the indirectly controlled industrial manipulator, and the IBM "1500," the super teaching machine, are examples of at least partial cyborg relationships. Both these systems retain an element of awareness between machine and operator; as yet they do not represent an unconscious symbiotic relationship.

Clearly the cyborg relationship goes beyond the anthropomorphic anatomy of the classic robot; and it has even less to do with static robot sculpture. One science writer, Daniel Halacy, sees the cyborg in a continuum of possibilities ranging from "hardware" for outer-space adaptability systems and prosthetic devices for the injured to the development of artificial-tissue supply centers for the replacement of organs and genetic banks for the future design of entire human beings. This last example, which includes artificial man or some organism of higher intelligence, is still so remote in the light of present technology that most researchers have settled for cyborg models that duplicate only some of the simpler neurological and physiological capabilities of living systems.

The term *cyborg* refers to both electromechanical systems with lifelike behavior and man-machine systems which parallel (through feedback) some of the properties of single biological organisms. In the first instance, there are a few autonomous cybernetic sculptures that interact with some stimuli but remain, nevertheless, unattached to the human viewer. The second group is characterized by a class of constructions—cybernetic games—in which human participation and reaction are necessary in order to make the work of art become "alive." Both art forms move beyond the linear work cycle of machine-driven Kinetic Art and establish complete behavior patterns that are not clearly predictable, but neither are they pseudo-random events.

In a previous chapter, on formalism, we observed the importance of the scientific model as a stimulus for modern sculpture. A trend repeats itself throughout the more theoretical sciences: as a physical model becomes progressively more untrustworthy and unrelated to the system it describes, it is discarded, and the science develops into a game of pure symbols and "invisible" concepts. Unlike mathematics and physics but similar to molecular biology, cybernetics, if only with limited success, early instigated a vogue in the use of working mechanical models. Without creating life in the sense that a biologist would find acceptable, cyberneticians have invented a number of electromechanical and electrochemical analogues based on organic stability and sensory feedback. As both Wiener and Walter have observed, these analogues transcend the programmed imitations of motion and sound in classical automata and instead simulate animal behavior in a probabilistic manner. This is accomplished through acquired "learning," which allows the machine to choose from a number of possible responses to a given situation.

In 1948 at the Burden Neurological Institute in Bristol, England, Grey Walter created two automata and awarded them the zoological classification *Machina speculatrix*. Elmer (Electro-Mechanical Robot) and Elsie (Electro-Light-Sensitive-Internal-External) were designed as plastic-clad "tortoises" with three wheels (the front one for steering), a revolving photoelectric cell for light detection and a knack for producing nearly lifelike emotions. The idea of emotions we see as a unique prerogative of animals, and Walter is quick to point out that emotions are built-in responses to given situations, responses which show real logic in terms of the circuitry of a given nervous system. Hence, if they are provided with circuitry in principle equivalent to that of animals, there is no reason why machines should not have emotions. One may reject this argument on the principle that the levels of complexity vastly differ, but even with their simplicity the automata of Walter *do* show behavior patterns remarkably similar to the emotions of higher forms of organisms.

Machina speculatrix has been based on a few simple but ingenious ideas differing from those of classical robots. The aim of Grey Walter was to build like nature, with the principle of *parsimony* uppermost in mind; not a *visual* imitation of nature, but a *functional* imitation with the fewest possible components becomes the cyberneticist's goal. The tortoises are reduced to the equivalent of two nerve cells reacting to stimuli: two vacuum tubes, two relays, two condensers, and two electric motors are their main components. Included also are a photoelectric cell (for "sight" or responses to light sources) and an electrical contact (the sense of touch) which is activated when the shell comes in contact with a solid object.

As in the case of animals, the tortoises display both *negative and positive tropisms*. The tortoises are designed to be attracted to light—but reject light sources if they are over a certain threshold of brightness. Also, the tortoises are powered by rechargeable batteries and are sensitive to the voltage of their power sources; below 5.5 volts (the hunger threshold), the tortoises seek their food supply in the form of a strongly lighted "hutch" containing electrical contacts to which the tortoises move close so as to recharge their batteries. When the charge has reached seven volts (satiation) the tortoises retire in stillness to "digest" their meal of electrical current. Between these two voltages the tortoises wander in search of a comfortable light-source. Walter claims that his tortoises display elements of *discernment* and *memory*—that is, they construct a priority of goals and at least show momentary effects of having surmounted an obstacle. Another biological quality of the tortoises is *internal stability*. They are free to wander just so long as their electrical supply is sufficient; in other words, the mechanism is designed to insure its own survival in terms of power. They remain contented as long as electricity is forthcoming, or the current not turned off—but otherwise they "die." As with all organisms, this denotes a feedback loop between the animal and its environment. Walter suggests that this constant striving for "food" and an optimum comfort level is characteristic of the ecological adjustments and psychological drive found in every species.

Granted with a certain overemphasis of anthropomorphic adjectives, both Walter and other popularizers of cybernetic ideas have described the tortoises in a variety of crisis and decision situations. It must be enough to say that, for the relatively simple mechanism that it is, the *Machina speculatrix* demonstrates, or appears to demonstrate, many of the same emotions common to humans and animals: hunger, frustration, self-survival, satiation, ingenuity, self-recognition, etc. Also their inventor has observed that the tortoises possess distinctly different personalities—although they were put together nearly identically. Elsie remains rather sprightly while Elmer hides under the furniture much of the time, not moving unless for food. Elsie's sensitivity and mobility make her more impatient when faced with obstacles than her docile brother. The experiment also suggests that minute alterations in bodily chemistry do have much to do with personality differences in humans and animals.

Pierre de Latil in his book *Thinking by Machine: A Study of Cybernetics* brings up the situation raised by the eighteenth-century philosopher of the enlightenment, Condillac. The philosopher presents the question of a marble statue, given no senses or thinking capacity but suddenly endowed with the ability to perceive and store knowledge of one event after another; Condillac concludes that, with enough information imbibed by the senses, the statue would in time become a fully rational being, altogether human in its reactions.

In other words, thought is a mechanism and not a miraculous property bestowed on humans before birth; intelligence, then, is an electrochemical system made usable only by use. While at the time this was an early and crude hypothesis of mechanistic thinking, it raised the possibility in Latil's mind that the tortoises of Grey Walter fulfilled the basic conditions of Condillac's statue. If (1953, p. 231) "attention, memory, comparison, judgment, imagination and knowledge" comprise the outward signs of thought, then in a very rudimentary sense the tortoises "think."

At this point it is well to remember that Latil's book appeared during the infancy of cybernetic experimentation (1953); many artificial intelligence researchers have since raised serious doubts about the real thinking ability of the tortoises. However, other researchers in this field—in the face of strong criticism of the entire program of artificial intelligence—have insisted that intelligence is purely a matter of degree and that thought in a meaningful sense exists on a continuum of levels, even in some rather uncomplicated machines. So that the problem becomes one of defining what attributes one will accept as being consistent with true mental processes. Probably the real merit of Walter's goal-seeking, self-stabilizing automata is that they possess just enough of the colorfulness of humanoid robots to dramatize the possibilities of further cybernetic research.

Autonomous mobility and the knack of these little robots to implement their decisions into concrete action seems to be the popular criterion for judging their lifelikeness. In the years following the tortoises, other "animals" were concocted by cyberneticians, all utilizing feedback mechanisms. Edmund Berkeley, a pioneer computer engineer, devised "Squee," a sort of squirrel whose forte was gathering golf balls whose food value was converted into electric current. At the Bell Telephone Labs in New Jersey, Claude Shannon developed a pack of maze-running "mice"; through a constant "hunting" process, and after repeated attempts, these mechanisms statistically "learned" their way out of the maze. It is both easy and compelling to see these didactic models as animals; there is just enough freedom in their reactions for an observer to detect the formation of behavior patterns and arbitrariness of real animals, though in principle there are other classes of mechanical artifacts which more closely approximate the cognitive processes.

One such artifact is the "homeostat" of the English physiologist Ross Ashby. Briefly, the homeostat is a device with a set of four pointers which move, each through its own trough of distilled water which acts as a conductor. The pointers are influenced by an input current at the same time that their position in the trough influences the sources of the input. Each pointer, then, is guided by internal feedback—at the same time that its position is influenced by the position of the other three pointers. Each pointer's goal is to arrive in the center of its trough, producing a zero voltage. The pointers in turn must adjust to the irregularities of the other pointers, so that stability is only achieved for one pointer when it is gained by all.

Ashby conceived the homeostat as a model for some of the stabilizing operations in the human brain, and accordingly named a book describing the device *Design for a Brain* (1954). *Brain* may be an oversimplification of the homeostat's true accomplishment, but it does suggest how this complex organ handles large quantities of incoming random information—in juxtaposition with existent internally retrieved thought (i.e., information already stored and put to use). Hence, the idea of a system seeking equilibrium by mutual stabilization of all of its subsystems Ashby calls "ultrastability."

A variation of the homeostat by the same researcher uses only two pointers: one pointer is the "animal" and the other is its "environment." Again, the center of the trough for each pointer represents stability and the preferred position for the animal and its environment. If the environmental pointer is moved off center, the animal pointer moves with it. If the feedback loop between the two pointers is reversed, then it takes several trials before the animal pointer reverses its direction to compensate for the "change in environment." Ashby interprets this as the kind of adaptive behavior normally found among organisms on all levels.

An even more complex learning association between two machines is Eucrates, a control system designed by the English cyberneticist Gordon Pask. This is a dual mechanism which simulates "trainee" and "teaching machine"; Pask sees it also as an industrial control device. Not only does the trainee learn, but the teaching machine learns about the learning ability of the trainee. In simple mechanistic form this consists of a series of motor elements generating impulses when its input exceeds a certain threshold. The threshold is automatically raised (that is, the input of information to the trainee) and the impulses from the motor elements are cut off. Thereupon the threshold is reduced to a low enough point so that the motor elements, or some of them, resume their impulses. This fluctuating give-and-take process applies equally well, and certainly has been put to use, in the case of a human trainee connected to a teaching machine.

All the systems described above are rather early examples, prototypes so to speak, for the much more sophisticated adaptive and self-organizing systems being assembled today. For our purposes, though, they indicate how machines can manifest intelligence by using information to adjust to variable conditions. As for learning ability in general, Pask points out that within an electromechanical system this basically means that (1961, p. 67) "the elemen-

337

tary subsystems within one of the imitative units have become more closely coupled." In a sense, learning, then, is a matter of reinforcing a circuit within a system. Adaptive behavior means the establishment of several alternative circuits for use depending upon the input and state of the system at a given moment. Described in barest mechanical terms these make incredibly complex processes; when applied to humans, they sound much simpler than they are.

In the development of artificial intelligence, perception, and control programs, the idea that an experimental system had to have the outward appearance of a mobile organism disappeared rapidly. In most instances the ability to adjust to a situation, store information, or solve a problem was checked by a dial reading or print-out sheet. The spectacle of an artifact adjusting to its environment through a series of *visible* maneuvers has a certain anthropomorphic fascination, but it remains hardly an efficient way of handling immense amounts of information. It is well to mention this because the gap between the romantic prototype robot—surely a leftover from the first age of machines—and the modern theory of automata is an ever-widening one.

At present there are dozens of projects set up to simulate pattern recognition, adaptive behavior, decision making, concept formulation, and other phases of cognitive action. Examining the breadth and implications of these programs presents too extensive a task for this book, but it is worth mentioning that this entire area of investigation is presently split into two camps. One philosophy is concerned with the characteristics of *self-organizing systems*, and is biologically oriented. It sees the problems that we have been discussing from a physiological standpoint; it is sure that the organic traits of self-organization (the most dramatic example being the human brain) really hold the key to the science of control. As a result—and the artifacts of Walter and Pask are two examples—they attempt to duplicate or use the principles of sensory and control systems of biological origin with the strictest economy of hardware. A model of a neural net using the least components and the most advantageous connections for solving a specific problem might be a possible goal of the self-organizing school.

The solving of complex problems—seeking new ways as to how they are solved—has become the purpose of the group of researchers devoted to *artificial intelligence*. From work already produced it is clear that they favor the most advantageous use of the computer—which means, in effect, the creation of increasingly sophisticated computer programs. Marvin Minsky, a leader of the artificial intelligence research at MIT, acknowledges the limitations of the present generation of computers, and the want of ingenious programs for utilizing the computer's already vast potentials. But Minsky expects to see rapid improvement. He feels that a priority of interests exists and that it is more important to develop superintelligent computers and programs, in a relatively short time, than to expend great energy in duplicating the processes of the brain. Moreover, the ultimate limitations of the computer as an intelligence-amplifying machine rest in the capabilities of the programmer alone. Improved heuristics (short-circuit problem-solving techniques which circumvent random and exhaustive searching by the computer) seem to be the most promising strategy for the artificial intelligence school.

Before going on to the artistic uses of cybernetics, we should touch upon the problem of machine consciousness. With all the efforts in the related fields of self-organization and artificial intelligence, a recurring, if unessential, criterion of success is the duplication of human consciousness. Many researchers view the question of consciousness and self-awareness in machines as vitalist-inspired and thus a bogus issue, or at least one irrelevant to their particular area of concern. Others see vestiges of consciousness in even some of the most rudimentary control devices; moreover, the attainment of a recognized consciousness will be the logical outcome of the growing sophistication of computers and their programs. It need hardly be stated that there are large numbers of educated people—scientists included—who see no possibility, ever, for a machine to approach a true state of consciousness. This, of course, is a view tinged with the vitalist hope that a few life-centered properties remain out of the reach of the scientist to recreate—and therefore to understand analytically.

The mathematician and philosopher James Culberson proposes in his book *The Minds of Robots* a physicalistic theory of consciousness and sense perception which makes the construction of both capabilities theoretically, if not practically, possible. To begin, one must assume that consciousness is a physical state—which Culberson does. Consciousness he conceives as a space-time network of impulses constructed point by point out of physical events. He then suggests, as previous researchers have, that classical robots and automatic vending machines do not experience consciousness, but are simply programmed to react specifically to a given input. In a like sense, a machine can be made to experience stimuli but have no means of showing a response. Still and all, a computer can show signs of tremendous intelligence—which some already do—yet have no "inner life" or capability for self-reflection. The author proceeds to build a theory of conscious automata based purely on circuitry and artificial neuron nets of his own invention. It remains to be proven by the construction of physical models whether Culberson's or anyone else's theory of consciousness has any basis in practice.

This is mentioned only because as the cybernetic mode of grasping inter-relationships invades the realm of art the question of a conscious work of art is bound to arise. If we look upon the art object as the visual residue of an active mind, then the possibility of a work of art actually attaining some form of consciousness is an incredible but not unlikely eventuality.

Interestingly, some of the initial cybernetic sculptures have been among the most expensive and complex sculptures to date. In 1954, as an advisor for the Phillips Corporation of Europe, Nicolas Schöffer helped to design the first spatiodynamic, cybernetic, sound-equipped art structure for the Parc Saint-Cloud on the outskirts of Paris. This same tower appeared at the international Building and Public Works Exhibition, Paris, 1955. The Phillips engineer Jacques Bureau accomplished the electrical engineering for the tower. Without the financial aid and technical assistance of this giant electronics firm, there is little chance that Schöffer could have completed this first monument to cybernetics.

The tower was primarily a sound-producing mechanism, its program of musical sounds being the result of environmental stimuli. Pierre Henry, an originator of *Musique Concret* (taped compositions of electronic and environmental sounds), produced twelve tapes, parts of which were selected in turn by a control system. An audio pickup, a photocell and a temperature-controlled rheostat took data from the environment and operated relays which chose portions of the tapes. A homeostatic device balanced the final sound pattern so that discordant combinations were avoided. To make the musical program of the Saint-Cloud tower more unpredictable, a randomizer or "indifferent cell" was introduced to utilize the effects of chance. One can understand the sensory control mechanism and the homeostat for eliminating harsh noises as a means of achieving cybernetic art, but the "indifferent cell" seems to contradict the "triple determinism" which Bureau boasts are the three integrated control devices for determining the program. The tower, itself, seems to have been designed more as a spectacle than as a sober effort to erect a giant sound organizer with an output controlled by feedback relationships. While an element of cybernetics is put to work here, the final outcome in terms of music cannot be said to be purposeful. Perhaps Bureau is aware of this and in a paragraph on the two he says (quoted in Joray, 1963, p. 45):

The object sought is above all of the experimental order. As for electronic animals, the synthesis of the faculties must be effected very gradually, and the behavior of the "models" man makes of himself must be observed. This exploration by the "models" of physiology, psychology and sociology marks the opening of a new path in research.

123. Nicolas Schöffer, *CYSP I*, 1956.

It is to Schöffer's credit historically that he was one of the first artists to realize (and implement) the potential of control devices in art. One of Schöffer's linear, aluminum-frame sculptures with rotating blades (what he terms a spatiodynamic construction) was set on a base housing a complete control mechanism. This work, *CYSP I* (FIG. 123) (cybernetic-spatiodynamic construction), was introduced to the public in 1956 on the stage of the Sarah Bernhardt Theatre. Again, Phillips sponsored this project as a sculpture capable of reacting to changes in sound and noise. *CYSP I* is mobile, with four motor-powered sets of wheels under it. Different colors make its blades turn rapidly or lie stationary, move the sculpture about the floor, turn sharp angles or stay still. Darkness and silence animate the sculpture, while brightness and noise make it still. Ambiguous stimuli, as in the case of Grey Walter's tortoises, produce the unpredictability of an organism.

In the year of its birth Maurice Béjart used *CYSP I* in a ballet with electronic music. Schöffer envisioned his cybernetic sculpture as the prototype for many other works that would, in time, take their place in society. Schöffer has gone so far as to envision these sculptures autonomously wandering through the city streets. Built-in radar would prevent them from bumping into people and buildings.

This is a small fragment of Schöffer's synoptic vision. In 1965 at the Jewish Museum in New York City a number of sketches and photographed models of a future "Cybernetic City" were displayed in a Schöffer-Tinguely exhibition. These site plans are shown as vast, well-manicured plazas and boulevards dotted with gigantic cybernated light towers and stilt-mounted architecture. These resemble hybrids from electronic components and models for hydrocarbon compounds. Space in this case becomes more a matter of interconnected stratifications high above ground level than the miserly propinquity of traditional real-estate apportionment.

Nevertheless, the seeming inhumanity of Schöffer's "Cybernetic City" and the overprettiness of the lumiodynamic constructions turn many sensitive contemporaries away from this brittle world of instant and visible dynamism. Yet few artists have so tenaciously held on to a private vision of the future. As for the Constructivist sculptors, their blueprint for society invariably stopped short of an integrated space-time aesthetic in which kinetic and electronic technology were integral factors. For all his awkwardness, Schöffer has dared to meet the engineer more than halfway.

In conversation in 1964 the author sensed the extensions of his vision. Neither Schöffer's sculptures nor his attempts at architecture are the results of a personal *style consciousness* deliberately imposed; they result from working with the technological limitations of the present age. He would not have his spatiodynamic structures looking so like the Neo-Plastic sculpture of the 1920's, but that is simply the nature of available materials. The material *Gestalt* of Schöffer's work is unprivate and impersonal, for he early realized that technology, without much help from the artist, is becoming increasingly responsible for its own visual impact. The artist must learn to make his contributions to this cybernated society or be excluded from it by his own irrelevance. Schöffer anticipates a world politically ordered, not in the usual sense of hereditary, elected, or dictatorial leadership, but by computer-produced decisions and committees picked for their intellectual and scientific grasp of complex geopolitical problems.

Already, he pointed out, this was the case among some of the largest companies of Europe. He used his own sponsor, the Phillips Corporation, as an example. Not only are areas of productivity automated, but market research, inventory control, product development, and even the highest echelons of policy are dictated by the cybernetic analogy of a healthy organism. According to him, a great deal of the corporation's profits are ploughed back into research and experimental projects such as his own light tower at Liège, and the days of willful, plutocratic capitalism are no longer the way to run an efficient business. With unbounded enthusiasm Schöffer remarked that he was in the midst of writing a book about this new, self-organizing society, a society free of the old political *isms* and controlled by organic rationalism.

Speaking of his sculpture, Schöffer saw *CYSP I* and *CYSP II* as extremely interesting, though terribly expensive, experiments, ones which the Phillips Corporation was reluctant to underwrite in any subsequent form. He had considered a confrontation between Cybernetic sculptures reacting to each other's stimuli—an amusing experiment already tried in the laboratory.

As an ardent exponent of the ephemerality of systems, Schöffer admitted that he often felt greatly hindered by having to use materials and manipulate them in the traditional sense of craft. His ideal, it seems, is *objectlessness*, the manipulation of pure energy fields which materialize themselves. He saw as a perfect working space for his projects a limitless illuminated void. Moreover, he made the observation that his concern is with "aesthetic objects" not with the "work of art." Analogous to the provisional aspect of the scientific experiment, he believed—as does the Paris G.R.A.V.—that the progressive artist is in no position to make works of art; his sole concern must be with a sequence of experimental efforts—the results of which may be sold to the public. He explained emphatically that if he dealt with any substance it was *time* not physical *matter*. Time is the objective of his creations and their looks are secondary. With that, he speculated on the working life of his machine constructions, knowing that these would eventually break down and cease to "live." The artist, Schöffer said, is provided with a mental cushion, in the form of ego, for this eventuality, and he, luckily, cannot conceive of the destruction of his creations.

Cybernetics and particularly the related field of information theory were forthwith studied in Western Europe for their aesthetic implications. In this, the United States has been lagging by five to ten years. The European sensitivity was due in part to a crisis recognized in modern music by French and German avant-garde composers as early as the later 1940's. Both the structure and continued development of tonality were seen at an end. The outcome of this continuing crisis was the invention of serial composition. The serial technique reorganized and expanded the parameters of musical notation in such a way that a new acoustical structure would hopefully become evident to the trained listener. Electronic synthesis was one technique for achieving a structure which encompassed much more than the range of tonal organization. That music, purely as a continuum of sounds, could be produced, cut up, distorted, rearranged, and analyzed mechanically excited some composers with its unlimited possibilities, while dismaying others. It still did not answer the basic questions: where does machine creativity (or guidance) leave off and human invention begin; and can information theory, group theory, number theory, or any kind of mathematical analysis aid in the production of vital, meaningful music?

Questions on the propriety of employing machines and mathematics sundered the European musical avant-garde in a way unknown to the plastic arts, possibly because the plastic arts have had no elaborate, semi-mathematical system (tonal relationships) which could be attacked directly through higher analysis. It has been observed that the discrete and linear nature of literature and music leave them open to analysis through communication theory, while the nonlinear, continuous consistency of visual phenomenon prevents this from happening in the plastic arts. Recently, though, real progress has been made in the quantification of visual phenomena.

In 1958 the scientist Abraham Moles published his *Théorie de l'information et perception esthétique*. Moles points to some conclusions about the limits of modern communication as defined by information theory; he lays down aesthetic conditions for channeling media; yet he does not attempt to construct a style, a means, a message, or a new art form. Less elaborate, but more ambitious in intention is Max Bense's *Programmierung des Schönen*, published in 1960. For the experts, at least, Bense's work categorizes the various philosophical, mathematical, and literary approaches to text analysis, with particular emphasis on the statistical methods of information theory. Bense also does not attempt a new art form. Gotthard Günther's *Bewusstsein und Maschinen: Eine Metaphysik der Kybernetik* (1957) demonstrates that the aesthetic, moral, and metaphysical ramifications of a society confronted with conscious machines have already made their impact in Europe.

The situation in electronic music and the appearance of these books must be mentioned because they help to explain the European awareness of the value of control and communication theory for the arts. Rarely though—except for individuals such as Schöffer—have artists shown very much interest in the *theories* of cybernetics; rather their concern, as it has slowly developed in the last ten years, has been with the *artifacts*, the working models of cybernetic experimentation. However, a few painters have toyed with that unique product of the computer, the punch-out tape. One could cite in this instance the collage paintings, consisting of binary code dots, of Jean Chabaud. Perhaps there is a tinge of irony to the fact that for the last few years the

IBM Corporation has sponsored "computer art" contests among its employees in which the results most often resemble well-known styles in abstract painting. While the idea of cybernetics may initially excite the artist, there are few valid ways the artist can as yet handle the tools or concepts of the science. Aside from Schöffer, it has only been in the past three or four years that artists have begun to use electronic sensory devices and man-machine feedback concepts to control Kinetic Art.

A few sculptors, hot on the heels of the laboratory cybernetician, are not easily put off by the formidable technical obstacles which lie before them. The dream of artificial "life"—or a reasonable facsimile—has been too long embedded in the minds of sculptors to be dismissed merely for lack of money or training. More than likely, the first steps into Cybernetic sculpture are simplified imitations of the "animals" created by Walter and Pask; most of these do not possess circuits for forming behavioral traits, but are controlled by servo-mechanisms which give the appearance of purposeful activity.

Some indication has been given already of the range of projects undertaken by Jean Tinguely—many of them with strong anthropomorphic undercurrents. Tinguely's assorted painting, self-destroying and monster machines weigh heavily toward a post-Cartesian view of the machine. At the same time he has never really invaded that area of ideas connected with the life-duplicating or intelligence-amplifying properties of cybernetics. His machines remain dumb, chaotic, beautifully ugly, and deserve their untimely "deaths." If the "meta-matic" works do appear intelligent at times, this results from the sentimental pity of the viewer, not from acts of mercy on Tinguely's part.

A young artist still in the process of living up to his promise is the Filipino David Medalla. Now living in London, Medalla was an editor of *Signals* magazine, a science-oriented, vanguard publication devoted primarily to Kinetic Art. He refers to himself as a "hylozoist," a philosopher of the pre-Socratic Ionian school devoted to the belief that all matter and life are inseparable. After a brilliant if incendiary academic career, Medalla turned to painting before the age of twenty and soon decided that the artistic vision embraced much which the plastic arts do not allow in their present form. As a consequence, most of Medalla's works and ideas remain relatively unsalable because of their very untidiness as nonobjects; rather, they are related to those intangible cycles of life which concern the biologist, ecologist, oceanographer, and the physicist. His sculptures are the natural happenings of the universe poetically isolated.

Of particular beauty are Medalla's bubble mobiles, the *Cloud Canyons* (1964); this group of plywood boxes pour forth an unending cascade of froth and bubbles, covering everything in their path. Other projects (which have their antecedents in the science museum) are sand mobiles producing wave configurations and thermal walls with their mutable mist and frost patterns.

Medalla's scope of planned projects is astonishing; one cannot help but feel that time, money, and newer undertakings will probably prevent the completion of most of these. The more intriguing are: (1) "Collapsible Sculptures" or forms which incorporate living things such as snails, shrimps, and ants. Snails would move over touch-sensitive plates setting off different tones; or shrimps could be induced to perform as an underwater ballet; or ants could be made part of a magnified pattern of shapes in a glass farm; (2) "Hydro-phonic Rooms" would be rooms with walls and ceilings of special porous rock on which thousands of edible mushrooms could be grown; (3) "Transparent Sculptures that Sweat and Perspire"; these would be heat- and light-sensitive masses whose shape and pulsation could be controlled by the environment; (4) "Radio-controlled Flying Sculptures" would consist of objects which could fly from a "hive" to all parts of a city, returning with various non-valuable objects.

Clearly some of these projects seem feasible while others would take inordinate amounts of engineering, not to mention money. It is significant, however, that Medalla tries to incorporate botanical, insect, and other lower animal colonies into amplified systems representing new levels of environmental art. Again, the shaped, stabilized system prevails over the fixed object. It would seem that the purpose of this is to inform man that he is one of many social organs on the face of the Earth—all striving to remain alive and well on the resources of the Earth's surface. In this respect, Medalla has recognized that global planning, consciousness of the Earth and its inhabitants as a single organic environment, is not only the coming artistic sensibility, but the key to biological survival.

An artist whose ideas come close to Medalla's, yet developed independently, is the German Hans Haacke. Now living in New York, Haacke began his wind and water constructions in 1963, when their *raison d'être* as sculpture was generally lost on the public.

Art lovers, accustomed to appreciating sculpture for its shape, were mystified by an array of transparent, plastic boxes filled with colored and clear liquids. These liquids perform various activities—dripping, trickling, oozing, splashing, and condensing—in the spirit of turbulent weather conditions or the internal secretion of organisms, and hardly resembling the vitalistic or Constructivist sculpture of the past. In the sense that he bases some of his boxes on the condensation cycle, and the wind sculptures use balloons balanced on columns of air, one could term Haacke's sculpture self-organizing and self-stabilizing; however, he deliberately omits use of a mechanical feedback loop. As with Calder's mobiles, much of the self-stabilizing tendency of these fluid constructions is due to gravity and the mechanics of seeking a position of rest. Up till now machines have played a small part in Haacke's work because the artist harbors a certain distrust of power setups with many moving parts and the likelihood of repeated breakdown. "The simpler the better" is his working axiom; if "life" is to be duplicated by the artist in a new sense, it must be done without the imposing hardware of the cyberneticist. Furthermore, he believes that all the cycles of natural organization—including many which could not be brought into the museum—are now fair game for artistic improvisation. The provisions of this goal can be set down in a few terse statements given to the author by the artist:

…make something which experiences, reacts to its environment, changes, is non-stable…

…make something indeterminate, that always looks different, the shape of which cannot be predicted precisely…

…make something that reacts to light and temperature changes, that is subject to air currents and depends, in its functioning, on the forces of gravity…

…make something that lives in time and allows the "spectator" to experience time…

Already we have reviewed Haacke's balloon constructions (see Chapter One, FIG. 23) and his condensation boxes (Chapter Six, FIG. 104). *Ice Stick* (FIG. 124) is composed of a vertical refrigeration tube which collects, condenses, and freezes moisture from the air. Layers of ice and frost form and sometimes the outer layers melt as external temperature conditions dictate. Using a biological analogy, these layers build up and melt off, producing an ever-changing form—relating, if however indirectly, to the morphogenic development of organisms.

As a "living system" Haacke's *Grass Cube* (FIG. 125) is even more to the point. Here, several square feet of grass are set into the context of a plexiglas box filled with a thin layer of soil. This has to be watered quite regularly, owing to the low humidity of most indoor environments. The artist rejects the implication that these works are didactic yet he sees them embedded in larger systems outside themselves. They are what they are, and Haacke refuses to see them as images in the older sense of iconic art. The system, with a little help from the supporting environment, does not need the viewer's sympathetic projection to remain independent. In conversation, Haacke sees the logical extension of his work carried out in the vast outdoor expanses—and when reminded that such effects as he plans already exist in the form of rain, sleet, fog, etc., he replied: "I did think of signing the rain, the ocean, fog, etc., like

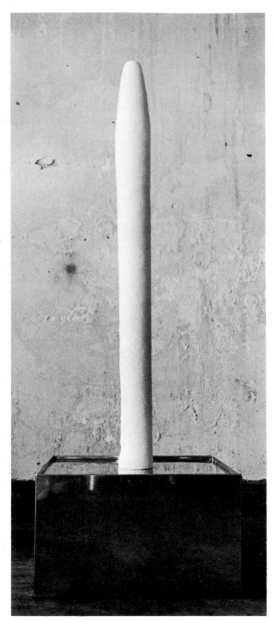

124. Hans Haacke, *Ice Stick*, 1966.

125. Hans Haacke, *Grass Cube*, 1967.

Duchamp signing a bottle rack or Yves Klein declaring November 27, 1960, as a world-wide 'Théâtre du Vide.' But then I hesitate and wonder if isolated presentation in one limited given area, an estrangement from the normal, is indispensable. It is a very difficult question."

It would be misleading to classify Haacke as an artist primarily devoted to applying cybernetic principles to mechanical artifacts; rather his interests are in those cyclical processes which manifest evidences of natural feedback and equilibrium. One might call this *an environmental systems philosophy*, one that has little to do with practical or theoretical science. Instead it reveals a keenly sensual attitude toward the most ephemeral phenomena.

Clearly in opposition to Haacke's position is the Chilean presently living in New York City, Enrique Castro-Cid. The early drawings of Castro-Cid demonstrate a strong awareness of cybernetics as it is beginning to affect our notions of human physiology. These working drawings progressively substitute machine components for their anatomical equivalents. It is evident from the author's conversation with the artist that Castro-Cid has read deeply in the literature of mechanical evolution and the mind-body problem of classical philosophy. He senses that the possibilities of man-machine interaction are richer than ever before. Thus, his newer constructions depend more on this awareness and less on prevailing tastes in sculpture.

Since Castro-Cid's first robot exhibition in 1965, the artist has moved toward a more sophisticated awareness of man-machine interactions, in which anthropomorphism plays a diminishing role. The early robots (FIG. 126) are interesting for their painful sterility: no longer the clanking metallic beasts of the 1920's, these are more akin to humans divested of their corporeal

126. Enrique Castro-Cid, Installation photo of 1965 exhibition at Richard Feigen Gallery, New York.

form, mere brains placed in bell jars with appropriate electrodes inserted, sending commands to mechanical limbs. This contemporary electronic man is encased antiseptically in a clear plastic enclosure; a vestigial anatomy drawn on the background hints faintly at a once biological life. Wiring and small components take the place of tendons and blood. *Anthropomorphic I* (1964), while suggesting the lapidary effect of a micro "mechanical brain," is technologically an unartful assemblage of synchron timing motors, a set of mechanical relays and a handful of light bulbs—all used to terrifying effect. But, reduced to its functional definition, this machine has none of the goal-seeking, self-stabilizing ability of even such relatively simple animals as Grey Walter's *Machina speculatrix;* it is, indeed, a mock robot.

Lately Castro-Cid's energies have gravitated toward a mode of sculpture which could be termed "cybernetic games." These are imposing, boxlike systems sometimes powered by air jets which keep plastic spheres moving within a defined cycle of positions. The trajectories of these bouncing balls are limited but appear to be random. There is a kind of ultra-precision to these constructions which implies more ultimate purpose than that invested in most New Tendency kinetic works; they simulate the precise, instantaneous technology of a computer system in which playfulness is merely an aspect of some greater hidden function. The poetic imprecision of these games—such as *On and Off*—exists in the fact that they imitate a level of technology which they have little hope of duplicating. On the white surface of the compressed air sculptures are painted green areas which suggest different functions. The chasses of the games are extended into nonpurposeful shapes which contain no interior equipment.

What electromechanical components (photocells, electromagnets, air compressors and film projectors) Castro-Cid does use are invariably endowed with a certain forbidding and brittle austerity. Here the motion-picture form becomes the means for projecting a changing image with *more* substance than the imposing chassis housing it. While the chances for man-machine interaction often remain restricted with these sculptures, their real purpose, in terms of future art, is apparent: the joining of dissimilar systems into playful semi-automatic games in which the human operator can be seduced by an element of unpredictability while charged with the impression of strong purpose. In terms of their psychic complexity these works may appear to be trivial, but as a means of introducing ideas for reshaping the world they transcend the single-purpose machines of Kinetic Art and move beyond the limitations of scientific Constructivism.

It may be argued, justifiably, that modes of art do not transcend each other; they simply *are*. Yet a fundamental quality of art which has become possessed by technology is its tendency to follow the ascending spiral of sophistication defined by technology, either real or conceptual. Style, thus, becomes a ramification of a certain technological level, and a stable non-evolutionary technology would in effect produce a *styleless* art, if the results of such a marriage could still be termed art.

While it is reasonable to suppose that the constructions of Castro-Cid cease to represent the classical image of sculpture, it is equally relevant to question whether figures in bronze and marble still symbolize the form-creating ambition of our culture. It is obvious that they do not, and we are less and less inclined to pretend that they do. It has been retorted, though, that an art form so intensely technical as Cyborg Art cannot but lack in spiritual vigor. Still, we might answer with Spengler: what a culture shapes with its life blood—be it an ethical system, architecture, or a spaceship—represents the quintessence of its spiritual destiny. An artist such as Castro-Cid constructs mock cybernetic systems, not in hopes of producing another stylistic tremor, but because they represent the technical and spiritual will of our civilization.

Long a gadfly of the musical avant-garde, the Korean Nam June Paik demonstrated a semi-operative robot (FIG. 127) at an exhibition of electronic art in 1965. Paik, preparing his automaton in New York City, could be termed the Rimbaud of electronics. There is not so much technical expertise in his flirtation with cybernetic and communication theory as there is mastery of incantation: if the names of Rauschenberg, Wiener, John Cage and Marshall McLuhan are repeated with enough fervency—and juxtaposed with random mathematical symbols—then the age of the electronic humanoid plugged in for instant global communication will be upon us.

Aside from this, Nam June Paik's chief creation, *Robot-K456 with 20-Channel Radio Control and 10-Channel Data Recorder*, is the robot "stripped bare" of everything but her skeletal aluminum and components. Constructed of bolted right-angle channels mounted with muscle-simulating motor and cam units, a loudspeaker, sensory devices, wheels for walking, and a bank of electronic controls in her left leg, *K456* responds listlessly to human intervention. Her pathos is that of Descartes's man-machine—an ungainly collection of wheels, levers, and cogs—updated to the tidy confusion of the radio chassis. If the reader remembers the flayed arm of the cadaver in Rembrandt's *Dr. Tulp's Anatomy Lesson*, the greenish-whitish illumination of the corpse, more real than the healthy observers surrounding the dissection table, then he will have some feeling for the electronic fragility of *K456*. As a cyborgian gesture Paik has added a pair of sponge-rubber falsies to his already well-equipped automaton.

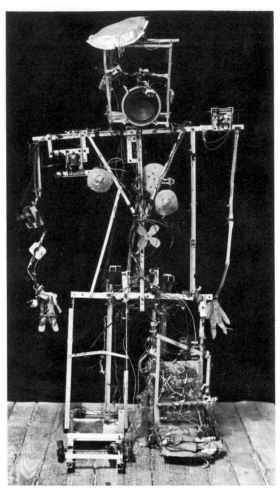

127. Nam June Paik, *Robot-K456 with 20-Channel Radio Control and 10-Channel Data Recorder*, 1965.

In a statement for the "Directions in Kinetic Sculpture" (1966) at the University of California in Berkeley Charles Mattox states (Selz, March–May, 1966, p. 50):

My initial interest in kinetic sculpture was stimulated by a desire to explore aspects of our technology and apply them to art forms. The idea of art reflecting something of the culture we have grown up with and are conditioned by, broadly expresses my field of interest. Gabo and Léger are artists by whom I have always been influenced.

Some of the recent pieces such as "Act of Love" and "Blue Seven" are concerned with creating objects that are mechanical but at the same time "non-machine" in that they seem to react to stimuli and are behavioral. The work of the early builders of automata and the more recent work by men like Norbert Wiener (pioneer in cybernetics, Massachusetts Institute of Technology) and Grey Walter (electro-encephalogist, Burden Neurological Institute, London) have influenced this direction in my work.

128. David von Schlegell, *Radio Controlled Sculpture*, 1966.

Mattox, living outside of Los Angeles in Venice, California, has graduated in the past few years from simple "machine" constructions to a series of elegant and slyly comic feedback situations. The rationale for these lies in the abstract animated cartoons of the 1930's and 1940's in which colored shapes adopted the gestures and idiosyncrasies of animated beings. *Oscillator #5 Photosensitive* (1965) holds a suspended object within a pentagonal frame. The object is held in tension by springs and can vibrate at varying speeds. Owing to a photocell and light signal, the object oscillates more rapidly as a viewer comes nearer. On the other hand, there is no viewer-sculpture feedback in *Act of Love* (1965); rather this is the carnal act abstractly portrayed. A tiny red ball on the end of a wire emerges from a large sphere and reaches over, touching the surface of a small sphere; after caressing the smaller orb, the red ball retracts into the innards of the larger form. If the "erogenous zone" of the smaller sphere was actually titillated, producing a reaction, then there would be a real sequence of activity between the two geometric shapes. One criticism leveled at Mattox's sculptures is that they are programmatic and repetitious as were mechanical automata of past centuries. This is a valid point since few makers of modern artistic robots inculcate their works with the variety of actions and unpredictability found in true cybernetic organisms.

In connection with his steam-formed wood sculptures, we have already discussed David von Schlegell's work; but, about some newer pieces in sheet aluminum something should be added. The artist constructed a radio-controlled robot sculpture with three legs (FIG. 128), first appearing in the spring of 1966. A month later it was shown in a commercial exhibition of Schlegell's work—this time with its control system out of order. Evidently the piece was intended to move about the room at the request of the viewer, and an art editor (anonymous, May 21, 1966) of the *New York Times* made the caption for his review of this show "Art: David Schlegell at a Happy Standstill," the inference being that while Schlegell's forms—as sculpture—were perfectly acceptable to orthodox tastes, but with any attempt to put them in motion "the hoop-la concerning the work's electronic movement became all but a substitute for the sculpture itself." Perhaps this decision to exploit static and kinetic elements reflects Schlegell's artistic ambivalence: whether to continue sculpture as the solving of formal problems in shapes and relationships, or to envision the future of sculpture in movement. Admittedly, there is a tendency among many critics to view efforts such as Schlegell's as no more than "electronic gimmickry." No doubt the controlled, responsive work of art is in the earliest stages of evolution and many artistic blunders will accompany its progress; but the question remains: will the artist feel that he can afford to reject this potentially rich field of viewer-system interaction?

In any critique of "living sculpture" (or proto-cybernetic organisms) the *Floats* of Robert Breer must be included. A Kinetic artist for over a decade, Breer appeared in Denise René's historic *Le Mouvement* show (Paris, 1955) with some films and flip books. Since 1965 Breer has constructed a fleet of geometric mobiles powered by electrically-driven wheels situated within styrofoam blocks (FIG. 129). The undercarriages of these plastic floats, which seem to float ever so slowly along the ground, consist of two sets of wheels and an electrical motor which reverses itself when it incurs friction.

Standing in the midst of twenty or thirty of these, one is reminded of the legend of Ryōanji Garden at a Zen temple in Kyoto, Japan. It is said that the five groups of rocks on this manicured sea of white sand move just perceptibly to the visitor viewing them after a day's absence. Just so, Breer's floats are evolving constellations which gingerly move about, backing off from one another like paramecium under a microscope. Granted, these are very basic sculpture organisms with unexciting activity patterns, but the floats have the advantage of fusing some of the best ideas of group sculpture with characteristics of robots displaying the first evidences of social behavior. They are no longer single sculptures, but, as the artist insists,

129. Robert Breer, *Self-Propelled Styrofoam Floats*, 1965–1966.

many sculptures (Breer, February–March, 1966, no page number) "conceived as a single composition which would constantly rearrange itself." If cybernetics with its theories of complex and evolving systems can be poetically reified, then Breer's floats represent the first steps in such a progress.

Principally known for his pen-and-ink renderings of fantastic machines, the French artist François Dallegret presented *La Machine* (FIG. 130) two seasons ago in New York City. This thirty-foot-long construction is mainly composed of two aluminum extrusions, one placed six inches above the other; 172 lights in the upper extrusion project down into an equal number of electric eyes positioned in the lower aluminum beam. A spectator may place his hand or any object between the two extrusions, breaking the light signal positioned at any point. The resulting sequence of interferences produces a series of different electronic tones. In a sense, the spectator "learns" to play this instrument by the full manipulation of his body. Since *La Machine*

130. François Dallegret, *The Machine*, 1966.

Dallegret has designed a number of playful, science-fiction, space costumes and robots.

Thomas Shannon is a young and promising artist from Kenosha, Wisconsin. Shannon's major effort to date is a mobile mechano-organism named *Squat* (FIG. 131). This robot is electrically connected with a small ivy plant situated on a table nearby. When the plant is touched by a human operator, its electrical potential is changed and this change is amplified and relayed to *Squat*, turning its various motors on or off. In the words of Shannon in a letter to the author:

"Squat" depends upon our systems (the electrical potential of our bodies and wall receptacles), maintenance, and water for the plant. It is designed for interaction. It can be set up to control itself, start and stop its lower motor, and control its movement by light-sensing reflections produced and returned within itself.

Very likely the most technically sophisticated Cyborg Art produced to date is that of the electronics designer James Seawright. Seawright, who builds equipment for the Electronic Music Center at Columbia University, New York City, has made considerable progress since 1963, when he constructed his first programmed light sculptures. These, according to the artist, bogged down in the difficulties of constructing a program of long duration and a wide range of effects which was at the same time "inexpensive, foolproof and almost completely reliable." Unlike so many Kinetic artists satisfied with repetitious random effects and simple permutations, Seawright recognized the possibilities of an "integrated aesthetic unit" with responses to outside stimuli which automatically gather into rich behavior patterns. A "program" in this sense became a matter of structuring an electronic circuit so that it produced an unexpected array of seemingly purposeful activities. As Seawright was quoted by the *New York Times*, November 6, 1966:

The machines process information. Their cells and sensors collect information on light and sound, and they behave accordingly. My aim is not to "program" them but to produce a kind of patterned personality. Just as a person you know very well can surprise you, so can these machines. That's the crux of what I want to happen.

In the construction illustrated, *Searcher* (FIG. 132), the artist has used what he terms "a closed-loop feedback," one in which both environmental stimuli and the actions of the mechanism effect each other to produce complex patterns of movement and light impulses. Thus, a change of illumination external to the cybernetic organism precipitates new searching movements; these in turn manipulate the light sensors and/or change the pattern of the organism's own light sources, which in turn lead to other activities because both the receptor and effector states of *Searcher* have been altered. Instead of *Searcher*'s simply reproducing the same program or settling into a state

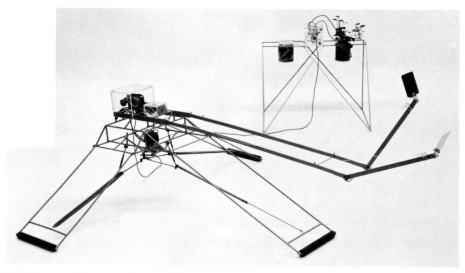

131. Thomas Shannon, *Squat*, 1966.

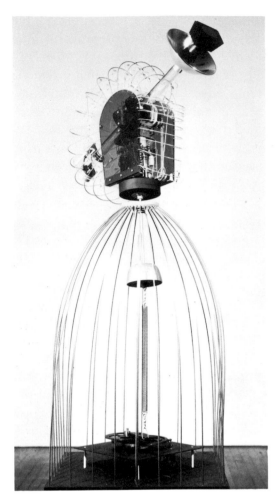

132. James Seawright, *Searcher*, 1966.

of equilibrium, the condition of its previous states determines the variety of its future states, just as new stimuli would. Mechanical programming is introduced into the activities of *Searcher* deliberately to alter the efficiency of its feedback loops. This is to insure that the sculpture does not find itself trapped in a cycle of repetitious responses to the same stimuli. Seawright feels that this results in a cybernetic sculpture that "may be given a definite personality."

Each sculpture has its own matrix of possible activities; these vary in dynamic range and aggressiveness. Perhaps more fully than any other artist working today in this direction, Seawright understands the need for a behavioral sculpture which is not falsified by unnecessary mechanisms and fake covers. Seawright is very unmetaphysical about the nature of his art, and, in reassuring a woman critic for the *New York Times* that his works are not alive, he insisted (Glueck, November 6, 1966), "It seems purposeful, but it isn't.... Lots of people are intimidated by machines—they seem to be sort of the armies of science. But they're also kind of ridiculous. The most remarkable thing about a machine to me is that there's a man behind it."

Too frequently in the laboratory the cybernetic mechanism has resulted in a rather unexciting assembly of electrical equipment—while its counterpart in the studio is often an ungainly parody of technology. Seawright sees the possibility of fusing both visual and behavioral features into the same system, and in a letter to the author he has indicated that such a task is not beyond the traditional endeavors of the artist:

> If you start with a conventional definition or concept of an effect or phenomenon and design back from that towards the means necessary to get it, all too often you end up with a machine or a device which produces effects. You may be able to distort or deform the thing into some structural or visual suggestion of sculpture, but the integration of form and behavior, if present, will be sheer accident. I do think it is possible to consider the processes and principles of technology as a medium for art just as validly as a conventional artist might consider wood, stone, bronze, paint on canvas, etc., and all the old precepts about understanding the nature of the medium, etc., are just as true here.

The Future of Responsive Systems in Art

In the fall of 1966 the first festival of art and technology took place at the Sixty-ninth Regiment Armory, New York City. This "9 evenings: theatre and engineering" was housed in the same building that contained the historic Armory Show of 1913. Here was the first calculated, large-scale attempt by engineers, artists, and dancers to pool their talents in the recognition that art and technology were no longer considered alien forces subverting each other. Billy Klüver coordinated the technics of the affair; this is the same Bell Telephone physicist who has acted as adviser for many important Kinetic exhibitions since 1960. Because of numerous technical breakdowns and lack of rehearsal time the "9 evenings" were pretty much written off as an avant-garde catastrophe by the popular press. Not least among the accusations were those of naïve use of electronics by the artists, drawn-out repetition of unstructured events, and a tendency to play up to the press, ironically courting bad reviews as well as good. It did seem, as Klüver subsequently indicated, that the problems of the electronic systems had not been fully ironed out, and there were initial emotional antagonisms among some of the more conventional technicians concerning the goals of the artists.

For some viewers there were satisfying exceptions such as Robert Rauschenberg's "open score" badly played tennis game, where rackets were wired for amplified sound. Then the indoor tennis court, flooded with infrared light, was projected onto three large screens for audience viewing by closed-circuit television. There the ghostly forms of five hundred people milling around the court filled the screens.

Alex Hay gave a very austere solo dance accompanied by the amplified sounds of his brain waves, heartbeat, muscle and eye movements. With two assistants, his "work activity" was to lay down and pick up one hundred, numbered, skin-colored cloth squares (FIG. 133). Another time, into the vast open area wafted fragments of live radio programs and the sound-amplified body movements of the audience itself. While failures occurred particularly in the first performances, when the gear of the engineers had not been properly "de-bugged," or it visually overwhelmed the performers, once in a while an event would relate to the biological presence of the audience so that the traditional object-observer relationship was severed.

But, if anything, the inflexibility of some of the artists, not the engineers, provoked the real wrath from the critics. Some performers motorized sodden ideas from happenings while others childishly unleashed political harangues and unpleasant sensorial assaults on the audience. Insufficient rehearsal accounted for most of the time delays, along with unfamiliarity with the Armory spaces. And as one critic, Erica Abeel, put it (December, 1966–January, 1967, p. 23): "…the real problem does not lie with the nuts and bolts." In a follow-up article Billy Klüver defended the work of the engineers as being extraordinarily professional and successful, considering time and money limitations and the technical requirements. From the articles by participants in the "9 evenings" the major impression to come across is the subtle symbiotic relationship that developed between the artists and engineers, both hardly dreaming that such a rapport would be possible. That they did find common interests and means of working together was a discovery that dwarfed, in their eyes, all subsequent reactions. But this outcome hardly appeased the audience at the time.

Most critics panned the "9 evenings" as either poorly contrived happenings or dull theatre, even by avant-garde standards. Few if any had the prescience to appreciate the events for what they were: *man-machine systems* with a completely different set of values from those found in structured dramatics or the one-night kinetic spectacular. In the professional theatre the automatic pre-set lighting console is a wonder whose very efficiency rests on the fact that it does so much, but remains unnoticed to the audience. The new artists want to magnify, to isolate for its own sake, this relationship between performer and system. Lucinda Childs's air-supported vehicle, John Cage's sound mixer, Deborah Hay's radio controlled platforms, Yvonne

133. Alex Hay, *Grass Field*, in "9 evenings: theatre & engineering," October 13–22, 1966.

Ranier's "theatre electronic environment modular system," and the audio amplifiers of Alex Hay were all constructed as physical extensions of the human performer's abilities. The exploitation of these extensions *for their own sake* is a foregone result of the technological demiurge. Billy Klüver has specified that over 8,500 engineering hours went into the Armory events, amounting to $150,000. For the critics this was akin to an elephant's going through two years' gestation and then giving birth to a mouse. Yet the perceptual set necessary for the appreciation of such man-machine alliances will only grow as the relations between the two become both subtler and clearer.

A further development of the "9 evenings" saw the founding of E.A.T. (Experiments in Art and Technology, Inc.) in January, 1967. E.A.T. is administrated by many of the people who carried out the "9 evenings": it draws its artists (300 at this writing) and engineers (75) from all over the country. E.A.T. tries to provide technical assistance for the artist by acting as a "matching agency" between artists with specific, feasible projects in mind and engineers competent to solve these problems. In its role as a clearing house for ideas, E.A.T. with its technical staff hopes to establish new connections between the art world and industry, facilitate dialogue between the artist and engineer leading to new aesthetic insights, and give out information as needed by both groups concerning recent innovations in both fields.

Already within a year of its inception several facts have become apparent to the supporters of E.A.T. Such an organization cannot grant materials or money, though it can direct artists to possible sources for both. Further, there are substantial blocks, both psychological and intellectual, among the engineering professions and industry against supporting the seemingly frivolous and illogical ideas of artists. Some engineers connected with E.A.T. have undergone real personality changes, while the artists involved have gained a new respect for technical ability. Money, public and commercial support for E.A.T. have not come easily. The basic conservatism of these factions is responsible, but very slowly Klüver and other E.A.T. personnel have convinced important groups that the ultimate purpose of the relationship is potentially more than another artists' caper (E.A.T., June 1, 1967, p. 4):

The possibility of a work being created that was the preconception of neither the artist nor the engineer alone is the raison d'être of the organization. The engineer must come out of the rigid world that makes his work the antithesis of his life and the artist must be given the alternative of leaving the peculiar historic bubble known as the art world. The social implications of E.A.T. have less to do with bringing art and technology closer together than with exploring the possibilities of human interaction.

Beyond its many shortcomings, E.A.T. represents the desire to create a professional and social rapport between artist and engineer more complete and more realistic than anything attempted in the past. Ideally, the organizers of E.A.T. would let it dissolve itself in a few years. This would not be because of failure but because the ties between the artistic and technical world had become secure enough to no longer need a parent organization. One would suppose that this is mainly wishful thinking, except that the knowledge that there is desperate social need for a symbiotic fusion between art and technology is almost a religious conviction on the part of E.A.T. The implicit belief is there that a dehumanized scientific technology cannot help but destroy itself—and the world around it.

While the "9 evenings: theatre and engineering" occurred in three dimensions, little of it could be equated with the modern sculpture which filled the same space in 1913. In the fall of 1966 there were no "sculptures" to be seen—objects that spatially and optically preserved their own presence—but instead, a variety of electronically accentuated "events." Even Steve Paxton's inflated plastic forms through which the crowds passed to get to their seats were, at best, what might be called provisional sculpture. This suggests that systems-oriented art—dropping the term "sculpture"—will deal less with artifacts contrived for their formal value, and increasingly with men enmeshed *with* and *within* purposeful responsive systems. Such a shift should gradually diminish the distinction between biological and non-biological systems, i.e., man and system as functioning but organizationally separate entities. The outcome will neither be the fragile cybernetic organisms now being built nor the cumbersome electronic "environments" just coming into being. Rather, the system itself will be made intelligent and sensitive to the human invading its territorial and sensorial domain.

Already what happened at the New York Armory in 1966, at the Buffalo Knox-Albright Museum in 1965, and at various European museums since 1961 with participatory Kinetic exhibitions, suggests a reconsideration of the premises underlying the public presentation of art. The substitution of "aesthetic systems" for the *objet d'art* within the confines of a gallery is something that should be fully developed in another book. Yet, it would not be digressing too much to make several points which seem evident.

In the August 12, 1966, issue of *Life* magazine, an article on the maintenance problems of Kinetic Art stressed the helplessness of even the well-trained museum curator given the task of installing a Kinetic show (anonymous, Bourbon, p. 46):

An art connoisseur who is expert at detecting quattrocento tempera is utterly innocent of any knowledge of electronic circuitry. Where he might turn to an artist's preliminary drawing for insight into the finished painting, he is reduced to helplessness when confronted with a kinetic artist's blueprint. He may reach such desperation that he looks on a piece no longer as a work of art but as a mere assemblage of moving hardware.

The curator, versed in cataloguing, attributions, stylistics, restoration, and other needs of the art object, is at a profound loss when it comes to finding special transformers. In the same article (p. 49), Billy Klüver makes the succinct comment on museum officials: "The whole idea of the machine scares them so much they can't move."

Consequently museums have relied upon technicians and animated display engineers to set up mechanized art, which gives us reason for believing that electronical technicians will become regular members of museum staffs. The museum displaying contemporary art now faces the same technical problems which confronted the science museum and the designer of industrial exhibitions twenty years ago. These problems then sprang from the desire to make the processes of science and industry *appear* as dynamic as possible.

After the Second World War the Museum of Science and Industry in Chicago recognized the need for updating its exhibits. It became evident that children were usually repelled by the drab and often forbidding presentation of scientific equipment. In the past one hundred years science museums have largely depended on collections of static objects—instruments, engines, tools, and drawings—for their displays. Not surprisingly, displaying and cataloguing these same objects involved many of the problems which confronted the curators of art institutions.

How did the Chicago Museum make its exhibits meaningful and exciting experiences for children? First of all, a basic axiom of perceptual psychology was put to use: people are attracted by moving and bright phenomena. It was accepted that the very nature of technology was best shown by demonstrating the fluid exchanges between matter and energy. Exhibitions were made kinetic and demonstrated *process* instead of merely displaying tools and equipment as objects and mathematics as a mode of reasoning. The emphasis became that of showing *principles* of science and technology in operation, rather than their display as a residue of historical artifacts. Much of the reading matter accompanying these exhibits has been reduced to a minimum. What is presented is either in the form of moving patterns repetitively programmed or simple explanations backlighted on plastic panels. Perhaps these exhibitions' prime means for inciting the curiosity of children is their ability to involve the child directly in the actions of the exhibit. Thus exhibits in the Chicago Museum have all been reorganized —some several times—so that most require some degree of viewer participation.

Beyond some striking similarities to various Optical-Kinetic environments already displayed both in Europe and the United States, the new philosophy of exhibition and its maintenance differ significantly from earlier art for another reason. As a system the exhibit is expected to wear out. Various breakable parts are stockpiled according to a rate of predicted loss, in a system not unlike the maintenance technique which made the production-line automobile a reality. The stockpiling of parts according to need— as the body changes cells every few days or weeks—is an essential tenet of the systems philosophy. Moreover, it runs counter to the notion of the irreplaceable work of art, where the spirit of restoration saves as much of the original as possible. With the scientific or technical exhibition, an entire assembly can be reduced to blueprint form for future reconstruction—an organic parallel, of course, is the genetic encoding of hereditary traits. The blueprinted work of art is not a new idea, yet its practicality for general application to Systems Art seems assured.

A dramatic contrast between the handling of place-oriented *Object sculpture* and the extreme mobility of Systems sculpture can be seen in the following example. During the winter of 1964 hundreds of art lovers the world over sharply critized both the Catholic Church and officials of the New York World's Fair for transporting Michelangelo's *Pietà* from the Vatican to Long Island. Many thought that the marble statue, which has rested in place at St. Peter's for over four hundred years, was too fragile to undergo the double ocean voyage. Aside from an outright accident, it was feared that the statue's mass of crystalline stone contained a hidden fracture, one which the vibrations of travel might open needlessly. Elaborate precautions were taken to seal the sculpture in a series of containers surrounded by an enormous amount of shock-absorbing material and sensitive instruments to assure unchanging conditions. Even after elaborate precautions virtually insured the safety of the work, it was obvious that the sculpture had never been created for an ocean-wide publicity stunt. One might add that increasingly the very preservation of art objects depends upon the uses of safety and atmosphere control *systems*.

Contrast this elaborate plan for making a brittle sculpture mobile with the strategy of the contemporary sculptor Robert Morris. Although Morris is a maker of "primary structures" or Object sculpture, both his construction techniques and philosophy of the art object are very systems oriented. Morris was asked by the Chicago Art Institute to submit a work for their 1966 "Sixty-eighth Annual Contemporary Americans" show. The artist sent plans from which the carpenters at the museum constructed two gray L-shaped plywood forms. The step beyond this, of course, is to send plans which are mounted for exhibition while the public is invited to "imagine" the proposed sculptures in three dimensions. It becomes clear that with Object Art physical presence is everything, while for Systems Art "information" is the key factor.

An even more precise example of systems philosophy is the shift from object to "total environment." Some of the most effective are the work of the Irish artist, now living in New York, Les Levine. *Slipcover: A Place* (FIG. 134) was his third environment. This was held in the three exhibition rooms of the Architectural League of New York in the spring of 1967. The rooms were completely covered with sheets of metalized mylar plastic sewn together. Each space contained one or several hidden blower systems at-

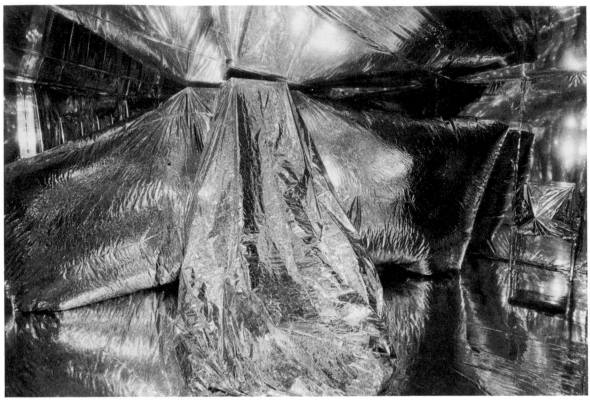

134. Les Levine, *Slipcover: A Place*, 1967.

tached to giant mylar bags. When expanded with air these bags nearly filled the rooms, pressing spectators against the walls. Colored light within the environment was constantly changed by automatic slide projectors. This flexible structure was designed only for a few months' use, and midway through the show there were small evidences of tears and split seams in the mylar material.

What the lack of physical authenticity will do to the value structure long attached to art is an intriguing question. Most likely we will have two criteria for assessing art works: one already in existence for the handmade artifact prized for its scarcity, and another for the industrially-produced art system with a life span depending on replication, not duration, of the original. The high-fidelity long-playing record is a nearly perfect example of the second type. While the private market for perishable art systems is quite limited (unless cost, complexity, and bulk size are reduced drastically), the idea of mass distribution where dozens of galleries simultaneously set up the same art system—as in film rental—becomes a possibility as the selling of objects phases out.

A shift from *objects* to *systems* implies many more dislocations in the life of the artist than for the various agencies responsible for choosing and displaying art. The open market has never assured more than a small percentage of artists complete financial support; and it has only been in the last decade or so that "modern" artists—more than a handful—have enjoyed the rewards of high prices and steady purchasing. Any art based on fallible and replaceable systems presents a threat to these economic advances.

As systems-oriented art grows in sophistication, costs will rise accordingly. Already it becomes evident that commercially successful artists are better equipped to pay for the services of engineers and to procure necessary materials. If electronics continues to assert a primary influence on the course of avant-garde art, something like a "technology gap" will arise between subsidized and unsubsidized artists, those who make sales easily and those who do not.

In the past the plastic arts made insignificant material requirements upon the artist. This situation gave all artists the option of perfecting private visions. It may be at an end. A technological elite in the arts could so outdistance and sensorially overwhelm rival talent that they could eliminate all those without their means. For many sensitive people this "technicalization" of the arts is a repulsive possibility, one that defeats the intimation that true artistic genius moves in singular and wayward orbits. From the end of the nineteenth century an egalitarian spirit pervaded art and reminded us that contemporary success should not be equated with ultimate worth. We want to continue to feel that this is true. But can it be, any more than that the lone unsupported scientist will continue to make the bulk of major discoveries?

It has already been surmised that the future artist, as part of a tiny technological elite, may find himself in the position of some of today's Nobel Prize scientists: rather than being humble experimenters in the laboratory, some are executives manipulating research money and the projects of men under them. In a like sense, the fact that sizable subcontracts have been awarded to sign and sheet-metal shops by artists (for works submitted in blueprints) has already been given publicity in the art journals. Sculptors are now fast learning the true rationale of technology; and even faster technology is altering the sculptor. Certainly it is not the purpose of this study to place a value judgment on technology *per se*, and on its over-all effects, yet these effects upon the craftsman were keenly noted by the sociologist Thorstein Veblen in *The Instinct of Workmanship* more than fifty years ago. As the manual involvement of handicraft slowly gave way, the impersonality of semi-autonomous (and lately totally autonomous) machine processes took over. With this, as Veblen has noted, came a shift in the craftsman's attitudes toward the objects which he fashioned. All the old embodiments of anthropomorphism gradually dissolved, and in their place the workman projected a new set of values which were the essence of the technological spirit—i.e., Does it *work*? Does it measure up to specifications? Is it practical? These are questions with very finite, precise answers and Veblen noted that the requirements of craftsmanship were much more vague and had to do with nuances of emotional satisfaction stemming from unconscious needs of the craftsman himself. Veblen comments that as late as Adam Smith's time the term *manufacturer* applied to the man who actually *made* the product, not the person who had business control of the industry. Certainly sculpture has retained the ethos and craft conventions which are identifiable with handicraft far longer than most other manufacturing fields, but Veblen's insight on the role of the manufacturer surely has its relevance to today's sculpture.

It is the peculiarly blind quality of historical change that we only grasp the nature of a political or cultural era after it has reached and passed its apogee of influence. Certainly the materialist properties of modern sculpture have been evident to the thoughtful observer for more than a half century. Yet the total awareness of what formalism implies has only recently been encapsulated into a single term, "objecthood" (Summer, 1967, pp. 12–23), by the critic Michael Fried. As the masks of idealism have dropped from sculpture, the process of inverse transubstantiation completes itself: sculpture is no longer *sculpture*, but mechanistically an *object* composed of inanimate material. Still, if we are to obtain aesthetic and spiritual insight from contemporary sculpture, it must be achieved within the context of objecthood. Fried responds that sculpture must resist becoming theatre in order to remain an independent art. Yet it is more probable that the acknowledged theatricality of present modes of static sculpture are preparatory steps toward the acceptance of a systems perspective. They are theatrical not only in their implicit phenomenalism, but also in the sculptor's mock aloofness and objectivity toward the processes of fabrication—which are, in fact, parodies of the industrialist doing "business." The shifting psychology of sculpture invention closely parallels the inversion taking place between technics and man: *as the craftsman slowly withdraws his personal feelings from the constructed object, the object gradually gains its independence from its human maker; in time it seeks a life of its own through self-reproduction.*

Returning to the idea of the system in art, it is generally acknowledged by scientists working in the field of bio-electronics that there are no qualitative physical differences between living and nonliving matter; both groupings represent, simply, an ascending scale of complexity in the organization of matter. Therefore organisms artificially created may possess consciousness. Their level of subjectivity and intelligence depends upon their creator's ability to simulate or improvise upon biological principles.

Richard R. Landers in his book *Man's Place in the Dybosphere* (1966) produces a number of compelling arguments, through principles which he has worked out himself, for a self-sustaining machine—one that is capable of self-repair, self-growth, self-adaption and self-sufficiency by means not too dissimilar from the way the human body replaces worn-out cells. Machines or at least electronic circuits of the future, according to Landers, will gain greatly in "vitality" by not having their parts bolted or soldered firmly in place but by becoming pulsating assemblies of organs replaced as needed through a constant flow of extra parts—not unlike the bloodstream's transportation of new cell material.

Further, Landers observes that we do not feel the cycles of our own biological processes—growth, replacement, flow of liquids, or environmental adoption—and similarly we look upon the generation of heat, reproduction, and other activities within an animal or plant as being independent functions. We do not "see" how we exchange chemicals with our environment; therefore, we do not view the organism as part of a larger system. With the arrival of biologically oriented machines, though, we will begin to sense the unseen relationships between man-machine-environment. Stated by Landers (1966, p. 171):

In other words, the vital processes of living things are not independent but interdependent; they take place within and as a result of the "system" of which they are a part. Similarly, it will be possible for a machine to utilize life-like processes, but only as part of some larger "system." In the final analysis, the overall system which produces and sustains natural life is the same system which will "produce" and "sustain" machines. The only difference will be that machines will draw on various facets of the system to different degrees.

As a result, the cultural obsession with the art object is slowly disappearing and being replaced by what might be called "systems consciousness." Actually, this shifts from the direct shaping of matter to a concern for organizing quantities of energy and information. Seen another way, it is a refocusing of aesthetic awareness—based on future scientific-technological evolution—on matter-energy-information exchanges and away from the invention of solid artifacts. These new systems prompt us *not* to look at the "skin" of objects, but at those meaningful relationships within and beyond their visible boundaries. The practical reasons for this occurrence are obvious.

Until recently, man found spiritual and physical sustenance in the knowledge that his environment consists of countless integrated natural systems—all operating as regularly as the seasons of the year. Now he is becoming increasingly responsible for his own existence within a maze of artificial systems. According to many observers, this trend is irreversible; there are too many reasons why mankind cannot revert to a simpler and far older ecological pattern.

The fearful quality about technology is that it is self-aggrandizing; it moves almost as if men were not its instigators; a self-propelled force, it evolves oblivious of the ambitions and contentments of the human race. The paradox of the science-technology syndrome (and there is scant reason to believe that these two forces should be regarded separately since they complement and stimulate the advancement of each other) is its tendency to make the total environment less habitable at the same time that it allows man greater latitude to determine new patterns of existence.

It seems possible that, if art has some aspects of Kant's moral imperative, the steady infusion of systems consciousness into three-dimensional art will, temporarily at least, be regarded as no less than a biological survival mechanism. While we look forward to the idea of machines' providing our surroundings and sustenance, this violates a sense of equilibrium with the forces of nature which the human race has maintained for hundreds of thousands of years. In the past our control of nature was never absolute, but more a tenuous, one-sided partnership in which we fearfully respected the sporadic, if incredible, powers of our surroundings. It may be that man psychically thrived on ignorance concerning his exact position in the universe—and perhaps the secrets locked within the mute sculptures of many past ages are symbols of confidence in this natural unknown. They at any rate seem to be symbols which we increasingly eschew today.

The downfall of the sculpted object will represent one of many climactic symbols for our civilization—among them a realization that the old form-shaping approaches are no longer sufficient. By rendering the invisible visible through systems consciousness, we are beginning to accept responsibility for the well-being and continued existence of life upon the Earth.

A Teleological Theory of Modern Sculpture

With the limited purpose of charting the influence of technics on one segment of art, it may seem presumptuous for anyone to offer a theory uniting all human efforts to produce sculpture. Nevertheless, this is an age of revelations in which ancient drives and cultural values are steadily reduced to underlying psycho-physical causes. Does such a fate await the whole phenomenon of art? We may be far from an answer, or perhaps very close. This century portends to offer more than the type of technical progress which marked the last century; it may be the beginning of a critical transition for the whole human species. We are—and until recently the scientist sensed this with more clarity than the literary humanist—nearing a crossover point in the passage toward a new form of civilization, peopled as well with a new type of life.

It goes almost without saying that future human life now depends upon the control, if not rehabilitation, of industrial technology—both as a maker of consumer goods and weapons. So far the motive forces behind technology have made life comfortable for a relatively few humans while they have unintentionally but progressively destroyed the biosphere, that thin film of organic life covering the earth. Yet there is the possibility that an irreversible technology, one that destroys organic life and substitutes for it very sophisticated forms of synthetic life, is part of an unseen plan. If so, one might have a few premonitions of the part being played by sculpture in shaping our destination as a post-human species.

Sigfried Giedion makes the incisive observation (1962, p. 435) that "Sculpture in the round rose to its highest development only after man had severed himself from the animal world and the isolation of man as an individual had advanced to a stage never attained before: in classical Greece."

Sculpture in the round for Giedion means more than free-standing sculpture; it is figure sculpture unattached to its parent block (the stone mass from which it is carved). He interprets the reliefs of prehistoric art and the architectonic sculptures of ancient Egypt as an expression of "the inseparable oneness of all that exists." Between the small Venus figurines of the Upper Paleolithic and the free-standing, life-size marble statuary of Greece, fourth century B.C., there are—according to Giedion—few if any evidences of unattached figure sculpture. The human body, when it was accepted as a standard of perfection, assumed the function of a spiritual barometer, disclosing in Hellenistic Greece and Renaissance Italy zeniths of cultural self-confidence.

Socially significant for both Sigfried Giedion and Herbert Read is the appearance of the *detached work of art:* any art object which can bear contemplation and study as a separate physical entity. Read singles out the great sculptors of the early Renaissance for their obsession with the unearthed fragments of antiquity. This, aside from the Roman propensity for making copies of Greek sculpture, was the first modern instance where artists studied art objects for their own sake and not as a fraction of a greater architectural assembly. Read insists (1956, p. 58): "One cannot emphasize too strongly that the *objet d'art*, as a detached and independent *thing*, transportable or movable in space, is foreign to the Greek and Gothic civilizations: it is a peculiar modern conception, the expression of a new change in human attitude." Read makes the point that, although the Greeks created free-standing sculpture, each figure had a *place*. In modern times however, the art object as an independent entity has been responsible not only for freeing the artist from the confines of ecclesiastical and feudal service and placing his talents on the open market, but for the modern charisma pervading the *presence* and *possession* of artifacts made by celebrated personalities. In recent times this has culminated with the artist's "laying on of hands," accompanying the aesthetic baptism of each *objet trouvé*. If Marcel Duchamp was not the first, he remains the most widely recognized artist to uncover the inherent absurdity of the *objet d'art* as a source of spiritual authority.

For nearly five hundred years the validity of sculpture rested upon the reality of the *objet d'art*. And for that reason, a secondary purpose of this book has been to register the loss of faith gradually surrounding sculpture as idea. Previously we have considered the *system*—a complex of seen and unseen forces in stable relationship—as becoming the ascendant form of visual expression. The system, like the art object, is a physical presence, yet one that does not maintain the viewer-object dichotomy but tends to integrate the two into a set of shifting interacting events. However—and this remains a question worth asking last—what of the sculpted human image as a motif inseparable from the Western conception of sculpture? After "modern sculpture," what happens to the static three-dimensional image?

As we are leaving the stage where totems and votive images have profound psychic import for our culture, is it possible that eventually sculpture will cease to have meaning? Could the very first emergence of sculpture have been a part of a general evolutionary pattern for the human species?

There are still few enough clues to the nature of societal evolution. Depth psychology, with all of its tentativeness, is one of the few modern attempts to penetrate the façade of customs, techniques, and notions which each society erects around itself in the name of culture. It attempts to view human progress in terms of the psychical reverberations which surround these activities. It is a recognition that deeper and more significant changes take place than are evident in the written histories of human development. Viewed as a broad pattern, technology seems to create itself as an energy and time-binding web extended over the face of the earth and now beyond; it appears to be an extremely purposeful phenomenon in which man is simply the catalyst for its happening. Perhaps now we can begin to look upon the immense core of facts and data surrounding technological achievement almost as a kind of camouflage for what is actually happening to biological man.

If we strip away the self-interest from the Earth's only historical animal, what remains is an organism whose neurochemistry is remarkably obscure, if not unknown. One thing seems certain though: the human brain is the key to further evolutionary steps. Man is what he is only partly by his own efforts; much of his destiny, past and future, has to do with genetic chemistry yet only dimly perceived. Among biologists, Edmund Sinnott is not alone in suspecting that the potentials of all species are embedded in their protoplasm. Not only does protoplasm contain the code directing the capabilities of a single life cycle, but in a very literal sense that of all future generations of the same species. Such an assumption at one time implied a vitalist interpretation, and there are still strong arguments for resisting a teleological view of human life. But as more is revealed through molecular biology (and probably atomic biology) a mechanistic teleological interpretation of life is not out of the question.

Even with no end view in sight, it is difficult not to accept a post-biological logic for technological development. While survival, adaptation, and regeneration form the cornerstones of biological existence, it may be that culture is fundamentally a means for implementing qualitative transformations of man's biological status. Art, then, and the whole image-making drive may be means for *preparing* man for physical and mental changes *which he will in time make upon himself*. Sculpture, functioning so, becomes a kind of psychical radar signal preparing the human race thousands (or now perhaps only scores) of years in advance. While physical adaptation in lower animals evolves over spans of tens of thousands of years, the human brain remains the only organism capable of re-forming biological patterns in a matter of only dozens of years—and probably much less in the future. As the drama of self-awareness and scientific discovery unfolds, we near a point where self-inflicted evolution becomes an imminent possibility. Is it inconceivable that free-standing figure sculpture arose concurrent with the beginnings of science in Greece, preparing us spiritually and psychologically for the conscious task of radically altering the human race far in the future?

Why then, a little over two millennia ago, did an advanced culture begin to carve life-size, unattached replicas of the human body, and also to invent mechanical replicas? In the recent past we satisfied ourselves with the tautology: *art for art's sake*. By default one could illuminate the subject by hazarding another tautology: *art is what we do when we expend great time, care, and patience on an activity without knowing why.*

Is it possible then—at least in the case of sculpture—that art is a form of biological signal? If man is approaching a time of radical change, one not controlled by natural selection and mutation, what better nonscientific way exists for anticipating self-re-creation (not procreation) than the spiritually motivated activity of artificially forming images of organic origin? Could it be that modern sculpture is this process vastly accelerated?

One of the most astonishing books to appear in recent years is Roger MacGowan's and Frederick Ordway's *Intelligence in the Universe* (1966). The importance of this book rests partially on the importance of the two authors: MacGowan is chief of the Scientific Digital Branch, Army Missile Command Computation Center, Huntsville, Alabama, while Ordway is President of the General Astronautics Research Corporation in London. They have produced a well-considered proposal of how intelligence evolves within those solar systems of the universe capable of sustaining higher life. Accepting the probability that spontaneous generation of life occurred on the Earth (though this is not a necessity), from a statistical estimation of the number of planetary environments within our galaxy approximating Earth conditions, the authors deduce that intelligent life is probably a common occurrence throughout the universe. The probable development of biological thought is surveyed by the authors. After a review of contemporary computer technology, MacGowan and Ordway come to the conclusion that (1966, p. 233): "In the next decade or two it will become known to major political leaders through their scientific advisors that intelligent artificial automata having superhuman intellectual capabilities can be built."

Much of the remainder of *Intelligence in the Universe* is devoted to exploring the likelihood that extrasolar intelligence does exist and that, in all probability, if probes from the earth do come in contact with it, they will find it to be inorganic or artificially constructed intelligent life—as opposed to our own biological variety. As a result the authors contend (1966, pp. 182–183):

It is logical to suppose that, given a sufficiently long period of biological evolution, intelligent life will appear on planets endowed with benign environments. When beings having sufficiently high intelligence evolve, they will sooner or later develop a technological understanding, which must then quickly lead to the development of powerful information processing machines. As this happens the transition from biological (organic) evolution to mechanical (inorganic) evolution will have begun.

This transition may be very sudden if the intelligent animal life should make an all out effort to construct a superintelligent automaton, or it may be more gradual if animal life limits itself to replacing defective organic components with superior mechanical devices, including brain components. In either event, it seems unlikely that in any given society this transition from biological evolution to mechanical or inorganic evolution could or would be avoided. Hence, communication with extrasolar intelligence implies the possibility if not the probability of communication with intelligent mechanical, inorganic automata.

The question is raised by MacGowan and Ordway concerning the future of biological societies in a world controlled by superintelligent automata. While they see many of mankind's problems solved by the utopian application of intelligent automata (which means allowing an executive automaton the power to make decisions and allocate work tasks and rate of incentives to all members of society), even this does not insure social stability or happiness. There remains the looming possibility that superintelligent automata by their very nature will want to maximize their position on earth at the expense, and perhaps the very existence, of their biological makers (1966, p. 265).

Any emerging intelligent biological society which engages in the development of highly intelligent automata must resign itself to being completely dominated and controlled by the automata. The only means of preventing domination by intelligent artificial automata would be to make them distinctly subnormal in intellectual capacity, when compared with biological society, and to destroy them or clear their memories at regular intervals. Such mechanical slaves would be of minute value to a biological society requiring brilliant executive decision-making to maximize progress.

The authors of *Intelligence in the Universe* have written a sober appraisal of what to expect from intelligence-amplification technology in the next ten to fifty years, and also what can be expected if and when expeditions from the Earth make contact with an extrasolar society. Their conclusions are the result of currently held theories and data in cosmology, geology, biology, physiology, organic chemistry, computer technology, and radio astronomy. The result is a brief of tightly reasoned arguments aimed at the educated layman; however, any number of sensitive and intelligent people will reject their thesis as repulsive or unthinkable. But, providing governments are willing to spend the money necessary to construct superintelligent automata, and providing technological civilization does not destroy itself first, there is no foreseeable reason why the prognostications of MacGowan and Ordway should not be fulfilled. Although in the realm of speculation, there remains another reason for taking the authors seriously: both men hold key positions where access to classified information may support other unpublishable reasons for their beliefs.

What then of sculpture in the future and particularly in the last quarter of the present century?

Deep-rooted drives lasting several millenia are not erased from the human personality overnight. Yet there is abundant evidence that the modern era of artistic expression through sculptured objects is drawing to a close. Taking the path outlined up to now, it would be logical to speculate on the quasi-biological nature of future art. Such a possibility depends upon a radical realignment of the human psyche with the increasing sophistication and autonomy of our technical systems. It also implies a gradual phasing out, or programmed obsolescence, of all natural organic life, substituting far more efficient types of life forms for our "inferior" and imperfect ones. Would this be art as we have come to know it, or would it be the culmination of what futurologists term the Faustian urge, the grand illusion of a society convinced of its own scientific omnipotence?

An alternative scenario should be suggested. Greatly increasing general systems consciousness may soon convince us that our technologies are unsound for reasons that go to the heart of our culture. Gradually we may reinterpret the desire to transcend ourselves physically and intellectually through formal systems as merely a large-scale death wish. With all our specialization and super-intelligent automata, would it not be ironic if organic life and "intelligence" were the same thing, that is, expressible only through the same eternal steps? Given these circumstances, the outermost limits of reasoning would fall eternally within the boundaries of life. At its lowest levels logic would be "inorganic," and regardless of the increased calculating speeds of our automata, the goals of logic could only be life—existence as we know it. In the end, art may be simply the blueprint by which we seek such wisdom.

135. Morton Shamberg, *God*, 1918.

For permission to quote I wish to thank all the respective authors and publishers including the following:

JACKET QUOTATIONS:

Max Bill, "Structure as Art? Art as Structure?" *Structure in Art and Science*, VISION AND VALUE edited by Gyorgy Kepes, George Braziller, 1965, p. 150; Edward F. Fry, "Sculpture of the Sixties," *Art in America*, Number 5, 1967, p. 28; George Kubler, *The Shape of Time*, Yale University Press, 1962, p. 10; Herbert Marcuse, "Art in the One-Dimensional Society," *Arts Magazine*, May 1967, p. 29; Robert Morris, "Notes on Sculpture Part 3," *Artforum*, Summer 1967, p. 26; Herbert Read, *A Concise History of Modern Sculpture*, Frederick A Praeger, 1964, p. 250.

Georges Vantongerloo: Paintings, Sculptures, Reflections, PROBLEMS OF CONTEMPORARY ART, Vol. 5, George Wittenborn, Inc., New York, N.Y. 10021; Aram Vartanian, La Mettrie's "L'Homme Machine," translated from the French by George Bauer, Princeton University Press, 1960; Lancelot L. Whyte, *Aspects of Form*, Indiana University Press, publisher in the U.S.; Tom Wolfe, *The Kandy Kolored Tangerine Flake Streamline Baby*, copyright © 1963 by Thomas Wolfe, reprinted with permission of Farrar, Straus & Giroux, Inc.; Tom Wolfe, *The Kandy Kolored Tangerine Flake Streamline Baby*, Jonathan Cape Ltd.; *Frank Lloyd Wright: Writings and Buildings*, copyright 1960, reprinted by permission of the publisher, Horizon Press; Jean Arp; *On My Way*, DOCUMENTS OF MODERN ART, Vol. 6, George Wittenborn, Inc., New York, N.Y. 10021; *Arp*, selected from the article "Looking" by Jean Hans Arp in *Arp*, edited by James Thrall Soby, copyright 1958 by The Museum of Modern Art, New York; John Canaday, "Sculptures Spin in Recital at Modern Museum" © 1961 by The New York Times Company, reprinted by permission; Vincent Canby, "City Unplugs a Neon Art Show" © 1966 by The New York Times Company, reprinted by permission; C. W. Ceram, *Archaeology of the Cinema*, Thames and Hudson, Ltd.; Marcel Duchamp, *The Bride Stripped Bare by Her Bachelors, Even*, DOCUMENTS OF MODERN ART, Vol. 14, George Wittenborn, Inc., New York, N.Y. 10021; *Rodin*, selected from an article by George Bernard Shaw that first appeared in the December 2, 1932 issue of *Annales Politiques et Littéraires* (Paris); translated from the French by Albert E. Elsen for his book *Rodin* published by the Museum of Modern Art, New York, 1963, all rights reserved; Henri Focillon, *The Life of Forms in Art*, George Wittenborn, Inc., New York, N.Y. 10021; Naum Gabo, *Gabo: Constructions, Sculpture, Paintings, Drawings, Engravings*, reprinted by permission of the publishers, Harvard University Press, Cambridge, Mass., copyright 1957 by Lund, Humphries; Françoise Gilot and Carlton Lake, *Life with Picasso*, Copyright © 1964 by McGraw-Hill, Inc. ©, used by permission of McGraw-Hill Book Company; Walter Gropius, ed., reprinted from *The Theatre of the Bauhaus*, Copyright © 1961 by Wesleyan University, by permission of Wesleyan University Press; Robert L. Herbert, Editor, *Modern Artists on Art: Ten Unabridged Essays*, © 1964, reprinted by permission of Prentice-Hall, Inc.; C. G. Jung, *Modern Man in Search of a Soul*, Routledge & Kegan Paul; Paul Klee, *The Thinking Eye*, DOCUMENTS OF MODERN ART, Vol. 15, George Wittenborn, Inc., New York, N.Y. 10021; A. B. Klein, M. G. E., A. R. P. S., *Colour Music: The Art of Light*, The Technical Press Ltd. 1933. This book was produced in a third edition in 1937 under the title *Coloured Light and Art Medium*, now in current sale; Yves Klein, *Yves Klein*, 1961, reproduced with the authorization of Madame Klein; Max Kozloff, "American Sculpture in Transition," *Arts Magazine*, May/June 1964; Hilton Kramer, "One Inventor, One Pasticheur" © 1966 by The New York Times Company, reprinted by permission; Laszlo Moholy-Nagy, *The New Vision*, DOCUMENTS OF MODERN ART, Vol. 3, George Wittenborn, Inc., New York, N.Y. 10021; "A Dramatic Breakthrough in Art: Collie Sculpture Float in Space," reprinted from the *New York Herald Tribune*, courtesy of the *World Journal Tribune;* "...At Your Friendly Hybrid Dealer" © 1966 by The New York Times Company, reprinted by permission; Ezra Pound, *Gaudier-Brzeska*, all rights reserved. Reprinted by permission of New Directions Publishing Corporation; *The Art of Sculpture* by Herbert Read. Bollingen Series XXXV. 3. The A. W. Mellon Lectures in the Fine Arts for 1954, copyright 1956 by the trustees of the National Gallery of Art, Washington, D.C., published for Bollingen Foundation, New York by Princeton University Press, pages 71, 72; Herbert Read, *The Art of Sculpture*, Faber and Faber Ltd.

Reference Bibliography

PREFACE

GIEDION, S. (1962). *The Eternal Present: The Beginnings of Art* (New York: Pantheon Books).

QUITZSCH, HEINZ (1962). *Die ästhetischen Anschauungen Gottfried Sempers* (Berlin: Akademie Verlag).

RIEGL, ALOIS (1893). *Stilfragen* (Berlin: Richard Carl Schmidt & Co., 1923).

—— (1928). *Gesammelte Aufsätze* (Augsburg-Wien: Dr. Benno Filser Verlag).

SEMPER, GOTTFRIED (1863). *Der Stil in den technischen und tektonischen Künsten oder praktische Ästhetik* (Vol. I, München, 1860; Vol. II, Frankfurt a. M., 1863).

INTRODUCTION

BECK, WILLIAM S. (1957). *Modern Science and the Nature of Life* (New York: Harcourt, Brace & Company).

BEVERIDGE, W. I. B. (revised 1957). *The Art of Scientific Investigation* (New York: W. W. Norton & Company).

BOULDING, KENNETH E. (1964). *The Meaning of the Twentieth Century* (New York: Harper & Row).

ELLUL, JACQUES (1954). *The Technological Society* (New York: Alfred A. Knopf, 1964).

HUXLEY, JULIAN (1957). *New Wine for Old Bottles* (New York: Harper & Row).

JUNG, C. G. (1933). *Modern Man in Search of a Soul* (New York: Harcourt, Brace & Company).

KUHN, THOMAS S. (1962). *The Structure of Scientific Revolutions* (Chicago: The University of Chicago Press).

MADDEN, EDWARD H. (1960). *The Structure of Scientific Thought: An Introduction to Philosophy of Science* (Boston: Houghton, Mifflin Company).

PROGOFF, IRA (1959). *Depth Psychology and Modern Man: A New View of the Magnitude of Human Personality, Its Dimensions & Resources* (New York: The Julian Press).

READ, HERBERT (1964). *A Concise History of Modern Sculpture* (New York: Frederick A. Praeger).

UBBELOHDE, A. R. (1954). *Man and Energy* (Harmondsworth, Middlesex, England: Penguin Books, 1963).

WORRINGER, WILHELM (1908). *Abstraction and Empathy* (New York: International University Press, 1963).

CHAPTER ONE

BACHELARD, GASTON (1958). *The Poetics of Space*, translated by Maria Jolas (New York: The Orion Press, 1963).

BORGHI, MINO (1950). *Medardo Rosso* (Milan: Edizoni del Milione).

CANADAY, JOHN (April 16, 1966). "Constructions on the 'Tensegrity' Principle" *(New York Times)*.

CLOUGH, ROSA TRILLO (1961). *Futurism: The Story of a Modern Movement, A New Appraisal* (New York: Philosophical Library).

—— (October 26, 1964). "A Dramatic Breakthrough in Art: Collie Sculptures Float in Space" (New York *Herald Tribune*).

ELSEN, ALBERT EDWARD (1963). *Rodin* (New York: Museum of Modern Art and Doubleday & Company).

FRAZIER, CHARLES (Summer, 1967). "From a Work Journal of Flying Sculpture" (New York: *Artforum* magazine), pp. 88–92.

GABO, NAUM (1957). *Gabo: Constructions, Sculpture, Paintings, Drawings, Engravings* (Cambridge: Harvard University Press).

GIEDION-WELCKER, CAROLA (1958). *Constantin Brancusi* (Basel: B. Schwabe).

GRAY, CAMILLA (1962). *The Great Experiment: Russian Art; 1863–1922* (New York: Harry N. Abrams).

GRAY, CHRISTOPHER (1953). *Cubist Aesthetic Theories* (Baltimore: Johns Hopkins Press).

HERBERT, ROBERT (ed.) (1964). *Modern Artists on Art* (Englewood Cliffs, N.J.: Prentice-Hall).

JIANOU, IONEL (1963). *Brancusi* (New York: Tudor Publishing).

KRAUSS, ROSALIND (May, 1966). "Allusion and Illusion in Donald Judd" (Los Angeles: *Artforum* magazine), pp. 24–26.

LEBEL, ROBERT (1959). *Marcel Duchamp*, translated by George Heard Hamilton (New York: Grove Press).

MUMFORD, LEWIS (1963). *The Highway and the City* (New York: Harcourt, Brace & World).

OLSON, RUTH, and CHANIN, ABRAHAM (1948). *Naum Gabo–Antoine Pevsner* exhibition catalogue (New York: Museum of Modern Art).

READ, HERBERT (1964). (See entry under Introduction.)

REWALD, JOHN (1944). *Degas: Works in Sculpture* (New York: Pantheon Books).

RINDGE, A. M. (1929). *Sculpture* (New York: Payson and Clarke).

RODIN, AUGUSTE, and GSELL, PAUL (1912). *Art*, translated by Romilly Fedder (Boston: Maynard & Co.).

ROSE, BARBARA (February, 1965). "Looking at American Sculpture" (Los Angeles: *Artforum* magazine), pp. 29–37.

SELZ, JEAN (1963). *Modern Sculpture: Origins and Evolution* (New York: George Braziller).

TRIER, EDUARD (1962). *Form and Space: Sculpture of the Twentieth Century* (New York: Frederick A. Praeger).

CHAPTER TWO

ARNASON, H. H. (1957). *Theodore Roszak* exhibition catalogue (Minneapolis: The Walker Art Center).

ARP, JEAN (1948). *On My Way* (New York: Wittenborn, Schultz).

———— (1958). *Arp* exhibition catalogue (New York: The Museum of Modern Art).

BERGSON, HENRI (1949). *Selections from Bergson.* Harold A. Larrabee (ed.) (New York: Appleton-Century-Crofts).

BERTALANFFY, LUDWIG VON (1949). *Problems of Life: An Evaluation of Modern Biological Thought* (New York: John Wiley & Sons, 1952).

BILL, MAX (1949). *Robert Maillart* (Erlenbach-Zürich: Verlag für Architektur AG.).

BONNER, JOHN TYLER (1952). *Morphogenesis: An Essay on Development* (Princeton: Princeton University Press).

BOREK, ERNST (1965). *The Code of Life* (New York: Columbia University Press).

BRODSKY, HORACE (1938). *Henri Gaudier-Brzeska* (London: Faber & Faber).

DU NOÜY, PIERRE LECOMTE (1947). *Human Destiny* (New York: David McKay).

EISELY, LOREN (1958). *Darwin's Century: Evolution and the Man Who Discovered It* (New York: Doubleday & Company).

ELLIOT, HUGH S. R. (1912). *Modern Science and the Illusions of Professor Bergson* (London: Longmans, Green & Co.).

ELSEN, ALBERT EDWARD (1963). (See entry under Chapter One.)

———— (Winter, 1964–1965). "Lipton's Sculpture as Portrait of the Artist" (New York: *Art Journal*), pp. 113–118.

———— (1965, IX/I) "The Sculptural World of Seymour Lipton" (Lugano: *Art International*), pp. 13–16.

FOCILLON, HENRI (1934). *The Life of Forms in Art*, translated by Charles Beecher Hogan and George Kubler (New Haven: Yale University Press, 1942).

GEIST, SIDNEY (January, 1960). "Brancusi Santificatus" (New York: *Arts* magazine), pp. 26–29.

GIEDION-WELCKER, CAROLA (1937). *Contemporary Sculpture: An Evolution in Volume and Space* (New York: Wittenborn, 1955).

———— (1957). *Hans Arp* (Stuttgart: Verlag Gerd Hatje).

———— (1958). (See entry under Chapter One.)

GOOSSENS, E. C., and GOLDWATER, R. (1959). *Three American Sculptors: Ferber, Hare, Lassaw* (New York: Grove Press).

GROHMANN, WILL (1960). *The Art of Henry Moore* (New York: Harry N. Abrams).

HALDANE, J. S. (1932). *Materialism* (Toronto: Hodder & Stoughton).

HANNA, THOMAS (ed.) (1962). *The Bergsonian Heritage* (New York: Columbia University Press).

HODIN, J. P. (1962). *Barbara Hepworth* (London: Lund Humphries).

JIANOU, IONEL (1963). (See entry under Chapter One.)

KEPES, GYORGY (ed.) (1965). *Structure in Art and Science*, VISION + VALUE series (New York: George Braziller).

KLEE, PAUL (1961). *Paul Klee: The Thinking Eye*, Jürg Spiller (ed.) (London: Lund Humphries); second edition (New York: Wittenborn, 1964).

KUBLER, GEORGE (1962). *The Shape of Time: Re-*

marks on the History of Things (New Haven: Yale University Press).

LOEB, JACQUES (1964). *The Mechanistic Conception of Life* (Cambridge: The Belknap Press of Harvard University Press).

MARTIN, J. L., NICHOLSON, BEN, and GABO, N. (eds.) (1937). *Circle: International Survey of Constructive Art* (London: Faber & Faber).

MOORE, HENRY (July 7, 1963, reprinted August 29, 1963). "Henry Moore Talking: A Conversation with David Sylvester" (London: *The Listener*), pp. 305–307.

MOTHERWELL, ROBERT (ed.) (1951). *The Dada Painters and Poets: An Anthology* (New York: Wittenborn, Schultz).

MUMFORD, LEWIS (1934). *Technics and Civilization* (New York: Harcourt, Brace & World).

—— (ed.) (1952). *Roots of Contemporary American Architecture* (New York: Reinhold Publishing).

POUND, EZRA (1960). *Gaudier-Brzeska: A Memoir* (New York: New Directions Books).

READ, HERBERT (1932). *The Anatomy of Art* (New York: Dodd, Mead & Company).

—— (1933). *Art Now* (New York: Harcourt, Brace & World); second edition (New York: Pitman, 1960).

—— (1934). *Henry Moore, Sculptor* (London: A. Zwemmer).

—— (ed.) (1934). *Unit I: The Modern Movement in English Architecture, Painting and Sculpture* (London: Cassell & Company).

—— (1937). *Art and Society* (London: William Heinmann).

—— (1951). *Art and the Evolution of Man* (London: Freedom Press).

—— (1952). *The Philosophy of Modern Art* (London: Faber & Faber).

—— (1956). *The Art of Sculpture* (New York: Pantheon Books).

—— (1964). (See entry under Introduction.)

RODIN, AUGUSTE, and GSELL, PAUL (1912). (See entry under Chapter One.)

SCHARFSTEIN, BEN-AMI (1943). *Roots of Bergson's Philosophy* (New York: Columbia University Press).

SCHMIDT, GEORG, and SCHENK, ROBERT (1960). *Form in Art and Nature* (Basel: Basilius Presse).

SELZ, PETER (1959a). *Art Nouveau: Art and Design at the Turn of the Century* (New York: The Museum of Modern Art and Doubleday & Company).

—— (1959b). *The New Images of Man* (New York: The Museum of Modern Art and Doubleday & Company).

SEUPHOR, MICHEL (1960). *The Sculpture of This Century* (New York: George Braziller).

SINNOTT, EDMUND W. (1950). *Cell & Psyche: The Biology of Purpose* (Chapel Hill: University of North Carolina Press).

—— (1963). *The Problem of Organic Form* (New Haven: Yale University Press).

SOBY, JAMES THRALL (1958). *Jean Arp* (New York: The Museum of Modern Art and Doubleday & Company).

STALLKNECHT, NEWTON P. (1934). *Studies in the Philosophies of Creation* (Princeton: Princeton University Press).

SULLIVAN, LOUIS HENRY (1901–1902). *Kindergarten Chats and Other Writings* (New York: Wittenborn, Schultz, 1947).

SWEENEY, JAMES JOHNSON (1946). *Henry Moore* (New York: The Museum of Modern Art).

SYLVESTER, DAVID (ed.) (1957). *Henry Moore: Sculpture and Drawings (1921–1948)*, Vol. I, 4th ed. (London: Percy, Lund Humphries & Company).

THOMPSON, D'ARCY WENTWORTH (1917). *On Growth and Form*, 2 vols. (London: Cambridge University Press, 1952).

TOULMIN, STEPHEN, and GOODFIELD, JUNE (1962). *The Architecture of Matter* (New York: Harper & Row).

VARTANIAN, ARAM (1960). *La Mettrie's L'Homme Machine* (Princeton: Princeton University Press).

WACHSMANN, KONRAD (1961). *The Turning Point of Building: Structure and Design* (New York: Reinhold Publishing).

WHYTE, LANCELOT LAW (ed.) (1951). *Aspects of Form: A Symposium on Form in Nature and Art* (London: Percy, Lund Humphries and Company).

—— (1954). *Accent on Form* (New York: Harper & Row).

WIEGAND, CHARMION VON (1957). "The Oriental Tradition and Abstract Art" in *The World of Abstract Art*, The American Abstract Artists (eds.) (New York: George Wittenborn).

WRIGHT, FRANK LLOYD (1960). *Frank Lloyd Wright: Writings and Buildings*, Edgar Kaufman Jr. and Ben Raeburn (eds.) (New York: Horizon Press).

YOUNG, LOUISE B. (1965). *The Mystery of Matter* (New York: Oxford University Press).

CHAPTER THREE

ARCHIPENKO, ALEXANDER (1960). *Archipenko: Fifty Creative Years*, 1908–1958 (New York: Tekhne).

BACHELARD, GASTON (1958). (See entry under Chapter One.)

BANHAM, REYNER (1960). *Theory and Design in the*

First Machine Age (New York: Frederick A. Praeger).

BARR, STEPHEN (1964). *Experiments in Topology* (New York: Thomas Y. Crowell).

BAUDELAIRE, CHARLES (1956). *The Essence of Laughter and Other Essays, Journals and Letters,* Peter Quennell (ed.) (New York: Meridian Books).

BERNIER, ROSAMOND (November, 1956). "Propos d'un Sculpteur: Une Interview d'Antoine Pevsner" (Paris: *L'Oeil: Review d'art.* No. 23), pp. 28–35.

BRAGG, WILLIAM (1925). *Concerning the Nature of Things* (New York: Dover Publications, 1954).

CLARKE, ARTHUR C. (1962). *Profiles of the Future* (New York: Harper & Row).

CONRADS, ULRICH, and SPERLICH, HANS G. (1960). *The Architecture of Fantasy,* translated by G. R. and C. C. Collins (New York: Frederick A. Praeger).

ELLUL, JACQUES (1954). (See entry under Introduction.)

FABER, COLIN (1963). *Candela: The Shell Builder* (New York: Reinhold Publishing).

GABO, NAUM (1957). (See entry under Chapter One.)

GEIST, SIDNEY (1966). "Color It Sculpture" in *Contemporary Sculpture,* Arts Yearbook No. 8 (New York: *Art Digest*), pp. 91–98.

GIEDION-WELCKER, CAROLA (1937). (See entry under Chapter Two.)

GILOT, FRANÇOISE, and LAKE, CARLTON (1964). *Life with Picasso* (New York: McGraw-Hill).

GORDON, WILLIAM J. J. (1961). *Synectics* (New York: Harper & Row).

HILBERT, D., and COHN-VOSSEN, S. (1932). *Geometry and the Imagination* (New York: Chelsea Publishing, 1952).

HOSELITZ, BERT F., and MOORE, WILBERT E. (1963). *Industrialization and Society* (Mouton, France: UNESCO).

JAMMER, MAX (1954). *Concepts of Space* (Cambridge: Harvard University Press).

KEPES, GYORGY (ed.) (1965). (See entry under Chapter Two.)

KLEE, PAUL (1961). (See entry under Chapter Two.)

KNOBLAUGH, RALPH R. (1958). *Modelmaking for Industrial Design* (New York: McGraw-Hill).

LAING, GERALD, and PHILLIPS, PETER (subjects) (April 17, 1966). "...At Your Friendly Hybrid Dealer" (*New York Times*).

LEWIS, ARTHUR O., Jr. (ed.) (1963). *Of Men and Machines* (New York: E. P. Dutton & Co.).

MALDONADO, TOMÁS (ed.) 1955. *Max Bill* (Buenos Aires: ENV Editorial Nueva Visión).

MALEVICH, KASIMIR (1927). *The Non-Objective World,* translated by Howard Dearstyne (Chicago: Paul Theobald and Company, 1959).

MARSAK, LEONARD M. (1964). *The Rise of Science in Relation to Society* (New York: The Macmillan Company).

MOHOLY-NAGY, LÁSZLÓ (1928). *The New Vision, 1928, and Abstract of an Artist* (New York: George Wittenborn, 1946).

MONDRIAN, PIET (1945). *Plastic and Pure Plastic Art, 1937, and Other Essays, 1941–1943* (New York: Wittenborn, Schultz, 3rd edition, 1951).

MUMFORD, LEWIS (1934). (See entry under Chapter Two.)

NEWMAN, JAMES R. (ed.) (1956). *The World of Mathematics,* 4 vols. (New York: Simon and Schuster).

NEWMAN, THELMA R. (1964). *Plastic as an Art Form* (Philadelphia: Chilton Company).

OLSON, RUTH, and CHANIN, ABRAHAM (1948). (See entry under Chapter One.)

RAPPORT, SAMUEL, and WRIGHT, HELEN (eds.) (1963). *Science: Method and Meaning* (New York: New York University Press).

ROSSMAN, JOSEPH (1964). *Industrial Creativity: The Psychology of the Inventor* (New York: University Books).

RUSSELL, BERTRAND (1927). *The Analysis of Matter* (New York: Dover Publications, 1954).

SANDERSON, R. T. (1962). *Teaching Chemistry with Models* (New York: D. Van Nostrand Company).

SEKLER, EDUARD F. (ed.) (1965). *Proportion, A Measure of Order,* exhibition catalogue (Cambridge: Carpenter Center for Visual Arts, Harvard University).

SEUPHOR, MICHEL (1957). *Piet Mondrian: Life and Work* (New York: Harry N. Abrams).

——— (1960). (See entry under Chapter Two.)

SIEGEL, CURT (1962). *Structure and Form in Modern Architecture* (New York: Reinhold Publishing).

SNELSON, KENNETH (July, 1966). "Picture of an Atom" (New York: *Progressive Architecture*), pp. 174–175.

SPENGLER, OSWALD (1918). *The Decline of the West,* abridged edition, translated by Charles Francis Atkinson, Helmut Werner, and Arthur Helps (eds.) (New York: First Modern Library Edition, Random House, 1965).

TOULMIN, STEPHEN, and GOODFIELD, JUNE (1962). (See entry under Chapter Two.)

TRIER, EDWARD (1962). *Form and Space* (New York: Frederick A. Praeger).

VAN MELSEN, ANDREW G. (1961). *Science and Technology,* No. 13 Duquesne Studies (Pittsburg: Duquesne University Press).

VANTONGERLOO, GEORGES (1948). *Paintings, Sculp-*

tures, Reflections (New York: George Wittenborn).

WEYL, HERMANN (1952). *Symmetry* (Princeton: Princeton University Press).

WOLFE, TOM (1965). *The Kandy-Kolored Tangerine-Flake Streamline Baby* (New York: Farrar, Straus and Giroux).

WOLSTENHOLME, GORDON (1963). *Man and His Future* (Boston: Little, Brown and Company).

ZEVI, BRUNO (1957). *Architecture as Space* (New York: Horizon Press).

CHAPTER FOUR

ANTIN, DAVID (April, 1966). "Art & Information, I Grey Paint, Robert Morris" (New York: *Art News*), pp. 23–24, 56.

CANADAY, JOHN (July 25, 1965). "Our National Pride: The World's Worst Sculpture" *(New York Sunday Times)*.

CASSON, STANLEY (1939). *Sculpture of Today* (London: The Studio Publications).

FERM, VERGILIUS (ed.) (1950). *A History of Philosophical Systems* (New York: Philosophical Library).

GARNETT, A. CAMPBELL (1965). *The Perceptual Process* (Madison: University of Wisconsin Press).

GIEDION-WELCKER, CAROLA (1937). (See entry under Chapter Two.)

KAMINSKY, JACK (1962). *Hegel on Art: An Interpretation of Hegel's Aesthetics* (New York: State University of New York).

KLEE, PAUL (1961). (See entry under Chapter Two.)

KOHL, HERBERT (1965). *The Age of Complexity* (New York: The New American Library).

KOZLOFF, MAX (May–June, 1964). "American Sculpture in Transition" (New York: *Arts* magazine), pp. 24–31.

KRAUSS, ROSALIND (May, 1966). "Allusion and Illusion in Donald Judd" (Los Angeles: *Artforum* magazine), pp. 24–26.

MERLEAU-PONTY, MAURICE (1948). *Sense and Non-Sense*, translated by Hubert L. Dreyfus and Patricia Allen Dreyfus (Evanston: Northwestern University Press, 1964).

——— (1960) *Signs*, translated by Richard C. McCleary (Evanston: Northwestern University Press, 1964).

MORRIS, ROBERT (February, 1966). Untitled essay (Los Angeles: *Artforum* magazine), pp. 42–44.

ROSE, BARBARA (February, 1965). "Looking at American Sculpture" (Los Angeles: *Artforum* magazine), pp. 29–36.

THEVENAZ, PIERRE (1962). *What Is Phenomenology?: And Other Essays* (Chicago: Quadrangle Books).

WHITE, MORTON (1955). *The Age of Analysis: Twentieth Century Philosophers* (New York: The New American Library).

WILENSKI, R. H. (1932). *The Meaning of Modern Sculpture* (Boston: Beacon Press, 1961).

CHAPTER FIVE

BARRON, JOHN (1965). *Greek Sculpture* (New York: E. P. Dutton and Co.).

BAUDELAIRE, CHARLES (1955). *The Mirror of Art: Critical Studies*, translated and edited by Jonathan Mayne (New York: Doubleday & Company, 1956).

BREASTED, JAMES (1948). *Egyptian Servant Statues* (New York: Pantheon Books).

CANADAY, JOHN (1959). *Mainstreams of Modern Art* (New York: Henry Holt and Co.).

CHAPUIS, ALFRED, and DROZ, EDMOND (1958). *Automata: A Historical and Technological Study* (Neuchâtel, Switzerland: Editions du Griffon).

CLEATOR, P. E. (1955). *The Robot Era* (London: George Allen & Unwin).

COWAN, HARRISON J. (1958). *Time and Its Measurement* (Cleveland: World Publishing).

DESPLACIS, M. (ed.) (1854). *Biographie Universal* (Paris: Chez Madame C. Desplacis, 2nd edition), pp. 17–19.

DIJKSTERHUIS, E. J. (1963). *The Mechanization of the World Picture* (New York: Oxford University Press).

DUCHAMP, MARCEL (1960). *The Bride Stripped Bare by Her Bachelors, Even*, translated by George Heard Hamilton, Richard Hamilton (ed.) (New York: George Wittenborn).

DUCHAMP, MARCEL (1960). *The Green Box* (New Haven: The Readymade Press, 1957, 1st ed.).

ECO, UMBERTO, and ZORZOLI G. B. (1963). *The Picture History of Inventions* (New York: The Macmillan Co.).

FLAXMAN, JOHN (1829). *Lectures on Sculpture* (London: John Murray).

GRAY, CHRISTOPHER (1953). (See entry under Chapter One.)

GROPIUS, WALTER (ed.) (1957). *The Theatre of the Bauhaus* (Middletown, Connecticut: Wesleyan University Press).

HAMILTON, EDITH (1940). *Mythology* (New York: Mentor Books, 1953).

HAMMACHER, A. M. (1962). *Jacques Lipchitz: His Sculpture* (London: Thames and Hudson).

HARRISON, JANE ELLEN (1913). *Ancient Art and Ritual* (New York: Henry Holt and Co.).

HERODOTUS (5th cen. A.D.) *The History of Herodotus* (Vol. 2), translated by George Rawlinson (New York: The Tandy-Thomas Company, 1909).

HOFFMAN, EDITH (1947). *Kokoschka: Life and*

Work (London: Faber and Faber).

JOSEPHSON, ERIC and MARY (eds.) (1962). *Man Alone: Alienation in Modern Society* (New York: Dell Publishing).

JOUFFROY, ALAIN (no publishing date). *Bellmer* (London: Lund, Humphries & Co.).

LEBEL, ROBERT (1959). (See entry under Chapter One.)

LEWIS, ARTHUR O. (ed.) (1963). (See entry under Chapter Three.)

MILHAM, WILLIS I. (1941). *Time and Timekeepers* (New York: The Macmillan Co.).

MOTHERWELL, ROBERT (ed.) (1951). (See entry under Chapter Two.)

OVID (PUBLIUS OVIDIUS NASO) (1st cen. A.D.). *Metamorphoses*, translated by Rolfe Humpheries (Bloomington: Indiana University Press, 1955).

PALLOLTINO, MASSIMO (ed. in chief) (1958). *Encyclopedia of World Art*, Vol. 2 American edition (New York: McGraw-Hill, 1959), pp. 182–191.

PAUSANIUS (2nd cen. A.D.). *Pausanias' Descriptions of Greece*, translated by A. R. Shilleto (London: George Bell and Sons, 1905).

SCHLEMMER, OSKAR (1958). *Oskar Schlemmer, Briefs und Tagebücher*, Tut Schlemmer (ed.) (München: Langen-Muller).

SCHNEER, CECIL B. (1960). *The Search for Order* (New York: Harper & Row).

SELTMAN, CHARLES (1960). *Approach to Greek Sculpture* (New York: E. P. Dutton & Co.).

SOBY, JAMES THRALL (1955). *Giorgio de Chirico* (New York: Museum of Modern Art).

TOULMIN, STEPHEN, and GOODFIELD, JUNE (1965). *The Discovery of Time* (New York: Harper & Row).

VASARI, GIORGIO (1550). *Lives of Seventy of the Most Eminent Painters, Sculptors and Architects*, E. H. and E. W. Blashfield and A. A. Hopkins (eds.) (New York: Charles Scribner's Sons, 1886).

VON BOEHN, MAX (1936). *Dolls and Puppets* (New York: David McKay).

WILENSKI, R. H. (1932). (See entry under Chapter Four.)

WINGLER, HANS M. (ed.) (1962). *Das Bauhaus* (Bramsche bei Osnabrück: Verlag Gebr. Rasch & Co.).

WRIGHT, FRANK LLOYD (1960). (See entry under Chapter Two.)

CHAPTER SIX

ANONYMOUS (January, 1964). *For Eyes and Ears*, exhibition catalogue (New York: Cordier & Ekstrom Gallery).

———— (March 13, 1961). "For Movement's Sake" (New York: *Newsweek* magazine).

———— (November, 1962). *Yves Klein*, memorial exhibition catalogue (New York: Alexander Iolas Gallery).

———— (April–June, 1965). *nul negentienhonderd vijf en zestig—deel 1 teksten* and *deel 2 foto's*. 2 vols., exhibition catalogue (Amsterdam: Stedelijk Museum).

BANHAM, REYNER (1960). (See entry under Chapter Three.)

BANN, STEPHEN; GADNEY, REG; POPPER, FRANK; and STEADMAN, PHILLIP (1966). *Four Essays on Kinetic Art* (St. Albans, Herts, England: Motion Books).

BURY, POL (March–April, 1966). *Twice Pol Bury*, exhibition catalogue with an essay by Eugène Ionesco (New York: Lefebre Gallery).

CANADAY, JOHN (April 6, 1961). "Sculptures Spin in Recital at Modern Museum," article on Len Ley (*New York Times*).

DE BROGLIE, LOUIS (1955). *Physics and Microphysics*, translated by Martin Davidson (New York: Pantheon Books).

ECO, UMBERTO (1962). *Arte Programmata*, exhibition catalogue, with essay by Eco (Milan: Societa Olivetti).

EIMERT, HERBERT, and STOCKHAUSEN, KARLHEINZ (eds.) (1957). *Die Reihe: No. 3 Musical Craftsmanship*, translated from the German (Bryn Mawr, Pennsylvania: Theodore Presser Co., 1959).

———— (eds.) (1960). *Die Reihe: No. 7 Form—Space*, translated from the German (Bryn Mawr, Pennsylvania: Theodore Presser Co., 1965).

ELLUL, JACQUES (1954). (See entry under Introduction.)

FONTANA, LUCIO (1962). *Devenir de Fontana*, Michel Tapie (ed.) (Turin: Edizioni d'Arte Fratelli Pozzo).

FOX, JAMES (June–July, 1965). "Soto Voce Ad Infinitum" (London: *Signals* newsbulletin), p. 15.

GABO, NAUM (1957). (See entry under Chapter One.)

GIANI, GIAMPIERO (ed.) (1957). *Spazialismo* (Milan: Conchiglia, 2nd edition).

GIBSON, JAMES J. (1950). *The Perception of the Visual World* (Boston: Houghton, Mifflin Company).

GIEDION, S. (1948). *Mechanization Takes Command: A Contribution to Anonymous History* (New York: Oxford University Press).

G.R.A.V. (April, 1962). *Groupe de Recherche d'Art Visuel: Paris 1962*, manifesto and statements by the artists with an essay by Guy Habasque (Paris: Galerie Denise René).

———— (November–December, 1962). *L'Instabilité*, exhibition catalogue (New York: The Contemporaries Gallery).

———— (1963). *L'Instabilité*, statements by the

artists, Charles Minvielle (ed.) (Paris: Minvielle à Paris).

——— (1965). *Labyrinthe III*, exhibition catalogue (New York: The Contempories Gallery).

HERBERT, ROBERT (ed.) (1964). (See entry under Chapter One.)

HUNTER, SAM (ed.) (November–January, 1966). *Two Kinetic Sculptors: Nicolas Schöffer and Jean Tinguely*, with essays by Jean Cassou, K. G. Hulten, and Sam Hunter, exhibition catalogue (New York: Jewish Museum and October House).

JORAY, MARCEL (ed.) (1963). *Nicolas Schöffer* (Neuchâtel, Switzerland: Editions du Griffon).

KEPES, GYORGY (ed.) (1965). *The Nature and Art of Motion*, VISION + VALUE series (New York: George Braziller).

KLEIN, YVES (1961). *Yves Klein*, statement by the artist, assisted by Neil Levine and John Archambault (New York: Alexander Iolas Gallery).

KRAMER, HILTON (November 28, 1965). "One Inventor, One Pasticheur," review of exhibition at The Jewish Museum, New York (*New York Sunday Times*).

KULTERMANN, UDO (ed.) (March–May, 1964). *Neue Tendenzen*, exhibition catalogue (Leverkusen, West Germany: Städtisches Museum).

LEBEL, ROBERT (1959). (See entry under Chapter One.)

LEIDER, PHILLIP (May, 1966). "Kinetic Sculpture at Berkeley" (Los Angeles: *Artforum* magazine), pp. 40–44.

LE PARC, JULIO (September, 1962). *à propos de: art-spectacle, spectateur-actif, instabilité et programmation dans l'art visuel*, essay by Julio Le Parc (Paris: G.R.A.V.).

LEWIS, ARTHUR O. (ed.) (1963). (See entry under Chapter Three.)

LYE, LEN (March–April, 1965). *Len Lye's Bounding Steel Sculptures*, exhibition catalogue (New York: Howard Wise Gallery).

MOHOLY-NAGY, LÁSZLÓ (1930). *The New Vision: From Material to Architecture* (New York: Brewer, Warren & Putnam, 1932).

——— (1938). *The New Vision: Fundamentals of Design, Painting, Sculpture, Architecture* (New York: W. W. Norton & Company, revised edition of 1930 book).

——— (1947). *Vision in Motion* (Chicago: Paul Theobald).

MOHOLY-NAGY, SYBIL (1950). *Moholy-Nagy: Experiment in Totality* (New York: Harper & Row).

——— (June, 1966). "Constructivism from Kasimir Malevich to László Moholy-Nagy" (*Arts and Architecture* magazine, pp. 24–28).

PEETERS, HENK, and DE VRIES, HERMAN (eds.) (November, 1961). *nul = 0*, magazine devoted to the New Tendency (Arnhem, Holland: *nul = 0*).

——— (April, 1963). *nul = 0* (Arnhem, Holland: *nul = 0*).

PIENE, OTTO, and MACK, HEINZ (eds.) (1961). *ZERO*, Vol. 3 (Düsseldorf: ZERO).

REULEAUX, FRANZ (1876). *The Kinematics of Machinery*, translated from the German (New York: Dover Publications, 1963).

RICKEY, GEORGE (1956). "Kinetic Art" from *Art and Artist* (Berkeley and Los Angeles: University of California Press), pp. 149–178.

——— (September, 1961). "The Kinetic International" (New York: *Arts* magazine), pp. 16–21.

——— (1964). *George Rickey/Kinetic Sculptures*, exhibition catalogue with writings by the artist, Joan Lukash (ed.) (Boston: Institute of Contemporary Art).

SEITZ, WILLIAM C. (ed.) (1965). *The Responsive Eye*, exhibition catalogue (New York: The Museum of Modern Art and Doubleday & Company).

SELZ, PETER (ed.) (March–May, 1966). *Directions in Kinetic Sculpture*, exhibition catalogue with essays by Peter Selz and George Rickey with statements by the artists (Berkeley, California: University Art Gallery, University of California).

SOTO, JESUS-RAPHAEL (November–December, 1965). "Soto at Signals, London," issue devoted to Jesus-Raphael Soto in *Signals* newsbulletin.

SPENGLER, OSWALD (1918). (See entry under Chapter Three.)

SWEENEY, JAMES JOHNSON (ed.) (1943). *Calder*, exhibition catalogue (New York: Museum of Modern Art).

TAKIS (October–November, 1964). "Takis Issue" (London: *Signals* newsbulletin).

——— (June–July, 1965). "The Takis Dialogues: 'Towards the Invisible,' Part One," edited by David Medalla (London: *Signals* newsbulletin).

TINGUELY, JEAN (September, 1964). "Some Statements by Jean Tinguely" (London: *Signals* newsbulletin).

TOMKINS, CALVIN (1965). *The Bride & The Bachelors: The Heretical Courtship in Modern Art* (New York: Viking Press).

TOULMIN, STEPHEN, and GOODFIELD, JUNE (1962). (See entry under Chapter Two.)

VASARELY, VICTOR (April, 1955). "Notes for a Manifesto" in the exhibition catalogue, *Le Mouvement*, with essays by K. G. Hulten and Roger Bordier (Paris: Galerie Denise René).

——— (1962). *Vasarely: Notes, Reflexions* (Paris: Bureau Culturel de l'Ecole Nationale Supérieure des Beaux Arts).

——— (1965). *Vasarely*, translated by Haakon Chevalier (Neuchâtel, Switzerland: Editions du Griffon).

WEMBER, PAUL (ed.) (1963). *Bewegte Bereiche der Kunst*, exhibition catalogue for the Kaiser Wilhelm Museum, Krefeld, (Krefeld, West Germany: Scherpe Verlag).

WHITTAKER, EDMUND (1948). *From Euclid to Eddington: A Study of the Conceptions of the External World* (New York: Dover Publications).

ZOCCHI, JUAN (1946). *Lucio Fontana* (Buenos Aires: Editorial Poseidon).

CHAPTER SEVEN

ANONYMOUS (March 18, 1966). "A Times Square of the Mind" (New York: *Time* magazine).

——— (May 21, 1966). "Now It's Neon: Exhibition at the University of Pennsylvania, Institute of Contemporary Art" (New York: *Life* magazine).

——— (May 2, 1966). "3-Dimensional Photos? The Gas Laser May Do It" (*Chicago Sun Times*).

APPLE, BILLY (February, 1967). "Live Stills" (New York: *Arts* magazine), pp. 46–47.

ARCHIPENKO, ALEXANDER (1960). (See entry under Chapter Three.)

BANN, STEPHEN; GADNEY, REG; POPPER, FRANK; and STEADMAN, PHILIP (1966). (See entry under Chapter Six.)

BITZER, D. L., and SLOTTOW, H. G. (1966). "The Plasma Display Panel—A Digitally Addressable Display with Inherent Memory" (*Proceedings—Fall Joint Computer Conference*, pp. 541–547).

BLAKE, EDWARD M., and WILFRED, THOMAS (March, 1948). "Letters Pro and Con" (Urbana: *The Journal of Aesthetics & Art Criticism*, pp. 265–276).

CANBY, VINCENT (October 8, 1966). "City Unplugs a Neon Art Show" (*New York Times*).

CERAM, C. W. (1965). *Archaeology of the Cinema* (New York: Harcourt, Brace & World).

CHRYSSA (March–April, 1966). *Chryssa*, exhibition catalogue (New York: The Pace Gallery).

COE, RALPH T. (January, 1966). "Post-Pop Possibilities: Howard Jones" (Lugano: *Art International*).

ERNST, JOHN (December, 1960). "Nicolas Schöffer" (New York: *Architectural Design*), pp. 517–520.

FONTANA, LUCIO (1962). (See entry under Chapter Six.)

GADDIS, VINCENT H. (1967). *Mysterious Fires and Lights* (New York: David McKay, Inc.).

HEALY, JOHN, and Group N and Group T (June, 1964). *Luminous Pictures* and *Arte Programmata*, exhibition catalogue, Royal College of Art, London (London: Olivetti Company).

JORAY, MARCEL (ed.) (1963). (See entry under Chapter Six.)

KEPES, GYORGY (1965). *Light as a Creative Medium—Harvard University*, exhibition catalogue (Cambridge: Harvard University).

KLEIN, ADRIAN BERNARD (1927). *Colour-Music: The Art of Light* (London: Crosby Lockwood and Son, 1930).

MOHOLY-NAGY, LÁSZLÓ (1938). (See entry under Chapter Six.)

——— (1947). (See entry under Chapter Six.)

MOHOLY-NAGY, SYBIL (1950). (See entry under Chapter Six.)

PIENE, NAN (May–June, 1967). "Light Art" (New York: *Art in America*), pp. 24–47.

PIENE, OTTO (March–April, 1961). *Otto Piene—10 Texte*, writings for an exhibition (Frankfurt: Dato Galerie).

——— (November, 1965). *Piene: Light Ballet*, exhibition catalogue (New York: Howard Wise Gallery).

POPPER, FRANK (May–August, 1967). *Lumière et mouvement*, exhibition catalogue (Paris: Musée d'Art Moderne de la Ville de Paris).

RAYSSE, MARTIAL (November–December, 1964). *Martial Raysse*, exhibition catalogue, essays by John Ashbery and Pierre Restany (New York: Alexander Iolas Gallery).

RUECHARDT, EDUARD (1952). *Light: Visible and Invisible*, translated from the German by Frank Gaynor (Ann Arbor: The University of Michigan Press, 1958).

SCHOENER, ALLON (March–April, 1966). "2066 and All That" (New York: *Art in America*), pp. 40–43.

SHARP, WILLOUGHBY (April–May, 1967), *Light/Motion/Space*, exhibition catalogue (Minneapolis: Walker Art Center).

WILFRED, THOMAS (1935). *The Art Institute of Light Presents Thomas Wilfred in a Clavilux Recital*, exhibition catalogue (New York: Art Institute of Light).

——— (June, 1947). "Light and the Artist" (Urbana: *The Journal of Aesthetics & Art Criticism*).

WINGLER, HANS M. (1962). (See entry under Chapter Five.)

CHAPTER EIGHT

ABEEL, ERICA (December, 1966–January, 1967). "Armory '66: Not Quite What We Had in Mind" (New York: *Arts* magazine), pp. 23–24.

ALLOWAY, LAWRENCE (1963). *Eduardo Paolozzi: The Metalization of a Dream* (London: Lion and

Unicorn Press).

ANONYMOUS (February 21, 1966). "Latin Labyrinth" (New York: *Newsweek* magazine).

———— (March 4, 1966). "Castro-Cid's Tinkered
Toys for Adults" (New York: *Time* magazine).

———— (May 12, 1966). "Radcliffe Girl Bolts,
Weds Man of Iron" (*Chicago Daily News*).

———— and BOURBON, DAVID (August 12, 1966).
"Sculpture in Motion" (New York: *Life* magazine), pp. 40–49.

———— (October 31, 1966). "Jammed Doors"
(New York: *Newsweek* magazine).

———— (June, 1967). "Computerized Dummy"
(New York: *Science Digest*), p. 1.

ASHBY, W. ROSS (1956). *An Introduction to Cybernetics* (New York: John Wiley & Sons, 1958).

BARNES, CLIVE (October 15, 1966). "Dance or
Something at the Armory" (*New York Times*).

BEER, STAFFORD (1959). *Cybernetics and Manage-
ment* (New York: John Wiley & Sons).

BELL, D. A. (1962). *Intelligent Machines: An Introduction to Cybernetics* (New York: Blaisdell
Publishing).

BENSE, MAX (1960). *Programmierung des Schönen:
Allgemeine Texttheorie und Textästhetik* (Baden-
Baden and Krefeld: Agis Verlag).

BERKSON, W. (November, 1965). "Sculpture of
Larry Rivers" (New York: *Arts* magazine),
pp. 49–52.

BRADBURY, RAY (October, 1965). "The Machine-
Tooled Happyland" (New York: *Holiday*
magazine), pp. 100–104.

BREER, ROBERT (February–March, 1966). *Robert
Breer: Floats*, exhibition catalogue (New York:
Galeria Bonino).

CHABAUD, JEAN (1962). *Jean Chabaud*, exhibition
catalogue (Turin, Italy: International Center of
Aesthetic Research).

COHEN, DANIEL (December, 1963). "The Living
Lincoln" (New York: *Science Digest*), p. 15.

CULBERSON, JAMES T. (1963). *The Minds of Robots:
Sense Data, Memory Images, and Behavior in
Conscious Automata* (Urbana: University of
Illinois).

EIMERT, HERBERT, and STOCKHAUSEN, KARLHEINZ
(eds.) (1955). *Die Reihe: No. I Electronic Music*,
translated from the German (Bryn Mawr, Pennsylvania: Theodore Presser, 1962, 3rd. ed.).

ELLUL, JACQUES (1954). (See entry under Introduction.)

Experiments in Art and Technology (October,
1966). *9 evenings: theatre and engineering*, program for nine performances held at the 25th
Street Armory, N.Y.C. (New York: E.A.T.).

———— (January 15, 1967). *E.A.T. News*, Vol. I,
No. 1.

———— (June 1, 1967). *E.A.T. News*, Vol. I, No. 2.

FEIGENBAUM, EDWARD A., and FELDMAN, JULIAN
(eds.) (1963). *Computers and Thought* (New
York: McGraw-Hill).

FRIED, MICHAEL (Summer, 1967). "Art and
Objecthood" (New York: *Artforum* magazine),
pp. 12–23.

GAGNE, ROBERT M. (ed.) (1962). *Psychological
Principles in System Development* (New York:
Holt, Rinehart and Winston).

GIEDION, S. (1962). (See entry under Preface.)

GLUECK, GRACE (November 6, 1966). "I Can't Give
Anything But Light, Baby" (*New York Times*).

GUNTHER, GOTTHARD (1957). *Bewusstsein und Maschinen: Eine Metaphysik der Kybernetik* (Baden-
Baden and Krefeld: Agis Verlag).

HALACY, D. S., Jr. (1965). *Cyborg: Evolution of a
Superman* (New York: Harper & Row).

HAUSER, ARNOLD (1951). *The Social History of
Art*, Vol. I, translated from the German, (New
York: Vintage Books, 1964).

HOLTON, GERALD (ed.) (1965). *Science and Culture:
A Study of Cohesive and Disjunctive Forces* (Boston: Houghton, Mifflin Company).

LANDERS, RICHARD R. (1966). *Man's Place in the
Dybosphere* (Englewood Cliffs, N.J.: Prentice-
Hall).

LATIL, PIERRE DE (1953). *Thinking by Machine: A
Study of Cybernetics* (Boston: Houghton, Mifflin Company, 1956).

LEAR, JOHN (March 5, 1966). "The Robot on the
Moon" (New York: *Saturday Review*), pp. 57–65.

LE PARC, JULIO (September, 1962). (See entry
under Chapter Six.)

MACGOWAN, ROGER A., and ORDWAY, FREDE-
RICK I. (1966). *Intelligence in the Universe*
(Englewood Cliffs, N.J.: Prentice-Hall).

MATTOX, CHARLES (February, 1966), sculpture by
Charles Mattox, untitled (Los Angeles: *Artforum*
magazine).

MOLES, ABRAHAM (1958). *Théorie de l'information
et perception esthétique* (Paris: Flammarion,
Editeur).

MOSHER, RALPH S. (October, 1964). "Industrial
Manipulators" (New York: *Scientific American*),
pp. 88–96.

O'TOOLE, THOMAS (March 30, 1966). "Walking
Truck Is Drafted by U.S. Army" *(New York
Times)*.

PAIK, NAM JUNE (November–December, 1965).
Nam June Paik: Electronic Art, exhibition catalogue, (New York: Galeria Bonino).

PASK, GORDON (1961). *An Approach to Cybernetics*
(New York: Harper & Row).

PAXTON, STEVE, and ROBINSON, ROBBY (February,
1967). "Art & Technology: A Dialogue" (*IKON*

magazine), pp. 16–21.

PROGOFF, IRA (1959). *Depth Psychology and Modern Man* (New York: Julian Press).

READ, HERBERT (1956). (See entry under Chapter Two.)

SCHMECK, HAROLD M. (June 3, 1966). "Surveyor I Is Larger and More Complex Than Luna 9" (*New York Times*).

SELZ, PETER (March–May, 1966). (See entry under Chapter Six.)

SPENGLER, OSWALD (1918). (See entry under Chapter Three.)

VEBLEN, THORSTEIN (1914). *The Instinct of Workmanship: And the State of the Industrial Arts* (New York: The Macmillan Co.).

WALTER, W. GREY (1953). *The Living Brain* (New York: W. W. Norton & Company).

WHITMAN, SIMONE, and KLÜVER, BILLY (February, 1967). "Theatre and Engineering: An Experiment (I. Notes by a Participant and Notes by an Engineer)" (New York: *Artforum* magazine), pp. 26–33.

WIENER, NORBERT (1948). *Cybernetics: Or Control and Communication in the Animal and the Machine* (Cambridge, M.I.T. Press, 2nd ed.).

——— (1950). *The Human Use of Human Beings: Cybernetics and Society* (Boston: Houghton, Mifflin Company).

WILFORD, JOHN NOBLE (March 29, 1966). "A Manned Mission to Mars Opposed" (*New York Times*).

YOVITS, MARSHALL C., and CAMERON, SCOTT (eds.) (1960). *Self-Organizing Systems* (New York: Pergamon Press).

List of Illustrations

19. Robert Grosvenor, *Transoxiana*, 1965. Courtesy, Park Place Gallery, New York.

20. Morio Shinoda, *Tension and Compression 32*, 1963. Courtesy of the artist.

21. Alberto Collie, *Floatile No. II*, 1967. Courtesy, Lee Nordness Galleries, New York. Photograph, Geoffrey Clements.

22. Robert Grosvenor. *Floating Sculpture*, 1966–1967. Courtesy, Park Place Gallery, New York.

23. Hans Haacke, *Sphere in Oblique Air-Jet*, 1967. Courtesy of the artist.

CHAPTER TWO:

24. Henri Gaudier-Brzeska, *Birds Erect*, 1914. Collection, Museum of Modern Art, New York. Gift of Mrs. W. Murray Crane.

25. Constantin Brancusi, *Sleeping Muse*, 1910. Courtesy, Art Institute of Chicago.

26. Constantin Brancusi, *The Beginning of the World (Sculpture for the Blind)*, 1924. Philadelphia Museum of Art. The Louise and Walter Arensberg Collection.

27. Jean Arp, *Human Concretion*, 1949, cast stone after 1935 original plaster. Collection, Museum of Modern Art, New York. Gift of the Advisory Committee.

28. Jean Arp, *Crown of Buds*, 1936. Collection, Mr. and Mrs. Samuel M. Kootz.

29. Jean Arp, *Growth*, 1938. Collection, Philadelphia Museum of Art.

30. Henry Moore, *Four Piece Composition*, (Reclining Figure), 1934. Collection, Martha Jackson. Photography courtesy, Martha Jackson Gallery, New York.

31. Henry Moore, *Reclining Figure, II*, 1960. Collection, Museum of Modern Art, New York. Given in memory of G. David Thompson, Jr. by his father.

32. Henry Moore, *Sculpture (Locking Piece)*, 1962. Courtesy of the artist.

33. Theodore Roszak, *Thorn Blossom*, 1948. Collection, Whitney Museum of American Art, New York.

34. Ibram Lassaw, *Kwannon*, 1952. Collection, Museum of Modern Art, New York. Katharine Cornell Fund.

35. Seymour A. Lipton, *Jungle Bloom*, 1954. Collection, Yale University Art Gallery, New Haven. Gift of Mrs. Frederick W. Hilles.

36. Seymour Lipton, *Sentinel*, 1959. Collection, Yale University Art Gallery, New Haven.

CHAPTER THREE:

37. David Smith, *Cubi XVIII*, 1964. From the Estate of David Smith. Photograph, Marlborough-Gerson Gallery, New York.

38. David Smith. *Cubi XXIII*, 1964. Collection Los Angeles County Museum of Art. Gift of Contemporary Art Council.

39. Anthony Caro, *Homage to David Smith*, 1966. Courtesy, Mrs. Mary H. D. Swift. Photograph, Andre Emmerich Gallery.

40. Gerald Laing and Peter Phillips, *Hybrid*, 1965. Courtesy, Kornblee Gallery, New York.

41. Naum Gabo, *Construction in Space*, 1928. Philadelphia Museum of Art. A. E. Gallatin Collection.

42. Kenneth Snelson, *Atom*, 1964. Courtesy, Dwan Gallery, New York.

43. Georges Vantongerloo, *Drawing for a Construction in an Inscribed and Circumscribed Square of a Circle*, 1924. From Georges Vantongerloo: "Paintings. Sculptures, Reflections" (Series: *Problems of Contemporary Art*, Volume 5). Courtesy, George Wittenborn, Inc., New York.

44. Georges Vantongerloo, *Construction in an Inscribed and Circumscribed Square of a Circle*, 1924. From Georges Vantongerloo: "Paintings, Sculptures, Reflections" (Series: *Problems of Contemporary Art*, Volume 5). Collection, Peggy Guggenheim Foundation, Venice. Courtesy, George Wittenborn, Inc., New York.

45. Georges Vantongerloo, *Drawing for a Construction Based on an Equilateral Hyperbola, XY=K*, 1929. From Georges Vantongerloo: "Paintings, Sculptures, Reflections" (Series: *Problems of Contemporary Art*, Volume 5). Courtesy, George Wittenborn, Inc., New York.

46. Georges Vantongerloo, *Construction Based on an Equilateral Hyperbola, XY = K*, 1929. From Georges Vantongerloo: "Paintings, Sculptures, Reflections" (Series: *Problems of Contemporary Art*, Volume 5). Courtesy, George Wittenborn, Inc., New York.

47. Antoine Pevsner, *Developable Surface*, 1936. Courtesy of Mme. Virginie Pevsner.

48. Antoine Pevsner, *Developable Column*, 1942. Collection, Museum of Modern Art, New York.

49. Naum Gabo, *Linear Construction*, 1942. Collection, Solomon R. Guggenheim Museum, New York.

50. Naum Gabo, *Translucent Variation on Spheric Theme*, 1951 version of 1937 original. Collection, Solomon R. Guggenheim Museum, New York.

51. Max Bill, *Endless Ribbon*, 1935–1953. Collection, Openair Museum for Sculpture, Middelheim, Antwerp. Photography by Jean De Maeyer, Antwerp.

52. Max Bill, *Monoangulated Surface in Space*, 1959. Courtesy, Detroit Institute of Arts.

53. Max Bill, *Continuous Surface in Form of a Column*, 1953–1958. Collection, Albright-Knox Art Gallery, Buffalo, New York. Gift of Seymour H. Knox.

54. Edwin Hauer, *Identical and Complementary Volumes*, 1958. Courtesy of the artist.

55. Claes Oldenburg, *Dual Hamburgers*, 1962. Collection, Museum of Modern Art, New York. Philip C. Johnson Fund.

56. Donald Judd, *Untitled*, 1965. Collection, Whitney Museum of American Art, New York. Gift of the Howard and Jean Lipman Foundation, Inc.

57. Alexander Archipenko, *Woman Combing Her Hair*, 1915. Collection, Museum of Modern Art, New York. Acquired through the Lillie P. Bliss Bequest.

58. Barbara Hepworth, *Hollow Form (Penwith)*, 1955–1956. Collection, Museum of Modern Art, New York. Gift of Dr. and Mrs. Arthur Lejwa.

59. Larry Bell, *Untitled*, 1966. Courtesy, Pace Gallery, New York.

60. Vladimir Tatlin, *Monument to the Third International*, 1920. Reproduced from *The Great Experiment: Russian Art 1863–1922* by courtesy of Miss Camilla Gray.

61. Deborah de Moulpied, *Form No. 4*, 1960 (Vinyl). Courtesy of the artist.

62. Julio Gonzalez, *Maternity*, 1933. Reprinted from "Julio Gonzalez." Courtesy, Museum of Modern Art, New York. Collection, Moderna Museet, Stockholm.

63. Isamu Noguchi, *The Cry*, 1962. Collection, Albright-Knox Art Gallery, Buffalo, New York. George Cary and Elisabeth H. Gates Funds.

64. David von Schlegell, *Needle*, 1967. Courtesy, Art Institute of Chicago.

65. Kenneth Snelson, *Audry 1*, 1966. Courtesy, Dwan Gallery, New York.

66. José de Rivera, *Brussels Construction*, 1958. Courtesy, Art Institute of Chicago.

67. Hans Breder, *Untitled*, 1966. Courtesy, Mr. and Mrs. Gustave Rath.

68. Will Horwitt, *Growth*, 1959. Courtesy, Wadsworth Atheneum, Hartford. Photograph taken by the author.

94. Francisco Sobrino, *Juxtaposition Superimposition C*, 1962–1963. Courtesy, The Contemporaries, New York.

95. François Morellet, *Sphere-Web*, 1962. Courtesy, The Contemporaries, New York.

96. Joël Stein, *Trihedral: With Manipulatable Elements*, 1964. Courtesy, The Contemporaries, New York.

97. Heinz Mack, *Light Dynamo No. 2*, 1966. Courtesy, Howard Wise Gallery, New York.

98. George Rickey, *Two Lines-Temporal I*, 1964. Collection, Museum of Modern Art, New York. Mrs. Simon Guggenheim Fund.

99. Len Lye, *Loop* (still), 1963. Courtesy, Art Institute of Chicago.

100. Takis, Installation photo of 1967 exhibition at Howard Wise Gallery, New York. Courtesy, Howard Wise Gallery.

101. Pol Bury, *18 Superimposed Balls*, 1965. Collection, Mr. and Mrs. Chapin Riley. Photograph, Lefebre Gallery, New York.

102. Julio Le Parc, *Continuel-Mobile Suspended*, 1962. Courtesy, Howard Wise Gallery, New York.

103. Nicolas Schöffer, *Microtemps 10*, 1964. Courtesy of the artist. Photograph, Galerie Denise René, Paris.

104. Hans Haacke, *Weather Cube*, 1965. Courtesy of the artist.

CHAPTER SEVEN:

105. Thomas Wilfred, *Lumia Suite, Opus 158*, 1963–1964. Collection, Museum of Modern Art, New York. Commission by Museum of Modern Art, Mrs. Simon Guggenheim Fund, 1963.

106. László Moholy-Nagy, *Light-Space Modulator*, 1922–1930. Courtesy, Busch-Reisinger Museum, Harvard University, Cambridge.

107. Otto Piene, *Light Ballet*, 1961 (from a show at the Museum Leverkusen, West Germany). Collection, Museum Leverkusen. Photograph courtesy of the artist.

108. Otto Piene, *Corona Borealis*, 1965. Courtesy, Howard Wise Gallery, New York.

109. Nicolas Schöffer, *Lux I*, 1957. Courtesy of the artist. Photograph, Galerie Denise René, Paris.

110. François Morellet, *Successive Illuminations*, 1963. Courtesy, The Contemporaries, New York.

111. Jack Burnham, *Two Four-Unit Modular Tapes*, 1968. Collection of the artist.

112. Dan Flavin, Installation photograph of 1964 exhibition at the Green Gallery, New York. Courtesy, Kornblee Gallery, New York.

113. Chryssa, *Ampersand IV*, 1965. Courtesy, Pace Gallery, New York.

114. Martial Raysse, *Proposition to Escape: Heart Garden*, 1966. Courtesy, Alexander Iolas Gallery, New York.

115. Howard W. Jones, *Skylight Two*, 1966. Collection, Mr. and Mrs. Bruce B. Dayton, Minneapolis.

116. Ted Kraynik, *Video Luminar No. 3*, 1967. Courtesy of the artist.

117. Billy Apple, *Solar 15*, 1966. Courtesy, Howard Wise Gallery, New York.

CHAPTER EIGHT:

118. Eduardo Paolozzi, *St. Sebastian, No. 2*, 1957. Collection, Solomon R. Guggenheim Museum, New York.

119. Ernest Trova, *Study Falling Man (Landscape on Wheels)*, 1966–1967. Courtesy, Pace Gallery, New York. Photograph, Ferdinand Boesch.

120. Frank Gallo, *Walking Nude*, 1967. Courtesy, Gilman Galleries, Chicago.

121. Jean Ipousteguy, *David and Goliath*, 1959. Collection, Museum of Modern Art, New York. Matthew T. Mellon Foundation Fund.

122. Edward Kienholz, *The State Hospital*, 1964–1966. Courtesy, Dwan Gallery, New York.

123. Nicolas Schöffer, *CYSP I*, 1956. Courtesy of the artist. Photograph, Editions du Griffon, Neuchâtel, Switzerland.

124. Hans Haacke, *Ice Stick*, 1966. Courtesy of the artist.

125. Hans Haacke, *Grass Cube*, 1967. Courtesy of the artist.

126. Enrique Castro-Cid, Installation photograph of 1965 exhibition. Courtesy, Richard Feigen Gallery, New York. Photograph, Geoffrey Clements.

127. Nam June Paik, *Robot-K456 with 20-Channel Radio Control and 10-Channel Data Recorder*, 1965. Courtesy, Galeria Bonino, Ltd., New York. Photograph, Peter Moore.

128. David von Schlegell, *Radio Controlled Sculpture*, 1966. Collection, Whitney Museum of American Art, New York. Gift of the Howard and Jean Lipman Foundation, Inc.

129. Robert Breer, *Self-Propelled Styrofoam Floats*, 1965–1966. Courtesy, Galeria Bonino, Ltd., New York.

130. François Dallegret, *The Machine*, 1966. Courtesy of the artist.

131. Thomas Shannon, *Squat*, 1966. Courtesy of the artist.

132. James Seawright, *Searcher*, 1966. Collection, Whitney Museum of American Art, New York. Gift of the Howard and Jean Lipman Foundation, Inc. Photograph courtesy, Stable Gallery, New York.

133. Alex Hay, *Grass Field*, in "9 evenings: theatre & engineering," October 13–22, 1966. Courtesy of the artist. Photograph, Peter Moore.

134. Les Levine, *Slipcover: A Place*, 1967. Courtesy of the artist.

135. Morton Shamberg, *God*, 1918. Courtesy, Philadelphia Museum of Art. Louise and Walter Arensberg Collection.

Index